DISCIPLINING THE POOR

DISCIPLINING
THE POOR

NEOLIBERAL PATERNALISM AND THE
PERSISTENT POWER OF RACE

JOE SOSS, RICHARD C. FORDING,
AND SANFORD F. SCHRAM

THE UNIVERSITY OF CHICAGO PRESS • CHICAGO AND LONDON

JOE SOSS is the Cowles Professor for the Study of Public Service in the Hubert H. Humphrey School of Public Affairs at the University of Minnesota. RICHARD C. FORDING is professor and chair of the Department of Political Science at the University of Alabama. SANFORD F. SCHRAM teaches in the Graduate School of Social Work and Social Research at Bryn Mawr College.

The University of Chicago Press, Chicago 60637
The University of Chicago Press, Ltd., London
© 2011 by The University of Chicago
All rights reserved. Published 2011.
Printed in the United States of America
20 19 18 17 16 15 14 13 12 11   1 2 3 4 5

ISBN-13: 978-0-226-76876-2   (cloth)
ISBN-13: 978-0-226-76877-9   (paper)
ISBN-10: 0-226-76876-7   (cloth)
ISBN-10: 0-226-76877-5   (paper)

Library of Congress Cataloging-in-Publication Data

Disciplining the poor : neoliberal paternalism and the persistent power of race / Joe Soss, Richard C. Fording, and Sanford F. Schram.
p. cm. — (Chicago studies in American politics)
ISBN-13: 978-0-226-76876-2 (alk. paper)
ISBN-10: 0-226-76876-7 (alk. paper)
ISBN-13: 978-0-226-76877-9 (pbk. : alk. paper)
ISBN-10: 0-226-76877-5 (pbk. : alk. paper)   1. Poverty—Political aspects—United States.   2. Paternalism—United States.   3. Poor—Political aspects—United States.
I. Soss, Joe, 1967–   II. Fording, Richard C., 1964–   III. Schram, Sanford.   IV. Series: Chicago studies in American politics.
HC110.P6D57 2011
339.4'60973—dc23
2011019001

CONTENTS

ACKNOWLEDGMENTS

T HIS BOOK IS THE CULMINATION OF A LONG JOURNEY THAT BEGAN IN 2002, when we first set out to study how welfare reform worked on the ground in local Florida communities. As the project grew in scope and ambition, we accumulated many personal and professional debts. As the book goes to press, we find that our gratitude extends to far more people than we can list here. At the outset, though, we want to publicly thank one another for a remarkable personal friendship and intellectual partnership. The pages of this book were written through almost-daily conversations that, in many respects, were their own reward. We each feel extraordinarily fortunate to have enjoyed a collaboration marked by generosity, respect, and an unflagging willingness to teach and learn.

For superb research assistance, we thank Linda Houser, Clare DiSalvo, Taina Maki, Sophia Peterson, Adam Butz, and Joan Schram. Special thanks also go to a number of individuals and organizations that went out of their way to support a project that never proved attractive to major funders. Jim Ziliak, Director of the University of Kentucky Center on Poverty Research, took a chance when he funded a small-grant proposal by Rich Fording to study race-based sanction disparities in the Florida Welfare Transition (WT) program. At the time, it was unclear how we would gain access to the contacts and datasets needed to complete the project. Jim's early gamble proved decisive in making our study possible. Mike Laracy of the Annie E. Casey Foundation played an equally critical role when it became clear that major funding would not be forthcoming and our project would have to proceed on a shoestring budget. Mike worked tirelessly to find the small infusions of funding that allowed us to expand our project and pursue a multimethod study of poverty governance. Maria Cancian and colleagues at the University of Wisconsin's Institute for Research on Poverty provided a small grant that made almost a full year of field research possible. Bryn Mawr College provided additional funds for field research and, most importantly, donated the staff time and computing resources needed to conduct a statewide, web-based survey of case managers in the Florida WT program. David Consiglio played an especially critical role in helping to design and administer the survey and its embedded experiments.

The analysis presented in the second half of this book would not have been possible without the support of many people associated with the Florida WT program. JenniLee Robbins of the Agency for Workforce Innovation was generous with her time as she helped us gain access to training sessions, board meetings, and frontline workers in one-stop centers throughout the state. Bill Hudgens of the Department of Children and Families provided crucial support by skillfully assembling administrative datasets and making them available to us in useable forms. Above all, we are grateful to the many administrators and frontline workers who took time away from their hard work in the WT program to share their hopes, beliefs, and frustrations in lengthy interviews. Thank you for all you taught us. Without your insights and assistance, this book would not have been possible.

For valuable feedback on our ideas, designs, and research papers, we thank Norma Altshuler, Jeremy Babener, Evelyn Brodkin, Sarah Bruch, Maria Cancian, Tony Chen, Adam Dahl, Sandy Danziger, Sheldon Danziger, Mary Jo Deegan, Phoebe Ellsworth, David Forrest, Jeremy Gordon, Clarissa Hayward, Matt Hindman, Christopher Howard, Vince Hutchings, Ryan King, Vicki Lens, Ann Lin, Julia McQuillan, Suzanne Mettler, Marcia Meyers, Don Moynihan, Erin O'Brien, Mark Peffley, Paul Pierson, Frances Fox Piven, Leslie Rescorla, Jodi Sandfort, Wendy Sarvasy, Marc Schulz, Kristen Seefeldt, Steve Smith, Dara Strolovitch, John Tambornino, Helen Tang, Anjali Thapar, Loïc Wacquant, Kathy Cramer Walsh, and Celeste Watkins-Hayes. Over the course of this project, we have also been buoyed by the support (and challenged by the questions) of countless students. Thank you for teaching your teachers so much.

We are especially grateful to John Tryneski, Rodney Powell, Larry Jacobs, Lisa Wehrle, our anonymous reviewers, and others at the University of Chicago Press for their terrific work in bringing this book to publication. The stylistic and intellectual shortcomings that remain in the text are undoubtedly fewer in number and far less egregious as a result of their efforts. We are also grateful to the publishers of earlier versions of material included in the book that appeared as: "Race and the Local Politics of Punishment in the New World of Welfare," *American Journal of Sociology* 116, no. 5 (2011):1610–57; "The Organization of Discipline: From Performance Management to Perversity and Punishment," *Journal of Public Administration Research and Theory* 21, no. 1 (2011):203–32; "The Third Level of U.S. Welfare Reform: Governmentality under Neoliberal Paternalism," *Citizenship Studies* 14, no. 6 (2010):739–54; "Deciding to Discipline: Race, Choice, and Punishment at the Frontlines of Welfare Reform," *American Sociological Review* 74, no. 3 (2009):398–422; "The Color of Devolution: Race,

Federalism, and the Politics of Social Control," *American Journal of Political Science* 52, no. 3 (2008):536–53; "Neoliberal Poverty Governance: Race, Place, and the Punitive Turn in U.S. Welfare Policy," *Cambridge Journal of Regions, Economy, and Society* 1, no. 1 (2008):17–36; and "Devolution, Discretion, and the Effect of Local Political Values on TANF Sanctioning," *Social Service Review* 81, no. 2 (2007):285–316.

Last but far from least, we thank our families, who endured the trials and tribulations of this collaborative research project for over nine years. Sandy thanks his wife Joan, who not only transcribed interviews but also had to talk about this project way more than she cared to. Rich thanks his wife Dana and his three children (two of whom were born on the eve of our first conference paper presentation!). Joe thanks his wife Kira for her love, support, wisdom, and laughter; he thanks his sons, Emil and Elijah, for tips on "sookling" in Florida, bad knock-knock jokes, awesome dance parties, and the joys of bedtime reading.

INTRODUCTION

P OVERTY IN THE UNITED STATES IS USUALLY THOUGHT OF AS A SOCIAL problem. In the occasional times when it rises to public attention, it troubles the conscience of a wealthy nation and calls forth the curative designs of social reformers. Passionate calls to end poverty frame public debates and fuel the efforts of many advocates and public officials. Yet poverty is more than a blight to be eradicated; it is also a problem of governance. The needs and disorders that arise in poor communities, and the difficulties they pose for societal institutions, must somehow be managed. In practice, social programs are rarely designed or evaluated as if the elimination of poverty were an attainable goal. Programs for the poor are used mainly to temper the hardships of poverty and ensure that they do not become disruptive for the broader society. They support the impoverished in ways designed to make poor communities more manageable and to shepherd the poor into the lower reaches of societal institutions. Poverty emerges occasionally in public life as a problem to be solved; the poor exist perennially as subjects who must be governed.

The central challenge of poverty governance can be traced to an apparent paradox. In capitalist democracies, the poor occupy a position that is both marginal and central to the social order. Out on the social periphery, they struggle to make ends meet in isolated neighborhoods and rural towns, under conditions their fellow citizens encounter mainly as news or entertainment. They are incorporated in partial ways, through precarious relationships to the routines and benefits that cement social order in the broader society. Yet the contributions of people who live and work in poverty are also essential for the smooth operation of societal institutions. The burdens they shoulder are indispensable for the quality of life that most residents of developed countries have come to expect (Gans 1972).

Thus, the most basic purpose of poverty governance is not to end poverty; it is to secure, in politically viable ways, the cooperation and contributions of weakly integrated populations. To meet this challenge, governments employ a variety of policy tools and administrative arrangements. They distribute relief to ease suffering and quiet disruptive political demands. They restrict aid to encourage the poor to take up work. They create incentives and services to smooth the path to preferred behaviors, and they police and imprison the poor for violations of law. They design social programs to teach prevailing norms, and they use surveillance and penalty systems to keep aid recipients moving along their designated paths. Through these and other methods, governments work continually to manage low-income populations and transform them into cooperative subjects of the market and polity.

Poverty governance, in this sense, is a perennial activity, yet its aims and operations are far from fixed. Its institutions keep time with the rhythms of political life. They adapt slowly to shifts in the organization of power and, on occasion, turn decisively to accommodate newly victorious interests and ideologies. Around the globe, efforts to govern the poor take different forms as public authorities struggle to navigate distinctive political, economic, and cultural dynamics. The compliance of the poor is never cemented, once and for all, through a seamless configuration of ideologies and institutions. To the contrary, the tactics of poverty governance are always unstable, and their power is never complete. They are contingent practices that evolve as public authorities cope with the internal contradictions of existing policies and work creatively to adapt to changing political pressures and institutional developments.

Over the past few decades, poverty governance in the United States has been transformed by the convergence of two reform movements. The first, often referred to as "paternalist," has promoted a more directive and supervisory approach to managing the poor (Mead 1997b). Citing images of disorder and dysfunction in impoverished communities, paternalists have argued that the state must meet its obligation to "tell the poor what to do" (Mead 1998). Thus, welfare programs have been recast to emphasize behavioral expectations and monitoring, incentives for right behavior, and penalties for noncompliance. Means-tested benefits of various stripes, from nutritional assistance to housing support, have been made conditional on good behavior. Tough new criminal justice policies have cracked down on illicit behavior and ushered in an unprecedented era of mass incarceration (Western 2006; Wacquant 2009).

The turn toward paternalism has intersected with a second development: the rise of neoliberalism as an organizing principle of governance. In the 1970s and 1980s, neoliberals initially adopted a laissez-faire stance, seeking to weaken the market-constraining effects of state regulations and the welfare state (Harvey 2005). Over time, however, reformers shifted to a more ambitious agenda (Peck and Tickell 2002). Today, neoliberalism encompasses a wide range of efforts to organize society according to principles of market rationality (W. Brown 2003). Rather than shrinking the state, neoliberals have worked to restructure it and harness its capacities. They have redesigned state operations around market principles and worked to make state officials more dependent on market actors to achieve their goals. Neoliberals have embraced the state as an instrument for creating market opportunities, absorbing market costs, and imposing market discipline (W. Brown 2006). Thus, core state functions, from war to welfare, environmental management to incarceration, have been contracted out to private providers. Policy authority has been decentralized and fragmented. Program operations have been restructured to emphasize competition and reward for performance.

The convergence of these two streams marks a significant moment in American political development: the rise of a mode of poverty governance that is, at once, more muscular in its normative enforcement and more dispersed and diverse in its organization. Poverty governance today is pursued through a diffuse network of actors who are positioned in quasi-market relations and charged with the task of bringing discipline to the lives of the poor.

Our book is the product of a sustained effort to make sense of this transformation. Bringing historical and theoretical analysis together with diverse sources of evidence, we seek to clarify the origins, operations, and consequences of neoliberal paternalism as a mode of poverty governance. The key features of our study fall into three broad categories. First, *Disciplining the Poor* is an effort to theorize how the present fits into a long history of efforts to regulate and reform low-income populations. The contemporary system is a blend of old practices and new political rationalities. To understand it, one must specify the elements of historical continuity and change that define its disciplinary project.

Second, unlike most research on "the politics of policy," our study does not adopt the vantage point of a single institution or stage of the policy process. Instead, we seek to draw multiple levels of governance into a common frame of analysis. Beginning with historical changes at the national level, we follow the path of governance down through a decentralized system. We trace its uneven development through state-level policy choices. We explore the differences that emerge as statewide policy designs give way to local strategies of implementation. Finally, we analyze how neoliberal paternalism gets put into practice, as street-level organizations and personnel carry out their work at the front lines of governance.

Third, our study seeks to clarify the central role that race plays in American poverty governance today. The racial character of the contemporary system is more than just a legacy of our troubled racial past. It is a reflection of how race operates today as a *social structure* that organizes politics and markets and

as a *mental structure* that organizes choice and action in governance. Racialized social relations and race-coded discourses provided essential resources
for the political actors who drove the turn toward neoliberal paternalism. In
this sense, race played a key role in shaping the governing arrangements that
all poor Americans now confront. The effects of race, however, have not been
limited to the broad direction of historical change. As we will see, racial factors go far toward explaining the systematic ways that governing arrangements
and outcomes vary across the contemporary system. Functioning as a socially
constructed "principle of vision and division" (Bourdieu 1990), race supplies a
powerful cultural frame and structural context for the contemporary practice
of poverty governance.

To set the stage for the study that follows, the remainder of this chapter
elaborates on each of these themes.

Historical Continuity and Change

Poverty governance today is not the sharp break with the past that many observers imagine, but it is also more than a simple recycling of old tactics. In
many respects, it is continuous with the long history of modern poor relief as
a mechanism for regulating the poor. The contemporary system incorporates
age-old strategies for enforcing work, including efforts to restrict and stigmatize
welfare receipt (Piven and Cloward 1971). It is a new chapter in the old story of
moralistic campaigns to "improve" the poor (Katz 1997), and it carries forward
the long history of efforts to regulate gender, family, and sexuality that feminist
historians have done so much to illuminate (Gordon 1994; Abramovitz 1988).

Advocates' claims of novelty aside (Mead 1998), the "new paternalism"
bears a striking resemblance to earlier forms of paternalism, including the
ideologies that attended nineteenth-century poorhouses, agencies for outdoor
relief, and scientific charity movements. Indeed, even the major areas of behavior emphasized in poverty policy today—work, sex, substance abuse, marriage,
child rearing, and so on—echo the main targets of earlier crusades to uplift and
normalize the poor.

In these and other ways, poverty governance continues to operate as a form
of social control, as Frances Fox Piven and Richard Cloward (1971) argued a
generation ago in their landmark study, *Regulating the Poor*.[1] Indeed, our empirical analysis suggests that Piven and Cloward's account of labor regulation
remains a vital resource for understanding poverty governance today. Work enforcement continues to be pursued, much as they argued, through efforts to

make poor relief less accessible and attractive than the worst available jobs. The administrative ceremonies of public aid continue to be rooted in Durkheimian rituals that stigmatize and deter welfare receipt. Much of welfare reform today can be interpreted as a classic case of "relief contraction," as Piven and Cloward use this term. By discrediting and deterring welfare usage, it forces desperate workers to accept the meanest work at the meanest wages.

Continuity can also be seen in the ambitious project of civic incorporation that informs neoliberal paternalism. Throughout its history, poverty governance has been an object of competing visions of the *civitas*—who we are and what we stand for, who should be included and on what terms, what we deserve and owe to one another (Heclo 1995). Programs for the poor have traditionally been organized to promote the specific conceptions of citizenship that have prevailed in particular eras—including the race, gender, and class biases they have entailed (Marshall 1964; R. Smith 1997; Somers 2008). Like generations of reformers before them, neoliberal paternalists have argued that meaningful civic incorporation can be achieved only by forcing the poor to confront a more demanding and appropriate "operational definition of citizenship" (Mead 1986). Behind the new policy tools and rhetorics, one finds an agenda that stretches back to the earliest days of Mothers Pensions in the United States. "Work first" strategies and "personal responsibility" contracts are new expressions of the old aspiration to make poor people into better citizens and strengthen their societal integration (Gordon 1994).

In this regard, neoliberal paternalism can be seen as an overt and ambitious effort to reshape the ways that poor people think about and regulate themselves. Yet this fact as well fails to set the present era apart. Poverty governance has always entailed more than just efforts to force the poor to adopt desired behaviors, regardless of their will. Its more ambitious goal, now as in the past, has been to transform the poor into new kinds of subjects who will *govern themselves* in preferred ways (Cruikshank 1999). Poverty governance today continues to operate as a "technical means for the shaping and reshaping of conduct"; it is an effort to reconfigure the ways that poor people freely choose to conduct themselves (Dean 1999: 17–18; Foucault 1991).

So what, then, has changed? Why should we see the rise of neoliberal paternalism as more than just old wine in new bottles? To clarify our answer, it is helpful to engage the most impressive recent effort to update Piven and Cloward's analysis, Loïc Wacquant's (2009) *Punishing the Poor*. Our analysis shares much in common with Wacquant's. We both argue that the key directions of change have been defined by neoliberalism and paternalism and that the system that has emerged is deeply racialized. We also agree that incarceration and punishment have come to play a more central role in poverty governance. Policing and corrections have become more prominent tools of social control, and criminal logics of violation and penalty have been imported into welfare programs. Together, these developments have given rise to a "double regulation of the poor." The "left hand" of the welfare state and the "right hand" of the carceral state now work together as integrated elements of a single system.

Within these broad lines of agreement, however, our account of historical change parts ways with Wacquant on a number of important issues. First, we adopt a different view of how neoliberalism and paternalism fit together and interact. Wacquant (2009: 19) conceptualizes neoliberalism as a destabilizing roll back of the activist welfare state: a retreat from state social functions and involvements in the market. Thus, the neoliberal state is defined by the "retraction of its social bosom" and the "amputation of its economic arm" (Wacquant 2008: 13). Penal modes of paternalism have been mobilized to contain the resulting social insecurities, especially the threat of disorder in poor black communities. In contrast, we argue that neoliberals have not dismantled the activist state; they have embraced its authority while working to redirect and transform it. In many respects, the neoliberal state is marked by *more* ambitious economic involvements and by *expansions* of social programs that target the poor. Neoliberal reforms have strengthened the state's capacities to serve markets, restructured its operations around market principles, and extended its reach through collaborations with civil society organizations.

In this sense, we offer an account of historical change that diverges from Wacquant's narrative of neoliberal rollback followed by penal-paternalist containment. Neoliberalism, as later chapters show, operates as an affirmative disciplinary regime in its own right. Likewise, the paternalist face of poverty governance cannot be reduced to the "fearsome and frowning mug" of punitive authority (Wacquant 2010: 217). In practice, paternalism brings authoritative direction and supervision together with moral appeals, social supports, tutelary interventions, and incentives in an effort to promote particular paths of personal reform and development. Neoliberalism and paternalism emerged together in U.S. politics and converged on a shared disciplinary project. Together, they have redefined poverty governance around a disciplinary agenda that emphasizes self-mastery, wage work, and uses of state authority to cultivate market relations.

Second, Wacquant (2009: 290) goes too far in arguing that conventional strategies of labor regulation have been "rendered obsolete" by the rise of a punitive neoliberal state. Our study demonstrates how old tools of labor regulation—barriers to welfare participation, low levels of aid, stigmatizing rituals, and so on—continue to be used as strategies for shoring up work effort among the poor. We update Piven and Cloward's (1971) analysis in a different way by showing how these old tactics have been augmented by changes in the basic goals and operations of welfare programs.

Historically, U.S. welfare programs "decommodified" labor by offering the poor a partial but significant reprieve from market pressures. Neoliberalism has undercut this decommodifying function by blurring the boundary between welfare receipt and labor market participation. Today, growing investments in poverty policies actively incentivize work and follow the poor into the workplace (through the Earned Income Tax Credit and transitional welfare benefits). Welfare programs for the unemployed have been redesigned to mimic the pressures and incentives of low-wage labor markets and to bolster these pressures with state authority. They strive to supply employers with labor on terms of their own choosing, and to actively groom, subsidize, and incentivize workers for transitions into jobs. The adults who participate in welfare programs today are not positioned outside the market; they are actively pressed into accepting the worst jobs at the worst wages. As a result, movements on and off the welfare rolls now provide a less reliable guide to the extent of labor pressures confronted by the poor. Today, work is promoted not only by limiting the reach and generosity of welfare programs (as Piven and Cloward argue) but also through affirmative uses of welfare programs as sites where state power is deployed to service markets.

Third, our analysis places political institutions, agents, and rationalities at the center of historical change. Wacquant treats the containment and control of marginalized racial minorities as a necessary feature of the social system. He offers a functional explanation for the rising "grandeur of the penal state" by stressing how this "fourth peculiar institution" was needed to take the place of its failed predecessors (slavery, Jim Crow, and the tightly bounded ghetto). Wacquant (2010: 217) cautions against overdetermined functional accounts and notes that changes in the state arose from political "struggles over and within the bureaucratic field." His study, however, provides no analysis of political agency on this front and asserts in numerous places that developments were "necessitated" in one way or another. By contrast, we treat the disciplinary turn in poverty governance as a contingent outcome and explain how specific political actors and changes in American politics converged to produce it. Indeed, we analyze neoliberal paternalism, not just as a political achievement, but also as a novel political rationality. Thus, our account of historical change emphasizes how new mentalities of rule are guiding the use of public authority and how, in a system of decentralized discipline, governance varies depending on specific configurations of political institutions and actors.

Fourth, Wacquant's analysis focuses on the substance and logic of *what* governing authorities are doing without giving equal attention to *how* they are doing it. By contrast, we conceptualize neoliberal paternalism as a change in the direction of poverty governance that is rooted in new ways of positioning governing authorities and organizing governing practices. As poverty management has been restructured through policy devolution, privatization, and performance systems, new strategies of social control have been applied to lower-level governing authorities as much as to the poor themselves. As we show in later chapters, new ways of organizing governance—benchmarks, incentives, contractual pay points, and so on—go far toward explaining the new patterns of treatment meted out to the poor. Accounts that ignore them misconstrue the direction of historical change and fail to explain (as one must) why practices and outcomes in the current system vary so greatly across states, localities, service providers, and frontline workers.

Last, Wacquant places punishment at the center of his account and engages the concept of discipline primarily to interpret the growing sovereign powers of the penal state. We agree that punitive policy tools and criminal logics of violation are key elements of the new system. But so are efforts to immerse the poor in new incentive systems, modes of pedagogy, and reformative experiences of market relations. Punishment is not the disciplinary alpha and omega of neoliberal paternalism, taking the place of an "American social state" that now lies in "ruins" (Wacquant 2009: 293). Penal logics operate within a much broader array of instruments that, collectively, are deployed to discipline the conduct of governing and governed subjects. Neoliberal paternalism is more than a coercive escalation of the state's punitive powers as a sovereign. It is a shift in the state's productive powers—that is, powers "bent on generating forces, making them grow, and ordering them, rather than impeding them, making them submit or destroying them" (Foucault [1980] 1990: 136). The disciplinary turn in poverty governance, in our analysis, entails the expansion of sovereign powers but, more fundamentally, is a project of *governmentality* focused on fostering particular forms of self-mastery and promoting a particular kind of wellness in targeted populations (Dean 1999).

The new modes of governance analyzed in this book are designed to foster new "mentalities of rule." Their purpose is to alter governing practices, not just by compelling desired action, but by reconstructing the ways that authorities understand themselves, their missions, and the problems and populations they act on (Dean 1999; Schneider and Ingram 1997). The ultimate purpose of these changes is to transform the poor themselves—to make them into the kinds of subjects who voluntarily embrace particular kinds of choices and behaviors. Neoliberal paternalism is, in this sense, an effort to discipline governing authorities so that they can be relied on to carry out the work of disciplining the poor. In poverty governance today, interventions that punish the poor work hand in hand with efforts to support and incentivize the poor, collectively serving a broader disciplinary agenda that specifies the creation of compliant and competent worker-citizens as its ultimate end (Korteweg 2003).

Following the Paths of Policy and Governance

Our goal in this book is to provide a critical analysis of how neoliberal and paternalist agendas fit together and get enacted as a concrete approach to governing the poor. Our approach to theory development emphasizes the value of paying close attention to what public authorities actually choose and do. The problem is that governance does not "happen" all at once in a single locale. It emerges through interactions across multiple levels of scale, and it takes on various forms as it moves out into separate jurisdictions. Federal policies get refined by state and local lawmakers; legislative intentions give way to the organizational realities of implementation; policies and rules get rewritten by the frontline workers who must decide how to interpret and apply them. To be persuasive, a theoretical account of poverty governance must be rooted in these everyday practices and robust enough to explain the variations that arise as governance filters downward and outward through the system.

Too often today, studies of governance are distorted by academic pressures to speak to the concerns that animate narrow subfields of inquiry. Specialists target particular institutions or stages of the policy process in isolation from others and focus on the particular methods and data sources that researchers have come to expect in their slice of the academy. This division of labor can produce valuable knowledge by subjecting individual pieces of the puzzle to intensive analysis. Yet it tells us little about how the pieces fit together as a coherent system of governance in a particular time and place. In this book, we forgo some of the benefits of specialization in order to pursue a more synoptic analysis of "administrative statecraft—the translation of politics into policy and routines that work on the ground" (Mead 2004a: 9). Our study follows governance down through the federal system, pursuing a consistent set of analytic goals as it tracks the cascade of political and administrative relationships that organize efforts to govern the poor.

In chapters 2 and 3, we chart the rise of neoliberal paternalism at the national level, specifying its key features and supplying a political explanation for its emergence after the 1960s. The first of these chapters emphasizes changes in the political economy of the United States; the second clarifies how racial politics played a pivotal role in the creation of neoliberal paternalism. In chapters 4 and 5, we elaborate on this historical narrative by adopting a state-level perspective on how poverty governance has changed over the past fifty years. We explain how and why strategies of poverty governance shifted in the states over time. We analyze the factors that led states to adopt different policies and governing arrangements, and we show how state choices accumulated to produce a deeply racialized pattern of policy regimes.

To extend our analysis to the local level, the second half of the book shifts to a more intensive study of poverty governance in the state of Florida, a national leader in the pursuit of neoliberal and paternalist reforms. After describing the Florida system and our approach to studying it in chapter 6, we organize the chapters in this section around four core elements of neoliberal paternalism. In chapter 7, we focus on local devolution, showing how social and political forces give rise to systematic differences in the ways that local authorities pursue the task of disciplining the poor. Chapter 8 explores the marketization of poverty governance, revealing how privatization and the "business model" have turned service provision into a site of profitable investment and a tool for servicing employer needs. Chapter 9 turns our attention to competitive performance systems, analyzing how pressures to meet numerical benchmarks motivate perverse organizational responses, discipline frontline workers, and ultimately promote tougher approaches to governing the poor. Chapter 10 rounds out this section by exploring the interplay of race and disciplinary discretion at the front lines of paternalist poverty governance.

In chapter 11, we conclude the empirical portion of our book with an analysis of how the rise of neoliberal paternalism has mattered—socially, economically, and politically—for the poor themselves. Chapter 12 reviews the major results of our study, specifies our critique of the current system, and suggests ways to develop a more just, caring, and democratic approach to poverty governance.

Over the course of these chapters, our study draws on an unusually diverse collection of data sources and analytic strategies. Poverty governance has many dimensions. To make sense of it, we have adopted a strategy of methodological pluralism. As we take up different questions and address different sites of governance, we draw together analytic approaches that rarely appear together in a single study. More methods do not guarantee a more valid or persuasive analysis. What they do offer is a way to avoid the blinders imposed by a single empirical standpoint, draw a broader range of dynamics into a common frame of analysis, and multiply one's opportunities for developing and challenging theoretical claims.

At the national level, we combine historical analyses of discourses, institutions, and interests with statistical analyses of public opinion surveys and program data. At the state level, we employ a variety of statistical models to clarify the dynamics of policy change across states and over time. In the second half of the book, we make extensive use of quantitative indicators drawn from administrative and contextual datasets. Our statistical analyses, however, are placed in dialogue with interpretive research based on more than three years of field research in the Florida Welfare Transition (WT) program. Evidence for this part of the project is based on in-depth interviews with case managers and administrators, observations of state and local program operations, attendance at state and regional training sessions, and documents produced by regional welfare offices and mass media sources. These data, in turn, are supplemented by results from an original statewide survey of WT case managers that included both conventional questions and random-assignment experiments. (The full statistical models for our analyses are available in an online appendix at http://www .discipliningthepoor.com.)

By applying this mix of methodologies across multiple levels of governance, our study draws several general properties of the system into sharper focus. First, poverty governance today operates as a cascade of policy choice points where relationships between higher- and lower-level actors tend to be structured in consistent ways. A common logic defines each link in the chain from national lawmakers to state officials to local boards to contracted providers to senior managers to frontline case managers to welfare clients. At each step, actors below control information needed by actors above and hold discretion over how to pursue preset goals. Actors above seek to discipline this discretion by setting benchmarks, controlling resources, monitoring performance, promoting particular discourses and frames, and deploying rewards and penalties. In this sense, the contemporary system is guided by a coherent governing logic that applies to public officials as much as the poor themselves. Neoliberal governance prioritizes freedom of choice for lower-level actors, yet it works through a panoply of tools to maximize the chances that these actors will "freely choose" courses of action preferred by agenda-setting actors above.

Second, variation and contingency are defining features of today's decentralized, choice-centered model of poverty governance. Neoliberal paternalism is not one thing; it is many things. It encourages states and localities to pursue different strategies for managing the poor. It paves the way for systematic but highly contingent racial disparities in treatment, without imposing a uniform racial system from above. It introduces new governing rationalities into older organizational cultures, in ways that lead to conflicted forms of consciousness and provide diverse resources for counterdiscourses. Indeed, our interviews with frontline policy actors belie any idea that neoliberal paternalism operates as an all-encompassing worldview faithfully enacted by street-level bureaucrats. To understand neoliberal paternalism, one must attend to its contradictions and contestation, as well as the ways actors subvert it and turn it to their own uses.

Third and finally, processes of accumulation play a key role in the outcomes produced by poverty governance today. As federal policies diffuse through successive arenas, they are elaborated in ways that deepen the system's disciplinary character. Actors above frequently structure and incentivize policy choices below to raise the odds of this outcome. But authorities at each level also act on their own priorities and needs, and often find it useful to layer more stringent program elements on top of the policies they inherit. A parallel process of accumulation works to deepen racial disparities. Looking across jurisdictions, the racial patterning of a single policy choice may appear modest in isolation, but repeated instances of this pattern combine to produce profound racial differences in policy exposure and treatment. Through "the ordinary acts of many people in many places, over time" (Pollock 2008: 11), small inequalities accumulate below the radar, compounding one another and the vulnerabilities of the most disadvantaged (DiPrete and Eirich 2006).

Poverty Governance and the Power of Race

A central claim of our study is that poverty governance in the United States today cannot be understood if one fails to appreciate its racial character. In the United States, race has always shaped governmental approaches to poverty and labor, welfare and criminal justice (Chad Goldberg 2007; Gabbidon and Green 2005). Yet the nature of this relationship has been far from constant. In the 1930s, it pivoted on overt forms of discrimination and the regional subjugation

of African Americans in southern systems of social caste and economic exploitation (Key 1949; Lieberman 1998; Katznelson 2005). In the 1960s, it was rooted
in the turbulent national politics of racial incorporation, as insurgent minority
groups mobilized to demand greater access to the civil, social, and political
rights of citizenship (Quadagno 1994). Poverty governance continues to reflect
the legacies of this racial history. Yet race also operates in new ways as a powerful force in contemporary social life, and the dynamics observed in earlier eras
provide an uncertain guide to how it shapes poverty governance today.

Since the 1960s, racial prejudice has declined and de jure discrimination has
become illegal (Schuman et al. 1998). Norms of equal treatment are now widely
endorsed, and overt expressions of racism are, in most public arenas, roundly
condemned (Mendelberg 2001). Racial minorities have entered the middle class
and become influential actors in major societal institutions (C. Cohen 1999;
Hochschild 1995). In administrative settings, the biases of white officials have
become less decisive as people of color have moved disproportionately into jobs
that focus on social problems in poor communities (Watkins-Hayes 2009).

Against this backdrop, the question of how race shapes American poverty
governance today poses an analytic puzzle of considerable political importance.
In the pages that follow, we take up a two-sided challenge: first, to explain how
race has shaped the construction of a new poverty regime, and, second, to explain how and when this regime generates systematic racial disparities. After
the 1960s, we argue, racialized political cleavages and institutional legacies
helped pave the way for neoliberal reforms, just as race-coded discourses fueled
the campaign for get-tough paternalism and underwrote the public's support.
As these agendas proceeded, state and local policy choices proved highly sensitive to the racial makeup of policy targets, giving rise to strikingly different governing regimes. At the front lines of implementation, race proved no less important: It operates today as a powerful force shaping administrative interactions
and guiding street-level decisions about who should get what, when, and how.

In these and other ways, we argue that race provides a key cultural resource
for the production of poverty governance. But poverty governance is also, in its
own right, a site where racial meanings and inequalities get produced. How is it
possible for racial disparities to emerge under the official cover of public policy
in an era in which laws rarely discriminate in overt ways and few public officials
can be described as self-conscious racists?

To answer this question, we begin from the premise that race is a socially
constructed form of classification that operates to structure social relations in
real and definite ways (Omi and Winant 1986; Bonilla-Silva 1997). Poverty gov-

ernance in the United States is "racialized," in the first instance, because racial categories play a key role in structuring the political and economic relations that define its aims, institutions, and operational context (Piven 2003). Because welfare-to-work programs function as labor market institutions, their practices reflect the continuing importance of race as an organizing feature of American labor markets (Brown et al. 2003; Holzer and Stoll 2003; Warren 2010). And because poverty policies are political creations, their design and implementation are shaped by the ways that racial distinctions matter for power, organization, and strategy in the polity (Frymer 1999; King and Smith 2005). In this sense, the roots of racial disparities in poverty governance lie outside its internal operations. The institutions and practices of poverty governance reflect the power of race as a structural feature of the American political economy and translate the racial terms of the broader social order into disparate outcomes for racially defined subgroups of the poor (Schram 2005).

Racial disparities do not flow directly from social structures, however. They depend, ultimately, on what specific human agents decide and do in the process of governing. As a result, one must specify how race operates, not just as a social structure coordinating human relations, but also as a cultural frame structuring perception and choice. To do so, we develop an original analytic framework: the Racial Classification Model (RCM) of policy choice, a general model of how and when racial categories can be expected to influence decisions related to policy design and implementation. The RCM extends a structural perspective on race by offering a more precise account of its subjective and intersubjective dimensions.

Building on theories of implicit social cognition (Winter 2008) and the social construction of target populations (Schneider and Ingram 1997), we argue that racial schemas can operate as powerful cognitive structures guiding perception and choice in poverty governance—even in the absence of overt prejudice, ingroup favoritism, or intentions to discriminate. That they *can* work in this way, however, does not guarantee that they *will*. Racial classifications provide just one of the many cultural frames available to authorities as they carry out their work. The key question, then, is why racial classifications sometimes rise above the alternatives and achieve priority as a foundation for thought, choice, and action in governance. The RCM offers a parsimonious framework for specifying the conditions that make this development more likely and the processes that generate racially disparate policy choices.

By testing the RCM in a variety of governing contexts, we show how racial disparities emerge as contingent but systematic outcomes depending on the characteristics of decision makers and policy targets, organizational contexts, and political environments. By applying a single framework across the entire system, we explain why race matters more in some contexts than others and how disparate policy choices accumulate to produce profound racial disparities. Indeed, the analysis we present should raise troubling questions for anyone who cares about social justice, civic inclusion, and democracy in America.

Conclusion: Analysis as Critique

A central goal of *Disciplining the Poor* is to provide a critical analysis of welfare reform—an analysis that not only explains how the poor are being governed and why, but also expands the space for political discourse by specifying a critique of contemporary practice. In this regard, we want to make clear from the outset that our critique does not reflect a preference for welfare over work or an antipathy toward efforts to encourage responsible and productive behavior. Work is necessary in all societies, so all societies must find ways to ensure that work gets done. Work is also an important part of human flourishing, so social justice is undermined when people are systematically denied the experience of meaningful work. In the United States today, work must play a central role in any plan to reduce poverty or, at a minimum, provide functioning pathways out of poverty. Our critique of poverty governance today, which we elaborate in chapters 11 and 12, begins from these premises and proceeds along four lines.

The first concerns the *terms* on which people are made to work. Like all labor-regulating institutions, welfare programs can promote just or unjust terms of exchange between employers and workers (Piven and Cloward 1971). Today, welfare agencies function as workforce intermediaries: They are designed to serve both employers and recipients, and to bring them together in employment relationships. Such intermediaries can do a great deal to align the needs of workers and employers in mutually beneficial ways (Dresser and Rogers 2003). But welfare programs today do nothing of the sort. They are designed to service the "low road" of capitalism by offering up labor on whatever terms the market will bear. They offer paltry benefits that set no meaningful floor under wages; they subsidize employers while asking nothing in return; they deploy state authority to force workers into jobs that ignore their needs and offer little hope for advancement. Welfare programs today demand "work first," while giving little serious attention to the disabilities, life problems, family needs, and resource deficits found among the poor. In the process, they actively diminish opportunities to acquire education and other forms of human capital that people need to get better jobs. Under the banner of "valuing work," we have constructed an aggressive work-enforcement system that rides roughshod over all countervailing values and willfully ignores the conditions of labor markets and poor people's lives.

Second, as students of politics, we emphasize that welfare programs are sites of politics that matter greatly for democracy, citizenship, and power in the United States. Accordingly, we highlight how neoliberal paternalism reduces citizenship to a market role and "de-democratizes" the citizenry in far-reaching ways. As a mode of poverty governance, it deepens the political marginality of the poor, channeling them into positions of civic inferiority and isolation. In welfare programs today, recipients have virtually no institutionalized ability to counter arbitrary exercises of power or to participate in the authoritative processes that govern them. Paternalists suggest that democracy will be well served by authoritarian policy designs that impose order on the lives of the poor. Yet no evidence suggests that welfare reform is producing civic incorporation on terms that comport with any reasonable conception of democracy. In poverty governance today, the values of work and responsibility are being used to justify surveillance practices, authority relations, and modes of civic positioning that are deeply anti-democratic.

Third, whatever one thinks about the values pursued by contemporary poverty governance, no reasonable standard of social justice can be reconciled with a system that systematically generates and tolerates racial bias. In the chapters that follow, we document how multiple features of the new policy regime function as mechanisms of racial inequality. Taken as a whole, we believe the empirical results offer a strong basis for concluding that governing authorities run a racialized system of poverty governance in the United States today. The design of this system facilitates the production of racial disparities at multiple levels, and the "taxes" imposed on people of color accumulate across these levels like compound interest. The problem is not that a few bad apples act as racists within the system. To the contrary, race is central to how the system operates; core features of the system contribute reliably to the production of racial disparities; and they do so regardless of whether specific actors in the system consciously approve of racially unequal treatment.

The final strand of our critique is perhaps the most damning for champions of contemporary welfare reform. Neoliberal and paternalist reforms, we argue, are failures on their own terms. The new system does not do what its advocates promise and, in fact, fails according to many of the standards they use to advocate for it. The efficient systems promised by champions of market-based reform routinely turn out to be unwieldy and inefficient. Contracting arrangements that were supposed to guarantee public accountability actually encourage scandals and corruption as they turn services for the poor into a corporate profit-making arena. At the front lines of welfare agencies, the tailored, personalized forms of client engagement promised by paternalists turn out to be "cookie-cutter" practices of regimented work enforcement. Performance management is supposed to promote rational innovation and learning in decentralized welfare systems, yet it more often works to promote conformity, inhibit learning, encourage goal displacement, and intensify the use of punitive practices. The inspiring image of the welfare poor being moved into jobs that carry them out of poverty and toward self-sufficiency has borne little resemblance to what welfare program leavers actually experience.

The list can go on. The point is that a close look at poverty governance reveals a system that fails by the very standards that reformers have used to sell and defend it. Indeed, it reveals a system that is operating in denial of social justice and contrary to democratic values. To point this out, one does not need to be "anti-work," resistant to the positive contributions of authority, or closed off to the potential upsides of recent reform ideas. Our critique of neoliberal paternalism is not a rejection of the potential values associated with work, responsible behavior, or civic obligation. To the contrary, we are critical of what has been created, and what is being done, in the names of these values—and in the names of us all.

THE RISE OF NEOLIBERAL PATERNALISM

I N THE RECENT HISTORY OF AMERICAN POLITICAL DEVELOPMENT, FEW changes have been as striking as the transformation of poverty governance. The state's new look can be seen in the shift to conditional, behavior-centered welfare provision (R. Weaver 2000), the spiraling numbers of poor people under correctional supervision (Western 2006), and a host of new arrangements that replace "rule-based, authority-driven processes [of governance] with market-based, competition-driven tactics" (Kettl 2005: 3). A great deal has been written about these changes and their socioeconomic effects. Yet their shared political sources and significance remain poorly understood. Lost in the divide that separates poverty studies from political science, the political origins and consequences of disciplinary poverty governance have remained obscure.

Indeed, when scholars turn to the question of *why* poverty governance has shifted direction, it is remarkable how little gets said about power and political action. Most accounts emphasize the effects of disembodied social forces, neatly cropping political agency out of the picture. Thus, dramatic changes in welfare systems are attributed to "shifting tides" that have swept across the developed nations, such as globalization and demographic transition (Gilbert 2002). New approaches to public aid are described as flowing logically from "changes in our understanding of the causes and consequences of poverty" (Danziger and Haveman 2001: 8). The rise of a new "Schumpeterian workfare post-national regime" is explained as a functional response to the evolving needs and crises of capital (Jessop 2000). The punitive turn in racial control is presented as a shift "necessitated" by new social insecurities (Wacquant 2009: 19).

Against this backdrop, we pursue two goals in this chapter. The first is to explain how the disciplinary turn was produced through organized efforts to redirect the exercise of public authority. In doing so, we emphasize that the politics of poverty is not an island unto itself, untouched by broader dynamics of power and conflict in the American polity. With few exceptions, studies of events such as the 1996 welfare reforms have tended to emphasize what is unique about poverty politics: the "traps" that stymie antipoverty efforts, the evolution of poverty policies and debates, and the changing networks of actors who have a seat at the poverty-policy table (R. Weaver 2000; Heclo 1994). Policy changes are analyzed as efforts to navigate the unique "helping conundrums" that arise from poverty and frustrate would-be reformers (Ellwood 1988). They are explained as products of the distinctive discourses and images that swirl around poor black women as "welfare queens" (Hancock 2004).

If new approaches to poverty had emerged in isolation, it would make sense to seek explanations within this domain alone. But they have not. Poverty governance was reconfigured as part of a much broader political campaign to redirect activist government in the United States (Pierson and Skocpol 2007). Its new look can be traced to the same political forces that have worked to deregulate industries, cut taxes, shift risks onto private actors, and weaken social protections for the middle class (Hacker 2006; Soss, Hacker, and Mettler 2007). The ambitious new schemes devised for the poor have reflected broader societal agendas; their success can be traced to larger changes in political mobilization and the organization of American politics.

Our second goal is to clarify the political rationality that underlies poverty governance today. As various policies change together in time, they rarely line up neatly to define a seamless new direction for the state. Each policy's trajectory is, in some measure, unique. To interpret changes in governance, one must seek out their commonalities and ask whether they exhibit a shared logic. Public policies are more than just political outcomes; they are frameworks that structure political relations and organize the exercise of public authority (Pierson 2006). Thus, the task of the political analyst is to clarify not just the sources of policy change, but also the political rationality of the resulting forms. In the absence of the latter, scholars describe the details of policy changes without explaining what they add up to and ultimately mean. In poverty governance, we argue, the key policy changes in recent years have reflected a coherent political logic rooted in neoliberalism and paternalism. These two analytic concepts provide essential tools for clarifying the ideological forces that have promoted policy change and the practical rationalities that organize governance at all levels of the system today.

Neoliberalism and paternalism are contested concepts, used by scholars in a variety of ways. To give them some precision, we begin by specifying the meanings we attach to them as modes of governance. In our second section, we analyze the political forces that drove the rise of neoliberal paternalism. We explain why poverty governance became a focal point for a broader political campaign and why programs for the poor were positioned as "low-hanging fruit" available for the political taking. Our third section specifies the changing contours of poverty governance, providing policy details to make the abstractions of neoliberal paternalism more concrete. Finally, in our last section, we theorize the present in relation to the past, clarifying the elements of historical change and continuity that define poverty governance today.

As we emphasized in chapter 1, race has played a central role in the rise of disciplinary poverty governance. In this chapter, we bracket the racial dimensions of this development in order to focus on the logic of neoliberal paternalism and its origins in a changing political economy. With this account in hand, chapter 3 presents a more sustained analysis of how racial politics facilitated the disciplinary turn and how race structures efforts to govern the poor today.

Neoliberalism and Paternalism

Neoliberalism is an intellectual and political movement that emerged in the late twentieth century to advance a radical market-centered agenda in global and domestic relations. Like all forms of liberalism, it prizes the "possessive individual" and privileges the freedoms associated with private property, market relations, and trade across nations. Yet neoliberalism should not be confused with classic forms of nineteenth-century liberalism for at least two reasons.

First, while liberal thought has often proposed an intimate relationship between political and market freedoms, neoliberalism goes further by treating market liberties as a model (and substitute) for political freedoms. Neoliberalism is an effort to extend the reach of market logic, applying it as an organizing principle for all social and political relations. As such, it represents a particularly muscular form of economic liberalism that goes far beyond traditional liberal claims for the compatibility of democracy and capitalism. Neoliberal governance privileges economic freedoms at the expense of political freedoms as well as democratic values such as universalism, egalitarianism, promotion of an active citizenry, and conceptions of a public good (W. Brown 2006).

Second, as a twentieth-century movement, neoliberalism departs in significant ways from eighteenth- and nineteenth-century laissez-faire doctrines of economic liberalism (W. Brown 2003). It is not a revival of the drive to limit state power so that markets can flourish independently. It is an effort to mobilize the state on behalf of the market and reconfigure the state as a quasi-market operation.

The confusion that surrounds this point today partly reflects the historical emergence of neoliberalism as an attack on the Keynesian welfare state and an effort to deregulate capitalism on a global scale. Intellectually and politically, neoliberalism developed as a challenge to the activist state's role as a "counter-vailing power" that used regulations and protections to temper the creative de-struction of capitalism (Galbraith 1952; Polanyi 1957). Its most important early theorist, Friedrich Hayek (1960), targeted Keynesian collectivism as the enemy of freedom and argued for easing state restraints on market inequalities. Its most prominent leaders in the 1980s, Ronald Reagan and Margaret Thatcher, empha-sized the need to liberate markets by reducing regulations and taxes, scaling back worker protections, and giving multinational corporations greater latitude (Harvey 2005). Similar themes animated the "Washington Consensus," which used organizations such as the World Bank and International Monetary Fund (IMF) to force governments in the global South to deregulate their economies (Stiglitz 2002; Peet 2003).

In all these developments, neoliberalism looks very much like a resurgence of laissez-faire, focused on "rolling back" state involvements in the market (Somers and Block 2005; Wacquant 2009). As forms of market fundamen-talism, however, the two diverge in significant ways. Laissez-faire doctrines presume that market relations emerge as natural modes of human interaction when people are freed from the distortions of the state. Neoliberalism holds, in-stead, that functioning markets are not natural outcomes that emerge by default (Klein 2007). Markets must be actively constructed; market behaviors must be learned; and once learned, they must be deliberately extended to new are-nas. Neoliberalism treats market rationality as a normative ideal to be pursued through applications of public authority and uses it as a preeminent standard for evaluating institutional designs and individual behaviors throughout society.

Thus, rather than limiting the state, neoliberalism envisions the state as a site for the application of market principles. Through contracting, decentralization, and competitive performance systems, neoliberal reformers work to "reinvent government" in ways that mimic market forms (Osborne and Gaebler 1992). Through privatization and collaboration, they make the state more reliant on market actors to achieve public purposes. Through discourses centered on cost and benefit, investment and return, neoliberalism renders government actions suspect when they cannot be justified through a market calculus. Efforts to deregulate markets persist but are blended into a broader project that embraces the activist state for alternative purposes: subsidizing market actors, stabilizing market disruptions, enhancing profits, absorbing losses, and expanding market relations. Above all, the state is charged with the task of fostering market ratio-nality itself—reconstructing institutions to encourage both the governing and the governed to think of themselves and behave as market actors. As Wendy Brown (2003: 9–10) explains:

> Neo-liberalism does not simply assume that all aspects of social, cultural and political life can be reduced to [a rational market] calculus, rather it develops institutional practices and rewards for enacting this vision. In contrast with the notorious *laissez faire* and human propensity to "truck and barter" of classical economic liberalism, neo-liberalism does not conceive either the market itself or rational economic behavior as purely natural. Both are constructed—organized by law and political institutions, and requiring political intervention and orchestration. Far from flourishing when left alone, the economy must be directed, buttressed, and protected by law and policy as well as by the dissemination of social norms designed to facilitate competition, free trade, and rational economic action on the part of every member and institution of society.

As the state is privatized, so too are the social problems of the citizenry. Matters of shared consequence, once addressed through public decisions about how to organize collective life, are recast as personal problems to be solved through rational individual choices. The democratic citizen, positioned as one who must act in concert with others to achieve preferred outcomes, is redefined as a consumer, worker, and taxpaying customer of the state. Citizens, in this guise, are investors who have a contractual right to expect efficient state actions that produce good returns. They are repositioned, through vouchers and choice programs, as individual consumers who pursue better outcomes by seeking goods from other providers (exit) rather than as co-participants deliberating and acting together to improve their shared institutions (voice). They are encouraged to help others, not by deciding how to organize their communities in a just manner, but by pursuing individual work as volunteers, charitable givers, and virtuous providers of services (Crenson and Ginsberg 2002). The competent and self-reliant market actor—working, investing, choosing, and assessing returns—is made synonymous with the good citizen.

The counterpart to the good citizen is, of course, the bad citizen, and neo-liberalism offers a moral and political vision in this regard as well. From Hayek (1960) onward, neoliberal discourse has valorized self-discipline as the sine qua non of freedom. Individuals, in this view, have a moral and political obligation to act as disciplined entrepreneurs. They must plan to meet their own needs, accept personal responsibility for their problems, and manage their daily affairs with prudence. The individual who does otherwise fails not just as an economic actor, but as a moral and civic being. This formulation has two key implications for governance.

First, it obscures the political dimensions of social problems by defining them as matters of personal choice. Insofar as "the rationally calculating individual bears full responsibility for the consequences of his or her action," the causal story of "a 'mismanaged life' becomes a new mode of depoliticizing social and economic powers" (W. Brown 2003). Of course, depoliticizing socially produced harms by framing them as personal matters is nothing new. Under neoliberalism, however, this old dynamic is set in motion and given greater reach through the broad application of a market frame. The default assumption is that the problems of the person are products of individual choice best resolved through individual efforts to seek solutions.

Second, this formulation turns efforts to promote disciplined entrepreneurial behavior into a primary task of governance in a free society. Without such discipline, the free citizen cannot exist. Thus, the state in a free society has an obligation to bring discipline to the lives of individuals so that, as competent market actors, they may function as full and independent members of society. To fulfill this responsibility,

> the state attempts to construct prudent subjects through policies that organize such prudence: this is the basis of a range of welfare reforms such as workfare and single-parent penalties, changes in the criminal code such as the "three strikes law," and educational voucher schemes. Because neo-liberalism casts rational action as a norm rather than an ontology, social policy is the means by which the state produces subjects whose compass is set by their rational assessment of the costs and benefits of certain acts, whether teen pregnancy, tax cheating, or retirement planning. (W. Brown 2003)

For low-income Americans, the neoliberal turn has converged with a second critical development: the rise of the new paternalism (Mead 1997b). As the term suggests, paternalism is rooted in a traditional conception of the father-child relationship. The child, in this view, lacks the capacity to know what is in her or his best interest and has yet to develop the self-discipline needed to act effectively on such knowledge. As an adult, the father is in a better position to know what is in the child's best interest. As a parent, the father has a moral obligation to act on this knowledge. He must use his legitimate authority to direct and supervise the child in ways that help her or him to flourish. For the child's own good, the father must at various times deny what the child wants, impose what the child resists, and punish what the child chooses to do.

Scholarly treatments of paternalism typically begin from a liberal view of adult citizens as independent individuals who, despite their imperfections, are in the best position to know their own interests. From John Locke's opposition to using the patriarchal family as a model for the state to John Stuart Mill's principle of free choice to Robert Dahl's arguments against ceding policy authority to expert "guardians," liberal political thinkers have consistently viewed paternalism as a violation of individual liberty that can be justified only in exceptional cases. As Mill (1983: 92) argued in *On Liberty*, "All errors which an individual is likely to commit are far outweighed by the evil of allowing others to constrain him to what they deem his own good." The narrow exceptions, for Mill, are defined by cases where individuals are incapable of exercising free choice—primarily children and, more infamously, "barbarians" who lack the civilization needed to make rational judgments. Liberals today justify paternalism by citing a wider range of factors that can impair or distort choice (Smiley 1989: 300; Thaler and Sunstein 2008). But their basic conception remains aligned with Mill's. Paternalism is "the interference with a person's liberty of action justified by reasons referring exclusively to the welfare, good, happiness, needs, interests or values of the person being coerced" (Dworkin 1971: 120).

In referring to paternalist *governance*, our use of the term departs from this liberal definition in three key ways. First, we begin with political relations rather than unencumbered individuals, emphasizing that paternalism is an authority relationship based on unequal status and power (Smiley 1989). It is not a form of "interference" with individuals whose desires exist, somehow, prior to social relations. Rather, as the father-child metaphor suggests, it is a relationship that makes the subordinate's development into a self-conscious project pursued by a directive and supervisory authority. Second, although paternalism can involve a "person being coerced," power may operate and be exercised in a variety of ways that do not require coercion (Hayward 2000; Barnett and Duvall 2005). Indeed, in Mary Jackman's (1994) view, the political importance of paternalism lies precisely in its capacity to make coercive force less necessary for the maintenance of unequal power relations. Third, because governing arrangements are always supported by multiple rationales, paternalist governance cannot be limited to activities "justified by reasons referring exclusively" to the well-being of the governed. In practice, it is motivated by a mix of public purposes, particularistic interests, and beliefs about what is good for the poor.

The new paternalism that informs poverty governance today follows the general logic of paternalism. Thus, its proponents begin from the very premise that liberalism rejects: The poor lack the competence needed to manage their own affairs. Although the poor may recognize what is in their interest, they lack the discipline needed to make "behavior consistent with intention" (Mead 1997b: 5). Their lives are disorderly to the point that no opportunity or incentive, however clear, can induce them to act in their own interest. The poor "need direction if they are to live constructively" (Mead 1997b: 2). Government must step in as a disciplinary authority, and must do so for the poor's own good. Asserting the necessity of a policy stance that "in effect treats adults like children" (Mead 1997b: 26), new paternalists argue that state agents must act as fatherly "authority figures as well as helpmates" (Mead 2004a: 158).

As a late twentieth-century development, however, the new paternalism has several features that distinguish it from earlier forms, including the extreme versions associated with American slavery (Genovese 1974) and European colonialism (Narayan 1995).

First, it is rooted in the context of contemporary citizenship and proceeds within a broader framework of institutionalized rights. Rather than denying the citizen's rights, it emphasizes civic obligations as a justification for enforcing behavioral expectations (Mead 1986). Unlike the paternalism of slavery or colonialism, the new paternalism is a project of civic incorporation that aims to draw its targets toward full citizenship. As such, it focuses on segments of the poor who are identified as being too irresponsible "to merit the esteem of others [or make] a community of equal citizens imaginable" (Mead 1997a: 229)—people such as "the homeless, criminals, drug addicts, deadbeat dads, unmarried teenage mothers, and single mothers claiming welfare-benefits who have by their behavior indicated that they do not display the minimal level of self-control expected of decent citizens" (J. Wilson 1997: 340–41).

The behaviors of these groups threaten not just their own interests, but also liberal-democratic aspirations for an inclusive and egalitarian political order. Thus, the new paternalism seeks policy arrangements that enforce a more appropriate "operational definition of citizenship" by making the extension of social rights conditional on the fulfillment of social obligations (Mead 1986). The poor are subjected to directive and supervisory governance not just for their own good, but equally for the good of society and democracy.

Second, the new paternalism emerged in the late twentieth century as a species of the political movement known as neoconservatism. In the United States, neoconservatives mobilized around the idea that the American state had allowed, and even fostered, a steep decline in social order and morality. In response, diverse interests came together under the banner of "a strong, state-led and -legislated moral-political vision" (W. Brown 2006: 697). Internationally, neoconservatives sought a more interventionist and empowered U.S. foreign policy rooted in moral purposes. Domestically, they promoted policies designed to restore "traditional" values and combat social disorder.

New paternalists applied this broader vision to the poor, assigning the state responsibility for causing (and now curing) the breakdown of morality and social order in poor communities. Contexts of social disorder undermine individuals' abilities to act on their interests and discipline their own behaviors. To foster individual competence, paternalists argue, poor communities must first be made secure, and the legitimacy and capacity needed for this task can be found only in a strong state. Thus, paternalists fold a broad agenda of social control into the rubric of exercising authority for the poor's own good. The disorders that have arisen from the poor's lack of discipline—non-work, criminality, teen pregnancy, single motherhood—must be met by "a strong state and a state that will put its strength to use" (Norton 2004: 178). For the poor's sake as well as society's, the state must employ directive social programs, strengthen policing and surveillance, and remove disruptive individuals through incarceration. Appraising America's poor urban communities in the 1990s, the paternalist Lawrence Mead (1997a: 230) concluded:

> It is difficult to recall an era of Western history when the restoration of order was so much an imperative in and of itself. Destitution no longer raises issues of justice. The only answer to poverty is a slow building up of community institutions to the point where they can again enforce the obligations of citizenship. Only if order is restored in cities, and especially if work levels rise, could the poor become more self-respecting. Only then could they stake claims on the collectivity as equals, rather than seeking charity as dependents.

Third and finally, as a late twentieth-century development, the new paternalism emerged in the context of "the therapeutic state" (Polsky 1991). Therapeutic state interventions aim to do more than just coerce individuals or alter opportunities and incentives. They aim to change a person's basic values and self-conceptions, reconstructing the citizen as a different kind of self-regulating subject (Cruikshank 1999). Drawing on a medical model, they assert the presence of a social or psychological pathology that expert authorities must "cure."

Thus, paternalists embrace public authority, not simply to impose choices on the poor, but to cure the deeper pathologies that prevent them from regulating their own conduct in competent ways (Schram 2000). "By bringing about profound changes at the most intimate levels of human experience, the state aims to integrate marginal citizens into the social mainstream" (Polsky 1991: 3–4).

Specified in these ways, neoliberalism and paternalism converge on a distinctive agenda for poverty governance. Together, they define a strong state-led effort to bring discipline to the lives of the poor so that they can become competent actors who recognize and act on their interests as freely choosing agents of the market. The link between neoliberalism and paternalism, Jacob Segal (2006: 327) explains, "lies in a common definition of freedom as a practice of efficient living that requires an inner discipline. Those who fail at freedom must be trained into it." Thus, *freedom* for the poor is pursued through modes of governance that discipline poor individuals and impose order on poor communities. "The discipline of civilization," neoliberals argue, "is at the same time the discipline of freedom" (Hayek 1960: 163). "Those who would be free," paternalists concur, "must first be bound" (Mead 1997b: 23). To expand freedom, the state must "tell the poor what to do" (Mead 1998).

Neoliberalism and paternalism also converge on the idea that governance itself must be transformed in order to more effectively manage the poor. Both promote efforts to extend the state's governing capacity by using privatization and collaboration to enlist civil society institutions. Paternalism emphasizes that such cross-sector collaborations must be state led, while neoliberalism emphasizes that they must be organized on market terms. But in this sense, they are complements. Just as neoliberalism blurs the boundary between state and market, "paternalism transcends the old opposition of the public and private sectors" (Mead 1997b: 11). The two converge as well on a preference for decentralization: to facilitate tailored, local forms of supervision and reform (paternalism) and to open governance up to greater entrepreneurial innovation and competition (neoliberalism). At the same time, both call for governance to be based on new forms of knowledge: greater surveillance and documentation of poor people's behavior, closer measurements to evaluate and incentivize performance in governance, more scientific analyses to create legible profiles of the populations being managed, and so on.

Above all, neoliberalism and paternalism converge on the priority of work compliance. Paternalists identify work as the most basic civic obligation and the root of a well-ordered life (Mead 1986). Cast as a necessary foundation for other virtues, the "work first" mantra unites moralists who differ in their ultimate ends. Whatever forms of self-discipline the poor may need, the state must begin by demanding "acceptance of the verdict of the marketplace" (Mead 1986: 87). And of course, it is this same verdict that neoliberalism prizes most. The neoliberal state is called upon to make the poor available to employers on terms set by the declining market for low-skilled labor. The state must teach the poor to conceive of themselves as market actors, and, to accomplish this goal, it must actively position its targets as actors in market relations.

At the intersection of these two rationalities, one finds a coherent project of *governmentality*, in the sense that Michel Foucault (1991) uses this term. In poverty governance today, efforts to compel compliant behavior (sovereign powers) and institutional techniques for reforming disordered individuals (disciplinary powers) are deployed together as productive techniques for managing behavior, fostering self-mastery, and promoting the wellness of targeted populations (governmentality). Poverty governance seeks to impose order as a condition of freedom and, in so doing, to bring order to the exercise of freedom. Its goal is to transform the poor into subjects who, under conditions of apparent autonomy, choose to act in ways that comply with market imperatives and political authorities. It is, in this sense, a regime of practice designed to "translate the goals of political, social, and economic authorities into the choices and commitments of individuals" (Miller and Rose 2008: 214).

Politics and the Transformation of Poverty Governance

As analytic concepts, neoliberalism and paternalism help clarify the disciplinary turn in poverty governance, but they do little to explain why it occurred. For that, one must look to the conservative resurgence in U.S. politics that reshaped public policy and drove economic inequality skyward after the 1970s. In the closing decades of the twentieth century, well-organized political actors mobilized against the activist state that had developed from the New Deal through the Great Society (Pierson and Skocpol 2007). Their grievances were not specific to poverty. They were a response to the major political victories of the preceding decades: expansions of the regulatory state, progressive taxation, and social protections (Pierson 2007); civil rights achievements (V. Weaver 2007); and revolutions in race, gender, and sexual relations (Luker 1996). The successes of the countermovements flowed from their deep resources and strategic creativity as well as from changes in the organization of U.S. politics. Their focus on poverty governance reflected the political utility of the "disorderly poor" as a vehicle for advancing their broader ambitions. Their outsized effects in this area reflected the political vulnerability of the poor and the weaknesses and choices of their opponents in this domain.

By the end of the turbulent 1960s, social movements had combined with Democratic Party control to fundamentally reshape the United States. The old racial order was upended, gender relations were recast, and new sexual and reproductive freedoms were reshaping the social landscape (King and Smith 2005; A. Davis 1983). The regulatory powers of government expanded in both depth and the breadth, reaching new dimensions of consumer protection, oc-cupational health and safety, and environmental protection (Melnick 2005). Citizenship and governance were redefined by a sweeping rights revolution that spread outward from civil and voting rights to a wide variety of anti-discrimination laws (Skrentny 2002). The national welfare state designed in 1935 grew dramatically in coverage, protection, and cost (Noble 1997).

In the mid-twentieth century, business interests adopted a posture of prag-matic acceptance toward social protections, recognizing the stability they af-forded and the political risks of attacking them. With most of the industrialized world still recovering from World War II, U.S. businesses could afford to be tolerant: They held a dominant position in global markets that generated sizable profit margins. Many firms also benefited directly from public programs that subsidized employee benefits and created markets for their goods. By the end of the 1960s, however, this relatively peaceful settlement had fractured. Global markets became more competitive and profits declined (Noble 1997). The bur-dens of regulation and social protection were more costly now, and they were expanding. Indeed, from 1969 to 1972 "virtually the entire American business community experienced a series of political setbacks without parallel in the post-war period" (Vogel 1989: 59). The political response from business was not long in coming.

The nascent political operations that business had developed in the early 1960s exploded into a fierce organizational offensive (C. Martin 1994). Be-tween 1974 and 1978, the number of corporate-sponsored political action com-mittees (PACs) grew from 89 to 784, with an additional 500 PACs emerging to represent trade associations and business interests (Conway 1986: 73). Older organizations like the Chamber of Commerce worked to increase their mem-berships and lobbying capacities, as new organizations like the Business Round-table were created to bring corporate leaders together as a more potent political force (Akard 1992). Offices representing business proliferated in Washington, where they paired the pursuit of insider influence with strategies for mobilizing grassroots support for legislative efforts (Vogel 1989).

Going on the offensive, business interests pushed a broad agenda (Ferguson and Rogers 1986; Vogel 1989; Akard 1992). They fought to cut tax burdens and shift them toward workers, deregulate financial markets, and weaken environmental and workplace protections. They moved to curtail worker power by undercutting labor unions and pushing aid recipients into labor markets. They worked to lower the costs of existing social supports and block the creation of new protections against changing societal risks. Together, these efforts restructured the American political economy in ways that allowed "the rich to pull away from the rest" (Bartels 2008). At the other end of the income distribution, their effects on poverty governance were amplified by the simultaneous rise of social conservatism as a potent political force.

In the mid-twentieth century, Christian fundamentalists generally disdained the worldly activity of political conflict. The first stirrings of change emerged in the early 1960s, in the form of outrage at the U.S. Supreme Court's ban on prayer in public schools. In the years that followed, anxieties rose steadily as women's rights and gay rights advanced, changes in sexuality and reproduction took root, and legalized abortion became the law of the land. A growing number of Christian leaders began to argue that the time had come "to get in there and fight" (Hodgson 1989: 174). In the 1980s, churches began to develop new capacities for local activism that would later be stitched together as a potent national network by Pat Robertson's 1988 presidential campaign and the drive to roll back abortion rights (Diamond 1995). By the 1990s, "the Family Research Council had 300,000 subscriber members in its communication bank, the Eagle Forum had 80,000 members, and the Christian Coalition could marshal 1.7 million donors and activists" (Heclo 2001: 181). Leaders such as Jerry Falwell and Ralph Reed moved aggressively to amass resources, build organizations, and, ultimately, remake state institutions and policies as instruments for the pursuit of moral purposes.

The social conservative movement drew the Christian Right together with other groups activated by perceptions of moral decline and social disorder. Neoconservatives, who began as disaffected liberals opposing communism, developed a broader agenda for using the American state to combat declining social order and moral restraint (Norton 2004). Racial conservatives, galvanized by civil rights victories, began to pursue a "law and order" campaign that identified social protest, civil disobedience, urban riots, street crime, and deviant behaviors in poor neighborhoods as related parts of a single problem: the breakdown of social order (V. Weaver 2007; J. Simon 2007). Together, these groups formed a powerful coalition pushing an agenda rooted in order, discipline, personal responsibility, and a moral state.

As conservatives and business interests mobilized, they sought more than just immediate policy victories. Adopting a longer view, they invested in efforts to transform the intellectual and organizational landscape of American politics. Corporations and wealthy conservatives, such as Richard Mellon Scaife, poured millions of dollars into the creation of new organizations (think tanks, foundations, and academic societies) designed to shift the terms of political debate and discredit Keynesian uses of the state. In the legal arena, they funded the rise of the Federalist Society and the law and economics movement (Teles 2008). More broadly, their investments produced a right-wing revolution in policy-focused think tanks (Rich 2004). At organizations such as the Heritage Foundation, American Enterprise Institute, and Cato Institute, conservatives turned broad ideas into detailed proposals, churned out research to support their agendas, and spent lavishly to spread their arguments through books, periodicals, and public events (Rich 2004). In the area of poverty governance, right-wing think tanks invested heavily in promoting welfare critics such as Charles Murray, Marvin Olasky, Lawrence Mead, and Robert Rector.

Conservative mobilization had equally profound effects on the party system. Opportunity came in the form of a fraying Democratic coalition. Support for civil rights in the 1960s badly weakened the party's "solid" hold on the South and on the loyalties of working-class white men. Capitalizing on this opening, business interests and conservatives did more than just increase their support for the Republican Party; they organized to push the party to the right. Conservative activists recruited far-right candidates and poured resources into their campaigns. New groups like the Club for Growth targeted moderate Republicans for elimination and funded primary challenges to replace them (Hacker and Pierson 2005). The result was a steep and asymmetric rise in party polarization. As its conservative southern members lost office, the Democratic Party's average ideological position moved slightly to the left. By contrast, the Republican Party shifted sharply to the right as it replaced its moderates with more aggressive advocates for markets and morality (Theriault 2006; McCarty, Poole, and Rosenthal 2006).

Conservative mobilization did little to move public opinion to the right (Fiorina 2004; Page and Jacobs 2009) or to shift public attention from economic to cultural issues (Stonecash 2000; Bartels 2008). It drove political change by underwriting the Republican Party's rise to power—supplying it with organized networks of business leaders and social conservatives and, perhaps more important, by providing unprecedented financial resources for political combat.

Indeed, conservatives benefited greatly from the rising political importance of money in the late twentieth century, as electoral campaigns and lobbying efforts became vastly more expensive. In 1980 and again in 1994, Republicans rode a wave of business money as corporate interests abandoned their usual pragmatic strategy of investing in both major parties (Piven 2007: 151). As money became more central to elections, spiraling inequality concentrated this resource at the top of the income distribution. In 2000, 95 percent of the people who gave $1,000 or more to a campaign came from the one-eighth of U.S. households with incomes over $100,000 per year (APSA Taskforce 2004). Both major parties reorganized their operations to reflect their growing dependence on affluent donors (Campbell 2007a). For Republicans, this focus fit easily into a pro-business policy agenda. For Democrats, it created significant cross-pressures and incentives to downplay questions of inequality, redistribution, and social protection.

The disciplinary turn in poverty governance was ultimately a product of these broad political developments, but it would be a mistake to think that the poor were simply swept up in this political wave, as one facet of change among many. From their inception, the rising conservative movements made the poor, and policies directed at the poor, a central focus of their political rhetoric and reform efforts. Indeed, the emphasis on poverty governance was no accident. It reflected the strategic utility of focusing on "the unruly poor" as a way to unite the emerging coalition and divide and discredit the opposition. By focusing on the poor, organized conservatives avoided the political obstacles they confronted in other policy domains and distracted attention from policy agendas that attracted far less public support.

The symbolic uses of the unruly poor were demonstrated as early as 1964, when Barry Goldwater and George Wallace campaigned for the presidency on "law and order" themes, with Wallace also demanding that welfare recipients be put to work. Although their campaigns failed, they succeeded in showing how a focus on social disorder could link political protest and street crime, capitalize on racial resentments, and lay blame at the feet of liberals. The lessons of their campaigns were not lost on leading Republicans. In 1968, Richard Nixon made law and order the centerpiece of his Southern Strategy for winning over disaffected white Democrats. In 1970, he followed up by declaring war on "the criminal elements which increasingly threaten our cities, our homes, and our lives." By the 1980s, conservatives had elaborated a rich narrative of "the

THE RISE OF NEOLIBERAL PATERNALISM · 33

underclass" that drew attention away from the structural problems of deindus-trialization and the compounding effects of racial segregation in American cit-ies (W. Wilson 1997; Massey and Denton 1993). Instead, this narrative blamed Great Society policies—coddling criminals, rewarding bad choices with hand-outs, and so on—for a rising tide of irresponsibility, promiscuity, violence, and welfare dependence. As president, Ronald Reagan extended the war on crime to a war on drugs and made the image of the "welfare queen" into a powerful metaphor for the idea that hard-working, law-abiding Americans were being exploited by the lazy and criminal poor.

The prominence of these themes in the conservative rise to power is best understood as a tactical response to the political opportunities and obstacles the coalition confronted. On the opportunity side, they offered a wedge issue almost uniquely well suited for exploiting post-1960s popular anxieties and divisions in the Democratic coalition. The race-coded themes of urban disor-der, crime, and welfare were aimed at the newly contested white electorates (in the South and elsewhere) who felt abandoned by Democratic support for civil rights, desegregation, busing, and affirmative action. Criticisms of wel-fare, a program that was now equated with poor single mothers of color (Han-cock 2004), played on diverse anxieties surrounding changes in gender roles, sexuality, and family formation. As the real wages of U.S. workers stagnated, images of lazy welfare queens provided a scapegoat for economic fears, chan-neling popular anxieties into anger at government for taxing working families to support the irresponsible poor.

At the same time, conservatives used their focus on the unruly poor as a way to put a populist face on their agenda, clothing it in anti-statist and anti-elitist rhetoric (Ehrenreich 1987). Welfare, in this frame, was not a hard-won protec-tion for poor workers and their families. It was the self-serving creation of a liberal "intelligentsia" that used big government to shower special benefits on the poor—at the expense of workers' checkbooks and most cherished values. In-deed, the image of a victimized "silent" and "moral" majority became a central trope of conservatism (J. Simon 2007). People who played by the rules were be-ing abused by the "illegitimate takings" of welfare freeloaders and violent crimi-nals (and later, undocumented immigrants). The earned and deserved rights of hard-working Americans were being ignored by liberal elites who cared more about the rights of the victimizers—the criminal defendants and welfare recipi-ents of the urban underclass. The interests of such ordinary Americans, in this frame, were equated with efforts to promote victims' rights, taxpayers' rights, and a society based on personal responsibility.

The conservative emphasis on poverty was not simply a matter of seizing opportunities, however. It also reflected the challenges that confronted an emerging coalition. Pro-market advocates and social conservatives have never been easy allies. Libertarian desires for free markets clash with the drive to create a moral-authoritarian state. Social conservatives recoil at the sight of corporations upending community traditions, promoting mass consumerism, and profiting from the sale of sex and sin. The growing alliance of the two movements depended on the suppression of divisive issues and the elevation of agendas valued by both wings. In this regard, poverty governance offered an inviting alternative. Reform in this area was a priority for two segments of the business community: low-wage employers eager to keep labor on the market and firms that stood to profit directly from privatization (Ehrenreich 1997; Piven and Cloward 1993). It was equally important to social conservatives, who were eager to bring vice and violence under control and to change welfare programs that they saw as encouraging marital breakdown, sexual promiscuity, and moral irresponsibility (Ehrenreich 1987; Gilder 1981).

In addition, the conservative focus on poverty governance emerged as a tactical response to the barriers the coalition confronted in other areas as it tried to reform the activist state. Even as Republicans gained control of elected offices, conservatives found that the state's expanded capacity and reach could not be easily repealed (Pierson 2007). The status quo bias of the U.S. political system, which had often thwarted efforts to expand the welfare state, now allowed retreating liberals to block efforts to dismantle it (Noble 1997). Rising party polarization made it more difficult to build bipartisan coalitions for policy change (McCarty 2007), and in many areas, the activist state had produced policy constituencies that now mobilized to defend their programs (Pierson 1994; Campbell 2003). Repeatedly too, conservatives found that Americans welcomed the rhetoric of personal responsibility more than policy changes that actually stripped them of protections and left them to fend for themselves on the market (Page and Jacobs 2009).

As Jacob Hacker (2004, 2006) rightly notes, these and other obstacles channeled the assault on social protections toward strategies of "stealth" (reducing protections below the public radar) and "drift" (preventing policies from adapting to evolving risks and needs). Poverty governance was a notable exception to this rule. Dramatic changes for the poor were pursued in the most visible ways and achieved with great fanfare. Several factors explain the discrepancy.

First, the poor provided a weak and isolated political target, unable to push back as others could. Stigmatized and lacking resources, the poor are rarely able to defend themselves in the policy process (Piven and Cloward 1977). And by the last decades of the twentieth century, organized allies were in short supply. Labor unions were in sharp decline and focused on their own problems (Goldfield 1989). Foundation-supported nonprofits that focused on poverty, such as the Children's Defense Fund, had no grassroots networks or mass memberships to mobilize (Skocpol 2003). The public interest organizations that proliferated on the left focused mainly on "quality of life" issues, devoting few resources to issues of economic distribution and protection (Berry 1999). Even social justice organizations, formed to advocate for groups such as women or racial minorities, tended to pay limited attention to welfare, treating it as a narrow subgroup issue with limited significance for their broader constituency (Strolovitch 2008).

Organizational weakness was compounded by institutional isolation, especially for clients in the Aid to Families with Dependent Children (AFDC) program. Over the course of the twentieth century, successive legislative actions segregated poor single women and their children from bona fide social insurance contributors (1935), the surviving dependents of deceased social insurance contributors (1939), and people with certified disabilities (1972). Thus, as the attacks on AFDC moved into high gear, recipients could not seek political cover through alignment with more positively constructed and powerful groups receiving aid from the state. Poor women with children stood alone, denigrated as a lazy and licentious racial other and contrasted with more deserving beneficiaries (Hancock 2004; Winter 2008). Common cause was further undercut by America's "hidden welfare state" of tax expenditures, which obscured the public supports going to non-poor families and made it appear that AFDC was unique in offering public support to able-bodied parents (Howard 1997; Hacker 2002). Coalition along gender lines was undercut by the paucity of child care and other supports being offered to working women, which made it seem like welfare clients received special treatment (Orloff 2002). And, of course, the design of the AFDC program itself kept recipients very poor, insecure, and mired in social crises (Edin and Lein 1997). In this policy context, calls for policy change came from across the political spectrum, and few allies could be found to oppose the conservative vision of change.

With the poor isolated by institutions, as well as social and residential segregation, Americans were encouraged to think about changes in poverty governance as if they mattered only for deviant others. Yet this was far from the case. The assault on the poor served as a symbolic vehicle for mobilizing opposition to the welfare state more generally and discrediting the ideas of political liberals.

It made iconic black images of dependent single mothers and criminally violent men into the symbolic faces of social entitlement and government support.

As Jacob Hacker (2006: 51) points out, the themes sounded in the anti-welfare campaign were only the most visible part of a "Personal Responsibility Crusade" that sought to undermine a wide array of collectivizing policies so that Americans would take greater ownership of their risks and choices. "By protecting us from the full consequences of our choices," reformers argued in areas from health care to pensions to child care, government supports erode "our incentives to be economically productive and personally prudent" (Hacker 2006: 38). The political spectacle constructed around the underclass served the broader effort, not just by using the deviant poor to legitimate its broad themes, but also by distracting attention from policy changes that were shifting risks onto the backs of working Americans. The symbolic image of counterproductive handouts to the poor focused public attention and framed an argument with far wider implications. Former Republican Congressman Dick Armey stated the point succinctly: "Social responsibility is a euphemism for individual *irresponsibility*" (Armey 1995: 317).

The conservative onslaught sowed division in the Democratic Party, not just in the electorate but also in the form of elite factions, such as the Democratic Leadership Council (DLC), that organized to push the party away from Great Society liberalism. Politically divided and outgunned, Democratic Party leaders fought back selectively as they engaged in a tactical retreat. On issues of greater concern to the affluent and well organized, Democrats worked aggressively to block or temper conservative legislation. In the area of poverty governance, they increasingly adopted a strategy of cooptation, seeking to evade the charge of being soft on crime and welfare by embracing milder versions of conservative proposals as their own.

Poor people, of course, had little ability to force the party to expend its dwindling political capital on their behalf. And with images of the poor increasingly racialized, a vigorous counteroffensive would have risked deepening the racial divides that threatened the party's coalition (Frymer 1999). Instead, leading Democrats began to argue that liberal positions on crime and welfare were costly political liabilities that undercut public support for party candidates and broader progressive agendas. By aligning themselves with efforts to transform poverty governance, they hoped to take the corrosive issues of race, crime, and welfare off the table—freeing the party from the wedge issues that Republicans had used so effectively and clearing the way for less "distorted" debates over work and poverty (Soss and Schram 2007).

Time and again, the same storyline played out on crime and welfare legislation. Badly damaged by the law-and-order campaigns, leading Democrats worked to counter the party's image as a weak link in the wars on crime and drugs. Thus, when the death of basketball star Len Bias set off a moral panic over crack in the summer of 1986, Speaker of the House Tip O'Neill moved quickly to make sure that Democrats would establish a strong anti-drug position before the upcoming elections. As a result, the Anti-Drug Abuse Act of 1986, which established mandatory-minimum drug sentences, was passed with less than a month of public deliberation, just in time for the November elections. As Dan Baum recounts (1997: 225):

> [Returning from the July 4 recess,] Tip O'Neill called an emergency meeting of the crime-related committee chairmen. Write me some goddamn legislation, he thundered. All anybody up in Boston is talking about is Len Bias. The papers are screaming for blood. We need to get out front on this now. This week. Today. The Republicans beat us to it in 1984 and I don't want that to happen again. I want dramatic new initiatives for dealing with crack and other drugs. If we can do this fast enough, he said to the Democratic leadership arrayed around him, we can take the issue away from the [Reagan] White House.

"The grand strategic game of realigning the image of the Democratic Party" reached its high point in the 1990s, under the presidency of Bill Clinton (R. Weaver 2002: 116). As a presidential candidate in 1992, Clinton combined populist economic appeals with efforts to establish himself as a New Democrat who would not be beholden to labor unions, racial minorities, feminists, environmentalists, or other groups viewed as "special interests" of the Democratic Party (Williams 2003). Clinton emphasized his credentials as a pro-death penalty, tough-on-crime governor. The crowd-pleasing centerpiece of his campaign, however, was his pledge to "end welfare as we know it" and tell the welfare poor, "two years and you're off."

Clinton's pledge would be put to the test four years later, after Republicans took over Congress in 1994 based on a Contract with America that promised to get tough with the poor. As Republicans seized control of the agenda, Clinton was forced to address welfare proposals that were far more stringent, and included far fewer supports, than the plans that he and his advisor David Ellwood had envisioned (Ellwood 1988; DeParle 1996). After contesting some of the most extreme provisions, Clinton ultimately came to the same conclusion that Tip O'Neill reached in 1986. To shed an electoral liability and clear the path for new policy efforts, Democrats would need to position themselves out front in abolishing "the welfare mess." Surveying voters for the upcoming election, Clinton's most trusted pollsters instructed him to "fast-track the Gingrich agenda" (Dick Morris), "transcend welfare politics" (Stanley Greenberg), and "clear the way for [the Democratic Party's] rejuvenated influence over ghetto poverty" (Dick Morris again).

As the election season moved into high gear, Clinton signed the Personal Responsibility and Work Opportunity Reconciliation Act (PRWORA), abolishing welfare as an entitlement and replacing it with a block grant to the states that emphasized work requirements, time limits, sanctions for noncompliance, and governing arrangements designed to promote privatization and performance-based contracting. For poor families in the new Temporary Assistance for Needy Families (TANF) program, the era of neoliberal paternalism was officially at hand.

Specifying Contemporary Poverty Governance

PRWORA was the most visible legislative event in the recent history of U.S. poverty governance. It also produced one of the most stunning policy effects: Between 1994 and 2008, the number of AFDC/TANF recipients in the U.S. declined by about 72 percent.[1] Focusing on these developments, many observers have described recent changes as a return to laissez-faire in which government retreats and the poor are left to fend for themselves in the market (Somers and Block 2005). Others, such as Loïc Wacquant (2009: 19), combine this narrative with a focus on rising correctional control: "As the state more completely sheds economic responsibility," it produces insecurity and disorder which, in turn, "necessitates the grandeur of the penal state."

In the area of poverty governance, however, the American state has not shed its economic responsibilities; it has recast and, indeed, deepened them. In this domain, as in many others, political challengers did not dismantle the activist state; they reorganized it and turned it to new purposes (Pierson and Skocpol 2007). The approaches to governance they put in place operate according to the logics of neoliberal paternalism described earlier, and they rely on a strong activist state in *both* the social welfare and penal-carceral fields. The key developments have not occurred along the quantitative dimension of more versus less state intervention. They have focused on how the state is intervening, for what purposes, and for whose benefit.

Poverty governance has been reorganized to replace centralized state control with decentralized cross-sector collaborations and to serve as a site of profitable investment for corporations such as Lockheed Martin, Maximus, Affiliated Computer Systems (ACS), and Corrections Corporation of America (CCA). Welfare investments that shield the poor from market pressures have, indeed, declined. But these resources and far more are being invested in neoliberal-paternalist governing strategies: policing, incarceration, and parole supervision; aid made conditional on behavior; social programs that emphasize direction, supervision, and penalty; policies that use tax dollars to subsidize wage costs; and a host of efforts to incentivize, enable, and enforce the placement of labor on the market.

The programs that have been curtailed mostly fall outside this rubric and target working-age, nondisabled Americans. In some cases, efforts to curb such protections have been overt. The Reagan administration cut federal investments in state unemployment insurance trust funds (Pierson 1994: 116–20); many states terminated or restricted their General Assistance (GA) programs (Gallagher et al. 1999); and in 1996, the federal government abolished the AFDC entitlement. Much of the erosion, however, was accomplished through strategies that blocked efforts to keep benefits aligned with inflation and coverage aligned with changes in labor markets (Hacker 2004). Even before welfare reform, the value of the combined AFDC-Food Stamp package had declined precipitously, mostly because lawmakers allowed the real value of AFDC benefits to decline by 42 percent between 1970 and 1996 (Pavetti 2001: 233).

Unemployment Insurance (UI), which serves a more economically diverse group, declined as well. The UI eligibility period and average replacement rate for wages held steady. But new policies restricted access by allowing employers to challenge their former workers' applications, and policy drift left workers unprotected in the fastest-growing sectors of the labor market (Fagnoni 2007; GAO 2000). Overall spending declined from $12,000 per unemployed worker in 1970 to less than $4,000 in 2000 (Massey 2007: 169), with most of the reductions coming from declining coverage of the lowest-wage workers (GAO 2000). By the 1990s, low-wage workers were twice as likely to be unemployed but, relative to other unemployed workers, were less than half as likely to receive UI (GAO 2000).

As supports outside the market dwindled, equally significant changes occurred in policies designed to incent employment and "make work pay." The crucial shift involved the decline of the minimum wage, which forces employers to bear the costs of increasing incomes, and the rise of the Earned Income Tax

Credit (EITC), which puts this burden on taxpayers. From 1968 to 2006, the real value of the minimum wage dropped from $9.30 to $5.15 per hour (from 45 percent to 28 percent of the average wage and from 93 percent to 50 percent of the poverty line) (Bartels 2008: 26; Massey 2007: 167–68). Faced with overwhelming public support for a minimum-wage increase (Bartels 2008), business interests pushed hard for the alternative strategy of expanding the EITC (Herd 2008). The EITC offers no protection for the unemployed and puts no floor under wages. Instead, by using tax revenues to augment wages, it strengthens work incentives for the poor and relieves wage pressures on employers. From 1975 to 2006, federal EITC spending rose from $5 million to $45 million (Scholz, Moffitt, and Cowan 2009). These investments substantially increased labor force participation among the poor (Grogger 2003; Meyer 2002) and led to reductions in market wages for low-skilled workers (Rothstein 2009).

The EITC is aimed at working-age, nondisabled adults who are in the labor market. On one side of this group lie target populations such as the disabled and elderly. Major programs for these populations continue to provide more generous nonmarket protections, but they have been reformed in recent years to present modest but clear work incentives (as is the case in Disability Insurance and Supplemental Security Income). On the other side, one finds means-tested programs for the working-age, nondisabled poor who lack a clear work attachment. Here, the work push is stronger and more paternalist. The best-known example is the TANF program, where poor families receive cash benefits that are time limited, tied to work requirements, and subject to sanctions for noncompliance (Schram 2000). TANF expenditures, increasingly run through for-profit contractors, have shifted away from cash aid and are now used primarily to fund services and classes that seek to eliminate work barriers and make labor more marketable (S. Allard 2009). These efforts are augmented by tax expenditures that subsidize the cost of hiring program leavers, offering employers up to $9,000 per hire under the Work Opportunity Tax Credit.

The work push is hardly limited to TANF, however. Since the passage of the Quality Housing and Work Responsibility Act of 1998, the federal government has required recipients of public housing aid to work or volunteer each month and has made TANF sanctions a basis for denying rent reductions due to lost income. Similar changes were made to food assistance. Today, recipients of the Supplemental Nutrition Assistance Program (SNAP, formerly known as Food Stamps) must register for work, accept suitable employment, and participate in work-promoting programs as a condition of aid. Working-age adults without children can receive SNAP for only 3 months in a 36-month period if they do not work or participate in a workfare program—a rule that parallels the strict work requirements imposed on adults without dependents in state GA programs (Gallagher et al. 1999). Similarly, since 1979 federal rules have promoted prison labor by allowing the sale, interstate commerce, and international export of goods made by prisoners. Between 1979 and 2005, "prison industries" contributed an estimated $97 million toward the costs of incarceration and $47 million in federal and state taxes (U.S. Department of Justice 2009). Over the same period, cheap prison labor was increasingly contracted to for-profit firms, with private prison operators such as CCA also profiting directly by using prisoners as maintenance workers (Kang 2009).

Under paternalism, work promotion has been accompanied by dramatic increases in procedures for monitoring and documenting poor people's behavior. Aid recipients have been increasingly subjected to drug testing, finger printing, and questioning regarding their sexual relations (to establish paternity and pursue child support). On the criminal justice side, the expansion of supervision has been greater still. Between 1970 and 2003, state and federal prison populations grew sevenfold, with most of the growth occurring among poor, undereducated, minority groups (Western 2006). Per capita corrections expenditure in the states rose from $23 in 1970 to $125 in 2001, from 1 percent to 3.5 percent of all budget outlays (Guetzkow and Western 2006).

In penal and welfare operations alike, the reach of state supervision has been growing beyond the limits of the official "participation spell." In some states, new forms of "post-exit paternalism" specify that welfare leavers must remain in their jobs to continue to receive transitional supports. Similarly, parole supervision has become more vigilant and has been applied to an escalating percentage of the post-prison population. In 2003, 4.7 million Americans were under probation or parole supervision, and the number of individuals leaving prison each year stood at 630,000 (quadruple the rate in 1978) (Travis 2005). More than 80 percent of people leaving prison were being placed on parole, and the number being sent back for parole violation was seven times higher than it had been twenty years earlier (Western 2006). Drug offenders receive especially close scrutiny in private "recovery houses," where they are monitored daily and risk a return to prison if they relapse (Fairbanks 2009). When prisoners finish "doing their time" today, they are typically released into "a closely monitored terrain, a supervised space, lacking much of the liberty that one associates with normal life" (Garland 2002: 178).

Neoliberal paternalism has guided equally important shifts in *how* poverty governance is organized and carried out. As the activist state has been turned to new purposes, it has been "rolled out" to diverse actors and locales through privatization and devolution (Peck and Tickell 2002). Emphasizing efficiency and performance, reformers have "reinvented government" as a diffuse network of governing relationships rooted in market principles. Increasingly, poverty governance is structured by contractual relations, decentralized to facilitate entrepreneurial innovation, and evaluated on market terms rather than democratic values.

The rolling out of poverty governance was driven by more than just ideology; it also served practical political purposes. Outside the elected offices of national government, the entrenched liberal state could not be easily purged of its established cultures, routines, and actors. Devolution and privatization shifted authority to sites with fewer barriers to establishing new governing logics. New performance systems facilitated outsourcing by establishing outcome-based logics of public accountability (distant from democratic control and transparency) that could be applied to private contractors as easily as state agencies. As governance became more decentralized, these performance systems also provided mechanisms for disciplining the operations of far-flung agents to improve the odds that principals' goals would be achieved.

Many of these developments have been accompanied by rhetorical attacks on "big government" that celebrate market efficiencies, local knowledge, and the compassion of nonprofit and religious organizations. The political salience of such appeals has obscured a more basic fact: Neoliberal paternalism is not about weakening the state; it is about strengthening the state as a disciplinary authority. New approaches to governing the poor have extended the reach of government via contractual relationships with market and civil society organizations. State powers of surveillance and discipline have expanded dramatically, even as the public sector has been attacked and prevented from growing to meet new needs.

Theorizing Historical Change and Continuity

Surveying these developments, it is tempting to posit a sharp break with the past. But poverty governance today is a blend of old and new. The challenge is to clarify how change has proceeded along the pathways marked out by historical continuity. To do so, we theorize the disciplinary turn as a point of transition in three long-standing functions of poverty governance: civic incorporation, social control, and the production of self-regulating subjects.

Neoliberal paternalism extends the long tradition of using poverty policies as tools of civic incorporation (Somers 2008). It shares this tradition with the War on Poverty of the 1960s, which pursued civic inclusion through efforts to expand rights and empower poor communities (Quadagno 1994; Cruikshank 1999). It also shares this tradition with earlier eras in which public policies shored up the privileged civic status of white males and sought to incorporate the poor in race- and gender-differentiated ways (Gordon 1994; Katznelson 2005). In each period, poverty governance has institutionalized a particular vision of citizenship: ideas about what civic membership entails, who is to be included, and on what terms. Neoliberal paternalism offers such a vision, and it plays a key role in the political rationality of poverty governance today.

Neoliberalism, as we have argued, recasts citizenship as a quasi-market role. Its citizens are not defined by their mutual engagement in a democratic mode of governance; they are identified by their discipline and prudence as consumers, workers, and taxpaying investors (Wolin 2008; W. Brown 2006). For the poor, this neoliberal vision is joined to a paternalist conception of citizenship that prioritizes the fulfillment of civic obligations. In T. H. Marshall's (1964) classic theory of citizenship, civic duties such as voting and working attach to individuals *because* they possess membership rights. Aside from obligations to obey the law, such duties are matters of civic expectation rather than state enforcement. Paternalists turn this conception on its head, making the fulfillment of obligations into a precondition for civic membership and an object of state enforcement (Mead 1986). Self-reliance as a worker and self-discipline as a community member are treated as "not just a moral good but a prerequisite for citizenship" (Mayer 2008: 167). They are necessary criteria for "moral standing" in the community of people who merit equal respect and can be presumed competent to participate in civic life (Mead 1992).

Guided by this vision, the old project of civic integration has shifted to emphasize the civic primacy of market competence and the necessity of modifying behaviors to meet civic expectations. Welfare programs have been redesigned to "require recipients to function where they already are, as dependents" (Mead 1986: 4), so they can become self-reliant workers who "live as full and independent citizens" (Novak et al. 1987: 5). Civic incorporation proceeds by positioning welfare recipients, not as bearers of rights or participants in governance, but as targets of direction and supervision (Mead 2005). Based on the premise that "the welfare problem [is] one of authority rather than freedom" (Mead 1986: 4), reformers have prioritized social order over social justice and civic compliance over civic engagement (Mead 1998).

Thus, attempts to engage and empower the poor have been displaced by efforts to reshape the ways that poor people manage themselves as individuals. Citizenship has been "reduced to self-care" (W. Brown 2006); self-care has been reduced to meeting one's needs through the market; and state authority has been redirected toward these ends. Uses of public policy to make "better citizens" have become, under this logic, indistinguishable from efforts to produce compliant subjects whose behaviors comport with market imperatives and political authorities.

The disciplinary turn in poverty governance has also reflected shifts in the race and gender dimensions of citizenship. During the Progressive era, for example, the reformers who championed Mothers' Pensions for poor women did so explicitly in the name of Republican Motherhood and the need to support women's special civic duty and right to care for the next generation of citizens (Skocpol 1992; Gordon 1994). Republican Motherhood, in turn, reflected the race-specific meanings of American citizenship that prevailed at the time (R. Smith 1997). Thus, the goal of facilitating gender-specific civic obligations contributed to both the provision of benefits outside wage work and the exclusion of racial "others" from the system—especially poor black women, who were valued more as workers than as mothers of citizens (Ward 2005).

By contrast, the neoliberal-paternalist vision collapses diverse civic values into a small set of foundational obligations. As we discuss at length in the next chapter, race no longer functions as a straightforward basis for exclusion; it operates as a more subtle cultural resource for the production of disciplinary modes of civic incorporation. Equally nuanced changes have occurred in the gender dimensions of civic integration.

Motherhood, for example, has not been abandoned as a civic good; it has been subjected to new terms of evaluation. The mother's nonmarket work, in caregiving and child rearing, has lost its status as a civic contribution meriting public support. But it has retained its status as a civic responsibility that poor women should be held accountable for—a practice to be monitored and disciplined. At the same time, wage work has been elevated as a new standard for judging the fulfillment of this duty. Thus, the welfare-reliant mother is framed as a civic failure, not just for dodging her own work obligations, but also for presenting her children with a bad role model, exposing them to shame, and failing to provide for their needs. The historically masculine role of the worker-citizen is impressed on poor women as a maternal obligation that they must fulfill, either by marrying a family breadwinner or assuming this role themselves (Korteweg 2003).

In this way and others, poverty governance has been transformed by what

Meda Chesney-Lind (1995) has called "gender equality with a vengeance," a historical pattern "whereby the replacement of gender difference with sameness [leads] to the more punitive treatment of women" (Haney 2004: 340). This change has involved more than as a simple matter of wage work becoming normative for all women in the wake of second-wave feminism. Now as in the past, race mediates the relationship between gender and civic enforcement efforts. Poor women of color predominate in the populations that fill women's prisons and welfare programs, and they prevail in the cultural images that have motivated policies to enforce work and personal responsibility (Haney 2004; Hancock 2004). As we shall see in later chapters, the civic-incorporation efforts directed at poor women today depend greatly on constructed images of blackness that frame poverty governance as a whole and underwrite its variations.

Different dimensions of historical development come into view if we shift our conceptual focus to labor regulation and social control. For centuries, poor relief has functioned as a key mechanism for regulating work behavior, and its logic has been firmly rooted in the "principle of less eligibility" (Piven and Cloward 1971). The principle, most clearly articulated in the English Poor Law Amendment Act of 1834, states that the condition of the aid recipient must never be "really or apparently" as attractive as the condition of the poorest worker in the lowest job. The principle acknowledged that welfare programs operated as politically defined sites of needs-based provision that shielded workers from pressures to sell their labor as a commodity at any price (Stone 1984). Expansions of relief protected workers and eased the wage-depressing effects of desperate competition by "decommodifying" labor (taking it off the market). Conversely, actions that reduced benefit levels, restricted access to aid, and stigmatized aid recipients undercut this decommodifying effect. Such practices shored up work effort by making public relief less viable as an alternative to the worst jobs and by linking it to a pariah status that self-respecting individuals struggled to avoid at almost any cost (Piven and Cloward 1971).

In the United States, decommodification has always been strongest in social insurance programs, where recipients have been protected by more secure eligibility rules and national structures of funding and administration. Programs for the poor were designed as more flexible tools of labor regulation that made aid more contingent on means tests, morals tests, and local administrative discretion. At times, their decommodifying effects have been negligible at best. In the first half of the twentieth century, for example, welfare programs in the South facilitated the exploitation of black agricultural workers by offering only a subsistence level of support when the fields lay idle. When hands were needed for planting or picking, local officials moved the poor off relief by applying vague eligibility rules, inspecting homes for moral violations, and, on occasion, simply shuttering the welfare office (Bell 1965; Piven and Cloward 1971).

As this example suggests, work enforcement has traditionally emphasized the *negation* of welfare as a viable alternative to the market. Even when work has been required as a condition of aid itself, as in the hard labor of the poorhouse, its main function has been to make relief unattractive to all but the most desperate claimants (Katz 1996). Such strategies of negation continue to play an important role in poverty governance, as illustrated by the withering of benefits for nonworking individuals and by the various forms of administrative legerdemain that have driven down the TANF caseload. Neoliberal paternalism is, among other things, a resurgence of efforts to undercut decommodification. But it also entails new developments that have made the principle of less eligibility less singular as a mechanism of work enforcement.

Today, efforts to negate welfare protections are complemented by more affirmative uses of welfare programs to service labor markets. Neoliberalism has blurred the boundary between the two, making welfare offices into helpmates for the labor market. When adults, mostly single mothers, apply for public aid today, they enter an arena that is organized to serve employers: Its purpose is to groom clients for employment, offer them up for hire, and press them into available jobs. Contemporary work requirements are designed to do more than just deter claimants. They are valued equally, if not more, as reformative regimens that immerse recipients in a tutelary market experience. Work activities in the TANF program function today as just one element of a broader regime of classes, incentives, penalties, and supports designed to create more attractive and compliant workers. The mission of the welfare office is to remove the recipient's "barriers" to work, teach her to be a self-disciplined market actor, and ensure that she pursues "work first."

In this manner, welfare participation has become, in its own right, a mode of labor market participation. Welfare agencies do not decommodify labor; they act affirmatively, and in collaboration with low-wage employers, to bolster its attractiveness as a commodity. Welfare programs have been turned into new sites of market activity. Their purpose is to supplement market pressures with state authority in order to hasten the movement of poor women into low-wage jobs. Paternalism has made the state into an agent of market discipline, "assuming the function that the workplace did before" (Mead 1997a: 229). Under neoliberalism, the boundary between state and market has eroded. Transitions into welfare receipt no longer diminish market pressures; transitions out do not ensure a weakening of state support and oversight.

The principle of less eligibility is also less decisive for labor regulation today because policing and corrections have become far more important tools of social control (Wacquant 2009). As labor markets for low-skilled workers disintegrated after 1970, wage work lost much of its power as a source of social order in race- and class-segregated areas of concentrated poverty (Wacquant 2009; Western 2006; W. Wilson 1997). The turn toward mass incarceration was a political response that concentrated, in a variety of ways, on poor, low-skilled men and women of color (Western 2006; Haney 2004). The carceral turn clearly intensified state social control, but it did so in ways that have had complex implications for labor regulation.

In the short term, of course, policies that warehouse large numbers of people in prison reduce the pool of workers available to low-wage employers (Western and Beckett 1999). In this regard, they do not promote wage work among the poor or strengthen competition for the worst jobs. In its broader dimensions, however, the rising tide of policing and corrections has enhanced work pressures in a variety of ways. Although we treat this issue more fully in chapter 4, two dynamics can be briefly noted here. First, like the variety of practices that deter welfare claims, muscular forms of policing and criminal punishment regulate labor by making alternatives to wage work less attractive. They raise the odds and costs of being penalized for the pursuit of illicit and informal alternatives to market income (A. White 2008). Second, prisoners actually make up a small percentage of the total population under correctional control (Western 2006). Far larger numbers are under community supervision in probation and parole programs that prioritize getting a job and holding onto it as an essential foundation for reintegration into the community (Rakis 2005). Here again, then, we find that neoliberal paternalism promotes work through a blend of strategies that negate alternatives to employment and work affirmatively to transform the poor into self-regulating subjects of the market (Haney 2010).

In addition to these parallels, the disciplinary turn in poverty governance has been marked by a new relationship between welfare provision and criminal justice. Under the "penal welfarism" that prevailed in the mid-twentieth century, liberal reformers drew social services into prison settings under the banner of rehabilitation (Garland 2002). In recent years, the direction of influence has reversed: Penal logics have been imported into the welfare arena, where they serve as adjuncts to the carceral system (Wacquant 2009). Movements between work and welfare have been relabeled as a form of "recidivism" (Guetz-kow 2006; ACF 1999). Welfare sanctions have been developed to shape client behavior through a logic of punishment for violation (Schram et al. 2009). State welfare programs use criminal records to exclude claimants (P. Allard 2002). They seek out criminal activity among recipients and prosecute failures to report income as a felony crime (Gustafson 2009). Welfare recipients' names are routinely shared with law enforcement and, under a project titled Operation Talon, public aid offices are used as sites for sting operations to arrest individuals with outstanding warrants (Gustafson 2009).

Through these and other developments, the penal and welfare systems have converged as symbiotic elements of a "double regulation of the poor" (Wacquant 2009). This convergence can be understood as gendered in four senses. First, its institutions have been built, politically, around gender-specific cultural images of poor racial minorities: the lawless, violent male of the underclass ghetto and the lazy and licentious welfare queen. Second, the system operates through gender-segregated institutions, with women making up roughly 90 percent of adult welfare recipients and men making up roughly 90 percent of prisoners (Haney 2004). Third, the direction of change on both sides has been toward a "masculinizing of the state" as a paternalist, behavior-enforcing custodian (Wacquant 2009: 15). The "nanny state" of welfare protections and prison rehabilitation programs has been supplanted by a "daddy state" emphasizing direction, supervision, and discipline (Starobin 1998). Fourth, historically masculine images of the worker-citizen have been elevated and universalized as a behavioral norm (Collins and Mayer 2010; Korteweg 2003). For former welfare recipients and prisoners, the sine qua non of civic reinstatement is the same: formal employment and wage-based support of one's children.

Finally, to clarify recent historical developments, one must also examine poverty governance as a site of productive power where particular mentalities of rule and modes of self-discipline are fostered (Foucault 1991; Dean 1999). Poverty governance proceeds today through a variety of efforts to produce subjects who, under conditions of apparent autonomy, can be relied on to choose in preferred ways. Reforms such as devolution and privatization have expanded the number and variety of choice points in poverty governance. The actors making choices among governing strategies have proliferated as policy authority has been rolled out to lower-level jurisdictions and diverse nongovernmental organizations. Welfare clients too have been repositioned as actors who, in a sense, are forced to make free choices. To receive aid, they must sign on as free parties to a contract, usually called an Individual Responsibility Plan. As

TANF participants, they must decide whether and how to fulfill their contractual obligations.

The counterpart to this expansion of "free choice" has been a proliferation of techniques designed to shape the ways that actors think about themselves and the decisions they confront. Throughout the system, authorities at higher levels work to structure and incentivize the choices made by actors below them. In classes for welfare recipients and training sessions for welfare case managers, instructors hammer home the importance of taking efficient steps toward improving the bottom line. Market rationality is promoted through performance benchmarks and penalties, financial incentives and managerial rituals, discourses that tout the "business model" of service provision, and symbolic celebrations of fast-food job placements as success stories.

Neoliberalism has been aptly described as "a political project that endeavors to create a social reality that it suggests already exists" (Lemke 2001: 203). Indeed, welfare programs today strive to turn welfare recipients into market actors by relentlessly insisting that this is what they already are *and have always been*. Their social responsibilities and needs are reframed as nothing more than aspects of their value as a worker on the market. Refracted through this prism, all facets of poor women's lives—mental illnesses, physical disabilities, educational deprivations, obligations to care for children or aged parents—are collapsed into the economic register, recast as "barriers" to work that must be overcome (Stone 2008). To turn recipients into subjects who will conduct themselves as market actors in the future, authorities work to reframe poor women's perceptions of their past. This rewriting of identity is well captured by the exhortations of a welfare "job club" instructor addressing a group of unemployed mothers in the TANF program:

> No one in this room has been out of work, the way we're going to write your resume. You're working in the house, you're a taxi driver, a budget planner, you volunteer at your children's school, you're a food preparer. You're self-employed, you're not receiving the income but you're working all the time. You have been successfully and diligently working daily. (Korteweg 2003: 468)

Like their clients, governing authorities at the front lines of welfare provision have been immersed in efforts to foster a market mentality. Caseworkers now hold titles such as "career counselor" and "financial and employment planner" and work with clients who have been relabeled as "customers" or "candidates" (as in job candidates). They join their clients as participants in the ritualistic signing of Individual Responsibility contracts. The sanctions they impose for noncompliance are framed as "wage deductions" for a client's failure to do her job.

Program managers are taught to embrace a forward-looking "business model" and to see themselves as serving local employers as much as aid recipients. One-stop centers are adorned with signs that promote market values and offer tips on how to market oneself by writing a better resume and dressing for success. Meeting spaces are labeled with titles like "The Excellence Room" and "The Opportunity Room." In these and other ways, welfare officials today are saturated in a discourse that continually reminds them: You work in a business; your business is to turn job candidates into employees; your relationship to the candidate is based on a contract; and it is your job to enforce the contract.

Such messages are rooted in a more basic organizational reality: Under the new regime of performance management, officials at the front lines have, in fact, been repositioned as actors in a quasi-market system (Radin 2006). Like the welfare recipients they serve, they confront financial incentives and penalties tied to documented outcomes that are closely monitored. In many states, local providers are explicitly placed in competition with one another, and, in all states, contracts for service provision base profitability on pay points that must be achieved through performance.

These performance systems, as we show in chapter 9, do more than hold providers accountable for outcomes. They bring a market-based form of discipline to the front lines of governance by focusing attention on performance benchmarks, competitive pressures, rewards and penalties, and the fact that everyone's behavior is being closely monitored and measured. Under this system, local providers learn quickly that they cannot meet their performance goals (and make their pay points) unless they use disciplinary policy tools to gain compliance from clients. In this way, neoliberal paternalism comes full circle, imposing a directive and supervisory form of market discipline on governing authorities so that they, in turn, can be relied on to impose a directive and supervisory from of market discipline on the poor.

Conclusion

The developments described in this chapter are best understood as political achievements with far-reaching political implications. As economic restructuring undercut wages and opportunities for the poor, political actors mobilized to shape the state's response. The systems they created were not necessitated by disembodied social forces, and they are not politically neutral in their effects. They were products of political action, and they represent a significant reordering of relations between state and market, between workers and employers, and especially between the poor and governing authorities.

Our telling of this story has focused on low-income Americans. It would be a mistake, however, to imagine that the developments we have described matter only for this group. Arguments that were honed and legitimated through a focus on the disorderly poor served as the template for a broader "Personal Responsibility Crusade" that has left working Americans far more vulnerable to the risks of modern life (Hacker 2006). President George W. Bush's vision of an "ownership society" signaled the broader ambitions of a neoliberal project that turns citizens into prudent market actors who bear personal responsibility for their problems and work to secure their own futures in individual rather than collective ways (Feldman 2006).

Increasingly, however, liberal Democrats have developed their own versions of neoliberal paternalism. A leading example is provided by the "libertarian paternalism" of Thaler and Sunstein (2008), which reframes collective policy questions as problems of individual choice and uses the cognitive biases revealed by behavioral economics to justify expert manipulations of "choice architecture." This is not the muscular brand of paternalism that poor people confront today, but it applies a governing logic to all Americans that is cut from the same cloth.

Likewise, neoliberal paternalism is not limited to the United States; it is a global shift in how the poor are governed. In the late twentieth century, rich nations, led by the United States and served by the IMF and World Bank, adopted a more directive and supervisory stance toward state-market relations in developing nations (Serra and Stiglitz 2008). The "Washington Consensus" on international development in the 1990s was of a piece with American welfare reform. In more recent years, wealthy nations have promoted Conditional Cash Transfers (CCTs) as a "global social policy" for the developing world, restructuring aid for the poor to incentivize compliance with a variety of public health, education, and welfare initiatives (Thompson 2007). Such "fast track" policies have spread to forty-two developing countries in recent years, where they have been elaborated in forms that are now being reimported to sites such as New York City (Peck and Theodore 2009).

In the developed world, "Model USA" has provided a template for the turn to "labor activation" policies across the Organisation for Economic Co-operation and Development nations (Piven 2002). Throughout Europe, public aid has been made more contingent on behavior and more focused on incenting labor participation (Torfing 1999). To be sure, the developed nations continue to differ systematically in their approaches to poverty governance (Esping-Andersen 1990; C. J. Martin 2004; Eichhorst, Kaufman, and Konle-Seidl 2008). Indeed, their patterning underscores a basic point of our analysis. Political challengers did not roll back the activist state; they reorganized and redirected it in ways that reflected the specific institutions and policy regimes they inherited.

By ignoring this fact, scholars enamored with the concept of globalization have frequently overstated the case for a worldwide convergence in social policy (Gilbert 2002). Global market integration has indeed contributed to the restructuring of welfare states. Its effects, however, have depended on the ways that political actors have responded within the contexts of their own institutions (Hay 2006). Political responses to the pressures of globalization have varied markedly across the wealthy democracies (Massey 2009). Likewise, political arguments that all states must bend to the "realities" of globalization, by subordinating social protections to labor market flexibility, have proved far more viable in some polities than others (Schram 2006).

The United States, with its historical emphasis on market conformity and collaboration, has been the predictable epicenter of the global turn to neoliberal poverty governance (Noble 1997; Katz 2002; Hacker 2002). When business interests and conservatives mobilized in the 1970s, they enjoyed an unusually hospitable environment for their political efforts. Isolated in the fragmented U.S. welfare state, the nonelderly, nondisabled poor were positioned as the "low-hanging fruit" for reformers—available to be taken without arousing more powerful constituencies. And in the wake of the turbulent 1960s, anxieties over social change, political unrest, and crime combined to give conservatives a powerful resource for discrediting Great Society liberalism and advancing a law-and-order agenda.

Political mobilization produced a new regime of supervision and discipline for the poor, organized by market logics and oriented to serve market needs. The new system does not represent a decisive break with the past. It remains rooted in the perennial projects of social control and civic incorporation, as well as the recurrent longing to turn the poor into new kinds of people. Echoes of eras gone by are abundant in poverty governance today. But the history of poor relief, like the development of the activist state, cannot simply be rewound to an earlier time. Significant changes have transpired in U.S. poverty governance. The rationality that binds them is neoliberal paternalism. Their implications for American democracy and society are, to say the least, far reaching.

THE COLOR OF NEOLIBERAL PATERNALISM

IN CHAPTER 2, WE ANALYZED THE RISE OF NEOLIBERAL PATERNALISM in a way that bracketed, for a moment, the racial dimensions of this development. We did so not because race has played a secondary role, but because its importance merits a chapter-length analysis in its own right. The disciplinary turn in poverty governance grew out of the changing racial order in American politics and society (King and Smith 2005). It was promoted through race-coded discourses that mobilized racialized images and understandings as potent political resources (Hancock 2004; J. Simon 2007). The path to reform was smoothed by the racial basis of existing institutions and by symbolic appeals to racial anxieties.

In principle, of course, neoliberal and paternalist ideas can be elaborated in nonracial ways. In practice, though, as a historical matter, neoliberal paternalism emerged in the United States as what Howard Winant calls a "racial project": It was "a discursive and cultural initiative, an attempt at racial signification and identity formation" that doubled as "a social structural initiative, an attempt at [racialized] political mobilization and resource distribution" (Winant 1994: 24). In the 1980s and 1990s, the campaign to reform poverty governance advanced through a "politics of disgust" that centered on threatening images of an unruly, pathological minority underclass (Hancock 2004; J. Simon 2007). Images of the deviant poor—out of order and out of control—fueled perceptions that a crisis was at hand and that immediate, far-reaching actions were needed. They also raised public tolerance for tough new policies by making them seem irrelevant to "Americans who play by the rules." The new regime would target the "others" of the underclass, whose deviance and dysfunction called for heavy-handed measures.

Yet it would be a mistake to reduce the racial origins of the disciplinary turn to its cultural and discursive dimensions alone. The success of race-coded discourses depended on a structural context of de facto residential segregation and institutional isolation for America's poor minority populations (Massey and Denton 1993; Brown et al. 2003). At a deeper level, the rise of neoliberal paternalism reflected the persistent power of race as a structure organizing social, political, and economic relations in the United States (Bonilla-Silva 1997).

As racial formations change over time (Omi and Winant 1986), they shape the economic and political foundations of poverty governance in different ways (Piven 2003). The system that emerged as part of the New Deal, for example, was built around the racial caste system of the South—an economy that ran on the exploitation of black agricultural labor and a one-party political system premised on racial domination and exclusion (Key 1949; Quadagno 1988; Lieberman 1998). The 1960s War on Poverty reflected dramatic changes in the racial order that emerged as African Americans migrated out of the South, racial movements demanded economic and civic incorporation, and the electoral circumstances of the Democratic Party shifted in racialized ways (Piven and Cloward 1974, 1977; Quadagno 1994).

Neither period offers a model of the racial order that fits the United States very well today. With de jure discrimination outlawed and overt exclusion discredited, members of subordinate racial groups have increasingly gained access to major societal institutions (C. Cohen 1999). Egalitarian racial norms are now widely promoted, and explicit racism is rarely tolerated in the discourses of the market and polity (Mendelberg 2001). As a result, the racial dynamics observed in earlier "big bangs" of policy development, such as the 1930s and 1960s, provide a highly uncertain guide for understanding the present.

In this chapter, we offer a historically specific account designed to clarify the foundational role of race in the recent transformation of poverty governance. To situate the present, we begin with a brief review of racial dynamics in the history of American social provision. Building on this account, the main sections of this chapter explain how race has operated in recent decades to pave the way for disciplinary poverty governance. Finally, we end the chapter by advancing an original framework for thinking about how race matters for contemporary *practices* of poverty governance. Building on theories of social construction and implicit racism, the Racial Classification Model (RCM) helps to explain why systemic racial biases continue to flourish in poverty governance—even in a "post–civil rights" era in which governing authorities exhibit declining racial prejudice and growing racial diversity.

Race and Poverty Governance in Historical Perspective

"The instinctive attitude of a great many," Marc Bloch (1953: 38) once wrote, is to "consider the epoch in which we live as separated from its predecessors by contrasts so clear as to be self-explanatory." Today, this "instinctive attitude" looms large as a stumbling block to understanding the racial basis of poverty governance. When the racial injustices of the past are not ignored, they are usually woven into linear stories of progress that celebrate the enlightened present. By suggesting that race matters "less" today, such stories obscure the possibility that race now matters in new ways, and in ways that reflect the legacies of earlier eras. More critical accounts that portray the history of U.S. social policy as an unswerving story of racism ironically have much the same effect. On both sides, such all-or-nothing stories distort the historical record and cloud its implications for social politics today. As Theda Skocpol (1995: 129) rightly notes:

> African Americans have not invariably been excluded from U.S. public social benefits, nor have they always been stigmatized when they did receive them. The overall dynamic since the Civil War has not been a linear evolution, moving from the exclusion or stigmatization of African Americans toward their (however partial) inclusion and honorable acceptance within mainstream U.S. politics and policies. There have been more ups and downs, more ironies and reversals, in the history of African American relationships to U.S. social policies across major historical eras.

Poverty governance has always served as a tool for incorporating and regulating marginalized groups (Heclo 1995; Gordon 1994). But marginalization itself does not have a static relationship to race, class, gender, or other axes of social division. Dimensions of social stratification intersect to shape poverty governance in historically specific ways because, in each era, they operate differently to define terms of societal membership, position groups in relation to societal institutions, and underwrite prevailing notions of obligation and deservingness.

Consider, for example, the complex ways that race intersected with class, gender, and citizenship in the early origins of America's "two-tier" welfare state of social insurance and public assistance programs (Nelson 1990). The earliest landmark event in social protections for men, the creation of Civil War pensions in the late nineteenth century, occurred in an era when overt white supremacy prevailed in most of American life. Yet the soldier's incorporation in the state's military apparatus, a central marker of masculine civic contribution, legitimated the extension of social protections across racial lines. Over 180,000 black Union veterans received the same eligibility for federal benefits as their white counterparts (Skocpol 1992: 138).

On the other side of the gender divide, when state-run Mothers' Pensions emerged in the early twentieth century, they reflected an even more complex mixture of racial dynamics. Mothers' Pensions were enacted in the Progressive era, partly to reduce the number of white children being placed in orphanages because their impoverished mothers could not care for them (Crenson 1998). The reformers who championed these pensions drew on a discourse of Republican Motherhood that identified women as the holders of a special civic duty (and right) to raise and care for the next generation of citizens (Skocpol 1992; Gordon 1994). Not surprisingly, this discourse reflected the racialized meanings of civic membership that prevailed at the time (R. Smith 1997; Ward 2005). The caregivers nurturing the future American republic were envisioned as white mothers. By supporting them, reformers sought to fight back the "race death" threatened by the growing ranks of "nonwhite" immigrants (Berg 2002; Ward 2005).

Mothers' aid was typically denied to black and Latina women, both because they were seen as undeserving and because their exclusion bolstered the prestige of the program as a support for "good mothers" (Bell 1965; Ward 2005). "Groups today regarded as minorities received only a tiny proportion of mothers' aid. In Los Angeles, Mexicans were excluded from the mothers-aid on the grounds that their inferior background made it too likely that they would abuse it. Sometimes minorities were excluded from programs; at other times programs were not established in locations with large minority populations" (Gordon 1994: 48).

At the same time, Mothers' Pensions also served as a vehicle for racial agendas that emphasized civic incorporation. Reformers promoted Mothers' Pensions as a tool for "Americanizing" Polish, Irish, German, and Italian immigrant families—groups that were viewed as "nonwhite" at the time and eventually made up a disproportionate number of recipients. Indeed, by emphasizing the potential for social and civic assimilation, Mothers' Pension advocates made arguments that positioned them as the racial liberals of their time.

> Conservatives tended to view non-WASPs as irremediably inferior. Liberals tended to regard them as inferior in culture but potentially responsive to a socialization that could bring them "up" to "American" standards. Mothers' aid supporters frequently spoke of building citizenship as one of the goals of the program, and they meant raising not only children but also mothers to that level. The supervision [of recipients] embedded in the mothers' pension plans aimed at raising recipients to "American" standards. (Gordon 1994: 47)

Reflecting this complex mixture of agendas, Mothers' Pensions were implemented in ways that varied greatly across communities and emphasized intrusive efforts to instill virtue and reform behavior. Yet their shared roots in the ideals of white Republican Motherhood also allowed these programs to serve as a foundation for more ambitious federal action in 1935.

The Aid to Families with Dependent Children (AFDC) program that ended in 1996 began as the Aid to Dependent Children (ADC) program, a minor element of the Social Security Act of 1935. The 1935 law established a two-tier system of provision, with social insurance programs controlled at the national level and public aid programs for the poor administered at the state and local levels. The two tiers divided along class, race, and gender lines. Social insurance programs focused on the families of white male workers. Job categories that included large numbers of women and people of color, such as domestic, nonprofit, and agricultural, were excluded from coverage (Lieberman 1998; Mettler 1998). Public assistance programs became the primary source of aid for poor female-headed families and nonwhite Americans (Gordon 1994).

The subsidiary status of the ADC program partly reflected the race and gender basis of prevailing civic hierarchies (Nelson 1990; Lieberman 2005). As Hugh Heclo (1995: 667–68) explains, the 1935 law cemented a particular "settlement of the social question" by giving civic priority to "the male breadwinner and the family dependent on his earnings" and specifying "the nation-state as the appropriate arena" of social protection for these citizens in full standing. Exclusion from the national social insurance programs reflected and, in the process, institutionalized the subordinate civic standing of women and racial minorities (Mettler 1998).

The segregation of programs for the poor, however, reflected more than just hierarchies in civic status. It emerged from material efforts to sustain the exploitation of cheap black labor in the Old South and unpaid women's labor in the family (Gordon 1994). The racial dimensions of this agenda were driven by southern white agricultural interests and their representatives in government. As plans for national social programs emerged in the 1930s, these actors mobilized to make sure that new forms of federal aid for the poor would not disturb the southern sharecropping system that relied on poor black families to work the fields (Lieberman 1998). They demanded and won a separate stream of federally funded programs for the poor that allowed the states to retain substantial control over eligibility, benefit levels, and program rules.

In the decades that followed, southern officials worked to ensure that black families had limited access to public relief, especially during planting and harvesting seasons. Work expectations, of course, attached to black women far more than white women. To enforce this norm, administrators applied "suitable home" rules, "man in the house" provisions, and other "morals tests" in racially biased ways (Bell 1965). The intricate rules provided a pretext for moving black women off the welfare rolls and making sure they were not secretly sharing their benefits with black men needed in the fields (Piven and Cloward 1988). To augment these strategies, some southern states moved to create "employable mothers" rules "in areas where seasonal employment was almost exclusively performed by nonwhite families" (Bell 1965: 46).

In all states, local ADC offices operated in discretionary, intrusive ways that contrasted sharply with the emphasis on rights and bureaucratic restraint found in social insurance programs. But because poor black women were concentrated in the southern political economy, they confronted variants of ADC that were stricter and more focused on labor regulation. Thus, the New Deal incorporated black mothers through state ADC programs that were segregated from national insurance, designed to support labor exploitation, and organized around rules that mothers in other parts of the country rarely encountered.

In the 1960s, the ADC program was renamed AFDC, and the patchwork quilt of local relief practices gave way to a more accessible and rule-based system. Once again, racial politics played a key role. The War on Poverty emerged from the tumultuous political struggles that allowed racial minorities to finally achieve meaningful citizenship in the United States (Quadagno 1994). Its legislative centerpiece, the Economic Opportunity Act of 1964, joined the Civil Rights Act of 1964 and the Voting Rights Act of 1965 to create a new system of civil, political, and social rights for racial minorities.

By the 1960s, large numbers of African Americans had migrated from the South to urban centers around the country, where they gained access to the ballot and became a more significant voting bloc for the Democratic Party. At the same time, disruptive social movements organized to push for civil rights, and later welfare rights, in ways that divided elites and put pressure on governments to take action (Piven and Cloward 1977). Across the states, these pressures drove sharp changes in rates of welfare participation and incarceration that tracked closely with levels of black insurgency and electoral power (Fording 1997, 2001). The War on Poverty became a key site for local political conflicts that pivoted on Black Power, white privilege, and competing visions of racial integration and justice in the new civic order (Quadagno 1994).

By the end of the 1960s, poverty governance had become more than a racialized field of practice; it was now a racialized object of political discourse and public perception as well (V. Weaver 2007; Kellstedt 2003). From the failed presidential campaigns of Goldwater and Wallace onward, the politics of poverty was reshaped by "law and order" calls to crack down on black criminality, welfare dependence, and social dysfunction (V. Weaver 2007). African Americans became the public face of welfare and crime policy, as their images increasingly prevailed in media stories on poverty (Gilens 1999). In the years that followed, the Democratic Party became closely associated with programs for the black poor, and attitudes toward blacks became a key predictor of white Americans' policy preferences, partisan loyalties, and voting behaviors (Carmines and Stimson 1989; Edsall with Edsall 1991; Kinder and Sanders 1996). Ironically, just as white racial attitudes were growing more tolerant (Schuman et al. 1997), "blackness" was becoming a more powerful frame for poverty politics (Winter 2008).

Race and the Rise of Neoliberal Paternalism

How, then, did race contribute to the rise of neoliberal paternalism? The most influential answer to date is offered by Loïc Wacquant (2009), who argues that the "penalisation of poverty" emerged as a fourth "peculiar institution" for "defining, confining, and controlling African Americans in the United States" (2001a: 98). The new regime, in this view, is the latest in a succession of systems for "the reproduction of ethnoracial hierarchy" (Wacquant 2001a) that that has included slavery (1619–1865), Jim Crow (1865–1915), and the racially defined ghetto (1915–68). With the demise of these earlier systems, Wacquant contends, the penal turn was "necessitated" by new social insecurities that emerged as poor minority communities suffered the effects of failing labor markets and fading social protections.

Although we agree that race played a key role in the rise of neoliberal paternalism, we are less inclined to see this development as a functional response necessitated by racial domination, rising insecurity, and the crumbling of older systems of racial control. The disciplinary turn in poverty governance, as we argued in chapter 2, reflects far more than a systemic need to "contain dishonored, lower-class African Americans" (Wacquant 2001a: 121). In this section and the next, we attempt to bring some precision to the claim that racial factors paved the way for neoliberal paternalism and should play a central role in efforts to explain this development.

Racial patterns of poverty in the United States are, in large measure, a reflection of the racial organization of labor markets and housing arrangements. Throughout the country's history, race has shaped the structure of opportunities for people to acquire marketable skills and convert them into decent jobs and wages. Between 1940 and 1970, black workers' incomes rose and the black-white wage gap fell, as manufacturing jobs proliferated and drove a broader expansion of opportunities and rewards for low-skilled workers (Ferguson 1996). After 1973, deindustrialization and global competition produced an era of income stagnation and declining job prospects for all low-skilled workers in the United States, but the effects on racial minorities were especially severe (W. Wilson 1997). People of color were concentrated in the low-skilled groups that took the heaviest toll under economic restructuring. As the competition for decent employment escalated, blacks lost jobs and wages at a faster rate than white workers who had similar demographic and skill profiles (Darity and Myers 1998). Residential "hyper-segregation," promoted by federal housing policies and banking practices at midcentury, accelerated these dynamics and concentrated their corrosive social effects in poor black neighborhoods (Massey and Denton 1993; Stoll 2010). The decimation that unfolded in these communities would eventually become the focal point for efforts to remake poverty governance, motivating calls for reform and framing public debates over the proper course of action.

These developments intersected with the post-1970 landscape of organized political competition in the United States, which was, in many respects, a legacy of the nation's troubled racial past. In Europe, for example, labor unions provided a powerful force opposing neoliberal responses to the declining fortunes of low-income workers. In the United States, labor unions were weakened from their inception by efforts to protect race-based labor exploitation in the South, which fragmented union efforts across the states and blocked their extension to many sectors (Western 1997; Warren 2010). Racial conflicts and racism divided workers and constrained the strategies adopted by union leaders (Goldfield 1997; Frymer 2007). At midcentury, fears that unionization would accelerate demands for civil rights led many southern Democrats to join the Republican push for new laws that drove steep declines in labor density and power (Katznelson 2005). Thus, by the time globalization pressures and neoliberal policy agendas began to spread across the developed world, labor unions in the United States were comparatively weak, increasingly in disarray, and largely ineffective as defenders of low-income populations (Massey 2009).

At the same time, conflicts in the 1960s effectively realigned party competition in the United States, making race into a more central organizing dimension for partisan loyalties, strategies, and issue positions (Carmines and Stimson 1989; Frymer 1999). "The decision by the Democratic Party to embrace civil rights in the 1960s promoted a mass exodus of southerners from the party, estrangement from blue collar voters in the north, and the end of the New Deal coalition" (Massey 2009: 21). To hasten these developments, Republicans invested heavily in campaign themes that focused on "inner city problems" and called for a restoration of "law and order" (V. Weaver 2007). Avoiding explicit appeals to racism, they attempted to peel off disaffected white Democrats by emphasizing race-coded wedge issues such as crime, welfare, teen pregnancy, busing, affirmative action, gangs, and the underclass (Mendelberg 2001; Kinder and Sanders 1996). In addition to moving racially charged issues to the forefront of poverty politics, the success of these wedge issues forced Democratic Party leaders to seek new strategies for neutralizing the damaging effects of race—a theme we will return to in the following section.

The new rights won by racial minorities in the 1960s recast poverty politics in ways that extended beyond the realignment of party competition. With new rights now established, white Americans increasingly concluded that equal opportunity had been achieved and, thus, poor minorities must be responsible for their own poverty (Kinder and Sanders 1996). The new rights also allowed better-positioned members of minority groups to enter dominant institutions and achieve middle-class status—a development that further isolated poor minority subgroups and reinforced perceptions that their poverty resulted from weak individual effort (Cohen 1999; Reed 2004). At the same time, the new rights accelerated two related processes that were already under way: rising numbers of racial minorities in programs for the nonelderly poor and a growing tendency to perceive policies for the poor through the lens of race.

In the early years of the ADC program, discrimination kept most eligible women of color off the rolls, resulting in a caseload that was 80 percent white in 1939 (Berrick 1995: 8). As African Americans migrated north, however, they began to enter the program in greater numbers. The political implications of this development were immediately apparent to senior administrators, who acted aggressively to counter the growing threat to the program's positive reputation.

As more African Americans gained access to ADC in the 1940s and 1950s, hostility to the program rose. Though the majority of eligible African American women did not receive ADC, opponents of welfare and African American rights nevertheless implied that welfare opened its doors to huge numbers of African American women. Welfare advocates were keenly aware of this misrepresentation. They feared its potential to destroy the program and hamper their bid to reform ADC. As a result, they developed a public relations strategy whereby they erased the race of ADC clientele. In their minds, destigmatizing welfare meant not only emphasizing "family" but also emphasizing the whiteness of ADC families. Only on rare occasions were ADC families revealed publicly as nonwhite families. (Mittelstadt 2005: 14)

The racial conflicts of the 1960s made a continuation of this "below the radar" strategy impossible, and the new rights they created made welfare more accessible to racial minorities (Quadagno 1994). Much as administrators had feared in the 1950s, AFDC quickly came to be viewed as a "black" program (Quadagno 1994). Public hostility toward the program rose precipitously, in a pattern that tracked closely with racial attitudes, and calls for welfare reform began to proliferate (Gilens 1999; Heclo 1994). As black welfare recipients grew in number outside the South, efforts to promote work followed their trail, spreading from the first "employable mother" rules in southern states to a series of federal initiatives (Mittelstadt 2005: 177–78). When early reforms failed to raise work levels much, federal lawmakers escalated their efforts. Work Experience Programs in 1964 were followed by the Work Incentive program in 1967, which was strengthened by new amendments in 1971 and again in 1981, which were then superseded by the Family Support Act of 1988 and ultimately by the TANF program in 1996.

A similar process—rising minority caseloads followed by a disciplinary programmatic turn—occurred in child welfare programs, especially foster care. As the foster care population doubled from 1982 to 1999 and became more concentrated in cities with large black communities, black children (17 percent of the nation's youth) became an astonishing 42 percent of the national caseload (Roberts 2002: 8). As the composition of the caseload changed, state foster care programs shifted from an emphasis on preserving families to a governing stance that focused on decisions about when to remove children from homes, terminate parental rights, and pursue more suitable candidates for adoption (Roberts 2002).

As racial minorities began to loom larger in program populations and political discourse, several structural forces combined to deepen the problems of poor urban minorities and raise their political salience. Residential segregation by race and class produced sharply delineated areas of concentrated urban poverty that were highly visible to the public (Massey and Denton 1993; Jargowsky 1997). The isolation and density of the poor in these neighborhoods functioned as force multipliers for the social disruptions that emerged when labor markets for less-skilled workers declined and stable manufacturing jobs gave way to low-wage, high-turnover service and retail jobs (W. Wilson 1997). As employment and wage prospects became increasingly "grim" (Holzer 1999: 2), "concentration effects" in poor minority neighborhoods produced a spiral of compounding social problems: physical disorder, drug abuse, health problems and high mortality rates, crime and violence, unemployment, family disruption, cycling between prison and neighborhood, early exits from schooling, residential instability, and so on (Sampson 2001).

Although the people of color who lived in such neighborhoods remained a small minority of the nation's poor, they became the primary focus of public discourse about poverty (Heclo 1994). The "pathologies of the urban underclass" took center stage in sensational media stories and became the leading frame for poverty research and policy debates (Jencks and Peterson 1991; Reed 1999: 179–96). Diverse societal issues, such as teen pregnancy and single motherhood, were swept into this frame in the 1980s, where they became repositories for public anxieties about the changing norms surrounding race, gender, and sexuality (Luker 1996).

As reformers mobilized to promote neoliberal and paternalist policy agendas, the race-coded urban underclass served as Exhibit A in their arguments for new governing arrangements. In a classic example of what Kingdon (2003) describes as a "window of opportunity" for preexisting policy solutions, reformers took broad agendas for reorienting governance and packaged them as specific solutions for the problems of concentrated urban poverty and social dysfunction.

The spectacle of underclass pathology was held aloft as proof that "permissive" social rights approaches failed the poor, public bureaucracies were inefficient and ineffective, and government was incapable of solving deep social problems on its own. To meet the challenges posed by the underclass, government would need to become more aggressive in enforcing social order, defining behavioral expectations, and demanding self-discipline from the poor. It would need to devolve policy authority so that governance could be tailored to meet the unique challenges arising in areas of concentrated poverty. It would need to embrace the "bottom line," results-oriented standards of market performance and draw on the capacities of for-profit, nonprofit, and religious organizations by contracting for their services.

This disciplinary turn was especially pronounced in the area of criminal justice, where racialized images of urban disorder were central to Republican "law and order" campaigns (V. Weaver 2007). As Nixon's war on crime begat

Reagan's war on drugs, the era of mass incarceration was ushered in by a host of new policies that increased the scope and severity of penalties and limited the potential for judges and parole boards to offer reduced sentences for rehabilitative or humanitarian purposes (Travis 2005). The new policies drove incarceration rates skyward and deepened class- and race-based disparities in imprisonment (Western 2006). Their origins, in turn, can be traced directly to the political uses of race in the shadow of urban deindustrialization and disorder. As Bruce Western (2006: 78–79) explains:

> Rapid growth in incarceration among young, black, noncollege men closely followed the collapse of urban labor markets and the creation of jobless ghettos in America's inner cities. The political context for the shifting demography of imprisonment [was] provided by a resurgent Republican party and a fundamental reform of criminal sentencing. Republicans' law-and-order politics grew out of reaction to the gains of the civil rights movement and anxieties about rising crime among white voters. Republican governors rejected rehabilitation, expanded prison capacity, and turned the penal system to the twin tasks of incapacitation and deterrence. Indeterminate sentences were discarded as legislators worked to limit the discretion of judges and parole boards. The growth in violence among the ghetto poor through the 1960s and 1970s stoked fears of white voters and lurked in the rhetoric of law and order. Crime, however, did not drive the rise in imprisonment directly, but formed the background for a new style of politics.

As the push toward neoliberal paternalism advanced as a racialized project, it also remade the meaning of race itself (Wacquant 2009). By altering the most salient images associated with racial groups, new poverty discourses and policies operated as "race-making" mechanisms (Lipsitz 1998). As public discourses focused on the dysfunctional black urban underclass, images of behavioral pathology became more central to the prevailing meaning of blackness itself. As race-coded appeals exploited racial anxieties, they also stoked these anxieties and turned them into more salient and powerful political forces. As the state moved to enforce work among low-income minorities, it strengthened the belief that members of this group would work only if forced to do so (Soss and Schram 2007). And as the state cycled vast numbers of black and Latino men between the prison and the ghetto, it bestowed the symbolic marker of a felony conviction in ways that deepened the stigma and costs of marginalized racial identities among the poor (Wacquant 2009; Pager 2007).

At the intersection of these developments, criminality and dependence became more central to the stigma of blackness and, politically speaking, "the poor became black" (Loury 2002; Gilens 2003). From 1950 to 1965, blacks were largely absent from media stories on poverty (Gilens 1999), and trends in racial attitudes were essentially uncorrelated with trends in welfare policy preferences ($r = .03$, Kellstedt 2003). After 1965, images of blacks predominated in media stories on poverty, especially when these stories focused on deviant and unsympathetic behaviors (Gilens 1999). Trends in racial attitudes became closely aligned with trends in welfare attitudes ($r = .68$, 1965–1996, Kellstedt 2003), and "welfare" became, for the first time, a pejorative term (Katz and Thomas 1998). Across the broad spectrum of poverty issues emphasized by Republicans, and especially in the areas of crime and welfare, racial cues emerged as powerful forces shaping policy preferences in the public (Kinder and Sanders 1996; Gilens 1999; Hurwitz and Peffley 1997; Gilliam and Iyengar 2000). The political importance of this development can be seen more clearly by taking a more focused look at how public support for paternalist welfare reform was mobilized in 1996 and operated in the years that followed.

Race and Public Support for Welfare Paternalism

After federal welfare reform passed in 1996, leading paternalists were eager to wrap their policy victory in the legitimating mantle of democratic responsiveness. Lawrence Mead (2001a, 2002), for example, hailed it as "a triumph for democracy" and hastened to add that public support for reform had little to do with race. To be sure, a majority of Americans disliked "welfare" by the 1990s and supported calls for work-promoting reforms. But as we have already seen, the origins of these public attitudes had a great deal to do with racial segregation, racial policy developments, and race-coded political rhetoric in the preceding decades (Loury 2002; Mendelberg 2001; Gilens 1999). In this section, we offer a more precise account of how race, public opinion, and party competition interacted in the political endgame that produced welfare reform. Racial politics, we argue, played a key role in the electoral strategies that set this endgame in motion, in the arousal of public demands that forced legislative action, and in the cultivation of public support for the paternalist regime that resulted.

By the 1980s, race-coded wedge issues had taken a heavy toll on the Democratic Party. In response, centrists at the Democratic Leadership Council (DLC) and elsewhere began to emphasize the electoral costs of racial liberalism and seek ways to neutralize the charge that Democrats were "soft" on underclass issues. In the presidential campaign of 1992, Bruce Reed and others at the DLC developed a strategy that sought to establish Bill Clinton as a "New Democrat" who would not be beholden to "special interests" such as women, blacks, environmentalists, and unions (Williams 2003).[1] Clinton tried to disarm Republican race baiting by condemning it as divisive politics (Mendelberg 2001: 104), and worked to connect with black voters through appearances in black churches and frequent discussions of his Christian faith, southern roots, and hard-working single mother. At the same time, he moved aggressively to assure white voters that he was not soft on race-coded underclass issues (Heclo 2001).

Indeed, three of the most memorable moments from Clinton's 1992 campaign clustered around key tropes of the "ghetto black" stereotype (rap music, violent crime, and welfare dependency) (see Devine and Baker 1991): his public reprimand of Jesse Jackson's Rainbow Coalition for issuing a speaking invitation to the controversial rap performer, Sister Souljah; his decision to fly home to Arkansas (unnecessarily) to preside over the execution of Ricky Ray Rector, a black man with limited cognitive functioning; and his repeated pledges to "end welfare as we know it" and to tell recipients "two years and you're off" (Williams 2003).

As Kent Weaver (2002: 116) rightly notes, the pledge to "end welfare as we know it" was not based on a specific policy agenda; it was a rhetorical move in "the grand strategic game of realigning the image of the Democratic Party on welfare issues." By aligning his rhetoric with Republican critiques, however, Clinton created a powerful, bipartisan message that the AFDC program was indefensible. Indeed, Clinton's pledge set in motion a period of escalating competition to get tough with welfare dependence—a competition that Republicans quickly showed they could win by calling for far more draconian measures than Clinton's divided Democratic coalition would permit.[2] As the contest intensified, news coverage rose sharply, with most stories pairing negative portrayals of the welfare poor with stereotypical images of poor black single mothers as "lazy and licentious" (Clawson and Trice 2000; Schneider and Jacoby 2005; Hancock 2004). The public's long-standing disdain for welfare became activated and more focused. A significant portion of the public was now paying attention, expecting federal officials to "reform welfare *in some direction*" and giving them good reasons "to believe that there was some political credit to be gained by ending it" (R. Weaver 2002: 119).

Figure 3-1 shows clearly the sharp arousal of public attention. The figure

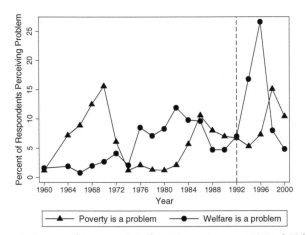

FIGURE 3-1. Perceptions of Poverty and Welfare Policy as Important National Problems: Responses to Open-Ended Questions, 1960–2000 (ANES)

presents trends over time in the percentage of Americans listing "poverty" and "welfare" in response to the American National Election Study's (ANES) open-ended question: "What do you think are the most important problems facing this country?"[3] Looking back to the War on Poverty era of the 1960s, one can see a decade-long pattern of rising public attention to poverty. The arousal of public attention in the 1990s looks quite different. When Bill Clinton made his campaign pledge in 1992, the percentage of Americans naming welfare as an important problem (7 percent) was lower than it had been a decade earlier and, in fact, was not significantly greater than the percentage citing poverty (6.7 percent). Over the next four years, this percentage skyrocketed to 26.6 percent—a figure that is more than double the largest previously recorded by the ANES.[4] Figure 3-1 also makes it clear that the sharp spike in public concern did not focus on "poverty and welfare issues in general." The rising chorus of condemnatory discourse focused public attention on the failings of the AFDC program and its recipients, without stimulating greater concern for poverty.

The table for the political endgame was now set. When President Clinton failed to introduce a welfare bill during his first fifteen months in office, Republicans proposed one that was more restrictive and less generous than any plan being considered in the White House.[5] By the time Clinton offered a proposal of his own, it appeared to be a pale imitation.[6] When Republicans took control of the U.S. Congress in 1994, the shift in agenda control was complete.

As Douglas Besharov noted in a 1995 op-ed titled "A Monster of His Own Creation," the aroused public now placed Clinton in a strategically disastrous position. Clinton elected to join Republicans in decrying the sins of the AFDC program. Having painted it as irredeemable, he was now trapped by the expectations he helped create. Although the public did not have strong preferences about which reform should pass (R. Weaver 2000: 191), its arousal made a defense of the existing program politically infeasible. "Republicans' control of the agenda meant that President Clinton would have to choose between approving a bill written largely on Republican terms and appearing to prefer the universally maligned status quo" (R. Weaver 2000: 195).

As the 1996 election approached, Dick Morris and other pollsters for the president surveyed the public to gauge the political costs of blocking welfare reform (Morris 1998). Even though Clinton had a twenty-point lead in the polls, Morris argued that the president needed to sign welfare reform as insurance for the election. Going further, he claimed that, by taking the welfare issue off the table, Clinton could "quiet racial disputes about social supports for the vulnerable" and "[clear] the way for [the Democratic Party's] rejuvenated influence over one of its central concerns, ghetto poverty" (DeParle 1999: 12; DeParle and Holmes 2000). On August 22, 1996, flanked by poor black women, Clinton signed on to the Republican's plan and turned their bill into law.

The aroused public that played such a crucial role in welfare reform represented far less than the citizenry as a whole.[7] It did not exist in 1992, and it disappeared shortly after 1996. For the brief time it lasted, however, it gave decisive first-mover advantages to Republicans and painted Democrats into a tactical corner. The key question, then, is *how* this segment of the public got activated. The answer, in short, is through a mobilization of racial bias.

Two analyses of data from the ANES time series provide evidence for this conclusion. The first and simplest is based on a series of three "snapshots" of the relationship between public perceptions of black laziness and perceptions of welfare as a major national problem. Drawing on the full cross-sectional samples available for 1992, 1996, and 2000, figure 3-2 presents two trend lines. The first traces the percentage of respondents citing welfare as a major national problem, shown earlier in figure 3-1; the second uses odds ratios from bivariate logit models to show, for each year, how well this perception of welfare is predicted by whether respondents perceived "most blacks" as lazy rather than hardworking. The close pairing of the two trends indicates that the mobilization and racialization of mass anxieties about welfare rose and fell in tandem during the 1990s. Both were weak in 1992 (and earlier); they rose precipitously together between 1992 and 1996; and both dissipated quickly once the antiwelfare campaign receded. The patterns strongly suggest that public discourse

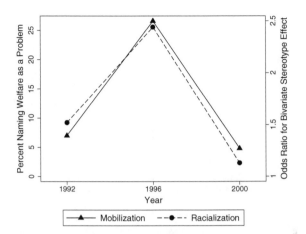

FIGURE 3-2. Perception of Welfare Policy as an Important National Problem and Its Relationship to the Black Laziness Stereotype, 1992–2000 (ANES)

Note: Data come from the American National Election Studies (ANES) time series, 1992–2000. The line for "mobilization" corresponds to the left axis and indicates the percent of respondents naming "welfare" in response to the open-ended question, "What do you think are the most important problems facing this country?" The line for "racialization" corresponds to the right axis and indicates the odds ratio produced by a bivariate logit model where black laziness stereotype (black minus white scores, recoded −1 to 1) is used to predict whether respondents named "welfare" as an important problem facing the country (0–1).

deepened the public's reliance on race as a frame for thinking about welfare, and did so in a manner that led growing numbers of Americans to see the program as a major national problem.

By drawing on a smaller panel of ANES respondents surveyed in both 1992 and 1996, it is possible to specify more precisely which segments of the public were mobilized. The panel data allow us to follow individuals over time and identify who shifted from being inattentive in 1992 to viewing welfare as a major problem in 1996. To clarify the pattern of activation, we rely on three separate panel analyses. Each produces the same results for a broad set of nonracial control variables. The odds of activation between 1992 and 1996 did not vary in any statistically meaningful way across groups defined by levels of family income, education, or southern residence. They were also statistically equivalent across groups defined by partisan and ideological identification, levels of media attention, and commitments to individualism and egalitarianism. The lone exception to this pattern is gender. Women were significantly more likely than men to be activated during this period—a pattern that underscores how changing gender norms (particularly related to work) contributed to public support for welfare reform (Orloff 2002).[8]

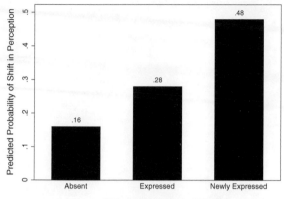

FIGURE 3-3. Relationship between Changing Perceptions of Black Laziness and Perceptions of Welfare Policy as an Important National Problem, Panel Data 1992–96

Note: Panel data come from the American National Election Studies (ANES) time series, 1992–96. All results are based on multivariate logit models predicting perceptions of "welfare" as an important national problem in 1996. "Status of Stereotype" groups are defined as follows: "Absent" indicates respondents who in 1996 identified blacks as no lazier than whites; "Expressed" indicates all respondents who in 1996 identified blacks as lazier than whites; "Newly Expressed" indicates the subset of respondents from this second group who in 1996 identified blacks as lazier than whites, but who in 1992 had not expressed this view. Control variables for all three models include respondent sex, education, family income, southern residence, ideological identification, partisan identification, level of media attention, support for individualism, support for egalitarianism, and perceptions of "welfare" as an important problem in 1992.

Turning to race, we find that concerns over welfare were significantly more likely to be activated among respondents who perceived "most blacks" as lazier than "most whites."[9] To clarify this dynamic, it is helpful to construct a hypothetical "average respondent" by setting all observed variables at their mean values and then predicting the probability of activation under three different stereotype conditions. Figure 3-3 presents the key results based on a simple criterion: When asked in 1996, did respondents score blacks as lazier than they scored whites?[10] The first bar, "Absent," indicates that an average respondent who did *not* do so would have a .16 probability of activation. The second, "Expressed," shows that this predicted probability rises to .28 for an identical respondent who differed only in describing blacks as lazier than whites. The third bar in figure 3-3, "Newly Expressed," is based on respondents who did not view blacks as lazier than whites in 1992, but came to hold this view by 1996. Thus, it indicates whether views of race and welfare shifted together in the mid-1990s, as both responded to anti-welfare discourses. The results indicate that anti-black and anti-welfare beliefs were, in fact, activated together. The probability of activation for the "Newly Expressed" group is .48. Thus, people in this group had roughly a 1 in 2 (50–50) chance of activation, compared to less than 1 in 6 in the "Absent" group and slightly more than 1 in 4 in the "Expressed" group.[11]

Our analysis of the ANES time series yields considerable evidence that the politically critical spike in public concern was rooted in a mobilization of racial bias. Nevertheless, the ANES measures offer a limited basis for assessing the racial sources of public support for *paternalist* reform. Individuals can view welfare as a problem, and even seek reductions in welfare spending, without necessarily favoring a more paternalist approach. To address this problem, we draw on a battery of questions included in the National Survey on Poverty Policy (NSPP) conducted by one of the authors in 2002. These items, which we use to construct an index of support for welfare paternalism, ask respondents to indicate on a 1–7 scale the degree to which they support or oppose policies that subject welfare recipients to (1) mandatory drug testing; (2) unannounced home visits to check for rule violations; (3) sanctions for noncompliance; (4) a family cap denying benefits to children born to current recipients; (5) a "man in the house" rule barring nonsupportive male residents; (6) mandatory classes on sex, marriage, and parenting; and (7) a suspension of rights to privacy in one's home.

Public support for such paternalist rules may, of course, reflect a variety of political values, such as individualism or egalitarianism. Relative to these alternatives, how much do racial attitudes matter? To answer this question, we rely on a second measure included in the NSPP. The Symbolic Racism 2000 (SR2K) scale is based on an eight-item battery of questions developed by Henry and Sears (2002). Rather than asking people to openly state stereotypical views, the questions solicit positions on issues such as whether blacks have gotten more than they deserve, whether black leaders have "pushed too fast," whether blacks do not do as well in society because they do not try hard enough, and whether blacks are responsible for creating the racial tensions that exist in the United States today.

To estimate the relative influence of racial attitudes, we include the SR2K scale alongside measures of four core values: individualism, egalitarianism, humanitarianism, and authoritarianism. Our models also control for respondent sex, age, education, marital status, family income, southern residence, party identification, and ideological identification. To clarify the new dynamics that arise when public attention is focused on questions of paternalism, we apply our model to the standard measure of welfare spending preferences (Gilens 1999) as well as our index of support for paternalism. Differences across the two models offer some insight into how the foundations of public preferences

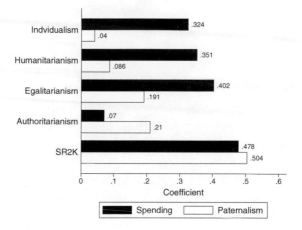

FIGURE 3-4. Value Effects on White Support for Welfare Paternalism and White Opposition to Welfare Spending, 2002

Note: Dependent variables are both coded to run from −1 to +1, and all independent variables are coded to run from 0 to 1. Bars represent absolute values for unstandardized coefficients. All effects are positive, with the exceptions of egalitarianism and humanitarianism (in both models). All effects are statistically significant, with three exceptions: authoritarianism (.07) in the welfare spending model and individualism (.04) and humanitarianism (.086) in the paternalism model. Control variables include measures for sex, age, education, marital status, family income, southern residence, party identification, and ideological identification.

shift when policy debates focus on the terms of welfare provision (paternalist versus rights orientations) rather than the extent of welfare provision (more versus less). Figure 3-4 presents the results of our full models.

In the darker bars in figure 3-4, we see that individualism, egalitarianism, and humanitarianism are all significant predictors of welfare spending preferences, while authoritarianism has no discernible effect. The effects associated with the SR2K scale are larger than what we observe for any of these core value measures. The lighter bars in figure 3-4 indicate how these measures relate to support for paternalist program rules. Here, the pattern of relationships differs considerably. When the focus is shifted to paternalism, we find smaller effects for individualism and egalitarianism, and the effect of humanitarianism is reduced to statistical insignificance. Authoritarian orientations, which had no discernible effect on spending preferences, emerge here as the second strongest predictor. The SR2K scale emerges once again as the strongest predictor, and, indeed, its relative importance is enhanced dramatically. In the welfare spending model, the coefficient for the SR2K scale is 67 percent larger than the average of the other four coefficients shown. In the model predicting support for welfare paternalism, the coefficient for the SR2K scale is 283 percent larger than the average of these other coefficients.

THE COLOR OF NEOLIBERAL PATERNALISM • 73

These results suggest a more precise interpretation of the "mobilization of racial bias" shown in figures 3-2 and 3-3. In the 1990s, calls for paternalist efforts to regulate behavior largely eclipsed the earlier focus of welfare debates on whether to reduce the size of welfare investments (Mead 2001a). The results in figure 3-4 suggest that this new frame, and not merely the rising intensity of the anti-welfare rhetoric, deepened the racial basis of welfare preferences in the public. Although they are based on data from 2002, they clearly imply that racial attitudes exert greater influence when the focus of welfare discourse shifts from spending to paternalism.

As a final step in specifying how racial attitudes have influenced public support for welfare paternalism, it is helpful to turn from the SR2K scale to a second set of measures included in the NSPP. In recent decades, the American public has overwhelmingly imagined the "typical" welfare recipient as a black woman.[12] And as theorists of intersectionality have long emphasized, we cannot assume that attitudes toward such a group, defined by a conjunction of race and gender dimensions, will take forms or have effects that are reducible to what we observe for a single dimension, such as race (Collins 1991; Crenshaw 1991; Cohen 1999; Sparks 2003; Hancock 2004, 2007; Strolovitch 2008).[13] Do perceptions of groups defined by race *and* gender influence public support for welfare paternalism in ways that are not captured by measures of racial stereotypes alone? In pursuing this question, we also extend our analysis beyond the stereotype of black laziness. As many feminist scholars have emphasized, sexual responsibility and sexual regulation were central to paternalist welfare discourse in the 1990s and to the reforms that resulted (Mink 1998; Anna Marie Smith 2007).

To capture these aspects of public opinion, we rely on a battery of questions in the NSPP that parallel the standard laziness stereotype item used by the ANES. The difference is that they substitute "sexually responsible" and "sexually irresponsible" for the traditional poles of the ANES "laziness" scale and ask for separate evaluations of black women, white women, black men, and white men.[14] Among white respondents, answers to these questions indicate a clear hierarchy of perceptions defined by both race and gender. White respondents are least likely to attribute sexual irresponsibility to white women (18.5 percent); the percentage then rises steadily from white men (35.5 percent) to black women (41.7 percent) to black men (55 percent). The differences across racial groups (23.2 percent for women, 19.5 percent for men) emerge here as slightly larger than the differences across gender groups (17 percent for whites, 13.3 percent for blacks), but differences across all groups are statistically significant.

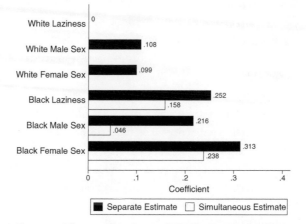

FIGURE 3-5. Stereotype Effects on White Support for Welfare Paternalism, 2002

Note: All bars represent unstandardized coefficients. Effects shown for all stereotypes of whites are statistically indiscernible from zero. Effects shown for all stereotypes of blacks are statistically significant, with one exception: the coefficient for black male sexual irresponsibility in the simultaneous estimation (.046). Control variables include measures for sex, age, education, marital status, family income, and southern residence.

Figure 3-5 presents results indicating the degree to which these four measures, as well as standard single-dimension measures of black and white laziness, predict support for welfare paternalism among white respondents. All estimates are based on models that control for differences in sex, age, education, marital status, family income, and southern residence (see Gilens 1999). The darker bars in figure 3-5 present results from six separate models, each of which examines a single stereotype in isolation from the others. One might think that paternalist regulations would be seen as more desirable by respondents who are more pessimistic about laziness and sexual irresponsibility as traits of "people in general," including white men and women. The results do not support this view. *None* of the measures for perceptions of whites emerges in our analysis as a significant predictor of white support for welfare paternalism.

By contrast, the same procedure indicates strong and significant relationships for all three perceptions of blacks: the conventional measure of laziness and both intersectional measures of sexual irresponsibility. The largest effect appears to be associated with the belief that black women tend to be sexually irresponsible, and this conclusion is corroborated by an analysis that includes all three measures in a single model. The results, shown by the lighter bars in figure 3-5, indicate that the stereotype of sexual irresponsibility among black women has a significantly larger effect than either of the other measures and, indeed, reduces the effect for perceptions of black males to statistical insignificance.

THE COLOR OF NEOLIBERAL PATERNALISM • 75

In sum, our analyses converge to provide powerful evidence that racial attitudes served as a primary cultural resource in the construction of public support for paternalist welfare reform. In the political endgame that led to federal reform in 1996, perceptions of welfare as a major problem spiked in a pattern that closely tracked the racialization of problem perceptions. The segment of the public that was mobilized by anti-welfare discourse came disproportionately from Americans who viewed blacks as lazier than whites—and especially from Americans who shifted toward stronger forms of this belief between 1992 and 1996.

Six years after the passage of reform, we find that, relative to other core values, racial attitudes consistently provide the single strongest predictor of welfare policy preferences. Moreover, they do so to a far greater degree when the focus shifts from spending to paternalism. White support for paternalism had no discernible relationship to beliefs about whites but was closely tied to stereotypes of blacks as lazy and sexually irresponsible. The strongest stereotype effects are observed when we attend to the intersection of race and gender that underlies the iconic image of the welfare queen as a black woman. Among the six stereotypes analyzed, the strongest predictor of white support for paternalism is the intersectional measure of beliefs about sexual irresponsibility among black women.

The Racial Classification Model

As the preceding sections have shown, race played a central role in the recent transformation of American poverty governance. In the chapters that follow, we turn from the creation of this regime at the national level to the ways that states and localities have used their discretion to design and implement its operation. To lay the groundwork for this analysis, we conclude this chapter by outlining a framework for thinking about how and when racial distinctions are likely to structure policy choices in poverty governance today.

Choice lies at the heart of politics and is a basic feature of governance at all levels of the policy process (Jones 2001). To note this fact is not to suggest that actors are free to address any issue at any time or that they make their choices as unencumbered individuals. As students of power have long noted, possibilities for choice may be rendered invisible by a variety of social constraints or actively suppressed by those who control agendas (Hayward 2000; Bachrach and Baratz 1962). When opportunities for choice do arise, actors inevitably respond to them in ways that reflect a host of factors, including the discourses, relations, routines, and structures in which they are embedded (March and Olsen 1989;

March 1994). Efforts to illuminate such dynamics are, in our view, part of what it means to analyze the politics of policy choice.

Whatever constraints and influences may be at work, however, public officials must ultimately *decide* how to design policies, organize their implementation, and apply them to specific people. Across levels of governance, racial factors can affect decisions in a variety of idiosyncratic ways. But as a large literature on social cognition demonstrates, it is also possible to specify general dynamics that explain why racial classifications influence political choices and why they are more likely to do so in some contexts than others. By focusing on these dynamics, it is possible to draw diverse policy activities into a common frame of analysis that clarifies how and when racialized policy outcomes are likely to emerge.

In proposing the Racial Classification Model (RCM) of policy choice, we aim to provide an analytic framework that is grounded in the structural changes that have reorganized American race relations in recent decades. The iconic image of racial bias in poverty governance is the white official who, acting on a conscious prejudice, intentionally discriminates against members of racial minorities. Today, however, civil rights are well established in law, overt racism is usually stigmatized, and egalitarian racial norms are widely endorsed (Mendelberg 2001). At the same time, the officials who govern the poor have become more racially diverse as members of marginalized groups have gained access to positions in relevant institutions (C. Cohen 1999). In this context, it has become harder to explain racialized policy outcomes as products of conscious intentions. It has also become less reasonable to rely on "white-centered" explanations that assume a white official, equate racial minorities with "outgroups," and focus on dynamics of ingroup favoritism, outgroup hostility, or "racial threat" (Allport 1954; Blalock 1967; Tajfel 1981). The prediction of such theories, mistaken in our view, is that racialized policy outcomes will fade into history as conscious prejudices recede and officials become more racially diverse.

By contrast, the RCM is rooted in theories of implicit racism and the unconscious ways that racial schemas, developed through cultural discourses and operating as shared cognitive frames, structure interpretation and choice (Quillian 2008; Winter 2008; Devine 1989). Building on Schneider and Ingram's (1997) theory of target populations, the RCM contends that policy choices are guided by actors' underlying assumptions about the people they target for policy action (Le Grand 2003). To a degree that these actors seldom realize, their assumptions about policy targets depend on salient social classifications and reflect the content of social group reputations. In this manner, racial categories can provide a powerful, though implicit, basis for beliefs about the "kind" of policy target being addressed and, thus, the type of policy action that is most likely to be effective. The model consists of three propositions.

(1) To be effective in designing policies and applying policy tools to specific target groups, policy actors must rely on salient social classifications and group reputations; without such classifications, they would be unable to bring coherence to a complex social world or determine appropriate action. Here, we assert two assumptions about policy choice. First, although policymakers and implementers have diverse motives (R. Weaver 2000: 30–31), we assume they desire to be effective when they apply policies to specific target populations (Schneider and Ingram 1997). Second, as they try to answer the question "what kind of policy will be effective?" officials are guided by their answers to more basic questions such as "what kind of group is this policy designed to influence?" and "what sort of policy tool is likely to move the members of such a group in the desired direction?" A policy tool that works for one group—a new incentive, opportunity, or education effort, say—can fail for another. Thus, attempts to choose effective policy actions depend on beliefs about "what kind" of group one seeks to influence.

By necessity, public officials make such judgments based on limited information. To do so, they rely on *social classifications* to identify the kinds of people being addressed and *group reputations* to intuit how such people are likely to respond to a particular intervention. Group reputations, in this sense, enable a kind of heuristic reasoning, allowing officials to fill in the detailed information they lack by extrapolating from what they think they know about the groups involved (Sniderman, Brody, and Tetlock 1991).

In emphasizing how racial categories can structure policy choice, the RCM follows a basic principle in the study of social cognition (Hogg and Abrams 1998). As George Lakoff (1987: 5–6) writes, "There is nothing more basic than categorization to our thought, perception, action, and speech. Without the ability to categorize, we could not function at all, either in the physical world or in our social and intellectual lives." This assumption is also consistent with bounded rationality approaches to decision making, which emphasize how reliance on social kinds and reputations allow for cognitive economy (H. Simon 1997; Jones 2001). Thus, the first proposition of the RCM asserts only that policymakers share a general property of human cognition and seek to make policy choices that will be effective for specific target groups.

(2) When racial minorities are salient in a policy context, race will be more likely to provide a salient basis for social classification of targets and, hence, to signify target differences perceived as relevant to the accomplishment of policy goals. While the first proposition of the RCM focuses on the categorical basis of choice, the second advances two arguments about race. First, however much race may be related to shared physical traits or cultural toolkits, it is fundamentally a form of social classification: It arises from social practices of categorization and is deployed as a means of organizing the social world (Jenkins 1997). The cultural boundaries that define racial categories function as potent "principles of vision and division" that situate actors in social relations and define their meanings for others (Bourdieu 1990; Brubaker 2004). Thus, the RCM suggests that racialized policy choices arise from the impact of one form of social classification on another—that is, policy actors' use of racial kinds to intuit the kinds of policy targets they aim to influence. Based on the racial composition of a target group, for example, a legislator may make important assumptions about participants' levels of human capital, tendencies toward social dysfunction or criminality, barriers to self-sufficiency, or vulnerability to labor market discrimination. An official charged with implementing policy may do the same when taking action on the case of an individual from a particular racial group. Thus, racial group reputations can guide assumptions about target characteristics at either the collective or individual level, and at any stage of the policy process.

Second, we assume that the salience of race varies across policy domains, time periods, and political jurisdictions. All else equal, we expect race to become more salient in a policy context as racial minorities come to figure more prominently in policy-relevant political events, media discourses, and target-group images. In hierarchical group relations, members of privileged group categories tend to be "normalized," while members of subordinate categories tend to be defined by the dimension of their "deviation" (Wildman and Davis 1996). Thus, while the presence of gay and lesbian individuals tends to raise the issue of "sexual orientation," this axis of identity is typically rendered invisible when only heterosexual individuals are under consideration. Likewise, although "gender" refers equally to men and women, masculinity and femininity, its salience is generally weak when men alone are under consideration. Following this logic, we assume that "race" is less likely to serve as a basis for cognition when whites predominate; it becomes more likely to structure thought and action as members of minority racial groups become more prominent in the events, discourses, or target groups associated with a policy. Under such conditions, it becomes more likely that racial distinctions will underpin the social classifications that guide interpretations and choices in policy settings.

(3) *The likelihood of racially patterned policy outcomes will be positively associated with the degree of policy-relevant contrast in policy actors' perceptions of racial groups. The degree of contrast, in turn, will be a function of (a) the prevailing cultural stereotypes of racial groups, (b) the extent to which policy actors hold relevant group stereotypes, and (c) the presence or absence of stereotype-consistent cues.* We assume that categorical contrasts are central to the ways that humans make sense of the world (McGarty 1999). Thus, the degree of contrast between two group's reputations is a critical mediating factor in the process that turns racial markers into usable pieces of information for identifying policy-relevant "kinds." When the perceived differences between groups are negligible, racial categories provide officials with little traction for making policy choices. Their heuristic value increases to the extent that a policy actor perceives meaningful group differences in characteristics relevant to the achievement of policy goals. As the perceived contrast grows larger, racial contrasts should offer a clearer basis for inferring target group traits, and racially patterned policy choices should become more likely.

The key question, then, is this: What influences the degree of policy-relevant contrast between racial groups? The RCM emphasizes three factors. First, because social groups carry different reputations in the broader culture, perceived contrasts will depend on which groups are salient in a policy domain. Consider, for example, reputations for preferring to be "self-supporting" versus preferring to "live off welfare." On this dimension, the gap between stereotypes of Asian and Euro-Americans is fairly small, while the gap between stereotypes of African and Euro-Americans is quite large (Bobo and Massagli 2001). Accordingly, in the context of welfare-to-work programs, the ratio of Euro- to Asian American recipients will be less likely to affect policy choices than the ratio of Euro- to African American recipients.

Second, the size of the gap between group reputations should also vary across public officials, depending on the stereotypes they hold. Systematic differences in racial stereotyping exist across groups defined by age, education, class, region, political ideology, and, of course, race itself (Bobo and Massagli 2001). Hence, the impact of racial classifications on policy choice should increase as the composition of decision makers shifts toward groups who embrace policy-relevant racial stereotypes to a greater degree.

Third and finally, stereotype activation should also depend on proximate contextual cues. Experimental research suggests that when immediate cues reinforce or appear to confirm group stereotypes, racially patterned responses become more likely. Thus, black defendants are more likely to receive the death penalty if they are perceived as having a "stereotypically black appearance" (Eberhardt et al. 2006), and the presence of a criminal record disadvantages black job applicants to a greater degree than their white counterparts (Pager 2003). Conversely, when stereotype-inconsistent cues are salient, they have the potential to diminish the odds of racially patterned responses (Valentino, Hutchings, and White (2002). Accordingly, racial group contrasts should be perceived as larger when officials confront stereotype-consistent cues.

Because the RCM is a cognitive model rooted in cultural frames and the goal of making effective policy choices, racialized policy outcomes can result from a variety of dynamics that fall outside its purview. Indeed, the earlier sections of this chapter point to many such dynamics. Electoral motivations may, for example, lead lawmakers to ignore the interests of minority groups who are positioned as "captured constituencies"—or to pursue policies designed to reassure white voters that they are not "beholden" to such interests (Frymer 1999; Williams 2003). Similarly, the balance of political pressures advanced by organized interests may exhibit racial biases that push officials to take racially patterned actions for reasons not covered by the RCM (Strolovitch 2008). The key contribution of the RCM is to suggest that, while such dynamics are often sufficient to produce racially biased policy outcomes, they are not necessary. Social structures give rise to mental structures that work in implicit ways to racialize policy choices and, thus, to produce racially biased policy outcomes (Winter 2008).

The same may be said for theories that emphasize white racism in policy settings. The cultural categories and reputations emphasized by the RCM are products of historical and contemporary racism. But we underestimate both the breadth and depth of their effects if we imagine that they are limited to actors who are white, who are consciously racist, or who feel hostile toward minority groups. Because the RCM makes no assumptions about the decision maker's racial status, it can be distinguished from accounts that focus on ingroup favoritism (Brewer 1999), animus toward outgroups (Allport 1954), and group threat (Blalock 1967). For this same reason, the RCM can be distinguished from models that emphasize decision-maker identity and argue that improvements in descriptive representation will result in better substantive representation for minorities (Swain 1995; Selden 1997). According to the RCM, minority representation in legislatures and bureaucracies may dampen, strengthen, or have no effect on racially patterned outcomes, depending on how minority perceptions of racial groups compare to majority perceptions. In poverty governance today, racial biases are not driven primarily by individuals who are conscious racists. They mostly arise "behind the backs" of officials whose ordinary interactions and choices are structured by race in ways that (more often than not) run contrary to their own racial values.

In the chapters that follow, we draw on the RCM to specify how and when racial disparities are likely to emerge in poverty governance today. The contingent predictions of the RCM—which suggest a variety of conditions that should mediate the production of racialized policy results—allow for empirical tests that are far more demanding than a mere demonstration that one group tends to fare worse than another. Indeed, our analysis raises the bar further by doing what few studies have done in the past: putting a single model of racial bias to the test at multiple levels of governance, based on numerous independent data sources, and using a variety of experimental and observational designs. As we will see in the chapters that follow, the results indicate that this simple cognitive model offers a surprisingly robust basis for explaining the when, where, and how of racial bias in the contemporary practice of poverty governance.

Conclusion

Neoliberal-paternalist poverty governance is rooted in, and justified by, a particular image of poor people. As described in chapter 2, this image should not be confused with the competent market actors presumed in laissez-faire ideology. In classic portrayals of *homo economicus*, all individuals, rich or poor, can be relied on to follow their natural propensities to "truck and barter" once they are freed from the distorting interventions of the state. The image of the poor that underlies neoliberal paternalism today is different. It identifies the poor individual as one who is suitable for incorporation as a responsible worker-citizen but who will be unlikely to make this transition unless the state acts on its obligation to impose social order and instill self-discipline. Neoliberal paternalism promises that, by becoming self-disciplined workers, the poor can achieve full societal membership. Their current marginality reflects the fact that they are undisciplined and irresponsible; their work ethic is underdeveloped; their sexuality is unrestrained; and, as a result, their communities are plagued by disorder and pathology.

In the U.S. context, a powerful cultural template for this image existed long before the rise of neoliberal paternalism. Its contours were cast in the crucible of American slavery, in the form of racial beliefs that legitimated paternalist white control over black populations within systems defined by labor coercion and sexual exploitation (A. Davis 1983; Collins 1991; Gilens 1999). Long after slavery ended, these beliefs persisted in the form of powerful "controlling images" of African Americans: not just the dependent and undisciplined worker requiring paternalist oversight, and not just the potentially violent black man, but also the hypersexual, unrestrained Jezebel, the Mammy whose appropriate role is to labor in the care of people outside her family, and the Matriarch who heads her family in ways that are neglectful of her children and threatening to potential male partners (Collins 1991; Jordan-Zachery 2009).

Thus, the images of the poor that justified the disciplinary turn in poverty governance in recent years did not emerge de novo as a rejection of liberal assumptions about individual competence. They drew on a powerful, preexisting set of cultural resources. Dysfunctional and gender-specific images of the black poor were generalized to the poor as a whole, in ways that constructed a policy target group consonant with neoliberal and paternalist rationalities.

The structural context for this development can be traced to the racial organization of American labor markets and the racially focused devastation that resulted from deindustrialization and declining demands for low-skilled labor. These developments combined with residential "hyper-segregation" to produce racially defined areas of concentrated poverty where social problems proliferated and compounded one another. The pathologies of "the underclass," in turn, became the basis for a powerful set of wedge issues that Republicans used to court disaffected Democrats in the white working class (especially in the South). The race-coded appeals of Republicans, and the defensive maneuvers of leading Democrats, proceeded on a political landscape defined by widespread racial anxieties and the institutional legacies of earlier eras of racial politics. Together, these racial forces paved the way for a transition to disciplinary poverty governance.

These developments suggest a great deal of continuity with the racial history of American poverty governance. Yet it would be misleading to treat poverty politics today as nothing more than the same thing all over again. Explicit forms of racism and racial exclusion have been replaced, for the most part, by implicit processes of racial cuing, interpretation, and action that coexist peaceably with institutionalized rights and the growing racial diversity of governing authorities. These dynamics of implicit racism lie at the heart of the Racial Classification Model and, as we will see in the chapters that follow, are central to the operation of poverty governance in the United States today.

RACE AND SOCIAL CONTROL IN
THE STATES, 1960-95

> There is a wise old saying in America, that "all politics is local"; there is a still wiser corollary, that all social control is local. All of the fundamental policies that regulate the conduct of American citizens and corporate persons *have been and still are made* by the state legislatures. State government in the U.S. is a *regulatory state*, and as a regulatory state it specializes in setting rules of conduct and backing those rules by sanctions. Thanks to its federalism, [the U.S.] meets the needs of social order through devolution.—Theodore Lowi (1998)

I N THE PRECEDING CHAPTERS, WE EXPLORED THE RISE OF NEOLIBERAL paternalism as a national political development. In this chapter, we begin our journey down through the system of poverty governance by examining state-level political developments during this transition period. In the American system of federalism, as Theodore Lowi (1998) notes in the quotation above, primary responsibilities for behavioral regulation have generally fallen to state and local governments. Nowhere has this been more the case than in the area of poverty governance. Prior to the 1930s, poverty governance was almost entirely a state and local affair (Katz 1996). Since that time, national policies have mostly served to structure, subsidize, and supplement state and local efforts. Thus, to understand the disciplinary turn, one must ask how prevailing state-level approaches were disrupted and how authorities responded to the resulting challenges.

Decentralized poverty management in the United States reflects more than a general tendency for states to take responsibility for maintaining social order (Lowi 1998). Because labor markets vary greatly across the states, national standards of provision make it harder to distribute relief in ways that are consonant with local market needs. As a result, the labor-regulating functions of welfare programs have always created pressures toward decentralization (Piven and Cloward 1971). Likewise, because state populations vary in their political orientations, decentralized policy control has protected federal officials from the divisive and electorally disruptive morality politics that often surround poverty. As Joel Handler (1995: 91) notes, "the more ambiguous or more deviant the perceived moral character of the poor, the more local the control of relief." In the United States, these two pressures toward decentralization have been reinforced by the politics of race and gender. When the federal government created national social insurance programs in the 1930s, it denied coverage to jobs filled primarily by women and people of color and left control over poor relief in the hands of the states. The resulting system was designed to accommodate racial exploitation and domination in the South (Lieberman 1998) and to cement a gendered "family wage system" focused on the white male breadwinner (Mettler 1998).

The tumultuous events of the 1960s marked a critical juncture in state-level governance of the poor. Until that time, state strategies closely followed the principle of less eligibility: Officials limited the accessibility and generosity of aid to ensure that it would not provide an attractive alternative to the lowest jobs in the state (Piven and Cloward 1971). Political and legal victories in the 1960s shattered this system and forced state officials to operate on a new landscape of federal rules and protections. Welfare caseloads "exploded," and, in the years that followed, states responded by offering reduced benefits. At the same time, as the race-coded law-and-order campaigns of Republicans made headway, state officials began to pass tougher criminal justice laws and build the infrastructure of mass incarceration. Together, these developments redefined the contours of poverty governance in the American states.

In this chapter, we make several arguments about how state-level efforts to govern the poor shifted from the early 1960s to the early 1990s. First, civil disruptions and civil rights victories in the 1960s changed the ways that states deployed beneficent and coercive tools of social control (Fording 2001)—or, as Bourdieu (1998) and Wacquant (2009) put it, the welfarist "left hand" and carceral "right hand" of the state. Second, the "right hand" began to carry more weight, as states abandoned the rehabilitative ideals of penal welfarism, shifted toward strategies of "governing through crime," and invested heavily in prisons to warehouse the poor (Garland 1990; J. Simon 2007; Wacquant 2009). Third, because state welfare programs were more constrained by federal rules, they took a less decisive disciplinary turn during this period. Legal and political victories in the 1960s made state welfare programs more accessible and generous. With access and due process rights institutionalized, state caseloads remained high in the years that followed. States responded by focusing on the second prong of the principle of less eligibility: reducing benefits to levels that would make the lowest-wage jobs more attractive.

Fourth, precipitous declines in benefits reduced the "work disincentives" of welfare but ultimately were not strong enough to move large numbers into the labor market. Thus, by the early 1990s, the disciplinary turn in poverty governance was decidedly uneven. On the carceral side, the transformation was firmly established. On the welfare side, the meager effects of benefit declines and soft work mandates were leading state-level officials (in Wisconsin, South Carolina, and elsewhere) to call for a more muscular approach. The states took the lead in creating new paternalist rules and laid the groundwork for federal welfare reform in 1996. Fifth, state-level responses varied greatly during this period, in a pattern that reflected the racialization of poverty governance. Trends in incarceration and welfare participation tracked patterns of black insurgency in the 1960s. In the years that followed, changes in welfare benefits, criminal laws, and imprisonment depended on the racial makeup of state populations. The rise of neoliberal paternalism was, in this sense, rooted in the interplay of racial politics and American federalism.

We begin with a brief historical overview of decentralization in poverty governance. We then turn to the political disruptions of the 1960s and their effects on the "left" and "right" hands of state social control. In the remaining sections, we analyze how states adapted to their new governing dilemmas in the 1970s and 1980s. We show how the state strategies that emerged were shaped by racial politics and how their patterning conformed to the logic of the Racial Classification Model (RCM) outlined in the preceding chapter.

A Brief History of Decentralized Poverty Governance

Localism is an enduring theme in the history of American poverty governance. Its origins can be traced to the early English system of poor relief, which colonists imported as a model for the New World (Quigley 1999). Local control of poor relief was initially rooted in two kinds of moral distinctions. The first, codified in the Elizabethan Poor Law of 1601 and the English Law of Settlement in 1662, drew a bright line between community members and "outsiders." The problems of the poor were identified as the independent responsibility of each local parish. On one side, the idea that no community should evade this responsibility established a moral imperative to provide relief. On the other, it provided a moral justification for denying relief to "strangers" who did not receive aid in their home parishes (Handler and Hasenfeld 1991).

The second divided local residents into moral kinds: the "deserving" and "undeserving" poor (Katz 1990; Trattner 1999). Evaluations of deservingness fell along many dimensions and were often rooted in differences of gender, race, ethnicity, and religion (Gordon 2002). The most basic distinction flowed from the expectation that able-bodied individuals should work. Thus, the "deserving" were typically identified as groups, such as the elderly, sick, and disabled, who had limited ability to work and, thus, were viewed as poor through no fault of their own. The nonelderly, able-bodied poor were seen as having no such claim. Accordingly, aid for this group was designed to impose stronger restrictions on access and generosity. Denials of aid were frequent, and the able-bodied could be subject to punishments as severe as execution if they were caught begging in public (as opposed to working or receiving organized public aid). To ensure that public relief would not be more attractive than the worst jobs, benefits for the able-bodied poor were kept well below local wages and provided under deeply stigmatizing conditions (Handler and Hasenfeld 1991). This "principle of less eligibility" was eventually codified in the English Poor Law Amendments of 1834, which declared that "the [relief recipient's] situation on the whole shall not be made really or apparently so eligible [desirable] as the situation of the independent laborer of the lowest class" (Piven and Cloward 1993: 35).

These basic principles of English poor relief guided state and local public aid in the United States from the eighteenth century through the early decades of the twentieth century (Katz 1996; Trattner 1999). When the federal government passed the Social Security Act of 1935, it expanded state relief programs and assumed partial responsibility for financing their operations. As it created new national social insurance initiatives, however, the 1935 law did little to overturn inherited traditions of local provision for the undeserving poor. Instead, the categorical architecture of the New Deal welfare system institutionalized distinctions between the deserving and undeserving by aligning them with the structure of American federalism (Mettler 1998; Lieberman 1998). Benefits for the deserving poor emphasized federal policy control and were designed primarily to protect and reward the contributions of white male breadwinners (Gordon 1994). These programs included the two new social insurance programs, Social Security Old Age Insurance (OAI) and Unemployment Insurance (UI), as well as three federally subsidized programs for the "deserving" poor that were administered in the states: Old Age Assistance (OAA), Aid to the Blind (AB), and Aid to the Permanently and Totally Disabled (APTD).

Separate state-level programs were established for Americans who lacked a disability, were not elderly, and fell outside the "white male breadwinner" model. For women and people of color, the decision to deny coverage to specific job categories meant that employment rarely translated into eligibility for social insurance (Lieberman 1998; Mettler 1998). Individuals who lacked a proven work history were similarly relegated to the inferior tier of state and local public aid programs (Heclo 1994). Thus, state-controlled Aid to Dependent Children (ADC) programs were created to provide cash benefits to poor children in single-parent (mostly female-headed) families, and state and local General Assistance (GA) programs were created as a catch-all income support for poor persons who were ineligible for other programs.

In this manner, the new system aligned the levels of the federal system with the deserving/undeserving distinction as well as with prevailing status divisions based on race, gender, class, and incorporation in the labor market. OAI was administered and funded entirely by the federal government, and payment levels were uniform across all states. In other programs for the deserving poor, states had a bit more control but had to operate within federal guidelines that ensured that benefits would be accessible and adequate. State ADC programs differed from these federally subsidized programs in three key respects: Their costs were reimbursed by the federal government at a far lower rate; their benefit levels did not have to stay above a federally specified minimum; and they were free to set eligibility standards with fewer federal constraints. GA was created as a state and local program in all respects. Subnational governments retained full control over GA eligibility criteria and benefit levels, and GA funding depended entirely on fluctuations in state and local fiscal circumstances.

Thus, prior to the 1960s, the undeserving poor confronted a patchwork quilt of state and local aid programs characterized by "length of residence requirements, pervasive invasion of privacy, and unregulated state discretion over eligibility conditions and the amounts of grants" (Rosenblatt 1982: 266). "Suitable home" provisions, for example, allowed ADC caseworkers to deny aid based on moral evaluations of a home's fitness for raising children. States and localities, free to set their own standards for suitability, frequently used these provisions to deny aid to unwed mothers (disproportionately black women). In 1954, Mississippi officials used this provision to cut 8,400 families from the ADC rolls (Ward 2005). In 1960, when Louisiana used a similar provision to shed 25 percent of its caseload, 90 percent of its terminations were justified by children born out of wedlock, and 95 percent of the terminated families were black (Nadasen 2005). By 1961, twenty-three states had a suitable home provision, including most of the southern states with large black populations. Other rules, such as "man in the house" and "substitute father" provisions, were used in a similar fashion. These provisions were enforced through "midnight raids" and caseworker surveillance, which served as deterrents to welfare participation in their own right.

To encourage work, some southern states also adopted "employable mother" and "suitable work" provisions that allowed local officials to deny aid whenever they determined that full-time work was available, regardless of the wage level.

Such determinations tended to coincide with seasonal needs for low-wage labor, especially agricultural needs during harvesting and planting seasons. And like suitable home provisions, work provisions tended to target black women, who were expected to remain in the labor force after giving birth. As one southern official explained at the time:

> The number of Negro cases is few due to the unanimous feeling on the part of the staff and the board that there are more work opportunities for Negro women and to their intense desire not to interfere with local labor conditions. [The staff and board see no reason] why the employable Negro mother should not continue her usually sketchy seasonal labor or indefinite domestic service rather than receive a public assistance grant. (quoted in Nadasen 2005: 9)

These sorts of expectations were rarely applied to white women, and, as a result, efforts to restrict eligibility and limit access exhibited a profoundly racialized pattern prior to the 1960s. They were most concentrated in southern states with larger black populations. Blacks were disproportionately poor in every southern state; yet, in each state, the black percentage of the ADC caseload remained well below the black percentage of the population (Lieberman 1998).

In addition to limiting access, state and local officials enforced work norms by suppressing ADC benefit levels. ADC benefits were kept very low, relative to wages in the worst jobs and relative to the benefits offered in programs for the deserving poor. In 1950, for example, average monthly benefits were $44 for OAA recipients, $47 for AB recipients, and $45 for APTD recipients. The average monthly benefit for ADC recipients, $21, was less than half as much. Because adult parents were not covered by ADC grants at this time, this benefit schedule meant that a family of three (one adult and two children) had to live on slightly less than what a single individual received from any of the other three public assistance programs. The average GA payment, $44 per case, was also quite low because, unlike the per-recipient payment schedules of the other programs, GA cases often consisted of an entire family.

Because local administrators held discretion in interpreting needs, actual payments often fell below formal benefit schedules. Indeed, a 1943 study found that, in contrast to the non-southern states, ten of the twelve southern states studied distributed ADC benefits in ways that delivered larger average payments to white families than black families.[1] In South Carolina, payments for whites exceeded those of blacks by an average of 38 percent (Lieberman 1998: 128).

Although racial factors made labor enforcement distinctive in the South, national patterns of benefit provision also followed the principle of less eligibility: State ADC benefit levels tracked state wage levels for less-skilled workers in a tight formation. Piven and Cloward (1971: 132) provide preliminary evidence for this claim by showing that agricultural wages and ADC payments were strongly correlated in the American states in 1951 and 1960. The agricultural sector, however, is more prominent in some states than others. To overcome this bias, we can rely on a measure that is more relevant to low-wage labor markets in all the states: the average monthly wage in the retail trade sector. Figure 4-1 compares this measure to the statutory ADC benefit level for a family of four (with no income) in welfare programs in each of the states for 1961. The results provide striking evidence that state benefit setting adhered closely to the principle of less eligibility in the period immediately preceding the upheavals of the 1960s.[2]

Two patterns in figure 4-1 stand out. First, wage and benefit levels are strongly correlated. The estimated regression line of .97 indicates that ADC benefits and retail wages tracked each other across the states, on average, in a near one-to-one fashion. Second, the maximum ADC benefit in every state was set at a level well below income offered by a full-time, low-wage job. Indeed, the average ratio of .60 suggests that the average ADC benefit was only 60 percent as generous as a full-time, low-wage retail job.

Because black women were more likely than their white counterparts to be

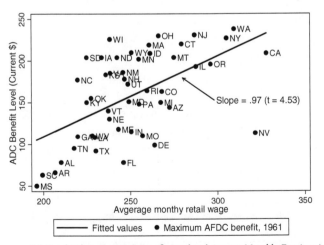

FIGURE 4-1. Relationship between ADC Benefit Level and Average Monthly Earnings in Retail Sector, 1961 (Current Dollars)

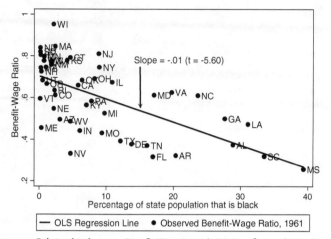

FIGURE 4-2. Relationship between Benefit-Wage Ratio (ADC Benefit/Retail Wage) and State Black Population, 1961

seen as suitable workers at this time, they were typically targeted for stronger work-enforcement efforts. The RCM suggests that the contrast in group reputations and norms should produce a racialized pattern of benefits relative to wages. If policymakers were more concerned about work disincentives for black women, we would expect them to set ADC benefits further below wage levels in states where blacks were more prevalent in the population. To test this expectation, we examine how the benefit-wage ratio (BWR)—that is, the ratio of the ADC benefit to the average retail wage—varied in relation to the black proportion of state populations in 1961. The results, presented in figure 4-2, strongly confirm our expectation. As one looks from left to right in figure 4-2, the black percentage rises and the BWR declines. In states where blacks made up 5 percent or less of the population, ADC benefit levels comprised, on average, about 70 percent of the retail wage level. Among the (southern) states where the black population exceeded 20 percent, the ADC benefit was only about 30 percent of the retail wage level. Thus, in addition to being targeted for a variety of tougher eligibility barriers, black mothers were also targeted for far stronger financial incentives to stay in the labor force.

Disruption, Federalism, and Poverty Governance in the 1960s

The long decade stretching from 1960 to the early 1970s marked a pivotal transition in American poverty governance. Like the earlier "big bang" of welfare state development in the 1930s, this period saw the creation of important new federal supports for the elderly and disabled poor. With the creation of Medicare in 1965, health-care coverage was extended to the elderly on a national scale. Social Security Disability Insurance (DI), created in 1956, was extended in 1960 to cover adults under the age of 50 who possessed sufficient work histories. Social Security OAI benefits were indexed to inflation in 1972, ensuring that legislative action would not be needed to counter the erosion of benefits. And finally, in 1972, the federal government replaced the OAA, AB, and APTD programs with Supplemental Security Income (SSI), a more generous program entirely funded and administered at the national level. In contrast to the New Deal era, however, the growing centralization and generosity of social protections in the 1960s did not bypass the able-bodied, nonelderly poor. The federal role in state welfare programs expanded, and did so in ways that made these programs significantly more accessible and generous.

A variety of factors undoubtedly contributed to these developments. Social commentators such as Michael Harrington (1962) helped focus elite attention on the scandal of poverty in an affluent society. Strong economic growth made a War on Poverty more affordable. Committed, skillful leaders in government worked strategically to achieve policy change. Of the many ingredients one might cite, however, none was more important than the pressures from below that came from the poor themselves. Changes in poverty governance during this period were, in large measure, a response to protest movements (including their litigation strategies) and urban riots that pushed public officials to take action. Political insurgency combined with electoral power to drive two key developments: an expansion of the federal role in state aid programs and state-level uses of welfare and incarceration to restore the social peace. Both responses would have profound consequences for poverty governance in the ensuing decades.

Throughout the 1960s, mass pressures for economic justice escalated through a variety of organized efforts. After winning major civil rights victories in 1964 and 1965, Martin Luther King Jr. and the Southern Christian Leadership Conference turned their attention to poverty and economic justice. Their demands for massive investments in the poor were echoed by more militant groups, such as the Black Panthers, the Revolutionary Action Movement, and a newly radicalized Student Nonviolent Coordinating Committee led by Stokely Carmichael and H. Rap Brown. By the mid-1960s, local welfare rights groups had begun to organize under the umbrella of the National Welfare Rights Organization. These groups differed considerably in their tactics and ideologies but, collectively, they posed a divisive threat to the fragile Democratic coalition, raised the specter of significant social unrest, and created powerful pressures for policy change.

The impact of these organized efforts was multiplied by the waves of urban riots that swept the country between 1964 and 1974. Decades later, it is easy to forget the scale and breadth of violence. In 1968, the Kerner Commission appointed by President Johnson released a stunning report on the disturbances. The report found that 164 major riots, spread across almost as many American cities, had occurred in the first nine months of 1967 alone. In 75 cities, the riots had resulted in over 80 deaths, many more injuries, and estimates of property damage in the hundreds of millions of dollars. To contain the most severe riots, local authorities often found it necessary to call in the National Guard and other reinforcements. Although the rioters were often portrayed as irrational, or as materially motivated looters, participants in different cities consistently cited political motivations rooted in similar grievances. Echoing black revolutionary leaders, their concerns focused on the criminal justice system and economic marginality.

How important were these mass pressures as a factor driving changes in poverty governance? Because scholarly treatments of this question have usually focused on the federal level, divergent answers have often seemed to be nothing more than differences of emphasis in historical interpretation. By analyzing how the fifty states varied in their responses, it is possible to get more empirical leverage on this question. Indeed, state-level analyses leave little doubt that trends in poverty governance were responsive to mass protest during this period.

The "relief explosion" of the 1960s occurred to a far greater extent in some states than in others. If, as Piven and Cloward (1971) argue, expansions of relief were deployed to pacify social unrest, Aid to Families with Dependent Children (AFDC) caseloads should have risen to a greater degree in states where disruption was more intense. In an analysis that controlled for a variety of factors related to welfare usage, Schram and Turbett (1983) found precisely this pattern. Indeed, relative to the other factors under study, the severity of rioting experienced in the 1965–68 period emerged as the single strongest predictor of caseload increases in state AFDC programs from 1969 to 1970 (and the second strongest predictor of caseload increases across the entire decade). Building on this work, Fording (1997) showed that changes in state welfare caseloads followed a clear political logic during this period, resulting in AFDC expansions under precisely the conditions suggested by theorists such as Piven and Cloward (1971) and Keech ([1968] 1981).

Specifically, the effects of black insurgency were contingent on two additional factors related to black political power: electoral access and relative share of the population. Where blacks lacked access to the ballot box, their protests did not signal a deeper electoral threat, and elected leaders were free to respond based on the preferences of empowered (white) voters. Under these conditions, levels of black insurgency had negligible effects on AFDC caseloads. By contrast, where blacks had achieved electoral incorporation, the political context was more conducive to insurgency effects. The size of the effects, in turn, depended on the black share of a state's population. If blacks made up a small percentage, insurgency produced modest expansions of the AFDC rolls. This effect diminished in states where black residents were somewhat more numerous. But in states where large black populations could exercise influence as voters, insurgent actions were followed by dramatic expansions in the AFDC rolls.

Extending this analysis, Fording (2001) showed that distributions of relief, which provided the "beneficent" side of state responses, were complemented by "coercive" uses of incarceration. In the absence of electoral power, waves of mass disruption were followed primarily by increases in incarceration, with few concessions in the form of expanded relief. But where electoral incorporation had been achieved, state responses to insurgency drew on both the "left" and "right" hands of state social control. Welfare and incarceration both expanded sharply to cover larger portions of the poor and, where black populations were larger, welfare expansions were less likely to be rolled back in the ensuing years. In states where all three elements of black political power were strong (electoral access, population size, and rates of insurgency), Fording (2001) found the most favorable responses of all: a "scissors" pattern that paired large, durable increases in welfare distribution with sustained decreases in incarceration levels.

The stark differences in responses clearly suggest that mass unrest created a new pattern of state-level social control. Federalism, however, is not just a system that allows states to pursue different strategies; it is also a relationship between levels of government. Along this dimension as well, political mobilization produced dramatic change. As civil rights leaders and social justice organizations pressed the national Democratic Party for more substantial action, black votes were becoming more important to the Democratic electoral coalition. In the early 1960s, the Kennedy administration began to formulate an ambitious anti-poverty agenda as a vehicle for responding to these pressures (Piven and

Cloward 1971). In the years that followed, the federal government produced a raft of new programs to support the able-bodied, working-aged poor, including Medicaid (1965), Food Stamps (1964), and Head Start (1964). Unlike earlier programs for this group, Food Stamps and Head Start would be entirely funded by federal government, and states would be given little discretion to set eligibility or benefit standards. Although the Medicaid program emerged from a more distinctive set of political developments (political maneuvering around the passage of Medicare), the design of this program shared the broader direction of change toward an expanded federal role. While states would retain some discretion over Medicaid, the federal government would absorb more than half the cost.

Shifts toward national policy control were more difficult to achieve in the AFDC program, where state discretion was already institutionalized (Lieberman 1998). To achieve it, activists pursued a two-pronged strategy. On one side, protest actions were combined with efforts to mobilize claims by the vast numbers of poor women who were not receiving aid. These tactics strained the meager capacities of state aid programs, disrupted local welfare operations, and created pressures for the federal government to step in (Piven and Cloward 1977). On the other side, welfare rights activists mounted an ambitious litigation campaign modeled after the legal strategies that had produced federal victories for the civil rights movement (M. Davis 1995).

The first signs of change appeared early in the decade. In 1961, a federal administrative ruling ended the "suitable home" requirement, and, in 1962, federal legislation expanded AFDC coverage to include parents of eligible children. As the decade unfolded, federal action escalated, topping out as the two-pronged insurgent strategy reached its peak. AFDC benefit levels increased throughout the 1960s, outpacing inflation. After federal passage of the Food Stamp Act in 1964, the overall value of the "welfare package" rose far more sharply than AFDC alone. Low-income families were now able to supplement AFDC's cash benefits with noncash Food Stamp (FS) transfers. The combined value of AFDC/FS benefits rose steadily over the next decade, and, with the welfare package now more adequate, so did the AFDC participation rate.

Rising caseloads reflected more than the draw of increased benefits, however. By the end of the 1960s, the welfare rights litigation campaign had begun to bear fruit (M. Davis 1995). Victories in federal courts ended the invasive and degrading "midnight raids" of welfare officials (1967), struck down "substitute father" and "man in the house" provisions (1968), ended length-of-residency requirements designed to deter welfare migration and program entry (1969), and gave welfare recipients due process rights to fair hearings in decisions re-garding benefit termination (1970). Together, these federal actions deprived the states of many of the tools they had been using to restrict access to cash aid and discriminate against poor women of color.

As new benefits came on line and old benefits became more generous and accessible, relief flowed to the poor at unprecedented rates. By 1975, welfare expenditures and participation rates had reached record levels, and welfare caseloads had become more racially representative of the poor than ever be-fore (Piven and Cloward 1993). The poverty rate declined steadily during this period, falling by half, from 22 percent in 1961 to around 11 percent in the mid-1970s.[3] Although economic growth undoubtedly contributed to this reduction in poverty, the combined effects of welfare expansions clearly played a major role (Stricker 2007).

Welfare and Poverty Governance in the States, 1970–95

In the last decades of the twentieth century, programs for more "deserving" subsets of the poor (elderly, disabled, and/or recently unemployed from a quali-fying job) exhibited a continued, if uneven, trajectory of centralization, stabil-ity, and growth. Federal involvements in these programs persisted, and benefits (even in the UI program) were steadily increased through automatic cost of living adjustments and state supplements (Burtless 1986; Scholz, Moffitt, and Cowan 2009).

After the era of disruption subsided, however, programs for the undeserving poor (nondisabled, nonelderly adults with less stable work histories) followed a different path. The AFDC program offers a case in point. With federal rules now protecting access, benefit levels became the primary focus of state efforts to limit the attractions of AFDC as an alternative to wage work. As figure 4-3 illustrates, the real value of AFDC benefits declined by almost half, from about $1,200 a month in 1970 to $624 dollars a month in 1995 (in constant 2007 dollars).[4] Because federal lawmakers did not index AFDC benefits to inflation in the 1960s, efforts to maintain benefits at 1970 levels required positive (and controversial) legislative action. In most cases, state governments did nothing, allowing inflation to cut into the real value of AFDC benefits. As the bars in fig-ure 4-3 indicate, however, clusters of states moved in several periods to extend the erosive effects of inflation by reducing the nominal amount of benefits.

In GA programs, where the events of the 1960s left unencumbered state control intact, opportunities for retrenchment were greater. As late as the mid-

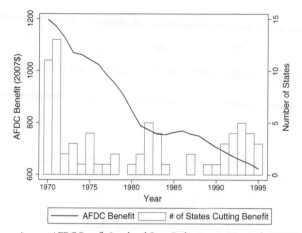

FIGURE 4-3. Average AFDC Benefit Level and State Reductions in Nominal AFDC Benefit Level, 1970–95

1970s, every U.S. state ran some type of GA program to provide aid to poor individuals and families who were ineligible for AFDC and SSI. Over the next twenty years, eighteen states abolished GA entirely, and GA benefits fell sharply nationwide (Uccello, McCallum, and Gallagher 1996).

Beneath these national trends, efforts to restore labor regulation after the 1960s followed a systematic pattern across the states. As we saw earlier in figure 4-1, state AFDC benefits were highly patterned at the dawn of the 1960s, tracking retail wages in close to a one-to-one relationship (.97) and averaging only 60 percent of these wage levels. Benefits and wages were, at this point, calibrated in precisely the manner suggested by the principle of less eligibility. Political disruption in the 1960s shattered this configuration. By 1976, state AFDC-FS benefits no longer followed state retail wages in lockstep: The relationship observed in 1961 (.97) was cut by more than half (.42), and state AFDC-FS benefits were now, on average, 81 percent of state retail wages.

If we look beyond the retail sector and incorporate wages for low-skilled workers in the agricultural and service sectors, the slipping hold of "less eligibility" becomes even clearer.[5] In 1976, the state-level relationship between low-skilled wages and AFDC-FS benefits was a paltry .21. The maximum AFDC-FS benefit was, on average, 91 percent of the average wage in jobs typically available to the poor. In fifteen states, the value of the benefit *exceeded* the value of the wages.[6]

These trends did not go unnoticed. State policymakers decried the rising generosity of welfare relative to work as well as the growth of AFDC caseloads and expenditures. In reality, the new "work disincentives" presented by higher BWRs were created by *two* trends: not just rising welfare benefits but also declining wages for low-skilled workers. The latter trend, however, was largely ignored in poverty debates. Despite popular support for raising the minimum wage, policies to raise the wage floor for low-skilled workers would not be forthcoming (Bartels 2008). Instead, state policymakers sought to restore the gap between welfare and wages by draining the real value of welfare benefits.

Although inflation did much of the work for them, the role of legislative action during this period should not be overlooked. Across all states and all years, AFDC benefits were left unchanged in only about 50 percent of the state-year combinations between 1970 and 1995. State governments cut the nominal AFDC benefit for a family of four on thirty-nine different occasions between 1970 and 1980, and on an additional thirty-five occasions between 1981 and 1995.

As they did so, benefit changes again followed a tell-tale pattern across the states, shifting to restore the calibration of benefits and wages that had been disrupted in the 1960s. Between 1970 and 1995, states cut the AFDC benefit by an average of $571 (in constant 2007 dollars), but the largest cuts occurred in states where welfare benefits had begun to approach wage levels for low-skilled workers. Among the twenty-six states that had a BWR above the national average in 1970, the average reduction from 1970 to 1995 was $717. Among the states with a BWR below the national average, the average reduction was only $401.

The pattern of benefit cuts, however, reflected more than just a shift back to less eligibility. Race took center stage in poverty politics after the 1960s, as blacks became more prevalent in welfare caseloads and pathological images of the black underclass prevailed in political rhetoric and mass media stories (see chapter 3). Although levels of overt racial prejudice were declining, perceptions of black laziness and irresponsibility were being cued, in a variety of ways, as frames for welfare policymaking (Gilens 1999; Peffley and Hurwitz 1999). Under these conditions, the RCM predicts that larger numbers of black welfare recipients would stoke fears about work disincentives and cue perceptions that the poor must be motivated to work. If this dynamic occurred, we should find that (a) the benefit reductions designed to make welfare less attractive were actually larger in states where blacks made up a higher share of the welfare caseload, and (b) this relationship was stronger in states where higher benefit-wage ratios made concerns about work disincentives more salient.

To test this interactive hypothesis, we rely on a multivariate model that controls for a variety of factors that might affect welfare benefit levels.[7] Focusing on the 1976–95 period, when benefit levels plummeted, we test whether decisions to change benefit levels were influenced by the racial makeup of welfare casel-oads and whether this relationship, in turn, was stronger in states with higher benefit-wage ratios.[8] Our results indicate that several factors made states more likely to cut benefits: decreasing tax revenues, rising AFDC caseloads, increases in Republican control of state government, and more conservative political ori-entations among state residents. Not surprisingly, state policymakers were less likely to cut benefits when the federal reimbursement rate increased.[9] These re-sults are all consistent with expectations as well as the results of past studies—a fact that raises our confidence that the model is well specified (R. Brown 1995; Hero 1998; Howard 1999; Orr 1976; Plotnick and Winters 1985; Wright 1976).

The key results, illustrated in figure 4-4, support our expectation that racial politics guided the effort to restore work incentives for the poor. Here, we see estimated results for two hypothetical "average" states (states with observed variables set at their means): one where blacks made up 10 percent of the AFDC caseload (Panel A) and an identical one where blacks made up 60 percent of the caseload (Panel B). In each case, we calculate estimates under three conditions: (1) a low BWR of .70, (2) a fairly typical BWR of 1.0, or (3) a high BWR of 1.2. Under each condition, the bars show the predicted probability that, in a given year, the state would cut the AFDC benefit, increase the AFDC benefit, or do nothing.

In Panel A, we find that when the caseload is only 10 percent black and the work disincentive is low (BWR of .7), the probability of the state increas-ing its nominal AFDC benefit is very high (.90). As the work disincentive in-creases, the probability of a benefit increase drops steadily. When confronted with a high BWR (1.2), the state becomes unlikely to raise its nominal benefit (.25) and instead is most likely to leave its nominal benefit untouched. In other words, a state with very few black recipients would be most likely to respond to a high work disincentive by allowing inflation effects to erode the real value of its AFDC benefit. Under no circumstance does our analysis predict that an "average" state with relatively few black recipients would be likely to take legis-lative action to decrease its nominal AFDC benefit.

Panel B provides results for an identical state where blacks make up 60 per-cent of the AFDC caseload. The predicted probabilities shift in a pattern that echoes what we see in Panel A, with two critical exceptions. First, with blacks making up a majority of the caseload, the effects of the BWR increase substan-

A

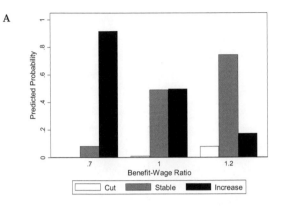

B

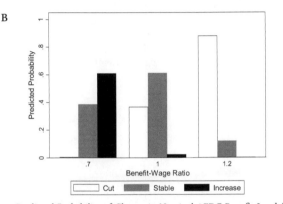

FIGURE 4-4. Predicted Probability of Change in Nominal AFDC Benefit Level (Decrease, Stability, Increase), by Racial Composition of the AFDC Caseload and Benefit-Wage Ratio, 1976–95 (A) Percentage of AFDC Caseload That Is Black = 10% (B) Percentage of AFDC Caseload That Is Black = 60%

Note: These estimated probabilities are based on a multivariate (ordered probit) model of state panel data for the years 1976–95. The dependent variable is the change in the nominal AFDC benefit level for a family of 4 (−1 = decrease, 0 = stability, 1 = increase). The model controls for the following state-level variables: per capita income, change in state tax revenue, Republican control of state government, state citizen ideology, the federal matching (reimbursement) rate, the state unemployment rate, the average benefit level in neighboring states, and fixed effects for states and years. The sample excludes Alaska and Hawaii.

tially. As in Panel A, we see that when the BWR is set at .70, an increase in the nominal benefit is the most likely outcome. Here, however, when the BWR is set at 1.0, the most likely outcome becomes no change in the nominal benefit. And most strikingly, when work disincentives are high (a BWR of 1.2), the state becomes very likely to take action to cut the nominal benefit, with a predicted probability of .85. Second, comparing Panel B to Panel A, we see that legislative actions to cut benefits are far more likely, and actions to raise benefits are far less likely, at all values of the BWR. Because the only difference between the two panels is racial composition, the differences indicate the direct and substantial effects of race. These results provide powerful evidence that, as state lawmakers reduced benefits, their adjustments were shaped by the interplay of racial politics and the principle of less eligibility.

These findings could, of course, be a spurious reflection of some kind of unique and unmeasured dynamic in the AFDC program. To check this possibility, we can look to see if the same forces also explain state decisions to dismantle GA programs during this period. Because all states had GA programs in the early 1970s, decisions to eliminate them from 1970 to 1995 can be analyzed by examining whether or not a state still operated a statewide GA program in 1996 (Uccello, McCallum, and Gallagher 1996). Unfortunately, available data do not allow us to measure state-level differences in the benefit levels and racial characteristics of state GA programs. As a "next best" substitute for the BWR used above, we capture state labor market pressures through a simple measure of wage levels for low-skilled workers (the denominator of the BWR). If states were motivated by concerns over work disincentives, actions to eliminate GA programs should be more common in states with relatively low wage levels for low-skilled workers. In lieu of program-specific data on racial composition, we rely on the black percentage of the total state population to test for racial effects.[10] Once again, our analysis controls for additional factors expected to affect provision of GA benefits.[11]

The key results are presented in figure 4-5, which shows the predicted probability of a "hypothetical average state" eliminating its GA program under various conditions defined by our two key variables. The probability of program termination rises sharply as the black percent of the population rises; it falls dramatically as the wages offered to low-skilled workers become more adequate. With the less precise measures available to us for the GA program, we do not find a statistically significant interaction of racial percentages and wage levels in this analysis. Nevertheless, the findings for GA elimination strongly corroborate our analysis of AFDC benefit reductions: the highest probability of GA elimination is predicted when state wages for low-skilled wages are at their lowest and GA recipients are most likely to be black.

Together, the findings shown in figures 4-4 and 4-5 underscore the centrality of race and less eligibility in the politics benefit retrenchment after the 1960s. By 1995, the safety net for the undeserving poor had eroded to the point that benefits lifted very few out of deep poverty. In the AFDC program, however, federal rules kept state benefits accessible and caseloads relatively high.

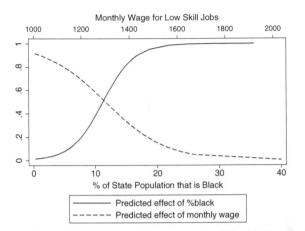

FIGURE 4-5. Predicted Effects of Black Population Percentage and Monthly Wage Level on Abolishing State GA Program by 1996

Moreover, even though benefits declined more steeply in states with higher BWRs, the state-level calibration of AFDC benefits and low-skill wages had not returned to anything like its earlier one-to-one relationship. The relationship between AFDC benefits and retail wages had been almost exact in 1961 (.97); it fell sharply by 1976 (.42); and it returned only slightly by 1995 (.54). The real value of welfare benefits dropped rapidly during this period, but so too did wages for low-skilled workers. The combined AFDC-FS benefit was, on average, 91 percent of the wage for low-skilled workers in 1976, and, despite steep benefit declines, it fell only slightly over the next two decades, coming to rest at 86 percent in 1995. In an era of declining wages, benefit cuts were not enough to restore work pressures. Calls for more fundamental reforms continued to escalate, and bigger changes in public aid for the undeserving poor were gathering momentum.

Incarceration and Poverty Governance in the States, 1970–95

The twenty-five years that followed 1970 marked a more decisive turn on the carceral side of poverty governance. In the AFDC program, federal rules limited state efforts to make welfare less accessible and more conditional. In the criminal justice field, however, the states were free to adopt more muscular approaches and, indeed, were pushed in this direction by national political developments. In the wake of civil rights victories and urban riots, Republican leaders demonstrated the electoral benefits of exploiting racialized anxieties over criminality and disorder. The law-and-order campaigns of Barry Goldwater and George Wallace were followed by Richard Nixon's declaration of a "war on crime" and Ronald Reagan's declaration of a "war on drugs." Conservative intellectuals, such as James Q. Wilson (1975), added fuel to the fire by declaring that rehabilitation efforts were an unmitigated failure that could be overcome only by tougher policies focused on incapacitation and deterrence. As debates about crime drove a wedge into the Democratic coalition, leading Democrats such as Tip O'Neill, Joe Biden, and Bill Clinton made tactical shifts toward the hard-line proposals of their conservative opponents.

The result was a spate of new federal policies that imposed tougher criminal penalties and expanded the incarcerated population (J. Simon 2007). Under the American system of federalism, however, the states held primary responsibility for crime policy. Thus, while the push to get tough on crime began at the national level, it would come to fruition in the states. It did so in short order, as Republican candidates adopted crime as a campaign issue in state elections and Republican governors began to push for changes in criminal justice policies. Under Governor John Ashcroft (1985–93), Missouri expanded the scope and severity of criminal penalties, spent $115 million on new prisons, increased its annual corrections budget from $87 million to $208 million, and experienced an 80 percent increase in its imprisonment rate (Western 2006: 60). In South Carolina, Governor Carroll Campbell (1986–90) led efforts to restructure sentences for drug offenders around mandatory minimums, no-parole clauses, and longer prison terms—producing a 39 percent increase in the imprisonment rate in just four years (Western 2006: 61).

As state lawmakers moved to get tough on crime, three dimensions of policy change compounded to drive up incarceration rates. First, a variety of new laws increased existing sentences and extended imprisonment to new categories of crime. "Moral offenses" related to drugs and sex were often singled out for particularly draconian measures (Wacquant 2009). Second, state lawmakers took action to ensure that tough new penalties would not be softened by tenderhearted judges or parole boards. To limit judicial discretion, they passed a host of new sentencing guidelines, truth-in-sentencing laws, and "three strikes" laws that collectively defined a new regime of determinate sentencing (Western 2006: 65). At the back end of prison stays, they moved to abolish or limit early parole, which had previously served a variety of rehabilitative, humanitarian, and incentivizing purposes. Instead, parole would now serve as a supervisory extension of the prison sentence, operating to cycle populations between poor minority neighborhoods and prisons (Wacquant 2009). By the end of the 1990s, more than 80 percent of people leaving prison were being put on parole, and the number of parolees sent back to prison for violations was seven times higher than it had been twenty years earlier (Travis 2005: 40). "With fully 54 percent of offenders failing to complete their term of parole in 1997 and parole viola- tors making up a third of all persons admitted in state penitentiaries every year (two-thirds in California), parole has become an appendage of the prison that operates mainly to extend the social and symbolic incapacities of incarceration beyond its walls" (Wacquant 2001: 113).

Third, to build the administrative capacities needed to warehouse large populations, state officials shifted budget allocations sharply in the direction of carceral investment. Between 1982 and 1997, state correctional spending grew 383 percent, while total state spending rose by only 150 percent (Wac- quant 2009: 153). Investments in new prison construction rose by 612 percent from 1979 to 1989, and, by 1992, four states—California, New York, Texas, and Florida—each spent more than a billion dollars per year on the operation of existing prisons (Wacquant 2009: 153–54). Prison growth was so dramatic that, by 1998, criminal corrections operations had become the third largest employer in the country—ahead of McDonalds and General Motors, and trailing only Wal-Mart and the temporary employment agency, Manpower, Inc. (Wacquant 2009: 158).

As corrections spending skyrocketed, fiscal patterns in the states under- scored the tight relationship between incarceration and welfare as instruments of social control. The growing cost of corrections put pressure on all areas of state spending, of course. Yet across state budgets, broad "crowd out" effects did not emerge. States that spent more on corrections did not, for example, spend substantially less on areas such as health care and education (Guetzkow and Western 2007). Instead, "bloated correctional spending primarily siphoned funds from welfare expenditures" (Guetzkow and Western 2007: 238). Na- tional trends underscore the shift. In 1980, the United States spent 58 percent more on AFDC than on jails and prisons; by 1995, U.S. spending on jails and prisons exceeded investments in AFDC (132 percent greater) as well as Food Stamps (69 percent greater) (Wacquant 2009: 159). As a percentage of federal spending on public housing, federal corrections expenditures rose tenfold, from 25 percent in 1980 to 246 percent in 1990 (Wacquant 2009: 160). Because these spending trade-offs focused so narrowly on "benefits for the 'undeserv- ing' poor," Guetzkow and Western (2007: 238–40) rightly conclude that they did not reflect a general, corrections-driven shortfall of resources; rather, they signaled a substantive shift in the ways that states were "dealing with poverty and the governance of marginalized populations."

Across the states, penal and welfare institutions were converging as "two components of a single apparatus for the management of poverty" (Wacquant 2009: 14–15). Although paternalism would not fully emerge in welfare policy until the 1990s, its rationality guided the expanding reach of police and prison operations throughout the 1970s and 1980s. As welfare supports weakened in these decades, the future of poverty governance was signaled more clearly by the law-and-order push to build "a strong state and a state that will put its strength to use" (Norton 2004: 178). Welfare programs would soon follow suit, joining penal and policing apparatuses as tools for "effecting the authoritarian rectification of behaviors [in] populations recalcitrant to the emerging economic and symbolic order" (Wacquant 2009: 14). As Loïc Wacquant (2009: 15) argues, in a passage that dovetails with our own analysis, the division of labor in this emerging "double regulation" was built on gender-specific variants of a common rationality:

> The public aid bureaucracy, now reconverted into an administrative springboard into poverty-level employment, takes up the mission of inculcating the duty of working for work's sake among poor women. The quartet formed by the police, the court, the prison, and the probation or parole officer assumes the task of taming their brothers, their boyfriends or husbands, and their sons. Within this sexual and institutional division in the regulation of the poor, the "clients" of both the assistantial and penitential sectors of the state fall under the same principled suspicion: they are considered morally deficient unless they periodically provide visible proof to the contrary. This is why their behaviors must by supervised and regulated by the imposition of rigid protocols whose violation will expose them to a redoubling of corrective discipline.

The upshot of this analysis is that welfare and criminal justice policies shifted in the late twentieth century as two parts of a single movement in poverty governance. If this argument is correct, then the same forces that led states to vary in their welfare strategies from 1976 to 1995 should have shaped outcomes on the carceral side as well. Our earlier analysis of welfare trends pointed to three key determinants of state variation: partisan/ideological control of government, the racial composition of policy targets, and labor market conditions for low-skilled workers. As states ramped up incarceration from 1976 to 1995, did their actions follow these same patterns?

We have already suggested a number of reasons to expect that race and partisan control mattered for state-level changes in incarceration rates. The law-and-order campaigns of the 1970s and 1980s were deployed as Republican electoral strategies; they used race-coded language to exploit racial anxieties; and they did so against a backdrop of racialized social disorder. Although many Democrats would eventually cooperate in the carceral turn, Republicans were the prime movers in the political actions that stoked fears of crime, focused electoral contests on law-and-order issues, and advanced punitive criminal justice reforms (Western 2006). Stereotypical images of threatening black men played a central role in these race-coded appeals, in media coverage of crime, and in public attitudes toward criminal justice policy (Mendelberg 2001; Gilliam and Iyengar 2000; Hurwitz and Peffley 1997).

The connections between incarceration and labor markets are less straightforward. Unlike welfare reform in 1996, tougher criminal laws were rarely sold in the political arena as a way to require the poor to work. Indeed, while prisons and welfare programs differ in many ways, they both have the effect of *removing* individuals from the reserve stock of labor available to employers. Thus, as imprisonment rates rise, they should draw poor people out of the low-wage labor pool, forcing employers to face tighter labor markets that push wages upward and bolster the bargaining position of workers (Piven 2010). From this perspective, mass incarceration seems to be an irrational work-enforcement strategy, and one is led to suspect that political forces unrelated to labor market needs must have driven its emergence.

Several observations counter this conclusion, however. Labor market theories of imprisonment suggest that, when work attachments weaken in poor communities, authorities tend to view the growing ranks of jobless young men as a kind of "social dynamite" that threatens a wave of crime and social disorder (Spitzer 1975: 645). To forestall this threat, they intensify policing in poor neighborhoods and penalties for criminal behavior (Western, Kleykamp, and Rosenfeld 2006). The resulting expectation-preemption dynamic can work as a mechanism to convert deteriorating labor market conditions into higher incarceration rates for low-income groups.

Beyond this dynamic, the rising tide of correctional control may serve labor markets in a variety of ways, despite the observation that imprisoned individuals are not standard participants in the labor market. A large percentage of the men who populate U.S. prisons today were not "removed" from the formal labor market by their incarceration; they were already surviving outside this system by pursuing informal or illegal sources of income (Venkatesh 2006). Against this baseline, tough criminal justice policies can operate in several ways to push men out of "off the books" activities and make them available to employers in the formal economy.

First, although they are not "standard" participants in the labor market, many prisoners are, in fact, available for employers to hire. Indeed, a growing number of "prison industries" offer incarcerated populations up to governments and corporations as cheap, easily controlled sources of labor (Kang 2009). Second, strong carceral strategies do not just send people away to prison; they cycle large numbers of people *through* prison (Travis 2005). At the prison-exit stage of this cycle, the vast majority of ex-offenders are now placed in parole arrangements that treat employment as the centerpiece of successful integration into the community (Rakis 2005). Parolees are typically pressured to take any available job, regardless of the terms. Probation programs, which hold an even larger portion of the convicted offenders under "community supervision," stress employment to an equal degree. The expansion of correctional control has created a community-supervision population that is triple the size of the imprisoned population. As a result, it has actually pushed more low-income men into work-enforcing supervision than it has pushed out of the formal labor market.

Third, muscular criminal enforcement can shore up work enforcement in poor neighborhoods by reducing the attractions of illicit income alternatives. To see how, recall how stigmatizing program conditions promote wage work by making welfare less attractive (Piven and Cloward 1971). Even when welfare benefits begin to encroach on available wages, the degraded *conditions* of benefit receipt continue to tip the scales in favor of low-wage jobs. Criminal justice policies can play a similar role when the jobs available in poor neighborhoods get so bad that opportunities in the underground economy become attractive. At such times, the degraded and dangerous conditions of prison signal the awful fate that awaits people who fail to play by the rules of the low-wage labor market. Aggressive approaches to policing and punishment make the worst "legitimate" jobs more attractive by raising the risks of illicit alternatives. This dynamic takes on an even stronger form for convicted ex-offenders: Their felony records limit them to the worst job openings (Western 2006), and their supervision makes imprisonment a far more likely outcome of underground involvements (Travis 2005).

For all these reasons, we should expect changes in state incarceration rates to reflect the same basic forces that we observed in our earlier analysis of welfare benefit and program cuts. Larger increases should track with Republican control of state government and with weaker labor market conditions. And once again, these effects should be stronger for blacks than for whites. Thus, the most dramatic expansions should have occurred when lower-class black men confronted deteriorating markets for low-skilled labor and conservative state governments.

To test these expectations, we conduct separate regression analyses of yearly changes in black and white state incarceration rates, 1976–95.[12] Our key predictors include Republican control of state political institutions (the governor's seat and legislature) and wage levels for low-skilled workers (as defined in our welfare analysis). To account for changes in imprisonment driven by actual changes in crime, we include a measure of the state crime rate. We also include race-specific measures of the drug arrest rate to capture the effects of this key mechanism for reducing the attractiveness of illegal work. Beyond these variables, we control for a wide range of factors that earlier studies have suggested may influence rates of imprisonment growth.[13]

Our results strongly confirm our race-specific expectations. Changes in white incarceration rates from 1976 to 1995 exhibit few significant relationships to our key predictors. Only changes in the crime rate and the presence of a Republican governor are associated with significant increases for this group. By contrast, we find consistently large effects on black incarceration rates. To illustrate, figure 4-6 presents the predicted effects associated with each of our key factors, controlling for the other variables in our models. To provide some historical grounding for this comparison, the results in figure 4-6 take into account both the extent of each factor's influence (as revealed by the coefficients in our regressions) and the actual changes over time observed for each factor (as revealed by shifts in the values of each variable, 1976–95).[14]

The results indicate that actual changes in crime rates played a relatively minor role in the states' sharp escalation of penal confinement during this period. Although the crime rate is a statistically significant predictor in both models, the average change in the crime rate during this period was near zero. Thus, the overall historical impact is estimated to be negligible. As the war on drugs intensified in these years, however, we see a strong, race-targeted effect for drug arrest rates. The expanding dragnet of drug-focused policing filled the prisons with black men without producing an observable effect on white incarceration rates.

A similar pattern can be seen for the crumbling labor market for low-skilled workers during these years. Consistent with "racialized labor-market" interpre-

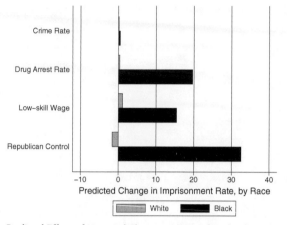

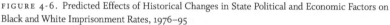

FIGURE 4-6. Predicted Effects of Historical Changes in State Political and Economic Factors on Black and White Imprisonment Rates, 1976–95

Note: This figure is derived from two state-level panel regressions of the race-specific imprisonment rate (i.e., the black imprisonment rate and the white imprisonment rate) on various state-level social, political, and economic variables (see online appendix for details). The bars in the graph are calculated by multiplying the regression coefficient for each variable by the 1976–95 change in the independent variable (averaged across states). The effect of Republican control represents predicted changes in imprisonment growth due to the observed 1976–95 change in Republican control of the governor's office, as well as the change in the percentage of state legislators who are Republican. All of the variables above had a statistically significant effect on black imprisonment growth. Of these variables, only the crime rate and Republican control of the governor's office had a statistically significant impact on white imprisonment growth.

tations of the carceral turn (Western 2006; Wacquant 2009), we find that declining wages for low-skilled workers had meager effects on white incarceration rates but led to dramatic increases in black incarceration rates. Finally, the largest historical effect observed here is political and, once again, is race-specific. Black incarceration rates rose sharply as Republicans made advances in capturing state gubernatorial and legislative offices, while white incarceration rates exhibited no discernible change. The critical role of electoral politics is underscored by a finding in this analysis that we do not show in figure 4-6: Increases in black incarceration rates were significantly larger in years when states held elections; white incarceration rates were immune to this effect.

Conclusion

In the decades leading up to the 1960s, poverty governance in the United States followed a well-worn path. Efforts to support and manage the poor were controlled at the subnational level and organized around distinctions of deservingness. Penal supervision encompassed a relatively small portion of the low-income population, and rates of imprisonment did not expand and contract very much as societal conditions changed over time. Welfare programs for the poor offered meager support, based on morals testing and means testing, and did so in ways that were closely calibrated to state and local labor markets. Work expectations focused primarily on black women and were expressed most clearly in the exclusionary practices and work-promoting rules of welfare operations in the southern states. Labor regulation was rooted chiefly in welfare institutions and pursued primarily by hewing to the principle of less eligibility.

From the 1960s onward, a series of developments intersected to transform this system. Political insurgency provoked strong responses from governing authorities, producing sharp shifts in welfare and incarceration that varied systematically across the states depending on the political power of African Americans. Mass disruptions and litigation campaigns pushed the federal government to impose new limits on state welfare programs, making it more difficult for state and local officials to selectively expel aid recipients in response to economic and political pressures. Collapsing labor markets for low-skilled workers undermined the economic viability of urban ghettoes and created a politically potent mixture of issues centered on race, poverty, and underclass pathology. In the wake of civil rights victories and civil unrest in the 1960s, Republican law-and-order campaigns exploited fractures in the Democratic coalition and turned racialized public anxieties into partisan victories. And as Democrats made tactical adjustments in response, political elites converged on tougher approaches to welfare and criminal justice.

Beginning in the 1970s, welfare and penal operations shifted in tandem as two elements of a single apparatus for managing the poor, and, as welfare supports eroded and imprisonment rates rose, poverty governance turned toward a "double regulation of the poor." Like Wacquant (2009), we have argued that race played a pivotal role in this transition. More than Wacquant, however, we have emphasized that the American system of federalism provides an essential starting point for understanding how poverty governance evolved from 1970 to 1995. Closer attention to federalism yields three important analytic payoffs.

First, it helps to clarify why state governments led the way toward tougher policies for the poor after the 1960s. Rhetorically, anti-welfare and law-and-order themes prevailed in national politics from 1964 onward. Yet the states were the prime movers in reshaping poverty governance from 1970 to 1990. Under American federalism, the states have always held primary responsibility for regulating conduct and maintaining social order and, relative to national government, have been far more vulnerable to both social disruption and business pressures (Lowi 1998; Noble 1997; Piven and Cloward 1971). In addition, while Republicans would not take control of the U.S. Congress until 1994, they held the balance of power in a considerable number of state governments during the preceding decades. As our analysis has shown, these were the states that took the lead in cutting welfare benefits and expanding prison operations.

Second, federalism provides the key to understanding why neoliberal paternalism emerged earlier and more forcefully on the carceral side, as opposed to the welfare side, of poverty governance. Under American federalism, the terms of federal-state relations, and the constraints they place on states, vary across policy areas and over time. In the criminal justice domain, federal actions in 1960s forced state police, courts, and prisons to operate within the constraints of new procedural rights. Yet national laws did little to disrupt state-level primacy in this area of governance or to impede the state actions that would lead in short order to an era of mass incarceration. National-level pressures on the states in this area primarily took the form of escalating declarations of "war" against crime, drugs, and social disorder.

On the welfare side, by contrast, a series of political and legal victories were institutionalized at the federal level in ways that imposed substantial constraints on state and local welfare practices. Federal laws and administrative rules made it difficult for states to restrict access to aid, drain welfare caseloads, monitor behaviors, or limit assistance to "suitable" recipients. To restore work pressures, states took action where they could, reducing AFDC benefits and, in some cases, ending the GA programs they operated outside federal oversight. But these actions paled in comparison to the rise of mass custody during this period. The full flowering of paternalism in welfare policy would not occur until later, and its arrival would be signaled by a return to state control in the absence of federally protected entitlement rights.

Third, close attention to state action in a federal system provides insight into the rise of neoliberal paternalism for a simple analytic reason: It allows us to observe changes in poverty governance repeatedly and under different social, political, and economic conditions. By doing so, we have substantially advanced the empirical basis for concluding that changes in incarceration and welfare provision were driven by a common set of forces. Moreover, the results of our analysis lend strong support to scholars, such as Western (2006) and Wacquant (2009), who have emphasized the explanatory importance of labor markets for low-skilled workers, partisan control of government, and inequalities rooted in racial classifications.

Thus, between 1970 and 1995, a relatively coherent set of forces drove substantial change in both penal and welfare operations in the United States, but their effects on the welfare side were limited considerably by federal protections won in the 1960s. As a result, while incarceration rates rose skyward, welfare caseloads did not fall from their historically high levels after the 1960s. Although the real value of state AFDC benefits fell by about half from 1970 to 1995, declining wages for low-skilled workers blunted their potential to make the worst jobs more attractive: Benefit-wage ratios did not return to the low levels that states had maintained in the past. At the same time, state benefits continued to be less responsive to (less correlated with) state wage levels than they had been prior to the mid-1960s. Against this backdrop, state governors increasingly sought to loosen federal constraints on state welfare operations— first by applying for waivers under the AFDC program and then by pushing for a more fundamental devolution of authority under the Temporary Assistance for Needy Families (TANF) block grant system. As we will see in the chapter that follows, this reassertion of state control would have far-reaching consequences for the development of paternalist welfare provision in the United States.

RACE AND FEDERALISM IN WELFARE'S DISCIPLINARY TURN

BY THE 1990s, THE DISCIPLINARY TURN IN AMERICAN POVERTY governance was well underway. Record numbers of the poor were under penal supervision; Aid to Families with Dependent Children (AFDC) benefits and General Assistance (GA) programs had suffered deep cuts; and federal officials had just passed the Family Support Act of 1988 to promote work and child support enforcement. The forces driving change, however, were far from exhausted. The 1990s would emerge as a decade of accelerating policy development that, ultimately, would institutionalize a new disciplinary regime for the poor.

The rapid pace of change in the 1990s is well captured by the trends shown in figure 5-1. In just a decade's time, the number of Americans receiving cash benefits from AFDC dropped by more than 50 percent, while the number incarcerated rose by more than 50 percent. Policy shifts this large are rare, to say the least, and their appearance together in time underscores the importance of analyzing the 1990s as a critical juncture in American poverty governance.

On their face, the falling welfare caseloads shown in figure 5-1 appear to indicate a restoration of the principle of less eligibility—that is, the idea that welfare should not be accessible or generous enough to offer an attractive alternative to the worst jobs in the formal economy (Somers and Block 2005; Pimpare 2004). There is some merit to this view. State actions in the 1970s and 1980s partially restored the calibration of benefits and wages that prevailed prior to the 1960s (see chapter 4). In the 1990s, benefit declines were bolstered by new rules designed to limit access and push recipients into the labor market. The resulting caseload declines were, in many respects, a classic case of throwing the poor out into the market (Piven and Cloward 1971).

But falling caseloads signaled more than just a return to less eligibility. They were byproducts of a more fundamental shift toward disciplinary poverty governance. In the 1990s, welfare programs were redesigned to serve as tools for cultivating market compliance and, ultimately, as state-run resources for employers. As new policies blurred the boundary between welfare operations and labor markets, movements across this boundary (caseload expansion and con-

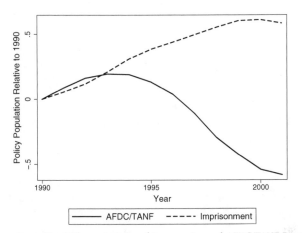

FIGURE 5-1. Proportional Change in Rates of Incarceration and AFDC/TANF Receipt, 1990–2001

Note: TANF caseload data are from the U.S. Department of Health and Human Services. Incarceration data are from the U.S. Bureau of Justice Statistics.

traction) became less decisive as a mechanism of labor regulation. Welfare itself became a way to motivate work and make the poor more attractive and available to employers. Welfare provision was reimagined as way to immerse the poor in a market experience and teach them self-discipline through paternalist direction and supervision.

In the twentieth century, the principle of less eligibility provided the default logic for state welfare provision—a guide that operated so long as it was not disrupted. In recent decades, two episodes of political mobilization changed national policy in ways that altered this logic. In the 1960s, mobilization from the left made benefits more generous and accessible and created new procedural protections. When the disruption receded, states returned to less eligibility, working to make AFDC less attractive than available jobs. Their efforts to do so were constrained, however, because (a) new federal rules limited their ability to make AFDC benefits inaccessible and (b) declining wages made it hard to push AFDC benefits much below the worst market offerings. AFDC caseloads failed to decline in the 1980s and actually rose in the early 1990s.

Policy change in the mid-1990s was driven by a second episode of political mobilization that disrupted the principle of less eligibility. In this case, mobilization came from the right and policy change institutionalized a muscular approach to disciplining the poor. When falling benefits failed to reduce AFDC caseloads, conservatives began to target the federal rules that held AFDC in place as a "decommodifying" program that pulled labor off the market. State officials descended on Washington in the early 1990s, seeking AFDC waivers that would allow them to make eligibility conditional on behavior modification. Pressures from these officials eventually combined with broader forms of mobilization to produce federal action in 1996. The AFDC entitlement and its constraining federal rules were replaced by a Temporary Assistance for Needy Families (TANF) block grant program that emphasized state and local governance.

The reform campaign restructured state policymaking around new federal goals and incentives. It also changed the underlying forces driving state action. When states initially pursued AFDC waivers in the early 1990s, they did so in a familiar pattern: Their requests continued to reflect the differences in racial composition, partisan control, and benefit-wage ratios (BWRs) that had driven state variation in the 1970s and 1980s. After 1996, however, disciplinary governance became a national political project. Key policy choices no longer reflected state BWRs, as one would expect based on the principle of less eligibility. States with high BWRs, of course, continued to feel economic pressures to restrict welfare usage. But now *all states* were being pressed, politically, to pursue the project of reforming the poor.

The widespread pressures flowed, first, from a racialized underclass discourse that demanded tough new strategies and, second, from partisan uses of this discourse for political gain. Overtaken by these forces, the principle of less eligibility became less singular (and hence, less discernible) as the basis of state policy choices. All states were now engaged in an effort to transform aid recipients into worker-citizens—not just to purge them from the rolls. Labor markets and partisan strategies now operated mainly as background factors. State variation flowed more directly from the racialized agendas that lay at the heart of the disciplinary project.

In the 1990s, the *direction* of change in state welfare programs reflected the political rationality that we have termed neoliberal paternalism; the *patterning* of change indicated the centrality of race for neoliberal paternalism itself. The institutional foundation for this pattern was American federalism, which functioned as a mechanism that converted racialized policy choices into a de facto system of race-targeted policies. State officials made different choices when their policy targets included larger numbers of African Americans, and these choices accumulated to create a deeply racialized structure of state policy regimes.

The Rise of AFDC Waivers

Under the federal limits imposed by AFDC rules, benefit levels became the focus of state efforts to restore the principle of less eligibility (see chapter 4). By the early 1990s, the limits of this approach were readily apparent. Rates of welfare participation remained high, and their persistence became a condensation symbol for the diverse anxieties provoked by images of social pathology in the underclass. Against this backdrop, a small group of state governors began to push for new freedoms to focus policy on the behaviors of the poor.

The foundation for this development was laid in 1962, when federal officials authorized section 1115 of the Social Security Act, allowing states to apply for waivers to experiment with welfare designs. For many years, federal constraints placed strong limits on waiver applications. State applicants had to show that their experiments would be cost-neutral for the federal government and would not violate the procedural protections won by the welfare rights movement. As a result, waivers were rarely pursued. In the 1980s, the Reagan administration began to encourage state applications and pushed federal administrators to approve them. The sea change, however, would not occur until the presidential election year of 1992.[1]

As Arkansas Governor Bill Clinton mounted a strong electoral challenge to President George H. W. Bush, he placed calls to "end welfare as we know it" at the center of his campaign (see chapter 3). Searching for a way to blunt Clinton's welfare strategy, and unable to pass new legislation so soon after the Family Support Act of 1988, the Bush administration turned to the AFDC waiver procedure as a way to signal its commitment to reforming the much-maligned program. In addition to encouraging states to apply, the Bush White House revised the cost-neutrality requirement. The new rules permitted experiments that would entail short-run costs so long as they, in theory at least, could generate long-run savings (Conlan 1998; Teles 1996).

As state officials responded to the call, their proposals initially focused on procedures designed to push AFDC recipients into the labor force, such as stringent work requirements, sanctions for noncompliance, and time limits for benefit receipt. By the early 1990s, however, the "work versus welfare" issue had been assimilated into a broader discourse of social pathology. The political focus was rapidly shifting away from objective features of the AFDC program and their relationship to work itself (Schram 1995). As Nathan Glazer (1995: 21) noted:

The issue has become what welfare symbolizes, not what it is. Welfare
has come to stand for the rise of a permanent dependent population cut
off from the mainstream of American life and expectations [and] for the
problems of the inner-city black poor. Ending "welfare as we know it"
seems to promise some relief from these social disorders.

On the national stage, conservative intellectuals worked to frame the problems of the black underclass as an indictment of liberal agendas and promote
them as a basis for new policy designs. Douglas Besharov called for greater
attention to the "worsening behavior" of the poor in areas beyond work: "The
out-of-wedlock birthrate is up (to 24 percent of all births nationwide), drug use
among inner-city parents and mothers is up, all these indicia of social problems are up" (Kershner 1991). Charles Murray (1984) argued that racial disparities had grown across a wide range of social pathologies, mainly because of
increasing welfare generosity and black women's reliance on AFDC. Lawrence
Mead (1986, 1992) argued that poverty was now rooted in a broad failure to
fulfill civic obligations that permissive social programs had fostered by failing
to demand self-mastery from poor minority populations. For Mead and others,
nonwork stood at the center of a broader web of social dysfunction that could
be addressed only by making state authority more demanding and putting some
muscle behind it.

Against this backdrop, state officials sought waivers for reforms designed to
modify a wide range of behaviors symbolically associated with the black underclass. In many states, political entrepreneurs promoted waivers by playing on
a combination of racial anxieties and fears that liberal welfare policies might
function as a "magnet" for poor families seeking to freeload off the taxpayers
(Peterson and Rom 1990). In Wisconsin, Republican Governor Tommy Thompson emphasized the social disorder of inner-city Milwaukee and the specter of
welfare migration from Illinois as central campaign themes. In California, Republican Governor Pete Wilson blamed the state's large budget deficits on welfare magnet effects, drawing cross-state welfare migration and cross-national
(undocumented) immigration together under a common narrative of "illegitimate takings" from taxpayers. In New Jersey, Wayne Bryant, a black Democratic
Speaker of the Assembly, pushed for waivers by decrying welfare as a "modern
form of slavery" that broke up black families.

Out of this ferment, waiver requests emerged as a paternalist strategy for
pushing the poor to make "better choices." In Wisconsin, Governor Thompson
drew national attention when he unveiled his "Learnfare" program in Wiscon-

sin, which made aid conditional on school attendance. In Maryland, Governor William Schaefer proposed a plan in 1992 that would cut AFDC benefits by 30 percent and restore this increment only in cases where recipients showed a pattern of "responsible behavior" by getting preventive health care, keeping children in school, and paying rent consistently. In California, Governor Wilson proposed family caps, earnings disregards to encourage work, and a system of benefit cuts that imposed larger reductions on long-term recipients and recipients who had recently arrived from other states. In New Jersey, Speaker Bryant proposed legislation that, among other things, imposed a "family cap" on additional benefits for mothers who gave birth to a child while already receiving welfare.

As the early adopters moved forward, they underscored the lesson that Bill Clinton had delivered in his 1992 presidential campaign: Targeting welfare for reform was a political winner. The lesson was quickly absorbed by governors in other states, who followed suit with welfare-bashing speeches and waiver requests of their own. As Kent Weaver (2000: 132–33) explains:

> Not only did waiver requests appear to offer political opportunities to claim credit, they offered evidence that a governor was trying to do *something* about a welfare system that was almost universally regarded as broken, insulating them from charges by political opponents that they were indifferent to the welfare mess. The long lead times [for approval] did little to discourage waiver requests, either: the requests allowed politicians to project an image of concern about the welfare problem with a very low probability that anything with negative consequences (negative evaluation results, for example, or increased homelessness among poor families) would occur in the political near term.

The Pattern of AFDC Waiver Adoptions

In the 1970s and 1980s, downward trends in AFDC benefits closely followed three factors across the states: the ratio of AFDC benefits to low-skilled wages, partisan control of government, and the racial dynamics of policy choice suggested by the Racial Classification Model (RCM). As states pursued AFDC waivers in the 1990s, their actions produced a pattern that can be used to assess political continuity and change against this baseline. Prior to federal welfare reform in 1996, did the shift in policy focus, from benefits to behavioral rules, produce a shift in the political underpinnings of state action?

To answer this question, we analyze state AFDC waivers during the crucial period running from January 1992, under the Bush administration, to September 1996, when the AFDC program was terminated. Our sample consists of all state-month combinations during this period; our outcome measure is based on state adoptions of a number of behavior-oriented reforms: time limits for termination or reduction of benefits, restrictions on JOBS[2] work exemptions, creation of JOBS sanctions, increases in earnings disregards to encourage work, family caps to deny aid to children born to women on welfare, elimination of rules to deny aid in cases with 100 hours or more of work, and creation of time limits for requiring work.

To estimate the effects of our key variables, we use an event history analysis that controls for a variety of other political and economic differences among the states.[3] These include the ideological orientations of state residents, indicators of social "pathologies" often associated with AFDC (welfare dependency, the unmarried birth rate, the AFDC caseload), state economic health (per capita tax collections), and indicators of a state's propensity to innovate.[4]

Our analysis yields several important results. To begin with, waiver adoption had no discernible relationship to a state's historical propensity toward policy innovation or the political orientations of state residents. Perhaps more revealing, waiver adoptions were unrelated to the objective levels of the various "social problems" emphasized by the political entrepreneurs who drove waiver efforts. By contrast, we find some evidence that waiver adoptions reflected fiscal pressures, as states with depleted tax coffers were significantly more likely to take action.

Turning to our main variables, we find substantial historical continuity. States with Republican governors were nearly twice as likely to adopt AFDC waivers as states with Democratic governors. The pattern from the 1970s and 1980s is also echoed in our results for racial composition and state BWRs. The joint effects of these two factors are illustrated in figure 5-2, which presents predicted survival rates under conditions defined by different combinations of their values.[5] For each combination, the curves indicate the proportion of states we would expect to have "survived" without a waiver adoption at a given point in time along the horizontal axis. As the curve declines, it indicates that fewer states are expected to forgo waiver adoption—that is, an increase in the proportion of states expected to adopt.

Figure 5-2 presents expected survival rates for four hypothetical states. In Panel A, the black percentage of the AFDC caseload is set at 10 percent, while in Panel B, it is set at 60 percent. In each panel, we plot the expected survival

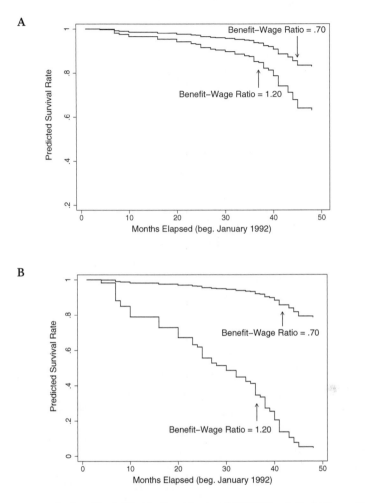

FIGURE 5-2. Predicted Survival Rate for State Adoption of AFDC Waiver, by Racial Composition of Caseload and Benefit-Wage Ratio, 1992–96. (A) %AFDC Black = 10%. (B) %AFDC Black = 60%

rate for one hypothetical "average" state with a BWR of .70 and one with a BWR of 1.20. We can begin by comparing Panels A and B to isolate the direct effects of race. Consistent with our earlier results for benefit trends, states with more black welfare recipients were significantly more likely to adopt a waiver, regardless of the value of the BWR. Similarly, but comparing the curves within each panel, we can see the direct effect of the BWR. As expected, the rate of waiver adoption is predicted to be substantially faster for an "average" state with a higher BWR (1.20), regardless of the racial composition of the rolls.

Perhaps the most striking feature of figure 5-2, however, is that the effect of the BWR (represented by the gap between the two curves) is significantly larger when the black percentage of the caseload is higher. Indeed, by the end of our sample period, nearly all of the states with the higher BWR in Panel B (where blacks make up a higher percentage of the rolls) are predicted to adopt a waiver. By contrast, with the racial composition set at the same level, only about 20 percent of states with the lower BWR are predicted to have done so. The magnitude of this joint effect is underscored by the comparatively small gap that emerges between the curves in Panel A, where African Americans make up only 10 percent of the rolls.

At one level, we interpret these findings as additional support for the RCM. Amid a highly racialized discourse of underclass pathology, state policy actions closely tracked the racial composition of policy targets. Moreover, the impact of racial composition was significantly enhanced by benefit-wage conditions that heightened concerns about work disincentives (and thus, made long-standing black stereotypes more salient and relevant). At a second level, we interpret these results as evidence of historical continuity in the early, state-led period of reform. As states took advantage of waiver opportunities in the early 1990s, their actions reflected the same political dynamics that guided state benefit-setting decisions in the 1970s and 1980s. Thus, as the scope of state discretion over AFDC expanded and the focus of policymaking shifted from benefits to behaviors, the basic logic of state policy choice remained largely unchanged.

Federal Welfare Reform

The Personal Responsibility and Work Opportunity Reconciliation Act of 1996 (PRWORA) nationalized and institutionalized the disciplinary program advanced by state waiver adoptions under AFDC. In doing so, it assimilated public aid for low-income families into the disciplinary stream of development that had overtaken state penal operations in the 1970s and 1980s. As Wacquant (2009: 79) notes, the policy changes embedded in PRWORA "converge[d] to treat—and in turn constitute—the dependent poor as a troublesome population to be subdued and 'corrected' through stern behavioral controls and paternalistic sanctions, thus fostering a programmatic convergence with penal policy." In chapters 2 and 3, we analyzed the national politics of this development in some detail. Here, we approach it from a state-level perspective to clarify how it created a new framework for state efforts to govern the poor in a federal system.

PRWORA restructured two political relationships at the heart of poverty governance: the relationship between federal and state authorities and the relationship between these authorities and low-income citizens. In both cases, it shifted governance toward a disciplinary model that uses incentives, penalties, and structural arrangements to shape the "free choices" of relevant actors. The disciplinary turn was clearly visible in the case of state-citizen relations. The TANF program was explicitly designed to reform the choices of the "dependent poor," who would now be addressed as deficient citizens and market actors. Welfare recipients would be disciplined through "contractual" obligations, incentives, tutelary efforts, and penalties for noncompliance.

What fewer observers noted was that PRWORA restructured federal-state relations in ways that drew on this same logic. Champions of welfare reform described it as a "devolution revolution" that would liberate creative state officials from oppressive federal rules. But PRWORA did more than transfer authority from one level of government to another; it restructured the relationship between levels of government. Under the new law, the states were forced to make policy choices in new areas, and their decisions were structured, incentivized, and constrained by new federal rules and performance benchmarks.

The flurry of state action after 1996 reflected the intersection of these two dimensions of change. On one side, PRWORA directed state authorities to shift the terms of their relationships with low-income citizens. The limited ethos of rights and opportunities that guided AFDC provision after the 1960s was supplanted by a new focus on enforcing obligations and rectifying behavior. The citizen's semi-entitlement to aid, backed by procedural protections, was abolished. Opportunities for job training, created eight years earlier under the JOBS program, met the same fate—as did the option of using public aid to support one's pursuit of higher education (Shaw et al. 2006). PRWORA included no significant provisions to create jobs or to promote the kinds of wages and working conditions needed by low-income mothers (Collins and Mayer 2010).

Instead, the new law identified work and marriage as the "foundation of a successful society" and directed states to focus on the twin themes of personal transformation and civic obligation. In designing TANF programs, state officials would have to decide how best to enforce work requirements and turn recipients into "job-ready" applicants for employers. They would have to create sanctions for noncompliance and devise schedules for their imposition and severity. Federal lawmakers encouraged the states to experiment with new behavior modification classes and behavioral conditions for eligibility. Federal performance reviews forced the states to institute new approaches to monitoring and documenting client behavior, leading some states to institute newly permitted procedures such as finger printing and drug testing.

As this description suggests, federal welfare reform did not seek to free the states; it sought to move them toward a more disciplinary approach to governance. PRWORA established a new "devolution settlement" that constrained, structured, and incentivized state choices along specific dimensions (Peck 2002). The earlier settlement established in the 1960s gave states limited freedom within a rule system designed to block the most exclusionary and invasive administrative strategies. In this sense, welfare rights victories placed federal rules in tension with the long-standing tendency for state and local authorities to pursue behavioral control (Lowi 1998). PRWORA reversed this polarity. It placed the weight of national government behind a disciplinary agenda and created a rule system designed to constrain liberal-minded state officials who might deviate from the new-paternalist script.

Thus, PRWORA barred the states from using their federal TANF funds to provide aid to recent noncitizen immigrants, people convicted of narcotics offenses under federal law, and teen mothers who did not live with their parents. It discouraged states from extending aid to new categories of recipients, while allowing them to deny aid to unwed mothers under the age of eighteen and to children born during a spell of welfare receipt. States could shorten but not lengthen the sixty-month federal limit on lifetime welfare participation; they could shorten but not lengthen the twenty-four-month federal timeline for requiring work participation.

In areas where the states were given broader discretion, they were subject to new structures and incentives designed to shape their choices. The open-ended entitlement to federal matching funds, a key support for states under the AFDC program, was abolished. In its place, the fixed allocations of the new block grant system gave states strong incentives to pare back services, prioritize cost-saving reforms, and limit the size of TANF caseloads. New outcome benchmarks, backed by "high-performance bonuses" and threats of funding reductions, encouraged states to seek budgetary returns by investing in initiatives that would achieve federal goals. By allowing states to fulfill their work participation requirements, in part or whole, by draining the TANF rolls, the "caseload reduction credit" created under PRWORA also incentivized efforts to slow program entry and speed up program exit.

In sum, PRWORA entailed a significant devolution of authority to the states but it should not be confused with a return to the pre-1960s era of nearly unfettered state discretion. Political mobilization in the 1960s expanded the national role in structuring state welfare provision. PRWORA did not reverse this development; it redirected it. After 1996, state efforts to discipline the poor would be driven by more than just state-specific economic and political conditions—or even competition with neighboring states. As states designed their new TANF programs, they enacted a national political project designed and incentivized by federal officials. Their policy choices are best understood as variations on the required theme of neoliberal paternalism.

State Policy Choices: Disciplinary TANF Provisions

It is tempting to view the two waves of state policy adoption that bracketed PRWORA as a single set of events. To do so, however, would be to ignore the restructuring effects of federal welfare reform. In the AFDC waiver period, state officials stepped forward for their own political and policy reasons, making the case that federal authorities should go along with their reform ideas. Thus, patterns of policy adoption reflected choices about *whether* to take action as well as decisions about how to take action. After 1996, TANF program design was placed on state legislative agendas throughout the country. The fifty states all confronted the same federal directives and incentives, and made their choices during the same brief window of transition between 1996 and 1999 (Soss et al. 2006). Despite these shared conditions, some states constructed far more disciplinary TANF regimes than others. Why?

To answer this question, we analyze how choices regarding disciplinary TANF rules were shaped by state-level social, political, and economic conditions. In addition to illuminating cross-state variation, this analysis again allows for an assessment of historical continuity and change. Over the past two chapters, we have identified a remarkably consistent triad of factors driving state trends in AFDC benefits, GA program cuts, incarceration rates, and AFDC waiver adoptions. Over a period spanning three decades, changes along all these dimensions reliably followed state-level differences in the racial composition of policy targets, partisan control of government, and market wages for low-skilled workers (measured relative to benefits in the case of AFDC). Did federal welfare reform alter the political dynamics of policymaking in the states?

To avoid an overly narrow portrait of disciplinary reform, we examine five policy choices that were highly salient in public debate and widely considered in the states after 1996.[6] The first focuses on efforts to end long-term "welfare dependence" by imposing lifetime limits on benefit receipt. In essence, states had to decide whether to embrace the federal lifetime limit of sixty months or exercise their option to impose a shorter limit. The second focuses on the sexual and reproductive behaviors of poor women. After 1996, states could elect to deter pregnancy and childbirth by imposing a family cap that denied additional benefits for children conceived by welfare recipients. Third, PRWORA required states to design sanction procedures to penalize recipients who failed to comply with new program rules. We analyze whether states chose to apply a "full-family sanction"—withdrawing the entire family's benefit on the first infraction—as opposed to a partial benefit sanction or a progressive schedule of increasing sanctions. Fourth, while federal rules required all states to impose TANF work requirements, states could choose to make this requirement more flexible by creating categories of temporary exemption (for a client caring for a child under twelve months of age). We rely on a scale based on twelve such categories, where higher values indicate greater "work requirement rigidity" (the number of categories that were *not* granted exemptions). Our fifth measure captures state decisions about how to limit TANF eligibility. Our scale is based on twenty-eight rules that either exclude individuals from eligibility (a stepparent) or create behavioral bases for denying eligibility (a child's poor school performance or attendance). Higher values indicate more restrictive eligibility standards.

In analyzing these five policy choices, we are most interested in the three factors noted earlier. As in our earlier analyses, we capture pressures related to less eligibility with the BWR—a measure of the ratio of welfare benefits to wages for low-skilled workers. To assess the impact of state officials' political orientations, we include a measure of state government ideology (Berry et al. 1998). We use this more sensitive measure, rather than a count of partisan control, to avoid lumping liberal and conservative Democrats together in the years that followed Bill Clinton's (and the Democratic Leadership Council's) embrace of welfare reform.[7]

Following the RCM, we expect state officials to adopt more disciplinary approaches when African Americans make up a larger percentage of program recipients. In addition, we extend our analysis after 1996 to address the rising salience of Latinos in welfare politics. Several observers have suggested that, as Latino populations have grown in the United States, perceptions of this group have become more important for the ways mass publics and elites think about welfare policy (Gilens 1999; Fox 2004). Anxieties about immigration helped fuel the campaign for federal welfare reform and, ultimately, immigrants (usually but not always presumed to be Latino) were singled out for some of the toughest policy changes passed under PRWORA.[8] Accordingly, we expand our tests of the RCM after 1996 to analyze whether policy responses to Latino targets paralleled responses to black targets.

In pursuing this test, we are guided by the RCM's prediction that racial effects on policy choices will be larger and more likely when the *gap* between policy-relevant group reputations is wider. In the welfare context, relevant stereotypes of blacks—low work effort, sexual irresponsibility, and so on—suggest a sharper contrast with whites than do relevant stereotypes of Latinos.[9] Accordingly, we expect the link between policy choice and racial/ethnic composition to be weaker and less consistent for Latinos than for blacks.

Beyond these variables, we include a number of additional predictors. In light of the political focus on welfare dependency and reproductive behavior, we include each state's caseload-to-population ratio under AFDC and the percentage of births attributed to unmarried mothers in each state. We test for continuity before and after 1996 by examining whether states that pursued AFDC waivers earlier went on to adopt more restrictive TANF policies. To account for electoral pressures, we measure the strength of interparty competition in each state and the degree of upper-class bias in rates of electoral participation. Finally, to capture the effects of economic and fiscal context, we include the state unemployment rate and a measure of each state's per capita tax revenues adjusted for interstate differences in cost of living.[10]

The most conspicuous result of our analysis is that very few factors appear to have had systemic effects on state policy adoption after 1996.[11] Consistent with the idea that states were now enacting a national political project, state lawmakers adopted policies in a pattern that had little grounding in the objective conditions they confronted. Across the five policy dimensions, most of our predictors yield no significant effects or only a single, isolated effect.[12] Outside our main variables of interest, only one factor emerges as a consistent predictor. States that achieved lower caseload-to-population ratios by 1996 were significantly more likely in the ensuing years to adopt full-family sanctions, restrictive eligibility rules, and rigid work requirements.

This last finding suggests some continuity in restrictive state orientations across the years that bracketed the passage of PRWORA. But nothing more specific is suggested by these results. Turning to our main variables, we find two more weak findings, but, in these cases, the null results suggest a striking historical development. In contrast to all our pre-1996 analyses of state welfare and incarceration outcomes, we do not find a single instance in which the adoption of a disciplinary TANF policy was significantly associated with state differences in the BWR. Deepening the contrast with the earlier period, these null results for the BWR persist across our models regardless of the racial composition of welfare caseloads. Combined with the weak effects of unemployment rates, these results suggest that labor market conditions and the principle of less eligibility became far less decisive in shaping state welfare policies after 1996.

A similar erosion of earlier dynamics is suggested by our results for political orientations in state governments. From the 1960s to 1996, Republican control of state government served as a reliable predictor of changes in poverty governance. In our analysis of TANF policy choices after 1996, this dynamic largely evaporates. On four out of five policy outcomes, we find no differences between ideologically liberal and conservative state governments. Only in a single instance, full-family sanctions, do we find that more conservative state governments were more likely to adopt a disciplinary TANF policy. Equivalent results emerge when we replace the government ideology measure with a measure indicating party control of state government.

Here again, the evidence suggests that a bipartisan "national consensus" to reform the poor, institutionalized and incentivized by PRWORA, overrode (at least for a period) the traditional mainsprings of state welfare provision. The states did not converge on a single approach after 1996. Rather, it seems that the differences in their approaches had little systematic basis. The lone exception to this pattern is the factor that provided the seedbed for anxieties over underclass pathology, welfare dependence, and social disorder—the same factor that provided the implicit subtext of Republican law-and-order campaigns and shaped the social composition of America's rising prison population. Race, which stood at the heart of the campaign for welfare reform, exerted a powerful and pervasive influence on state TANF choices.

Across all five policy choices, we find that states were more likely to adopt disciplinary program features if blacks made up a larger percentage of the welfare caseload. The scale of these effects is illustrated in figure 5-3, which presents predicted outcomes for a hypothetical "average" state (all other variables in our models are set at their means). Moving from left to right, we see how predicted outcomes shift as the black percentage of the caseload rises in this "average" state. Panel A shows results for our dichotomous policy choices: full-family sanctions, family caps, and early lifetime limits. When the black percentage is low, the predicted probability of adoption is quite low in all three cases, ranging from about .05 to .20. As the black percentage rises, the probability of strict sanction adoption escalates rapidly, followed at a lag by the predictions for time limits and family caps. When the black percentage is at its highest observed values, full-family sanction adoption is predicted to be a near cer-

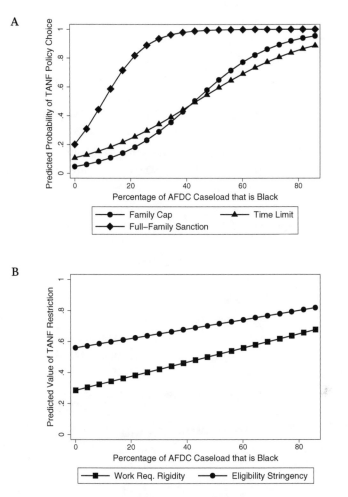

FIGURE 5-3. Effects of Black Caseload Percentage on Restrictive TANF Policy Choices in a Hypothetical Average State. (A) Family Caps, Time Limits, and Full-Family Sanctions. (B) Work Requirement Rigidity and Eligibility Restrictions.

tainty; predicted probabilities for family caps and time limits are only slightly less extreme.

Panel B presents our results for work-requirement rigidity and eligibility restriction. To make the results easier to compare, we have converted the scales for these variables so that they indicate the number of provisions adopted in each state as a proportion of the maximum number adopted in any state. Once again, we observe a clear relationship between racial composition and policy adoption. Our "average" state is predicted to adopt about 58 percent of the eligibility restrictions when the black percentage is at its minimum, compared to about 81 percent when the black percentage rises to its maximum. The effects are even stronger for decisions to maintain rigid work requirements. With the black percentage at its minimum, the state is expected to favor more rigid provisions only 25 percent of the time. With the black percentage at its observed maximum, the predicted rate rises to about 65 percent.

These results provide dramatic evidence that the "blackness" of welfare caseloads mattered greatly for the ways that states pursued the disciplinary agenda set by federal lawmakers in 1996.[13] By comparison, the effects associated with Latino prevalence in state welfare caseloads appear quite meager. As expected, they are weaker and less consistent than the effects associated with African Americans. Although the coefficients for Latino percentage are positive in four of our five models, the estimates reach statistical significance in only one case: the adoption of time limits shorter than the federal requirement.

Scholars such as Martin Gilens (1999: 71) have good reason to speculate that "as the country's Latino population continues to grow, attitudes toward welfare and poverty may become as strongly associated with perceptions of Latinos as they are now with perceptions of blacks." In the years that followed federal welfare reform, however, state decisions to adopt disciplinary TANF policies were overwhelmingly influenced by the relative prevalence of African American program participants. Variations in the Latino portion of the caseload appear to have made far less difference. And in a striking reversal of poverty governance over the preceding thirty years, blackness drove patterns of behavioral reform in ways that appeared newly detached from partisan politics and the principle of less eligibility.

State Policy Choices: Second-Order Devolution

The choices that states confronted after 1996 were a result of what students of federalism call "first-order" devolution—a shift in responsibilities from the federal level to the states. In the years that followed, state officials faced a parallel question regarding "second-order" devolution: Should a state govern its TANF program directly from the center, or should it shift primary responsibility to local authorities and try to shape their actions through structures and incentives? For several reasons, an analysis of state decisions in this area has the potential to advance understandings of the turn to neoliberal paternalism.

First, as described in chapter 2, devolution is a central feature of the neoliberal vision of poverty governance. Although other elements of this vision, such as privatization and performance management, will occupy our attention in later chapters, they are difficult to observe at the state level. By contrast, second-order devolution of TANF authority provides a sharp and measurable reversal of state operations under AFDC. Over the lifespan of the AFDC program, the clear trend was toward "second-order centralization," with seventeen states moving from an emphasis on local control to greater state supervision and no states moving in the opposite direction (Adkisson and Peach 2000). After 1996, many observers predicted that first-order devolution would lead seamlessly to second-order devolution in the states (Nathan and Gais 1999). Events, however, did not cooperate. Under TANF, second-order devolution turned out to be an important political choice, not a natural or inevitable outgrowth of reform.

Second, social control theorists have long emphasized how the localization of policy authority facilitates the regulation of moral conduct and labor participation (Lowi 1998; Handler and Hasenfeld 1991; Piven and Cloward 1971). Echoing this perspective, Gainsborough (2003: 618) suggests that second-order TANF devolution represented "a shift in emphasis away from the needs of the poor toward the needs of local employers." Such arguments stand in sharp contrast to leading accounts of local devolution, which portray it as a politically neutral effort to enhance effectiveness and efficiency or as a way to promote more tailored responses to local preferences and problems (Dye 1990; Rivlin 1992; Kettl 2005). In such accounts, the paired historical emergence of paternalism and devolution appears to be an unrelated coincidence. By contrast, social control theorists suggest that decisions to localize poverty governance make the paternalist features of TANF programs into more flexible and far-reaching disciplinary regimes.

Third, by analyzing second-order devolution, we extend our study of racial effects from the selection of disciplinary rules to the design of governing structures. The provisions analyzed in the preceding section were explicitly debated as tools for rectifying behavioral pathologies—disorders that, as we have seen, were disproportionately attributed to African Americans. In this sense, one does not have to reach far to see how larger numbers of black welfare recipients might make their passage more likely. The case of second-order devolution is less straightforward because advocates typically promoted it by criticizing "one size fits all" approaches and citing racially neutral values such as community involvement, efficiency, and effectiveness. Thus, if one follows the political discourse, it seems reasonable to think that race might shape choices among disciplinary rules but have little effect on choices regarding devolution. With racialized questions of behavior less prominent, one might also imagine that decisions regarding devolution were shaped by a broader array of state-level factors.

Between 1996 and 2001, most states opted against second-order devolution or pursued only a "slight" form of it (Gainsborough 2003). Fourteen states reversed the trend under AFDC by devolving primary authority over TANF to local authorities. In eight of these states, county officials gained control over welfare spending (through block grants) as well as TANF work requirements, sanctions, time limits, and the use of one-time diversion payments (Gainsborough 2003). In the other six, primary authority was devolved to local/regional governing boards that control programs related to both TANF and the Workforce Investment Act. Such boards consist of a mix of public and private officials, with most states requiring that at least half the board's members come from the local business community (Gainsborough 2003). Although they represent a minority of all states, this group of fourteen states includes six of the eight most heavily populated, making the impact of second-order devolution quite substantial.

Did states localize TANF operations in patterns that reflected racial classifications and the political and economic factors emphasized by theories of social control? To pursue this question, we conducted a logistic regression analysis, where the outcome was coded 1 for the fourteen states that engaged in significant devolution between 1996 and 2001 and 0 for all other states. To capture the expectations of social control theories, we included measures of four relevant factors. If pressures for labor regulation rise when employers confront labor scarcity (Piven and Cloward 1971), then second-order devolution should be more likely in (a) states where employers confront tighter labor supplies, as indicated by a lower unemployment rate; and (b) states with higher per capita rates of welfare participation, as indicated by AFDC caseloads. At the same time, social control theories suggest that welfare arrangements will tend to be responsive to actual or potential lower-class political power (Fording 2001; Piven and Cloward 1971). Following this logic, as well as recent supportive evidence (Avery and Peffley 2005), one would expect second-order devolution to be more likely in states that exhibit a higher degree of upper-class bias in electoral turnout.

Finally, extending the argument that penal and welfare operations have become linked mechanisms within a "double regulation of the poor" (see chapter 4; Wacquant 2009), we include a direct measure of the rates at which different states have invested in corrections spending (see Jacobs and Helms 1996; Rose and Clear 1998). Outside social control theory, there are few reasons to expect a relationship between this measure and TANF devolution decisions. By contrast, social control theory suggests that TANF devolution should be more likely in states that devote a higher percentage of their direct expenditures to corrections.

Given prevailing stereotypes of African Americans (Gilens 1999; Schuman et al. 1997), the RCM suggests that when officials confront larger numbers of black welfare recipients, they become more likely to perceive themselves as making policy for "tough cases" who present stronger barriers to the achievement of welfare-to-work policy goals. Accordingly, they become more likely to see tough disciplinary rules as reasonable, desirable, and necessary. This narrative points to a straightforward interpretation of the results presented in the preceding section. But how might it explain decisions to pursue second-order devolution?

The RCM suggests that, as state officials survey their local jurisdictions, race can operate below the level of conscious reflection to provide cues regarding the "kinds" of welfare recipients that prevail in one place versus another. Thus, in a state where residents' racial characteristics do not vary much across local jurisdictions, officials are more likely to perceive recipients' needs and traits as fairly consistent across the state. When racial minorities are concentrated in some areas rather than others, however, officials become more likely to perceive the sorts of meaningful local differences that make it sensible to pursue distinctive approaches in different locales.[14] Such perceptions will tend to suggest the desirability of policy devolution for reasons that appear, to the actors themselves, purely pragmatic and appropriate.

At the same time, the RCM predicts that racial salience will depend on the relative size of minority populations. If a state has a very small minority population, its distribution across localities should matter less because race itself is less likely to be salient. As minority percentages rise, policymakers should become more aware of local differences in racial composition. As a result, the RCM points to an interactive dynamic. Devolution should be more likely in states that exhibit greater variance in the minority share of county populations. This "racial-dispersion effect" should become weaker as the minority share of the total state population decreases; it should intensify as the minority share of the state population rises.

Returning to the RCM's emphasis on the gaps between group reputations, we can also specify separate predictions for blacks and Latinos. Prevailing stereotypes regarding work motivation and personal responsibility imply that black-white contrasts are larger than Latino-white contrasts (Fox 2004). Thus, just as state choices regarding disciplinary rules were more responsive to blacks than Latinos, we expect the interactive relationships specified above to be significantly stronger for blacks than for Latinos.

Finally, our model also includes measures to test whether second-order devolution was more likely in (a) states with a history of welfare innovation, as indicated by earlier requests for AFDC waivers; (b) states that had more ideologically conservative government officials; (c) states where administrative capacities are supported by higher per capita tax revenues; and (d) states where centralized governance is complicated by lower population densities.

Among this last set of variables, several noteworthy results emerge. Although conservatives have often taken the lead in pushing for policy devolution (Conlan 1998), we find no evidence that differences in state government ideology mattered for decisions to devolve TANF authority. Instead, states were significantly more likely to pursue second-order devolution if they had taken earlier steps to adopt AFDC waivers, if they had lower population densities, and if they had higher per capita tax revenues to invest in local capacities.

Turing to our key results, we find strong evidence that state decisions to localize TANF authority followed the dynamics suggested by social control theorists. Second-order devolution was significantly more likely in states that had tighter labor markets and higher welfare caseloads. TANF operations were also more likely to be localized in states that had a stronger upper-class bias in voter turnout. And as expected, states that invested more heavily in corrections were more likely to localize welfare governance.

The empirical tests of the RCM yield equally strong results. As expected, we find significant effects associated with the black percent of the state population, the dispersion of black populations across counties (as measured by the coefficient of variation), and their interaction. Figure 5-4 illustrates the joint effects of the two racial factors. To produce the three curves shown here, we once again constructed a hypothetical "average" state by setting all other variables at their mean values. We then set this state's level of racial dispersion (variation across counties) at a low, medium, or high level (25th percentile, median, and 75th percentile, respectively). Finally, for each level of dispersion, we calculated how the predicted probability of second-order devolution changes as the black percentage of a state's population rises.

Consistent with our expectations, levels of racial dispersion have no discernible effects when the black percent of the state population is at its minimum. Looking rightward, however, clear differences emerge. As expected, larger

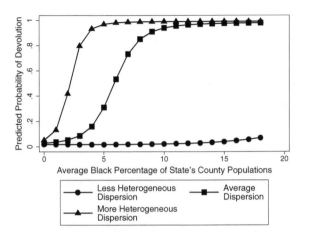

FIGURE 5-4. The Effect of Black Percent of State Population at Different Levels of Black Dispersion

percentages of black state residents have a weak effect on the probability of devolution when black populations are relatively evenly distributed across counties (25th percentile). When the dispersion of black residents is more uneven, however, the predicted probability of devolution rises steadily along with the black percentage of the state population. The effect is dramatic even at just the median level of dispersion. It increases further when dispersion is set at the 75th percentile.

To provide a further test of the RCM, we replaced our black population measures with parallel measures of prevalence and dispersion in state Latino populations. As expected, this substitution weakened our results substantially. The performance of the model as a whole declined (the PRE dropped from .68 to .46); Latino prevalence and dispersion yielded no significant results; and their interaction was statistically significant but quite small.[15]

In sum, recent state decisions to localize welfare operations appear to have been highly racialized and rooted in social control. Of course, devolution "in general" may serve a variety of purposes in a federal system, many of which can be progressive or democratic (Freeman and Rogers 2007; Fung 2004). The disciplinary turn in poverty governance, however, was far from a general case. As states took up this project, their decisions to devolve welfare authority did not emerge as politically neutral efforts to enhance effectiveness and efficiency. They emerged as ways to structure the pursuit of a highly racialized project of social control.

Cumulative Effects and Racialized Policy Regimes

Policy choices are more than just outcomes in the political process. They are active forces in the ordering of political relations that define civic status and position social groups in relation to governing authorities (Mettler and Soss 2004; Soss and Schram 2008). Just as racial inequalities can shape social policies, social policies can structure racial inequalities (Schram 2005). From this perspective, our empirical results do more than just reveal the political effects of race on poverty governance; they raise the specter of policy-based racial inequity.

If states with more black residents choose distinctive TANF rules, the ultimate (even if unintended) effect may be to create a system in which African Americans are located in distinctive institutions. Indeed, if policy choices follow a consistently racialized pattern, small differences may add up to produce dramatic disparities. On average, African Americans may be exposed to tougher rules implemented with more local discretion. In this section, we analyze how choices regarding devolution and disciplinary rules combine to generate racially patterned policy regimes. The results point to a deep interplay of race, localization, and social control.

We can begin by taking a closer look at how state decisions to discipline and devolve relate to each other. As the states shifted toward neoliberal paternalism, did decisions to devolve program authority emerge as a structural counterpart to more stringent disciplinary rules? Figure 5-5 shows how the predicted probability of second-order devolution varied across groups of states defined by their adoptions of the five disciplinary rules analyzed earlier. The horizontal axis indicates the stringency of state TANF regimes based on a scale that awards one point each for adoptions of a family cap, time limits shorter than the federal requirement, full-family sanctions, a work requirement rigidity score higher than the median, and an eligibility restriction score higher than the median.[16] The curve in figure 5-5 shows a nonlinear relationship, with the states that adopted the most disciplinary program rules being significantly more likely than others to devolve TANF authority to the local level.

With this evidence as empirical support, we can create a more comprehensive measure of "devolution and discipline" in state TANF programs. Our regime scale awards states one point for pursuing second-order devolution as well as one point for each of the five disciplinary program rules.[17] Using this measure, we examine differences in the types of TANF regimes that black and white recipients confronted after the post-1996 wave of state policy choices. To do so, we rely on official data for the racial characteristics of TANF program

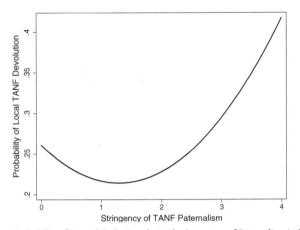

FIGURE 5-5. Probability of Second-Order Devolution by Stringency of Paternalism in State TANF Rules

participants in each state in 2001. Preliminary analyses of the separate policy elements indicated modest but consistent differences, with black families more likely than white families to be exposed to localized, disciplinary governance. Figure 5-6 shows how small but reliable racial differences in policy exposure concatenate to produce dramatic racial disparities across state TANF regimes.

The horizontal axis of figure 5-6 indicates how many of our key program elements a given state employs: five have none; eight have one; eight have two; eleven have three; eight have four; and seven have five or six. Panel A presents the average black and white percentages of state TANF caseloads for each regime type. Here, we see that modest but consistent differences can combine to produce an intensely racialized pattern. White families average 69 percent of the caseload in states that have none of these program elements, while black families account for only 6 percent of these states' caseloads. As one looks to the right, toward the most devolved and disciplinary regimes, the white percent falls as the black percent rises. In state regimes that fall into the two most disciplinary and devolved categories on our scale, whites average just 31 and 34 percent of the caseload while blacks average 57 and 58 percent of the caseload.

Panel B turns from state averages to national patterns, answering the question: Of all U.S. families participating under each regime type in 2001, what percent were white and what percent were black? Here again, the results are striking. Of all U.S. families who participated in TANF programs without *any* of these regime elements, 63 percent were white while just 11 percent were black. This 52 point white-over-black gap evaporates immediately as one looks

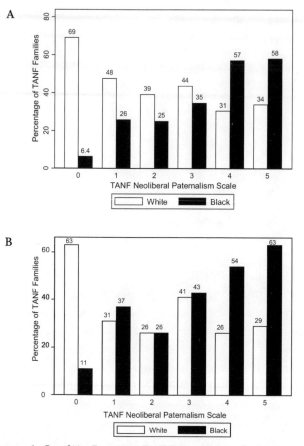

FIGURE 5-6. Cumulative Exposure to TANF Program Features by Race, 2001. (A) Average Racial Composition of State TANF Policy Regimes. (B) National Racial Composition of TANF Policy Regimes

rightward. Black and white families have roughly equal exposure to the next three regime types. In the second most devolved and disciplinary regime type, however, blacks make up 54 percent of all families while whites make up only 26 percent. Of all the families in the United States who were exposed to the most extreme regime type, 63 percent were black while just 29 percent were white. Here, we see a key dynamic related to racial inequality in the contemporary United States: Large disparities emerge not in the visible form of a single decision, but from the less visible accumulation of smaller differences (Lin and Harris 2008; Pollock 2008).

With these results in hand, we can take a final step in analyzing the conjuncture of race, poverty policy, and social control. Building on our earlier analyses, we can return to the idea that the disciplinary turn in poverty governance has involved a racialized convergence of penal and welfare operations. In this view, African Americans have become disproportionately subject to policy regimes that emphasize a combination of carceral control and locally managed welfare discipline. Figure 5-7 offers a stunning, and deeply disturbing, confirmation of this argument. The horizontal axis here replicates the TANF regime measure use in figure 5-6. The bars in figure 5-7 indicate the average black percent of population for states with each TANF regime type (labeled on the left-vertical axis). The dots plotted in the figure show, for each TANF regime type, the average percentages of state populations that were under correctional control in 2007. Patterns of correctional control appear to track closely with both the black percent of state population and TANF regime types. This apparent relationship is confirmed by the curved line in the figure—a simple quadratic slope generated by regressing correctional control rates on our TANF regime scale and its square. The relationship between correctional control and TANF regime type is very strong: the R-squared for the quadratic slope is .76.

Taken together, the results in this figure suggest a strong state-level pattern of racialized social control. Looking across the American states, one finds a tightly configured relationship consisting of higher black population rates, more stringent and locally controlled TANF regimes, and more aggressive applications of correctional control. No single picture can capture the complex developments

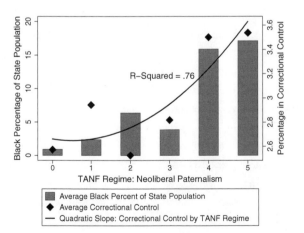

FIGURE 5-7. Black TANF Caseload and State Incarceration Rates by TANF Regime Type

in governance that we set out to explore in this book. But figure 5-7 brings vivid detail to some major themes of our analysis. Neoliberal paternalism is a decentralized, disciplinary mode of poverty governance; it seeks to instill and insist on preferred behaviors among the poor; it weaves penal and welfare operations together as instruments for this project; and its construction and operation are both fundamentally entwined with race.

Conclusion

By any measure, the 1990s qualify as a critical juncture in the development of American poverty governance. As incarceration rates rose by more than 50 percent during this decade, welfare provision was reconfigured to follow a disciplinary logic. Welfare programs that had focused on processing needs-based eligibility claims were recast as overt sites of personal and behavioral reform. In this chapter, we have analyzed this disciplinary turn from the perspective of American federalism. As Lawrence Mead (1996: 588) has rightly pointed out, "today's welfare reform is an exercise, not in economic transfer, but in state building." At the heart of this state-building effort is a rewriting of the "devolution settlement" that structures relations between national and state governments (Peck 2002). Federal welfare reform in 1996 is best understood as an effort to both expand and discipline state freedoms in the welfare arena so that states, in turn, can be relied on as vigilant and creative "free actors" pursuing efforts to discipline the poor.

As the 1990s began, state officials continued to labor under the national framework of procedural constraints secured by welfare rights activists in the 1960s. AFDC benefits had already dwindled to penurious levels, but caseloads remained high and federal rules impeded state efforts to impose behavioral conditions on welfare receipt. The 1992 presidential election broke this impasse. As Bill Clinton rode toward office on his pledge to "end welfare as we know it," President Bush countered by encouraging state waiver experiments under the existing AFDC program. From 1992 to 1996, a growing number of states stepped forward to turn client behaviors into targets of modification and grounds for exclusion. If the rising emphasis on behavior signaled historical change, however, the patterning of state waiver adoptions indicated continuity. As states pursued AFDC waivers, their actions followed the familiar patterns revealed in our analysis of benefit cuts and incarceration increases in the 1970s and 1980s. Republican state officials led the way, and the tough new rules emerged disproportionately in states where higher BWRs combined with higher percentages of black welfare recipients.

In this sense, state waiver adoptions reflected the partisan uses of welfare reform as well as the racialization of age-old efforts to enforce the principle of less eligibility. Given the consistency of these dynamics from the 1970s to the mid-1990s, it would not have been surprising to find them at work again after 1996. PRWORA, however, entailed far more than an expansion of state discretion. It placed the full weight of national government behind the disciplinary agenda of neoliberal paternalism, and it applied new structures and incentives to enlist all states in the national project of reforming the poor. Acting within this framework, and guided by a moral fervor to end permissiveness, state officials took up their task in ways that overrode the traditional determinants of state policy choice.

In addressing the most disciplinary policy tools, states acted in ways that were largely detached from differences in the objective conditions they confronted. Tougher approaches did not reflect higher observable rates of "social problems" among the poor. More tellingly, they had no discernible relationships to the BWRs and partisan/ideological differences that had shaped state action in the preceding decades. Across all the states, policy adoption was driven by a cresting moral and political enthusiasm to get tough with the poor.

The discourses that drove this enthusiasm often emphasized "perverse" work incentives (Somers and Block 2005), but the broad themes of dysfunction and reformation that stood at their center cannot be reduced to this old less-eligibility trope (Schram 1995; Hancock 2004; Sparks 2003; A. M. Smith 2007). Under welfare reform, work continues to be promoted through the principle of less eligibility and Durkheimian rituals designed to stigmatize and deter welfare claims (Piven and Cloward 1971). But welfare reform was more than an effort to deter, exclude, and punish—more than an effort to enforce work by applying the sovereign's power to coerce. The new disciplinary rules were designed to remake the poor as a population of self-disciplining citizens and laborers. Accordingly, state decisions to adopt them reflected the deeply racialized nature of the reformative project itself.

As we have seen in earlier chapters, race served as a key cultural resource for actors promoting the disciplinary turn in poverty governance after the 1960s. Throughout the 1970s and 1980s, race consistently shaped poverty governance as states cut welfare benefits, filled prisons, and pursued behavior-focused AFDC waivers. By the 1990s, images of dysfunction in black communities stood at the center of poverty discourse. The heated campaign for welfare reform placed these images at the forefront of national consciousness, producing a sharp spike in public perceptions of welfare as a major national problem (see chapter 3). This was the political context in which states began to select TANF policies in the wake of PRWORA—a context that was implicitly but deeply rooted in the idea that state authorities needed to reconstruct the disorderly lives and dysfunctional subjectivities of the black underclass.

Across all five of the disciplinary provisions we examined, we find that tougher rules were more likely to be selected by states where African Americans made up a higher percentage of the welfare rolls. These findings fit the predictions of the Racial Classification Model (RCM) in straightforward ways. Digging deeper, we find that racial/ethnic biases in policy selection vary in more subtle ways that lend support to the RCM. Consistent with the RCM's emphasis on reputational gaps, we find that racial/ethnic biases are weaker and less consistent for Latinos than for blacks. Turning to decisions about how to structure TANF governance, we find that states were significantly more likely to pursue second-order devolution if black populations were larger (raising their salience) and more unevenly distributed across localities (raising perceptions that local clienteles would require different approaches).

The results underscore important political features of federalism and devolution in the context of American poverty governance. Under welfare reform, first-order devolution provided the structural foundation for racialized patterns of disciplinary policy choice. Patterns of second-order devolution reflected and deepened this intersection of race and social control. Localization of TANF operations tracked the distribution of black populations; it was highly responsive to the predictors emphasized by social control theory; and it became concentrated in the states that embraced the most disciplinary TANF rules. As race shaped state policy choices along multiple dimensions, consistent racial differences in policy exposure concatenated to generate profound disparities in the policy regimes that black and white TANF recipients confront. In this sense, federalism served as a key mechanism for the racialization of neoliberal paternalism in practice. Racial groups in the United States are equal before the law but unequally distributed across the states. This fact explains how, under the cover of policies that are officially race-neutral, policy regimes have emerged in ways that suture together larger black populations, higher rates of carceral control, and more devolved and disciplinary welfare programs.

STUDYING POVERTY GOVERNANCE IN FLORIDA:
WHY AND HOW

IN RECENT DECADES, THE AMERICAN STATES HAVE DIFFERED SYS-
tematically in their approaches to governing the poor. As we have seen,
their strategies have been deeply entwined with the politics of race and social
control. Poverty governance, however, is more than a matter of policy choice. It
is a practice that emerges in local arenas, as policy designs get interpreted and
applied by authorities closer to the ground. In an era of policy devolution and
privatization, these tasks have been rolled out to a diverse array of organizations
and communities, where local officials work to convert policy mandates into
concrete rules, routines, and administrative actions.

Local operations of this sort, by definition, are rooted in particular locales
that differ from the nation as a whole. To study them intensively, one must
choose a site. In this chapter, we explain why we use Florida as our research
site, why our study focuses on sanctioning practices in the Florida Welfare
Transition (WT) program, and how we have collected and analyzed evidence
regarding local governance. In the process, we describe features of the Florida
system that provide essential background for the chapters that follow.

Case Selection: Why Florida?

Florida does not represent a "typical" case of poverty governance in the American states. Indeed, because state policies vary so greatly across so many dimensions, it is not clear that any state could be described in this manner. The key
question is not whether particular states are typical; it is whether their distinctive features make them more or less useful for studying how neoliberal paternalism proceeds in practice. Florida, we argue, offers a variety of advantages in
this regard. The policies adopted in this state make it a leading-edge case in the
disciplinary turn, where one can encounter neoliberal and paternalist governance in particularly sharp focus.

In Florida, we can observe how *all* the defining elements of neoliberal paternalism operate together in strong form. Strategies that exist in varying shades of
grey in other states—and thus have a less certain relationship to neoliberal and
paternalist rationalities—can be discerned with great clarity in Florida. Indeed,

celebratory assessments of the Florida welfare system validate its status as a leading effort to realize the aspirations of contemporary poverty governance. The Florida WT program has been hailed for its successes and held up as a model to be emulated elsewhere. Federal officials have repeatedly singled it out for high-performance bonus awards and encouraged other states to move their operations in its direction. Thus, while no state can represent all states in a statistical sense, Florida provides a strong basis for "analytic inferences" about how neoliberal paternalism proceeds as a regime of practice.[1]

For our purposes, five state characteristics stand out. First, Florida has been a leader in devolving policy control to the local level and integrating welfare and work programs under the authority of regional workforce boards. Second, it has pursued a strong program of privatization, outsourcing service provision through contracts with for-profit and nonprofit organizations. Third, it has developed an ambitious performance management model that uses state-of-the-art information systems to track key actors and reward or penalize their efforts to meet benchmarks. Fourth, it is a national leader in the use of sanctions (penalties for noncompliance) to bring client behavior into line with expectations. Fifth, as a large and diverse state, Florida offers an excellent site for exploring the effects of local differences in social, economic, and political environments.

After 1996, a number of states extended "first-order" (federal-to-state) devolution by pursuing "second-order" (state-to-local) devolution (Gainsborough 2003). Florida was one of twenty states that took this route. Going further, it elected to close the state's local welfare offices and integrate local TANF operations into the twenty-four Regional Workforce Boards (RWBs) that had been created as part of the Workforce Investment Act of 1998 (see figure 6-1).[2] In Florida, RWBs are incorporated public-private partnerships that include local representatives of business, labor, and nonprofit organizations. By law, however, they must be composed so that employers make up a majority. During the period of our study, RWBs held primary authority for designing Local Operating Procedures in the WT program and for negotiating contracts with for-profit and nonprofit service providers.[3] Like other aspects of the Florida system, the use of RWBs to integrate and control programs for low-skilled workers has been highlighted by federal officials as an innovation that other states should strive to emulate (Austin 2005).

In Florida, the RWBs that contract with private providers are overseen not by state agencies, but by a statewide public-private corporation called Workforce Florida, Inc. (WFI). WFI is authorized to set statewide implementation rules and guidelines. It partners with a second entity, the Agency for Workforce In-

Florida's Workforce Regions

1. Escarosa Regional Workforce Development Board, Inc.
2. Oklaloosa-Walton Jobs & Education Partnership, Inc.
3. Chipola Regional Workforce Planning Board
4. Gulf Coast Workforce Development Board
5. Big Bend Jobs and Education Council, Inc.
6. North Florida Workforce Development Board
7. Florida Crown Workforce Development Board
8. First Coast Workforce Development, Inc.
9. Alachua, Bradford Workforce Development Board
10. Citrus Levy Marion Workforce Development Board
11. Workforce Development Board of Flagler and Volusia Counties, Inc.
12. Workforce Central Florida
13. Brevard Workforce Development Board, Inc.
14. Pinellas Workforce Development Board
15. Hilsborough County Workforce Board
16. Pasco-Hernando Jobs & Education Partnership Regional Board, Inc.
17. Polk County Workforce Development Board, Inc.
18. Suncoast Workforce Development Board, Inc.
19. Heartland Workforce Investment Board, Inc.
20. Workforce Development Board of the Treasure Coast
21. Palm Beach County Workforce Development Board
22. Broward Workforce Development Board
23. Miami-Dade & Monroe County Jobs & Education Partnership
24. Southwest Florida Workforce Development Board

FIGURE 6-1. Florida's Workforce Regions

novation (AWI), that holds responsibility for administrative coordination across the twenty-four local RWBs. (For example, WFI establishes statewide guidelines for sanction processes; RWBs amend these through local operating procedures; AWI tracks local sanction rates and other aspects of RWB performance, reporting its results at regular intervals.) The Florida Department of Children and Families (DCF), a conventional state agency, is limited to two tasks: receiving the federal TANF block grant and authorizing eligibility determinations. Taken as a whole, the Florida welfare system stands out among the states as a strong model of privatized and decentralized program control (Botsko, Snyder, and Leos-Urbel 2001: 7).

As it devolved and privatized poverty governance, Florida also designed one of the nation's toughest TANF programs. After 1996, it adopted "some of the strictest time limits and work requirements in the nation" and strengthened its requirements by creating "few possibilities for exemptions" (Botsko, Snyder, and Leos-Urbel 2001: 4). Statewide, WT clients must document at least thirty hours of work activities per week to remain eligible for aid, and many regions have opted to raise this requirement to forty hours. Failures to comply with these and other program requirements are penalized by benefit sanctions that, as we describe below, fall at the strong end of the national continuum and are imposed with greater frequency than in most other states.

In the Florida WT program, strong forms of devolution, privatization, and work enforcement coexist with one of the nation's most extensive systems of performance management. Under this system, each region must work to meet performance benchmarks in specific areas defined by the statewide board. The board negotiates with each RWB to establish a region-specific set of performance goals. After efforts to meet these goals are measured, state-level officials use them to evaluate and rank regional performance. RWBs use the same measures to determine whether service providers are fulfilling the terms of their contracts.

AWI tracks regional performance on a monthly basis, reporting results via its website. The centerpiece of this system is "the red and green report," which ranks the twenty-four regions based on performance scores and applies colors to indicate standing: red for regions in the bottom quartile, green for those in the top quartile, and white for those in between. Green scores can qualify a region for program-improvement funding and for entry into competitions for additional resources allocated by WFI. For for-profit and nonprofit service providers, red scores can mean the difference between contract renewal and termination. Between these extremes, contracted service providers typically lose "pay points" as a result of weak performance rankings, and regions are likely to get unwanted scrutiny from the state board if their performance rankings fall.

Finally, the attractions of Florida as a case for analysis are bolstered by its remarkable racial and political diversity. The state's racial diversity is amply demonstrated by the composition of its welfare caseload. Between January 2000 and March 2004, 36.2 percent TANF adults were black, 33.7 percent were white (non-Latino), and 28.5 percent were Latino. Moreover, the racial composition of the caseload varied greatly across the state's counties, with the white (non-Latino) proportion of recipients ranging from a high of 89 percent (Gilchrist County) to a low of 4 percent (Miami-Dade County)—a fact that offers considerable advantages for analyzing how race relates to patterns of welfare implementation.

Florida's political diversity is equally striking, as evidenced by recent voting returns in presidential elections. Over the last three presidential elections, the average Democratic share of the two-party vote across Florida's sixty-seven counties has been approximately 44 percent, with a healthy standard deviation of 9.2 percent. The most conservative counties have delivered an average Republican vote share as high as 75 percent (Okaloosa, Santa Rosa, Clay), while the most liberal counties have provided Democrats with vote shares as high as 69 percent (Broward, Gadsen). In combination with the strong features of the Florida WT program, racial and political variation across the state provide an ideal setting for studying how race and politics matter for the decentralized governance of disciplinary welfare-to-work programs.

Why Sanctions in the WT Program?

Within the Florida WT program, our analysis focuses on the use of sanctions as a disciplinary policy tool. Sanctions are penalties that reduce or terminate welfare benefits in cases where clients are deemed to be out of compliance with program requirements. They are, in many respects, the neoliberal-paternalist tool of discipline par excellence—the threat that puts muscle behind directive program rules and incents client cooperation with supervisory administration. In the paternalist frame, sanctions are conceptualized as a tutelary "stick" that authorities use to impose consequences when clients fail to meet their obliga- tions. With the "carrot" of benefits made conditional on good behavior, sanc- tions allow officials to send a clear message about the costs of failing to meet expectations. In the neoliberal frame, sanctions are valued as tools for imposing a market logic on welfare participation and providing clients with a market ex- perience. In this rendering, benefits are conceptualized as wage-like payments to clients who complete their work activities; sanctions are cast as "wage deduc- tions" analogous to what workers experience when they miss work hours or fail to complete their jobs in a satisfactory manner.

Prior to 1996, sanctions were used infrequently and applied only to the bene- fits of the adult head of a household, not the entire family (Bloom and Winstead 2002). They became far more important under the TANF program because new rules specified stricter work requirements, set narrower exemption criteria, made a broader scope of behaviors subject to sanction, and gave states more options in designing penalties (Hasenfeld, Ghose, and Larson 2004). Perhaps most important, federal rules required state TANF programs to meet specific quotas for the percentage of recipients participating in work-related activities. Sanctions are now the primary disciplinary tool available to administrators as they seek to motivate the client behaviors needed to meet these quotas. They are most often applied when recipients fail to complete required hours of par- ticipation in countable work activities such as job search, job readiness classes, vocational education, training, community work, and paid employment.

Welfare providers can use a variety of administrative strategies to remove noncooperating clients from the rolls (Brodkin 2008), but sanctions are clearly cardinal primary tool of disciplinary welfare provision. Among scholars, there is broad agreement that sanctions have played a key role in transforming welfare from a system focused on cash benefits to one focused on enforcing work (Pavetti et al. 2004). Between 1997 and 1999, nearly 500,000 families lost benefits due to sanctions—approximately one-quarter of the caseload reduction for that period (Goldberg and Schott 2000). The states with the strictest sanctions experienced caseload declines as much as 25 percent greater than those reported by states with the least stringent sanctions (Rector and Youssef 1999). Indeed, some suggest that the *threat* of sanctions may be responsible for even greater numbers of recipients leaving the rolls and for declines in the numbers of poor families applying for welfare assistance (Lindhorst, Mancoske, and Kemp 2000). Studies also suggest that being sanctioned significantly increases hardship among recipients (Reichman, Teitler, and Curtis 2005; Stahl 2008).

Here, as in other aspects of TANF policy, Florida has emerged as a national leader. To begin with, its sanctions are more severe than the tools in most states. Under welfare reform, seventeen states, including Florida, adopted "immediate full family sanctions" that remove the entire TANF family from the rolls at the first instance of noncompliance. Eighteen states adopted a "gradual full-family sanction," which potentially has the same effect, but only after continued noncompliance. The remaining states chose to employ a "partial sanction" of benefits, which usually reduces only the adult portion of the grant.

Although it imposes full-family penalties at the first infraction, Florida uses sanction duration as a way to raise penal severity when violations accumulate. First infractions terminate cash aid for ten days; second and third instances result in terminations of one month and three months, respectively. For two reasons, most penalties applied in Florida are first sanctions and, thus, fall at the shorter, ten-day end of this continuum. First, clients who receive a second or third sanction, by definition, must have received a first sanction. Second, if clients amass a six-month record of unbroken compliance in the wake of a sanction, the prior sanction is "forgiven" and any future sanction is treated as a first occasion (AWI 2004a; Fla. Stat. § 414.065). Based on data gathered by the U.S. General Accounting Office, it appears that Florida falls near the middle of the pack for sanction duration: "In 23 states, benefits are restored fully as soon as compliance occurs. In another 21 states, the first sanction continues for 1 month or until families return to compliance, whichever is longer, while the remaining 7 states extend the length of the first sanction for a minimum of 2 or 3 months" (U.S. General Accounting Office 2000b: 17).

In practice, however, it should be noted that statewide rules define minimums rather than definitive penalty periods in the Florida WT program. Individuals must reestablish compliance to reinstate aid, and this process is subject to great variation under local operating procedures. As we will see in chapter 9, returns to compliance can be delayed considerably by red tape and administrative intransigence. Moreover, when clients have been under a sanction for more than thirty days, they must document their return to compliance *and* submit a new Request for Assistance (RFA) *and* pass through a fresh face-to-face application interview (Fla. Stat. § 445.024).

The severity of a state's sanction policy also depends on the scope of benefits affected. In addition to terminating the full-family cash benefit, Florida is one of twelve of states that takes away a family's Food Stamp grant when a TANF sanction is imposed (U.S. General Accounting Office 2000b). Because this grant is often larger than the monthly TANF benefit, its inclusion in the sanction can result in a devastating loss of income. Children under 16 may continue to receive their portion of the Food Stamp grant if a family relative or community member from a charitable organization agrees in writing to serve as a "protective payee" acting in their best interests (Fla. Stat. § 414.065). If no protective payee is approved, the entire family loses food assistance for the entire month at the first infraction, even if the sanction is only for ten days.

Finally, in addition to having relatively strong sanctions, Florida imposes sanctions at a very high rate. Between 2000 and 2004, sanction rates in the Florida WT program were fairly stable, with seasonal fluctuations falling around a mean of about 3,200 sanctions per month. Figure 6-2 presents this trend, along with the trend for nonsanction TANF exits. The WT program averaged about 5,800 nonsanction exits per month during this period. Thus, between 2000 and early 2004, more than one-third of all monthly exits in Florida were due to sanctions.

Efforts to compare state sanction rates are complicated by differences in the severity of state sanction policies and in the ways that states calculate their sanction rates. The available evidence, however, suggests that Florida sanction rates fall at the high end of the continuum. While sanctions account for about one-third of all Florida case closings, federal data indicate that they accounted for only 7 percent of all case closings nationwide in 2002 (U.S. Department of Health and Human Services 2004).

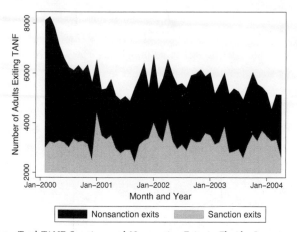

FIGURE 6-2. Total TANF Sanctions and Nonsanction Exits in Florida, January 2000–March 2004

As an alternative measure, Pavetti and colleagues (2004) recommend following a single cohort of clients over an extended period of time and calculating the rate at which they incur sanctions. Based on this method, they measure the sanction rate in three states that, like Florida, employ immediate, full-family sanctions. Following the cohort of adult recipients who entered TANF in November of 2001, they find that over the next eighteen months, 13 percent of the New Jersey cohort and 17 percent of the Illinois cohort were sanctioned. In South Carolina, where clients could be observed for only ten months, 5 percent incurred sanctions. Using the same November 2001 cohort, we calculated comparable sanctioning rates in Florida. After ten months, 43 percent of the cohort had been sanctioned at least once, and, after eighteen months, 47 percent had been sanctioned. In both cases, the Florida rates far exceed those produced in other states.

Finally, because of its decentralized governing arrangements and diverse community characteristics, Florida provides a superb opportunity to analyze variation in the use of sanctions. Between October 2001 and March 2004, the state as a whole sanctioned 38.2 percent of the WT caseload on average each month. Yet as the table indicates, the twenty-four regions varied greatly in their sanction rates during this period, ranging from a low of 25.5 percent in Region 6 to a high of 52 percent in Region 17. Some of this variation, of course, may be traceable to differences in client behaviors across the regions. Under second-order devolution, however, there are ample opportunities for local sanctioning practices to be influenced by regional differences in political culture, labor

Average Monthly Sanction Rates across Twenty-four Workforce Regions in Florida

Region #	Name	
6	North Florida Workforce Development Board	25.47
5	Big Bend Jobs and Education Council, Inc.	30.31
12	Workforce Central Florida	32.76
23	Miami-Dade & Monroe County Jobs & Education Partnership	33.82
7	Florida Crown Workforce Development Board	33.83
9	Alachua, Bradford Workforce Development Board	33.95
2	Oklaloosa-Walton Jobs & Education Partnership, Inc.	33.95
24	Southwest Florida Workforce Development Board	34.48
20	Workforce Development Board of the Treasure Coast	34.72
11	Workforce Development Board of Flagler and Volusia Counties, Inc.	37.12
21	Palm Beach County Workforce Development Board	37.33
	Statewide Average	38.18
18	Suncoast Workforce Development Board, Inc.	38.28
15	Hillsborough County Workforce Board	38.58
10	Citrus Levy Marion Workforce Development Board	38.61
3	Chipola Regional Workforce Planning Board	39.09
4	Gulf Coast Workforce Development Board	39.16
19	Heartland Workforce Investment Board, Inc.	41.08
14	Pinellas Workforce Development Board	41.43
8	First Coast Workforce Development, Inc.	41.67
13	Brevard Workforce Development Board, Inc.	43.48
1	Escarosa Regional Workforce Development Board, Inc.	44.40
22	Broward Workforce Development Board	45.09
16	Pasco-Hernando Jobs & Education Partnership Regional Board, Inc.	45.72
17	Polk County Workforce Development Board, Inc.	51.97

Note: The sanction rate is the average percentage of the caseload that is sanctioned each month during the period October 2001–March 2004.

market conditions, population differences, provider types, and local operating procedures. In the chapters that follow, we take advantage of these variations to examine how differences in local environments intersect with client characteristics to shape the distribution of sanctions.

Mixed Methods of Data Collection and Analysis

In studying the Florida WT program, we have adopted a question-driven approach that does not privilege any particular method or logic of inquiry. Data sources and tools of analysis always offer partial glimpses of social phenomena—

both in the sense that they are incomplete and in the sense that they favor particular dimensions over others. Studies that use different methods often differ as well in their logics of inquiry and criteria for persuasiveness. Efforts to clarify these differences are good for a pluralistic and vibrant social science, but they can also spill over into a kind of intellectual policing that suggests scholars must choose a camp: You must conduct your study within a single approach, this view suggests, or else risk incoherence. By contrast, we are impressed by the potential for different methodologies—say, statistical modeling and interpretive field research—to inform one another in ways that make each better and, collectively, yield a richer portrait of the phenomenon under study.

Pursuing this possibility, we adopted a wide array of empirical strategies based on their potential to complement one another and offer distinctive insights into our research questions (Shapiro 2007; R. Smith 2002). To illuminate the Florida WT program from a variety of angles, we assembled a diverse body of evidence based on statistical analyses of administrative and contextual datasets, in-depth interviews with state and local implementers, direct observations of state training sessions and local program operations, analyses of documents produced by state and regional offices, and a statewide survey of welfare case managers that included both conventional questions and random-assignment experiments.

The classic approach to combining such methods is to "triangulate findings" by seeking out instances where they converge on a single conclusion (King, Keohane, and Verba 1994). In some cases, we follow this strategy. By focusing narrowly on the empirical *products* of different methods, however, this image can obscure the deeper ways that mixed-methods strategies can alter the *process* of research. In this project, we moved forward with our various investigations simultaneously, drawing on insights from each to guide our next steps on the others. Statistical analyses and observations of training sessions presented us with puzzles that led us to ask case managers new questions. Interviews led to discoveries that forced us to extend our statistical research to new areas and respecify models that had once seemed satisfactory. As our interpretations of actors' understandings evolved, we found that "settled" findings might have alternative meanings and devised new ways to adjudicate among them. In this sense, our methods did not provide independent sources of evidence to be triangulated; they functioned as *interdependent* streams of activity that shaped one another (and our broader agenda) through a process of incremental learning and revision.

Our statistical analyses are based on administrative data for all clients who participated in the WT program from January 2000 through December 2004. In addition to providing detailed measures of clients' individual and family characteristics, these data provide the best possible record of case openings and closings, including sanction outcomes. To explore local influences on sanctioning patterns, we merge these individual-level data with contextual measures of regional, county, and organizational characteristics. In addition, to examine the effects of performance systems, we employ data from official AWI performance assessments.

To analyze local operations and the understandings that guide them, we conducted intensive field research in four of Florida's twenty-four workforce regions from February 2005 to January 2008. The four regions were selected to provide a range of implementing environments. One included a major urban center; the second offered a densely populated suburban area; the third consisted of a less-populated collection of suburbs; and the fourth was a rural area made up of a string of small towns. The four regions vary greatly in their racial and ethnic makeups, prevailing political orientations, and histories of for-profit, nonprofit, and governmental service provision. Over the course of our study, however, all four regions eventually contracted with for-profit providers to run their one-stop centers—primarily Arbour/Rescare, which served as the main provider in sixteen of the twenty-four Florida regions.

During the three years of our field research, we conducted in-depth interviews with state-level officials, regional board members, program supervisors, and case managers. We observed sanction training workshops for frontline case managers, meetings of region-level staff, and intake and orientation sessions with new WT applicants. In addition, to gain insights into local operations and their variation, we collected and analyzed documentary evidence from regional memoranda, reports, and websites for all twenty-four workforce regions in 2009 and 2010.

In the four workforce regions selected for intensive study, we conducted over sixty in-depth interviews with all relevant frontline workers.[4] To put greater pressure on our interpretations, two of the three investigators conducted interviews separately, at first in different regions and then with the same workers in a given locale. At each stage, the two interviewers compared findings and debated possible interpretations—asking how differences in personal style might be influencing the interviews, identifying points of interpretive agreement, and specifying tensions that merited further investigation. All interviews were recorded and transcribed verbatim for analysis. Analysis of the interviews, which took place throughout the course of the study, focused on three primary goals:

(1) ascertaining the nature of key work routines, organizational operations, program procedures, and attendant local norms; (2) developing an interpretive account of actors' understandings and their relations to choices and behaviors of interest; and (3) forging a dialogue in which our ongoing field research informed and directed our statistical analyses, and our ongoing statistical analyses raised new questions for exploration in the field.

Finally, to obtain a larger sample of case manager views and gain the advantages of inference associated with an experimental design, we administered a web-based survey to WT case managers throughout the entire state of Florida. In addition to posing a variety of conventional questions regarding case manager characteristics, attitudes, and beliefs, the survey included a series of random-assignment experiments designed to yield insights into how race and presence of discrediting markers influence sanction decisions at the front lines.

Together, these sources of evidence allow for an unusually rich analysis of how outcomes vary across locales and emerge from the understandings and routines that shape practice at the front lines of provision. At the same time, they supply the materials needed to clarify the logics, operations, and contradictions of neoliberal paternalism as a regime of practice. Chapters 7 through 10 are organized around four key dimensions of this regime, with each focused on a specific aspect of neoliberal paternalism. Chapter 7 focuses on *local devolution*, seeking out the forces that give rise to systematic differences in local efforts to discipline the poor. Chapter 8 explores *marketization*, revealing how service provision has been privatized as a site of profitable investment and redesigned as a tool for servicing employer needs. Chapter 9 focuses on *performance systems*, analyzing how pressures to meet numerical benchmarks motivate perverse organizational responses, discipline frontline workers, and promote higher sanction rates. Chapter 10 concludes this section of the book by exploring the interplay of *race and disciplinary discretion* in caseworker-client relationships at the front lines.

THE LOCAL POLITICS OF DISCIPLINE

POLICY DEVOLUTION HAS BEEN A HALLMARK OF THE DISCIPLINARY turn in poverty governance. Under welfare reform, federal officials have set goals and used benchmarks and incentives to structure choices at lower levels of government. But within this framework, they have given broad freedoms to state and local officials, who are expected to tailor governance to their own particular needs. In chapter 5, we saw how this dispersion of authority led to systematic differences in program design across the states. Choices about how to organize Temporary Assistance for Needy Families (TANF) provision consistently responded to the "blackness" of welfare caseloads, and a host of modest differences accumulated to produce a highly racialized pattern of policy regimes. Policy designs, however, are ultimately just frameworks for governance. They are not the human activity itself. In this chapter, we turn to the local operations that put neoliberal paternalism into practice. We analyze how local forces interact with client differences to shape program implementation in a highly decentralized system of disciplinary poverty governance.

To do so, we focus on patterns of sanctioning in the Florida Welfare Transition (WT) program. When adults (mostly single mothers) enter the WT program, they sign an Individual Responsibility Plan (IRP) that places them under a variety of contractual obligations. They agree, for example, to document their participation in required work activities each week; they promise to be timely in meeting with case managers, reporting changes in household status, and attending classes on how to organize their lives and market their labor. Sanctions are the "sticks" that put muscle behind such program rules. In Florida, they allow frontline workers to withhold all TANF and Food Stamp benefits at the first instance in which a client is deemed to have fallen out of compliance.

Sanction decisions are supposed to respond directly to objective client behaviors. In this sense, they should reflect nothing more than individual differences. In practice, however, local sanction processes can be organized in a variety of ways and influenced by a wide range of environmental factors (Pavetti et al. 1998). By exploring these influences, this chapter reveals continuities in governance that extend from state policy choice to local implementation. In chapter 5, we saw that second-order devolution emerged in states that adopted the most disciplinary TANF rules and had larger, less evenly distributed black populations. In what follows, we show how these decisions to localize program control facilitated racialized patterns of disciplinary action at the front lines of welfare provision. Our analysis reveals that sanction patterns today are shaped by a complex interplay of client traits and local forces.

Welfare officials do not inevitably sanction clients of color at higher rates. Indeed, sanctions are imposed with little racial bias in some contexts and target whites disproportionately in some instances. The patterns do not indicate a pervasive dynamic of racial prejudice and discrimination. They point to a more subtle process in which racial categories emerge, under particular circumstances, as implicit structures for policy choice. Sanctions are applied to clients, we show, in a pattern that closely conforms to the contingent logic of the Racial Classification Model (RCM). Client race can matter more or less depending on how contextual factors affect the salience and contents of racial categories as frames for decision making.

The analysis that follows can also be seen as a critique of studies that misconstrue sanctioning by focusing narrowly on individuals. Sanction decisions are products of *governance*. They take on different patterns depending on how policy authority has been structured, and they respond systematically to local political and economic conditions. To clarify these dynamics, we begin by analyzing sanction patterns in the Florida WT program. Turning to the national level, we show how outcomes in Florida reflect the state's decision to adopt second-order devolution as a governing structure. In states that share this design, we find politically contingent patterns of racial disparities that closely resemble the Florida results. In states where local actors have not been given primary authority over operating procedures, these biases are diminished.

Organizations, Environments, and Sanction Implementation

Welfare sanctions are generally thought of as responses to individual behavior. In neoliberal discourse, they are framed as "wage deductions" for clients who, like irresponsible employees, fail to do their jobs. For paternalists, they are a tutelary response to individual noncompliance—a swift consequence for the client's failure to meet his or her personal responsibilities. Most scholarly studies implicitly share this individualizing frame by asking "who is likely to get sanctioned" in the TANF program. Thus, the main contribution of the literature to date has been to show that sanctioned clients tend to resemble long-term welfare recipients in terms of their marital status, age, family size, education level, work experience, and race (Wu et al. 2006; Pavetti, Derr, and Hesketh 2003; Hasenfeld, Ghose, and Larson 2004; Kalil, Seefeldt, and Wang 2002; Koralek 2000).

Over the next few chapters, we offer an alternative view that emphasizes how patterns of disciplinary action are shaped by governing structures, implementing organizations, and local environments. Before taking a closer look inside welfare-to-work organizations, we focus here on the environmental forces that impinge on their operations. In doing so, we draw on a number of key insights from welfare history and public administration scholarship.

Prior to the 1960s, unfettered local implementation was a defining feature of public aid programs in the United States (Katz 1996). Throughout this period, administrative rules and actions were highly responsive to pressures that came from community employers and political actors (Bell 1965; Ward 2005). Local control made welfare offices more vulnerable to local interests that worked to "shape relief practices in accord with widely different labor practices so as to mesh with local labor requirements" (Piven and Cloward 1993: 130–31). In the process, it embedded welfare implementation in the racial structuring of local political economies. Surveying this history of local influence, Robert Lieberman (1998: 229) concludes: "The distinction between national and local control and the extent of decentralized bureaucratic discretion have been crucial in determining how social policy treats African Americans."

The lessons of this history are reinforced by a broader conclusion in the field of public administration: Organizations that implement public policy tend to operate as "open systems" that are highly responsive to their environments (Meier 1993; Keiser and Soss 1998). Administrators must serve "many masters" at once and are subject to pressures from a variety of actors who have a stake in the outcomes they produce (Derthick 1990). Agency personnel are usually drawn from nearby communities and, as a result, tend to share local political orientations and cultural beliefs (Khademian 2002). Organizational norms and ways of "making sense" tend to get constructed out of cultural resources that are inherited from the broader community (Weick 1995; J. Martin 1992; M. Feldman 1989). Over time, as managers work to navigate changing local conditions, their organizations tend to develop in directions that accommodate and adapt to their "political and task environments" (Hrebiniak and Joyce 1985; Meier 1993).

Under welfare reform, these sorts of dynamics have been given greater running room by the push toward policy devolution. In all states today, local TANF officials have some level of discretion over program elements that affect the rate and incidence of sanctioning. They interpret state guidelines and convert them into local operations; they decide how to inform clients about program rules and sanction steps; they design procedures for monitoring compliance and notifying clients of impending violations; and so on. Thus, even when TANF offices operate under the same state guidelines, field studies find that sanction philosophies and practices tend to vary dramatically across local organizations (Pavetti et al. 1998).

Second-order devolution deepens the opportunities for local influence. Under this design, primary authority is placed in the hands of local county officials or regional workforce boards (RWBs). In the Florida WT program, for example, RWBs develop independent local operating procedures (LOPs) that modify basic features of the statewide sanction guidelines. The LOPs vary greatly across the state and can define penalty criteria as fundamental as whether a client must document forty as opposed to thirty hours of work activity each week to avoid a sanction.

In sum, there are a number of good reasons to analyze sanctions, not just as events that happen to some clients more than others, but as outcomes of governance. To do so, one must examine how client characteristics interact with organizations and their environments to produce systematic patterns of disciplinary action.

Local Political Environments and Sanctioning in the WT Program

The twenty-four workforce regions that implement the Florida WT program vary widely in their sanction rates (see table on p. 149). Client characteristics also vary across the regions, and may do so in ways that lead to different rates of rule violation. Thus, differences in sanction rates tell us little about whether local forces influence approaches to disciplining the poor. To assess this possibility, one must examine individual differences alongside contextual factors. In this regard, we are particularly interested in how penalty rates may be shaped by local political orientations.

Conservatives and Republicans were the driving political forces behind the disciplinary turn in poverty governance (see chapters 2–4). From the 1960s onward, they deployed law-and-order themes for electoral gain and pushed for more muscular approaches to work enforcement. In the states, they worked to expand correctional control and extend its logic of violation and penalty to welfare. In our analyses, Republican/conservative control of government consistently predicted state-level increases in incarceration, decisions to end

GA programs, benefit cuts in the Aid to Families with Dependent Children (AFDC) program, and adoptions of full-family sanctions under the TANF program.

If policy implementation follows legislative action as a continuation of "policy-making by other means" (Lineberry 1977), we should expect related patterns to emerge as local officials put this disciplinary project into practice. In conservative regions, disciplinary goals should enjoy greater "buy in" from local administrators and should be bolstered by stronger local pressures to use "sticks" rather than "carrots" to promote client compliance (Ridzi 2009). After accounting for client differences, we should find regional patterns of sanctioning that reflect the political dimensions of the disciplinary project.

To test this proposition, we merged individual-level measures from WT administrative data with contextual indicators of local characteristics. To measure local political environments, we created a county-level conservatism index based on local support for eighteen constitutional amendments that appeared on statewide ballots from 1996 to 2004. We validated this index by comparing its values to average Republican vote shares in Florida counties (presidential elections, 1996–2004) and to survey data showing rates of liberal-conservative self-identification in eight Florida counties (1996–2004). (For details, see Fording, Soss, and Schram 2007.)

In addition to this index, our models control for a number of other county characteristics that might affect sanction rates: the nonwhite percentage of residents, total population size, unemployment rate, poverty rate, average wage in food service and drinking establishments (annual), and number of TANF-receiving adults per 100,000 residents. These county-level variables were merged with administrative data that cover the entire Florida WT caseload, indicate the timing and location of sanction decisions, and measure client characteristics at the individual level.[1] Our individual-level control variables include client sex, age, marital status, number of children, age of youngest child, wage income, and race/ethnicity.

Based on these measures, we conducted an event history analysis (EHA) of sanction outcomes for clients in the WT program. Like multiple regression, EHA allows us to estimate how different variables affect an event of interest (a sanction). Instead of just predicting whether the event occurred, however, EHA explains variation in the amount of time that elapses between a starting point and the event's occurrence. For this reason, EHA is sometimes referred to as "duration analysis" (in economics) or as "survival analysis" (in medicine).

We use EHA to analyze sanction outcomes for all clients who entered the

WT program for the first time during the twenty-four-month period from January 2001 to the end of December 2002. The starting point for each client is the month of first enrollment. Our outcome variable takes on a value of 1 in the month that a client is sanctioned and a value of 0 in all preceding client-month combinations.[2] Thus, our EHA sheds light not only on why some clients get sanctioned while others do not, but also on why some clients get sanctioned more quickly than others.[3]

Our results confirm what previous studies have shown: Sanction rates vary significantly depending on client characteristics (Born, Caudill, and Cordero 1999; Koralek 2000; Westra and Routely 2000; Hasenfeld, Ghose, and Larson 2004; Kalil, Seefeldt, and Wang 2002; Keiser, Mueser, and Choi 2004; Wu et al. 2006). They are significantly more likely to be applied to the small number of men in the WT program, relative to the large majority of women. They are also more likely to be imposed on clients who have older children, clients who live in two-parent families, younger clients, and clients who have lower levels of human capital (as measured by wage income and education). In addition, we find that sanctions are applied more frequently in counties with higher poverty rates, higher population densities, and larger per capita TANF caseloads. (Although we control for client race in this analysis, we leave discussion of these results for a more detailed analysis below.)

Turning to political differences, we find that clients who participate in more conservative counties have a significantly greater risk of being sanctioned in every observed month of the participation spell, relative to similar clients in more liberal regions. To clarify how the effects of local political ideology accumulate over the course of a twelve-month TANF spell, figure 7-1 plots cumulative "survival rates." For each month of the spell, the curves indicate the probability that a typical client would "survive" in the program this long without being sanctioned. For purposes of this illustration, we estimate survival curves for a "typical" TANF client, which we define as a thirty-one-year-old single white woman with one child (aged three to four years), twelve years of education, and an average level of wage income in the quarter preceding the current month. We plot two survival curves for this hypothetical client: one assuming that she resided in the most liberal county in Florida and a second assuming that she lived in the most conservative county.

The survival curves show that, from the first month onward, the "typical" client has a lower probability of surviving without a sanction if she participates in the more conservative county. Over the course of the participation spell, risk disparities accumulate to produce large differences by the twelfth month. If our

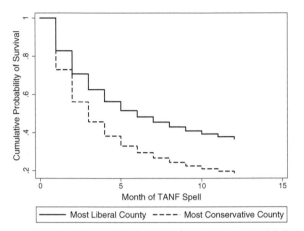

FIGURE 7-1. Estimated Cumulative Survival Function for a Typical TANF Adult, by Local Political Ideology

Note: Survival functions are estimated for a thirty-one-year-old single white woman with one child (aged three to four years), twelve years of education, and an average level of wage income in the previous quarter.

typical client participated in the most conservative county, she would have a .20 probability of surviving through the twelfth month without a sanction. If she participated in the most liberal county, she would be twice as likely to survive through the twelfth month without a sanction (.40). Given the stringency of the WT program, relatively few clients are able to participate for twelve months in any county. Regardless of which month one uses as the endpoint of observation, however, our results clearly show that politically conservative counties sanction at higher rates, and this effect accumulates over the course of the spell. As poverty governance has been rolled out to local authorities, disciplinary practices have become highly contingent on politics and place.

Client Race as a Contingent Source of Vulnerability

Our findings so far underscore the importance of attending to local political differences and stages of the participation spell. In turning to the racial dimensions of disciplinary practice, then, we must consider how these factors might intersect with client race to shape sanction patterns. Three conditional propositions from the RCM suggest expectations. First, larger disparities in treatment should emerge when the racial/ethnic groups in question provide a sharper contrast of policy-relevant reputations. Second, racial biases in treatment should be more likely when client traits supply authorities with stereotype-consistent cues—that is, traits that align with and evoke policy-relevant racial stereotypes. Third, racial biases should be more likely when beliefs about policy-relevant racial differences are more prevalent among governing authorities and, thus, more available as frames that might be tapped by contextual cues.

The first proposition suggests that white-black disparities should be larger than white-Latino disparities. Relative to whites, blacks are far more likely to be seen as exhibiting low work effort and motivation, irresponsible behavior, and preferences for long-term welfare dependence (Gilens 1999; Schuman et al. 1997). Latino stereotypes tend to fall somewhere in the middle, offering a smaller negative contrast with whites (Fox 2004).[4] Thus, the RCM suggests that black-white biases should be larger and more consistent than Latino-white biases.

The second proposition suggests that client race and spell duration should interact to influence sanctioning. For decades, long-term welfare "dependency" has functioned as a race-coded keyword of welfare discourse (Fraser and Gordon 1994). It draws old racial stereotypes of laziness together with images of "welfare queens" living off the dole and discourses of addiction and pathology (Gilens 1999; Hancock 2004; Schram 1995). Thus, in the welfare-to-work context, longer participation spells are likely to function as cues that evoke policy-relevant racial stereotypes. The RCM suggests that as spells lengthen, implicit racial frames will be activated more often and racial gaps in treatment will widen.

The third proposition directs us to ask how local authorities differ in their racial beliefs. Based on our earlier results, differences across liberal and conservative political environments appear to merit special attention. In principle, there is no reason why conservatives should hold more negative views of racial minorities. Indeed, there are good reasons to distinguish between the two when trying to explain policy preferences (Sears, Sidanius, and Bobo 2000). In practice, however, conservatism and race became deeply entwined in American politics over the past few decades (see chapter 3). As Republicans made extensive use of race-coded electoral themes, party competition became more racially aligned (Carmines and Stimson 1989). Ideological conservatives became more likely than liberals to hold negative views of welfare recipients *and* to see African Americans as lazier than whites (Domke 2001; Federico and Sidanius 2002; Gilens 1999; Glaser 1994; Johnson and Marini 1998; Oliver and Mendelberg 2000).

Figure 7-2 illustrates this relationship based on pooled National Election Studies (NES) data from 1996, 2000, and 2004 (the period of our analysis).

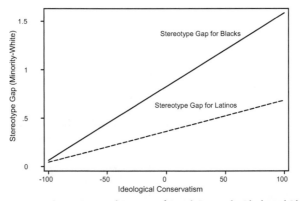

FIGURE 7-2. Average Gap in Perceived Laziness of Racial Groups, by Ideological Identification of Respondents

Note: The vertical axis is the stereotype gap and is computed as the difference in the mean assessment of laziness for each pair of target groups (the mean score for blacks/Latinos minus the mean score for white), where the laziness scale is coded as follows: 1 = hardworking through 7 = lazy. As scaled, the stereotype gap is a measure of the degree to which respondents view blacks (or Latinos) as lazier than whites. The measure of conservatism is computed as the feeling thermometer score for conservatives minus the score for liberals. The lines in the graph represent the predicted relationship between conservatism and the stereotype gap for each group, based on a bivariate regression that utilizes pooled data from the National Election Study (1996, 2000, 2004). Each slope value is statistically significant ($p < .01$).

The NES includes a series of separate questions that ask respondents to place "most" blacks, Latinos, and whites on a seven-point scale running from "hardworking" to "lazy." By subtracting respondents' placements of whites from their placements of blacks and Latinos, respectively, one can calculate a "stereotype gap" for each pair. Figure 7-2 shows the relationships we observe when we regress these stereotype gaps on a measure of each respondent's feelings toward liberals and conservatives.

The results highlight three key points. First, among the most extreme liberals, virtually no racial gaps exist in expressed endorsements of laziness stereotypes. Second, among moderates and conservatives, black-white gaps are consistently larger than Latino-white gaps. Third, as one looks from left to right, moving toward the conservative end of the ideological spectrum, both stereotype gaps grow consistently larger. This last result is consistent with evidence from a wide range of national surveys conducted from 1990 onward and can be confirmed separately in all regions of the United States.[5] Indeed, an AP-Yahoo Poll conducted in September 2008 by Paul Sniderman and colleagues offers a more comprehensive view of the ideological contrast. Relative to liberals, conservatives in the national survey were less likely to see African Americans as law abiding, determined, friendly, dependable, intelligent at school, smart at every-

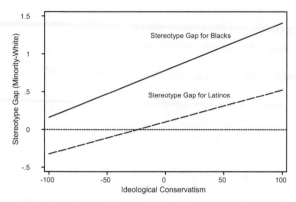

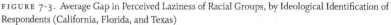

FIGURE 7-3. Average Gap in Perceived Laziness of Racial Groups, by Ideological Identification of Respondents (California, Florida, and Texas)

Note: The vertical axis is the stereotype gap and is computed as the difference in the mean assessment of laziness for each pair of target groups (the mean score for blacks/Latino minus the mean score for white), where the laziness scale is coded as follows: 1 = hardworking through 7 = lazy. As scaled, the stereotype gap is a measure of the degree to which respondents view blacks (or Latino) as lazier than whites. The measure of conservatism is computed as the feeling thermometer score for conservatives minus the score for liberals. The lines in the graph represent the predicted relationship between conservatism and the stereotype gap for each group, based on a bivariate regression that utilizes pooled data from the National Election Study (1996, 2000, 2004), with the sample restricted to respondents in California, Florida and Texas. Each slope value is statistically significant ($p < .01$).

day things, and likely to be good neighbors; they were more likely to see African Americans as violent, boastful, complaining, lazy, and irresponsible.

For our study of Florida, further precision is offered by figure 7-3, which shows the pattern of NES stereotype gaps observed in the three American states with the largest Latino populations (California, Florida, and Texas).[6] The results are almost identical to those shown in figure 7-2. The key difference is that among the most liberal respondents, the Latino-white stereotype gap is actually reversed. Extreme liberals in these states actually tend to view Latinos as slightly *more* "hardworking" than whites. By contrast, our three-state sample produces results for the black-white stereotype gap that closely resemble the results from our national sample.

Based on this evidence, the RCM suggests that racial disparities in sanctioning (a) should be larger in more politically conservative communities and (b) should fade or even reverse (in Latino-white comparisons) in the most liberal environments. As noted earlier, a variety of dynamics may drive this relationship: local pressures on implementation, local recruitment of agency and RWB staff, the translation of local racial beliefs into organizational cultures, and so on. For all these reasons, the RCM suggests that race will be more likely to guide sanctioning, and thus racial disparities will be larger, in more conservative political environments.

Preliminary support for this expectation can be found in a study of welfare sanctions in Missouri (Keiser, Mueser, and Choi 2004). Dividing the state into seven broad geographic regions, and controlling for client- and county-level factors, the study finds that racial differences in sanction rates track with levels of political conservatism. Although they fit the RCM's predictions, these results have several limitations that can be overcome in an analysis of the Florida WT program. First, minority populations are larger and more widely dispersed in Florida than in Missouri. As a result, we can examine racial effects in a larger number of local contexts and observe them at a lower level of aggregation that is both administratively and politically meaningful (the county). Second, because Florida is a racially diverse state, we can test our disparate predictions for blacks and Latinos rather than being limited to the black-white comparison observed in Missouri. Third, by employing an event history design, we can directly observe how racial effects vary across the participation spell and control for this dimension of risk in assessing the interplay of client race and local conservatism.

Race, Politics, and Participation Spells:
Conditional Tests of the RCM

With these expectations in hand, we can return to the WT administrative data analyzed earlier. Because we have variables measured at two levels of analysis (individual and county), we take the additional step here of subjecting our data to a different modeling approach: a discrete-time multilevel EHA of sanction initiation (Barber et al. 2000). The variables included in our models are the same as we described for our earlier analysis. The results for individual-level client characteristics, based on a multilevel approach, parallel those presented earlier.[7]

Figures 7-4 and 7-5 present our key results for the interplay of client race/ethnicity, local political ideology, and participation spell length. Each figure presents separate panels for three points in the participation spell (three, six, and nine months) and shows the predicted relationship between local conservatism and the group-specific probability that a sanction will be imposed.[8] The most striking pattern here is that local political differences consistently matter more for black and Latino clients than for white clients. At every stage of the spell, conservatism raises sanction rates to a greater degree for blacks and Latinos than for their white counterparts.

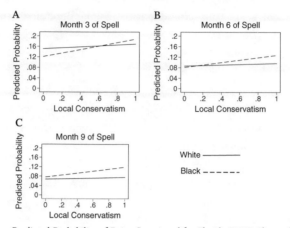

FIGURE 7-4. Predicted Probability of Being Sanctioned for Florida TANF Clients, by Race, Local Political Environment, and Month of TANF Spell. (A) Month 3 of TANF Spell. (B) Month 6 of TANF Spell. (C) Month 9 of TANF Spell.

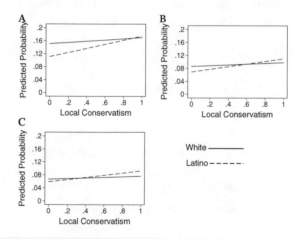

FIGURE 7-5. Predicted Probability of Being Sanctioned for Florida TANF Clients, by Ethnicity, Local Political Environment, and Month of TANF Spell. (A) Month 3 of TANF Spell. (B) Month 6 of TANF Spell. (C) Month 9 of TANF Spell.

At the left side of each panel, we can see that racial biases in sanctioning are highly contingent. At all three points in the participation spell, the most liberal counties are predicted to sanction Latino clients less frequently than white clients (figure 7-5). Indeed, because differences across local contexts and spell periods cancel out, we find no significant differences in the overall rates at which white and Latino clients are sanctioned. These results are largely consistent with the survey evidence just reviewed: Latino-white stereotype gaps are consistently smaller than black-white stereotype gaps, and, in states with larger Latino populations, liberals tend to view Latinos as more hardworking than whites.

An isolated echo of this pattern can be seen even in the black-white comparison shown in the top panel of figure 7-4. At the earliest stage of a spell that takes place in the most liberal county, we find that black clients are actually less likely to be sanctioned than their white counterparts. Several factors may contribute to this result. First, this is precisely the condition that RCM suggests should be most favorable to black clients. Survey data suggest that strong liberals perceive little or no difference in black and white "laziness" and, in the earliest months of benefit receipt, black clients do not possess the stereotype-consistent cue of a longer participation spell.

Second, the earliest period of the spell is a transitional stage where clients learn about the strict terms of WT participation. In our field interviews, WT officials at all levels reported that when new clients learn about the program, many opt not to return—despite their successful application for benefits. Among other things, the clients learn that between 120 and 160 hours of work activity will be required each month for a payment of only $240. According to WT officials, clients who have a viable income alternative, even if it is quite meager, often respond by electing to take their first check and never come back. In the local parlance, this decision to opt out is referred to as "self-sanctioning" because it results in a standard sanction off the rolls but, critically, is not the result of a discretionary decision by a case manager. Abundant evidence, of course, demonstrates that labor markets and social networks are more likely to provide income alternatives for low-skilled whites than for low-skilled blacks (Brown et al. 2003; Lin and Harris 2008). As a result, higher rates of self-sanctioning among white WT clients may be enough to produce a "white-over-black" pattern of overall sanction rates under the isolated conditions where the RCM predicts that the two groups will be sanctioned at a more or less equal rate.[9]

Taken as whole, our analysis of black-white disparities provides strong support for the RCM. The results suggest that the effects of client race are doubly mediated. First, movement from a liberal local environment to a conservative environment raises the probability of a black or Latino client being sanctioned, not just in absolute terms, but also relative to non-Latino whites.[10] Second, this dynamic is contingent on spell length. As spells increase from three to nine months, the *absolute* risk of a sanction decreases for all groups (as indicated by the falling intercept values in the panels). Sanction rates (which may be bolstered by self-sanctioning) are highest during clients' earliest months. Declines in these rates over time, however, exhibit a clear racial bias. As white clients move from their third to ninth months, their predicted sanction rate drops by approximately 56 percent (for an ideologically moderate county). The reduction for blacks over this same period is only about 33 percent.

Because of this disparity, the prediction lines for black sanction rates rise faster than the lines for white sanction rates as one moves down through the panels of figure 7-4. By the sixth month of the spell, in the most conservative counties, the predicted probability of a sanction is 30 percent greater for black clients than for white clients. By the ninth month, black clients are predicted to be sanctioned more than whites in *every* county. In the most conservative counties, their predicted sanction rate rises to a level that is approximately 70 percent higher than that of whites.

In sum, our results largely confirm the conditional predictions of the RCM. Sanction rates for black and Latino clients depend on local political orientations in ways that sanction rates for non-Latino whites do not. Longer participation spells also enhance black and Latino sanction rates relative to those for non-Latino whites. The backdrop for these dynamics, however, is not a relentless pattern of inferior treatment for clients of color. Overall sanction rates for Latino and white clients are quite similar, and, in some instances, Latinos are less likely to be sanctioned than their white counterparts. Black-white sanction disparities emerge as stronger and more consistent in this analysis. In all but the most favorable circumstance (a brief participation spell in a liberal county), sanction rates are always predicted to be higher for black clients than for whites. When black clients participate for longer spells, cuing images of "dependency," their sanction rates rise relative to whites, and do so most sharply in the most conservative counties.

Coherence and Patterning in Local Disciplinary Regimes

Our results so far suggest that individual clients encounter different approaches to sanctioning depending on the county in which they participate. Collectively, they raise the question of whether second-order devolution in Florida has led to the construction of distinctive local regimes of poverty governance. This development would be highly consistent with our analysis in chapter 5. Under first-order devolution, we found that states constructed racialized policy regimes that blended tougher, more localized TANF programs with stronger correctional control. To see if local implementation followed this pattern, it is useful to set aside individual-level data for a moment and analyze county-level data for evidence of local regime differences.

In chapters 4 and 5, we presented several kinds of state-level evidence for the claim that neoliberal paternalism has entailed a racialized convergence of penal and welfare operations. In the 1980s and 1990s, incarceration rates and welfare programs shifted in response to the same state-level forces, exhibiting a special sensitivity to the interplay of the benefit-wage ratio (BWR) and race. After 1996, states designed their TANF programs in ways that closely followed differences in their carceral strategies and black population percentages. In the Florida WT program, do local differences in sanction implementation flow from similar "regime dynamics" that link welfare provision to a conjunction of race, penal operations, and BWRs?

Consistent with our strategy in chapter 5, we analyze implementation regimes by focusing on the black-white differences that produced stronger results in our earlier analyses. In addition, given our analysis of spell-length effects and "self-sanctioning" dynamics, we adopt an outcome measure that captures black-white sanction disparities observed in each county after the third month of the participation spell. Two predictors of this outcome are of central interest. First, we extend our earlier emphasis on the benefits and wages *available* at the state level by constructing a parallel measure of benefits and wages as components of *income* at the county level.[11] For each county, we calculate the income benefit-wage ratio (IBWR) for blacks as the number of black households receiving income from public assistance divided by the number with income from work-related earnings. Thus, higher values indicate higher rates of reliance on welfare benefits relative to earnings. As a control variable, we construct a parallel measure for white households in each county.

Second, we extend our earlier focus on state incarceration levels by constructing a related implementation measure: county arrest rates. Our primary measure is calculated as the number of times black individuals were arrested in a county divided by the number of black county residents. As a control variable, we employ a parallel measure of arrest rates for white county residents. Finally, we include an interaction term to test whether the relationship between black arrest rates and WT sanction disparities intensifies in counties where blacks exhibit greater reliance on welfare benefits relative to earnings. The additional control variables for our regression analysis include the county population size, the county unemployment rate, the county conservatism index, the black percentage of the county population, and the county crime rate.[12]

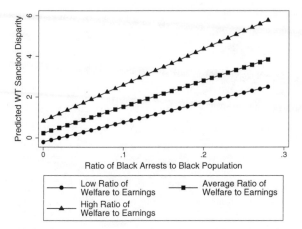

FIGURE 7-6. Black-White Sanction Disparities by Black Arrest Rates and Benefit-Wage Ratios in Black Household Incomes (Florida Counties)

Controlling for these factors, we find significant effects in the expected direction for all three of our main measures: the black IBWR, the black arrest rate, and their interaction. Figure 7-6 presents a graphic illustration of these results, providing strong county-level corroboration for our earlier findings at the state level. For a "typical" Florida county (one with mean values on all control variables), we observe how predicted black-white sanction disparities shift across the values of our two interacting variables. To ease interpretation, figure 7-6 shows estimated sanction disparities covary with black arrest rates at three levels of the IBWR: the 25th percentile (low), the median (average), and the 75th percentile (high). At all three levels of the IBWR, we can see that counties that arrest blacks at higher rates are significantly more likely to sanction black WT clients at higher rates than whites. Thus, local implementation follows the state-level pattern established in chapter 5: a race-specific convergence of disciplinary practices across the penal and welfare domains.

The three slopes shown in figure 7-6 allow for further insight into how this relationship shifts depending on levels of the IBWR. The slopes indicate that a statistically significant relationship persists at all three levels. The arrest-sanction linkage intensifies, however, as black households in our "typical" county become more reliant on welfare benefits relative to market earnings. As labor-market participation weakens as a source of income for black households, we observe a tighter conjunction of escalating black arrest rates and black-white sanction disparities. In addition to matching the conditional predictions of the RCM, these complex patterns underlie a more straightforward relationship confirmed by a separate analysis (not shown): The counties that produce larger black-white arrest disparities tend to be the same counties that produce larger black-white sanction disparities.[13]

Together, this evidence suggests considerable continuity in the patterning of disciplinary regimes. At both the state and county levels, and in policy choice as well as implementation, we find that more disciplinary welfare approaches converge with tougher approaches to criminality in ways that are racially patterned and responsive to the benefit-wage relationship. Neoliberal paternalism is a system of dispersed and variegated disciplinary practices. The best evidence we can muster suggests that it takes on distinctive and coherent forms in different jurisdictions—linking penal and welfare operations, and becoming more intense when public aid levels appear to pose a greater threat to labor discipline among African Americans.

Second-Order Devolution as a Governing Structure: National Evidence

Our analysis of Florida WT data suggests that client race affects sanctioning in a manner that is highly contingent on local political environments. There are good reasons to suspect Florida may differ from other states in this respect. By pursuing a strong form of second-order devolution, Florida officials have given local authorities greater latitude in designing and implementing LOPs. Does the adoption of second-order devolution, itself a racialized practice (chapter 5), create the "conditions of possibility" needed for local political differences to shape the racial basis of sanction implementation?

To explore this possibility, we can turn to national data on sanctioning in state TANF programs. Administrative data from the Florida WT program allow for a far more detailed analysis of sanctioning dynamics. National-level data, however, offer the best available opportunity for assessing the extent to which results from Florida hold in other states.

As a first step, we can consider the direct relationship between race and sanctioning across the American states. After 1996, states with larger black caseloads were more likely to adopt the strictest TANF sanctions. As a result, by 2001, black TANF recipients had become more likely than their white counterparts to be exposed to the stiffest penalties (see chapter 5).[14] Does racial composition have a similar effect on the rate at which officials impose sanctions on TANF clients? A preliminary answer to this question can be obtained by analyzing data from the U.S. Government Accountability Office (GAO) that identify

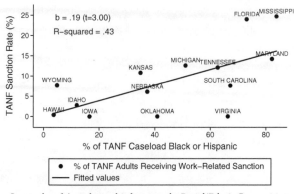

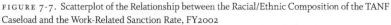

FIGURE 7-7. Scatterplot of the Relationship between the Racial/Ethnic Composition of the TANF Caseload and the Work-Related Sanction Rate, FY2002

Note: The sample for this analysis consists of the fourteen states that enforced immediate, full-family sanctions in 2002. The horizontal axis is computed as the sum of the percentage of TANF families who are African American and the percentage who are Hispanic, based on data reported for April, 2002. The vertical axis is the percentage of cases closed due to a work-related sanction during FY2002. These data are reported in the *Sixth Annual Report to Congress*, published by the Office of Family Assistance in the Department of Health and Human Services (http://www.acf.hhs.gov/programs/ofa/data-reports/annualreport6/ar6index.htm).

the racial composition of each state's welfare caseload and the *overall* sanction rate in each state. Figure 7-7 presents a simple bivariate analysis showing how state sanction rates covary with the nonwhite proportion of the TANF caseload, focusing on states that have adopted the strictest sanction policies.[15] The results suggest a strong relationship between racial composition and sanctioning.

The implementation pattern shown in figure 7-7 is consistent with our earlier analyses of state policy choice in chapter 5: In states where racial minorities are more prevalent in the welfare caseload, authorities tend to adopt a tougher disciplinary stance toward welfare recipients in general. Beyond this observation, however, the aggregate data summarized in figure 7-7 are quite limited. They tell us little about whether states are actually sanctioning black and Latino recipients more often than whites or whether the effects of race vary across local jurisdictions. Without accounting for the many other ways clients may differ, figure 7-7 merely indicates that states with larger nonwhite caseloads, for some reason, sanction more frequently.

To dig deeper, we can turn to a national dataset assembled by the Office of the Assistant Secretary for Planning and Evaluation (ASPE) in the Department of Health and Human Services. The data include measures of clients' characteristics and county locations. Unlike the GAO data, the ASPE data do not cover the full universe of TANF cases in each state. They are based on probability samples of TANF families collected separately by each of the fifty states in each

year from 1999 through 2005. The data are collected to facilitate federal evaluations of state TANF program performance and consist of two types of samples:
active cases and closed cases. The closed-case samples are most helpful for our
purposes because they indicate the specific reason why each client's case was
closed: leaving welfare for employment, getting married, or being sanctioned,
among others. This "reason for closure" measure allows us to construct a dependent variable that distinguishes sanctioned clients from all other program
leavers. Pooling all closed-case samples for the entire 1999–2005 period, we
analyze all adult TANF leavers identified by the state as the head of the household. Using this definition, and accounting for missing data, our dataset consists
of approximately 195,000 TANF adults residing in nearly 2,700 counties.

The ASPE dataset does not allow us to strictly replicate our Florida analysis
and should not be expected to yield identical results. To begin with, our fifty-
state analysis is limited to closed cases, while the Florida WT data allowed us to
observe open as well as closed cases. In addition, because the national data are
based on cross-sectional observations, we cannot observe or control for the ways
that sanction dynamics vary across the participation spell. Finally, although we
control for a number of relevant client traits, our individual-level measures are
not identical to the ones employed in the Florida analysis.[16] With these caveats
noted, the ASPE data allow for a limited replication of our Florida results and
provide the best opportunity to analyze how the effects of local political environments may depend on second-order devolution (hereafter, SOD).

Our results confirm that national sanction patterns are significantly related
to a number of individual-level factors. Across both SOD and non-SOD states,
the probability of being sanctioned is higher for clients who are younger, who
are citizens, who have older children (SOD states only), and who possess less
human capital (as measured by education level and earned income). On the
whole, these results comport with our results from Florida. Several findings
diverge, however. For example, gender has no discernible influence on sanctioning in SOD states, and, in non-SOD states, women are more likely than men
to be sanctioned. In addition, in non-SOD states, we find that single parents
are more likely (rather than less likely) to be sanctioned. Finally, we find that
clients who receive disability benefits or live in public housing are significantly
more likely to have left TANF due to a sanction, perhaps reflecting significant
employment barriers among these clients.

Among our contextual measures, we find that sanction exits are significantly
more likely in counties with larger black populations (across all states) and in
counties with larger Latino populations (in non-SOD states). These results did

not emerge in the stronger models we were able to specify in our analysis of Florida WT data. But they are consistent with the broader pattern of racial-composition effects observed in state policy choice (chapters 4 and 5) and in our analysis of GAO data on sanction rates.

Turning to client race, we find results that closely match our findings in the Florida WT program. Here, as there, the direct effects of client race are statistically insignificant when other factors are controlled for and county ideology is set at a typical (politically moderate) level. And once again, we find that the effects of client race are mediated by local political context. The key difference in the national analysis is that black-white sanction disparities do not appear to be contingent on local political environment in all states. Consistent with our expectations, more conservative local environments raise sanction rates for blacks relative to whites *only in the subset of states that have adopted SOD.* Thus, while individual-level biases in administrators' decisions may contribute to racial disparities in sanctioning (see chapter 10), it appears that the adoption of a decentralized governing structure is a precondition for the emergence of politically patterned racial differences in local sanction rates. Finally, in yet another echo of our Florida findings, the pattern for black clients fades in the case of Latino clients. Latino sanction rates do not covary with local political environments, regardless of SOD.

Figure 7-8 presents a graphic illustration of our results for states with SOD. The figure shows the predicted probability of a sanction exit for a typical client, by the race of the client and the local political environment.[17] Consistent with our Florida results, we see that the predicted probability of a sanction is roughly similar for black and white clients if they reside in a strongly liberal county. As county conservatism rises, racial disparities quickly emerge in the anticipated direction. In the most conservative counties, the predicted probability of a sanction exit is approximately 70 percent greater for black clients than for white clients.

Together with our more detailed analysis of Florida data, the national results strongly suggest that SOD paves the way for race-based sanction disparities in more conservative communities, where antiblack stereotypes are more likely to prevail. No single analysis can be definitive. But our confidence is raised by the consistency of findings across two very different datasets, levels of analysis, and modeling approaches. Today, as in the past, administrative decentralization matters greatly for how African Americans are treated in welfare programs (Lieberman 1998). In the post–civil rights era, however, the dynamics of this relationship have become more implicit and contingent. Consistent with the

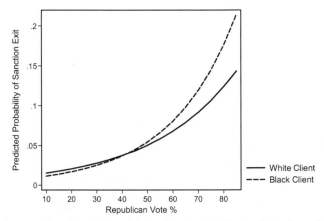

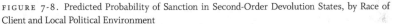

FIGURE 7-8. Predicted Probability of Sanction in Second-Order Devolution States, by Race of Client and Local Political Environment

Note: Predicted probabilities were calculated based on the results presented in the online appendix, for the SOD sample of states.

RCM, racial disparities do not flow automatically from the devolution of authority to local actors. Indeed, they do not appear at all in some localities and for some minority groups. For African Americans who participate outside the most liberal local environments, however, SOD provides an institutional foundation for stronger and more racially focused disciplinary action.

Conclusion

Historical changes in poverty governance depend on shifts in policy implementation as well as policy design. Looking across the developed nations, for example, observers who focus narrowly on policy designs have tended to see a global "convergence" of welfare states (Gilbert 2002). As Cathie Jo Martin (2004) has shown, however, policy similarities often obscure persisting differences in governing practices. In nations with divergent political profiles and institutional histories, administrators have put similar policies to very different uses as they have interpreted and operationalized the broad mandates of lawmakers (Martin 2004).

In this chapter, we have presented evidence that similar dynamics have occurred within the state of Florida and across the United States more generally. The more muscular stance of American poverty governance today was set by national and state policy designs, but it was not set in stone. Governance is ultimately a practice not a policy—or more precisely, it is a collection of practices structured by policy frameworks. As one follows the path of neoliberal paternalism down from national and state policies to local practices, its diversity comes into sharper view.

The coherence of neoliberal paternalism lies not in the uniformity of governance across contexts, but in the consistency of the forces that explain its variations. At the national level, the disciplinary turn in poverty governance was driven by conservative political actors who exploited deeply racialized anxieties and problems in an era of faltering markets for low-skilled labor. In our analyses of state policy choices and local implementation practices, these same three factors have cropped up time and again to explain differences across jurisdictions. Wherever we have looked, variations across time and place have converged to reveal neoliberal paternalism as a racialized political project of market discipline.

In the Florida WT program, RWB officials and welfare providers enjoy broad freedoms under a strong system of SOD. These freedoms are, above all, openings for local influences on implementation. Drawing on "open systems" theories, we have suggested a variety of reasons to expect welfare administrators to respond to their local environments (Meier 1993). As we will see in chapter 8, these general dynamics have been bolstered in the welfare case by neoliberal shifts in program mission that encourage frontline officials to service local employers and labor markets. In principle, sanction usage is supposed to stand outside these various local influences, operating as a direct response to objective instances of client noncompliance. In practice, we find that it does not.

Under SOD, politically conservative communities have been able to pursue a more aggressive approach to sanctioning. But this development has not affected all clients equally. Non-Latino white clients in the WT program can participate in the most liberal or the most conservative county of Florida without experiencing a discernible change in their risks of being sanctioned. Local conservatism leads to a higher risk of being sanctioned only when the client in question is black or Latino.

The same point can also be made in reverse: Client race influences sanctioning primarily in Florida's more conservative counties. This finding dovetails with our broader argument that, in the post–civil rights era, racial factors shape poverty governance in implicit and highly conditional ways. Indeed, the null findings presented in this chapter closely adhere to the contingent propositions of the RCM. Racial biases in sanctioning are relatively unlikely in the most liberal environments and are minimized when participation spells are shorter. Latino-white sanction disparities are, in comparative terms, fairly weak and inconsistent. Stronger disparities emerge under the facilitating conditions specified by the RCM: when black and white clients (a larger stereotype gap) participate in more conservative counties (a higher rate of stereotype acceptance) and accumulate longer spells of program participation (a stereotype-consistent cue).

Turning to national data, we see how the neoliberal emphasis on policy devolution restructures governance in ways that facilitate such racial dynamics. At a simple descriptive level, states with larger black caseloads have imposed sanctions at higher rates. Looking more closely, however, we find that racial disparities in sanctioning emerge across U.S. counties in a politically contingent manner that depends on SOD. For all that has changed in American racial politics, Robert Lieberman's (1998) observations about the historical links between decentralized policy control and racial bias remain as relevant today as ever.

Finally, our analysis of sanction patterns has also corroborated a broader argument that we share with Loïc Wacquant (2009). Under neoliberal paternalism, welfare practices have converged with policing and penal operations as entwined elements of a racialized "double regulation of the poor." In the Florida WT program, larger black-white sanction disparities are produced by the same counties that produce larger black-white arrest disparities. Consistent with our broader analysis, this relationship emerges in stronger forms in counties where black households draw more of their incomes from public benefits, relative to market wages. Here, as in earlier chapters, we find that the potent mixture of blackness and conditions that appear to threaten labor compliance produces an escalating convergence of penal and welfare discipline.

THE MARKETIZATION OF POVERTY GOVERNANCE

NEOLIBERALISM HAS RECAST AMERICAN POVERTY GOVERNANCE along many dimensions. In the preceding chapter, we explored the dynamics of policy devolution, and, in the next, we turn to competitive performance systems. The present chapter focuses on *marketization*: the drive to reconstruct poverty governance so that it follows market principles, becomes more reliant on market actors, services labor markets, yields profits for investors, and works to construct self-disciplined low-wage workers. We use the term *marketization* to signal changes that are both narrower and broader than privatization through outsourcing (Winston et al. 2002). They are narrower in the sense that we are interested in the marketization of *poverty governance*, a domain where problems are complex, goals are contested, and processes and outcomes are hard to evaluate. Outsourcing may have advantages in some cases where tasks are straightforward, outcomes are easily measured, and competing vendors are plentiful (refuse collection, janitorial services, and asphalt laying) (Bendick 1989; Donahue 1989; Hodge 2000). We focus here on the marketization of complex human services that differ greatly from such tasks.

At the same time, marketization encompasses far more than outsourcing or public-private collaboration. Cross-sector collaboration is an American tradition that dates back almost as far as regulatory and reformative poor relief itself (Katz 2002: 171–94). Nonprofit community organizations have long played a valuable role in poverty governance. Our analysis focuses on more novel features of neoliberal poverty governance: contracts that promise revenues in exchange for performance, operations that focus on servicing and subsidizing market actors, the conversion of welfare provision into a profitable domain of corporate investment, and so on. In what follows, we explore the rise of a broad market rationality that recasts traditional models of the welfare state and underpins a distinctive regime of practice for governance.

Classic models of the welfare state emphasize the boundary between the market's work-based system of distribution and the state's needs-based system of social protection (Stone 1984). Welfare programs historically functioned as "decommodifying" spaces where qualifying citizens were shielded from pressures to sell their labor at whatever prices employers would pay (Esping-

Andersen 1985). To enter the welfare system was to exit the labor market. Thus, conflicts over social protections historically centered on how the boundary between the two systems should be drawn (Stone 1984) and how needs-based benefits should compare to work-based benefits in terms of accessibility, generosity, and stigma (Piven and Cloward 1971). Market pressures shaped welfare policy and administration, and citizens were divided across programs based on work histories. But welfare programs were not structured internally as markets; their services were not organized around the needs of employers; and private providers were not incentivized as investors pursuing organizational revenues and returns for shareholders.

As neoliberalism has extended market rationality to new domains, it has eroded the state-market boundary emphasized in such accounts of the welfare state. Needs-based aid for the poor has been retrofitted as a market transaction rooted in financial incentives, penalties, and profits. The state's authority is deployed not to relieve citizens from market pressures, but to reinforce these pressures on behalf of employers. Norms and expectations from the business world have recast the organizational cultures of welfare providers, just as norms and expectations from the low-wage labor market have reshaped the terms of program participation for welfare recipients.

In the Florida Welfare Transition (WT) program, officials at all levels refer to this new stance as the *business model*, a term they contrast with the discredited Aid to Families with Dependent Children (AFDC) program's *social work* culture of handouts and paper pushing. The business model is innovative and results oriented. The social work model is a misguided "old school" ideology: the failed mantra of long-term bureaucrats who enabled long-term welfare dependency. The business model's narrow emphasis on work attachment is seen as more focused and realistic than the social work model, which is disparaged as a boundless and unrealistic commitment to caretaking and coddling. As one case manager put it, "We're about employment now, not solving the social service problems of the world."

As we will see, the business model is far too monochromatic to describe the conflicted views that frontline workers express in interviews. Case managers do not approach their work as faithful adherents to this worldview. They cite the business model as descriptive shorthand for the organizing realities that define their work conditions. They invoke it matter-of-factly to name the project they have been hired to advance. They embrace it as the opposing and only alternative to the failed welfare culture that preceded it.

Among the changes signaled by the business model, none is more important than the shift toward viewing employers and low-income families as "dual clienteles" of the Temporary Assistance for Needy Families (TANF) program.[1] The new ethos is well captured by a program director at Maximus Inc., a for-profit service provider for Wisconsin's version of the TANF program, W-2: "I think there's two ways to look at the W-2 program. One is as an economic program designed to allow participants to become more a part of the economic fabric of the community. The second—maybe just as motivating—is to get a low-cost workforce into the economy so that employers don't have to pay ever-increasing wages" (Collins and Mayer 2010: 55). Indeed, a central conceit of neoliberal welfare reform, belied by centuries of labor history, is that the interests of employers and recipients-cum-workers are indistinguishable. In this frame, the success of each depends on the other, and both benefit from a thriving local economy in which businesses profit, grow, and expand their workforces. Thus, efforts to service employers are just a proactive way of serving recipients.

A parallel substitution occurs on the other side of the welfare relationship, as service provision shifts from government agencies to for-profit corporations. The intellectual roots of this shift can be traced to Milton Friedman's ([1962] 2002) argument that free markets offer a dynamic solution to the inefficient and unresponsive tendencies of "governmental monopolies." In the 1980s, this argument was expanded by conservative think tanks and promoted by the Reagan administration's President's Commission on Privatization. In the 1990s, New Democrats joined the cause, as the Clinton administration pushed for broad efforts to "reinvent government" as a consumer-oriented collaboration of state and civil society (Osbourne and Gaebler 1992).

In the welfare arena, privatization was touted as a way to escape the "fundamentally flawed" culture of AFDC bureaucracies, gain the cost-saving efficiencies of market competition, and harness the local capacities of nonprofit and religious organizations. When welfare reform passed in 1996, it opened up vast new opportunities for profitable investment. Leading estimates placed the market potential of social-welfare operations at $15 billion, out of a projected $30 billion for all state and local service contracts (Sanger 2003: 96). Attracted by the "possibility of big profits and high-flying stock prices," corporate suitors flooded state capitols in what *Time* magazine aptly termed a "welfare-management gold rush" (A. Cohen 1998; see also Ehrenreich 1997). And they did so mostly below the public radar. Mass media devoted little coverage to welfare outsourcing and typically framed it in positive terms that made churches, charities, and local nonprofits into the public face of privatization (Brophy-Baermann and Bloeser 2006).

By 1997, all states but one contracted out some portion of welfare services (U.S. General Accounting Office 2002). By 2001, more than a quarter of all TANF contracts had been given to for-profit companies, while faith-based organizations received only 7 percent (GAO 2002). Today, IBM, Affiliated Computer Systems (ACS), and Electronic Data Systems Corp. (EDS) each earn more than $1 billion annually from state and local contracts; Accenture Ltd. and Maximus Inc. reap annual earnings between $500 million and $1 billion (*Washington Technology* 2009). The rapid growth of Maximus Inc. has been especially striking, leading a major outlet for contracting news to conclude: "If there is any doubt that welfare 'reform' has become a fruitful business, consider these numbers: Maximus grew from a $50 million operation in 1995 to $105 million in 1996 and to $319 million in 1999, a 36.8 percent sales growth over 1998" (*Washington Technology* 2009). In 2008, Maximus Inc. took in $745 million in revenue, almost $553 million of which came from state and local contracts (*Washington Technology* 2009).

In what follows, we explore how marketization has transformed welfare provision. We begin with national developments in the area of "waste, fraud, and abuse," contrasting the increasingly punitive approach to recipient fraud with the proliferation of corrupt profiteering among corporate providers. We then focus on Florida to look more closely at how a highly privatized welfare system operates in practice. In our third section, we show how the Florida WT program has been recast as an effort to service and subsidize low-wage employers. Finally, we turn to organizational culture, showing how the business model supplies a practical rationality for governance and lies uneasily beside other commitments in frontline workers' belief systems.

The Neoliberal Turn in Waste, Fraud, and Abuse

Provider corruption and claimant fraud are old themes in American welfare politics. Their prominence can be traced back at least as far as the Civil War Pensions of the nineteenth century, which were assimilated into party patronage operations in ways that created lasting anxieties over corruption in big social programs (Skocpol 1992). As the welfare state grew in size and popularity, images of ill-gotten gains offered conservatives an attractive way to discredit social protections without directly threatening benefits that most Americans valued and relied on.

Charges of widespread fraud also served as a pretext for purging welfare caseloads and tightening eligibility procedures (Piven and Cloward 1971). Like the "suitable home" and "employable mother" rules that served a similar purpose in the South, anti-fraud campaigns tended to focus on areas with larger black caseloads (Neubeck and Cazenave 2001: 92–109; Kohler-Hausmann 2007). They also tended to target providers as much as beneficiaries, framing the two as collaborators in fraud. In 1962, for example, Senator Robert Byrd (D-WV) held dramatic public hearings to pursue his suspicion that lax, liberal social workers were abetting widespread welfare fraud among the predominantly black aid recipients of Washington, D.C., (Neubeck and Cazenave 2001: 92–109). At the hearings, Senator Byrd made the broader frame of his inquiry explicit: "It is about time that we stop encouraging indolence and shiftlessness, and that we quit furnishing money, food and rent for indecent mothers and paramours who contribute nothing but illegitimate children to the society of this federal city, most of whom end up roaming the streets and getting arrested for various crimes" (Reese 2005: 116).

In the wake of the welfare rights movement, anxieties over fraud emerged again in the 1970s as an entry point for efforts to curtail welfare. In debates over the Family Assistance Plan in 1972, Senator Russell Long (D-LA) charged that "the welfare system, as we know it today, is being manipulated and abused by malingerers, cheats, and outright frauds" (Gustafson 2009: 654). Four years later, in the presidential nomination campaign of 1976, Ronald Reagan coined the term *welfare queen*, drawing on the widely publicized cases of two women convicted of fraud: the "welfare queen of Chicago," Linda Taylor, and her "Cadillac-driving" counterpart from Compton, Barbara Jean Williams (Gustafson 2009: 655). When Reagan took over the presidency in 1981, he quickly initiated efforts to root out waste, fraud, and abuse in welfare programs.

By the 1990s, AFDC benefits had fallen to levels that would not cover basic family necessities, and welfare recipients had become increasingly reliant on hidden income supplements that were forbidden under AFDC rules (Edin and Lein 1997). State responses offered a stark illustration of how welfare operations turned toward penal logics in this decade (Wacquant 2009). During the wave of AFDC waiver experiments in the mid-1990s, twenty-four states empowered new "preeligibility" fraud investigation units to pursue evidence of deceit through administrative records, home visits, and interviews with relatives, neighbors, employers, and landlords (Gustafson 2009: 659). After federal reform in 1996, the intermeshing of welfare and criminal justice systems accelerated and reshaped efforts to combat fraud.

The new law made individuals ineligible for aid if they were wanted by authorities for an outstanding felony warrant or a parole or probation violation.

The new "fugitive felon" rules effectively stripped welfare recipients of the privacy protections that shield financial and governmental information for other Americans. Welfare records and Social Security numbers could now be routinely matched to criminal justice information systems, without probable cause or judicial procedure (Gustafson 2009: 668–69). In addition to providing a tool for purging caseloads, the new process significantly raised the risks of welfare claiming for poor adults with unresolved criminal justice issues. To bolster the combing of welfare records, authorities also began to use social welfare offices as sites for sting operations to capture fugitive felons (Gustafson 2009: 669–70).

Cases of welfare fraud took on a more criminological meaning during this period and were drawn into the orbit of "zero tolerance" law enforcement. The 1996 law required states to design their own fraud prevention programs. A number of states, including some of the most populous,[2] adopted new biometric imaging procedures (Gustafson 2009: 674). By photographing and/or fingerprinting applicants, officials argued they would improve their ability to catch fugitive felons and "double dippers" using aliases to receive benefits from multiple jurisdictions. These police-style processing techniques rarely uncover fraud, despite their considerable cost. The California State Auditor (2003), for example, found that the state paid a private corporation $31 million for its finger-imaging system, and was paying $11.4 million per year to operate it, but typically found only one "duplicate" case per month that was worthy of further investigation.

Today, most fraud cases arise from more mundane actions, such as a client's failure to document changes in household composition or income status on a monthly report form. The consequences of such failures can be shockingly large. Instead of just leading to a loss of benefits, they can now be pursued as felony offenses by welfare fraud investigation units housed in district attorneys' offices (Gustafson 2009: 685). When reporting failures have benefit effects that are too minimal to justify criminal prosecution (less than $400), California follows a "three strikes and you're out" rule that imposes a lifetime ban on benefit receipt (Gustafson 2009: 685).

A conspicuous feature of this crackdown on recipient fraud is its contrast with the corporate fraud that has been facilitated by welfare reform. Because disciplinary poverty governance is an administration-intensive enterprise (Mead 2004a), its rapid rise in the 1990s called for capacities that few states possessed. On the penal side, states filled the gap by hiring for-profit providers such as Corrections Corporation of America (CCA) to build, staff, and operate new prisons (Wacquant 2009: 151–91). On the welfare side, federal reform called on the states to carry out a bold new agenda but invested little in the public sector capacities needed to do so. Thus, the turn to outsourcing was more than just a product of pro-market ideologies and corporate efforts to open new markets. In the states, it was a practical administrative necessity.

To quickly attract the capacities they needed, state officials offered contracts that promised substantial profits and limited red tape and regulation. The deals often became sweeter in negotiations, where inexperienced public officials had to work out the fine print with seasoned veterans of corporate bargaining. The resulting contracts usually provided public funds in decidedly "slushy" forms that invited waste, fraud, and abuse. Benchmarks were set for performance outcomes, but few procedures were created to track the use of public funds or monitor implementation processes. Indeed, because the federal law stated that welfare performance goals could be met through caseload reduction credits, private providers who shed large numbers of recipients could skirt even this minimal form of accountability.

Corruption and profiteering have been abiding themes of neoliberal economic reform in the developing world (Holmes 2006; E. Brown and Cloke 2005). They have also plagued U.S. military operations in recent years, as warfare and policing abroad have become more reliant on corporations such as Blackwater Inc. and Kellogg, Brown, and Root (Whyte 2007; Avant 2005). In domestic policy as well, neoliberalism has produced a seemingly endless cycle of deregulation and reregulation centered on "private abuses of the public interest" (L. Brown and Jacobs 2008).

In welfare, as in these other areas, outsourcing was advanced by framing prevailing conditions as a "crisis" that could be solved only by unleashing the dynamic capacities of loosely regulated markets (Klein 2007). Privatization was touted as a solution to the whole "welfare mess" of long-term dependency, bureaucratic waste, and client fraud. Indeed, one of the ironies of neoliberal reform is that corporate providers often hawk their wares by promising to do a better job combating bureaucratic waste and client fraud. ACS, for example, advertises its innovative solutions designed to "eliminate inefficiencies, analyze data for potential fraud, monitor online transactions to ensure appropriate use, and perform other functions to safeguard against fraud, waste, and abuse of government programs" (ACS 2009).

In reality, outsourcing has brought new capacities to the crackdown on recipient fraud, while initiating a far more expensive era of corporate malfeasance. By focusing on just a few of the most successful ongoing players (as opposed to the failures of smaller, discredited contractors), it is possible to suggest the broad scope and scale of this development.

In 1994–95, Governor George W. Bush led a failed effort to privatize Texas welfare services by hiring one of his major campaign contributors: the defense contractor, Lockheed Martin (Walters 2007). A decade later, Texas awarded a five-year, $899 million contract to a team of contractors led by Accenture Ltd., paying the group to screen welfare cases and run four regional call centers (in place of public welfare offices). Thirteen months into the contract, Accenture was cashing state checks without fail, but thousands of unprocessed applications had piled up; call centers were ignoring calls; and legitimate benefit claims were being mistakenly denied—sometimes with tragic consequences.[3] Amid growing outrage at what *Governing* magazine called a "multimillion-dollar meltdown," the state was forced to terminate the contract (Walters 2007). Yet even as the state "scrambled to rehire state employees to clean up the call-center mess, it was contracting out again" (Walters 2007). Accenture Ltd. went on to win lucrative new contracts in California and other states, while Texas offered a profitable new contract to Maximus Inc. to take over the call centers and other operations (Walters 2007).

In 2006, an IBM-led team that included ACS beat out Accenture Ltd. for a ten-year, $1.16 billion contract to process Food Stamp, Medicaid, and TANF applications through centralized call centers in Indiana (M. Smith 2006). The contract was promoted by Family and Social Service Administration Secretary Mitch Roob, a former employee of ACS, and in March 2007 more than 1,500 state employees were forced to leave unionized public jobs for nonunion positions at ACS (DeAgostino 2005). Under the new arrangement, Texas-style problems quickly emerged. Applicants were routinely sidetracked by lost documents, lengthy hold times, delays in application processing, and mistaken denials of eligibility (Kusmer 2007). The statewide automated call distribution systems failed "approximately twice a month, losing all calls in progress" (Kusmer 2007). Meanwhile, an Associated Press review in August 2009 revealed that the state's costs had risen $180 million (15 percent) beyond the price of the original contract (Kusmer 2007). In October 2009, Governor Daniels terminated the contract with the IBM-led group. Although he publicly declared that the outsourcing plan was a "flawed concept," the state quickly announced that it would establish new contracts with some of the for-profit providers that had worked with IBM, including ACS (Schneider and Ruthhart 2009).

As a purveyor of waste, fraud, and abuse, however, no corporation has succeeded in the welfare arena like Maximus Inc. In 1993 and 1994, problems with Maximus forced the state of Arizona to refund $250,000 in child support payments, doubled the cost of child support collection in Mississippi, and produced a scandal in West Virginia when it was revealed that a state supervisor (on a project that Maximus was bidding on) had been paid as a Maximus consultant. Despite this record, Maximus emerged as a go-to provider after welfare reform. In 1997, the company went public with an $87 million stock offering, as it won lucrative welfare contracts in states such as Connecticut and Wisconsin. After just three months of service in Connecticut, Maximus was over a month late in processing client checks and had a backlog of unprocessed applications. The company determined that it would have to hire additional staff to fix the problems, at a cost that would have yielded losses of $500,000 per month. Critics charged that Maximus "underbid, over-promised and didn't deliver," but the company succeeded in obtaining a $6 million (50 percent) increase in payments from the state (McGowan and Murphy 1999).

In Wisconsin, Maximus generated even larger scandals. In 2000, it was charged with "skimming" its most work-ready welfare recipients and funneling them into its own temporary employment subsidiary, MaxStaff (Millard 2000). Later, it was revealed that the wife of Jason Turner, a key architect of Wisconsin welfare reform, held a private meeting with Maximus officials that led to the hiring of her father as a consultant. Public dismay grew deeper still when the Legislative Audit Bureau uncovered malfeasance so significant that the state sought to withhold or recover $7.6 million in unearned payments. According to the audit, Maximus had spent $51,000 to pay employees seeking new contracts in other states, $196,000 on advertising to promote the Maximus brand, $15,741 on a staff party at an expensive resort, more than $23,000 to hire singer Melba Moore and a group of clowns to entertain corporate clients and staff, and $23,637 for corporate promotional items such as fanny packs and golf balls (DeParle 2004).

In New York City, Maximus built on its ties to Jason Turner, who had moved from Wisconsin to become the city's welfare commissioner. In the bidding process for a large welfare contract, it was revealed that a close friend of Turner's, Tony Kearney, was paid by Maximus while he served as a consultant to the city. Kearney was assigned to an office on the same floor as Turner's and was allowed to sit in on meetings that city officials held with Maximus's competitors. When these and other problems were revealed by the city's comptroller, Alan Hevesi, reporters dug deeper. They quickly found that when Maximus requested to be paid $4,620 per job placement, city officials had responded by *raising* the amount to $5,000 (Lipton 2001). Hevesi ultimately failed in his effort to block the Giuliani administration's contract with Maximus, which would remain in place until Mayor Bloomberg ended it in 2002 (Cooper 2002).

Just five years after welfare reform, in 2001, state and local governments were spending about $1.5 billion of public TANF funds per year on contracts with private service providers (U.S. General Accounting Office 2002). There is little evidence that this wave of outsourcing improved services for poor families or raised the efficiency and effectiveness of public investments. Instead, it created a permissive environment for profiteering and waste, fraud, and abuse that stood in stark contrast to the crackdown on welfare recipient fraud. Today, California welfare recipients can be charged with a felony crime for receiving as little as $400 in undue benefits, while corporate provider scandals that cost the public millions of dollars produce no criminal charges whatsoever. Neoliberal welfare reform has created two worlds of waste, fraud, and abuse: a disciplinary regime of heavy surveillance and penalty for poor families and a weakly regulated landscape of profits and corrupt spending practices for corporate service providers.

Privatizing Governance in the State of Florida

Like other states, Florida turned to outsourcing at the same time that it cracked down on fraud among welfare recipients. In the WT program, fraud penalties now follow a "three strikes and you're out" model that new applicants learn about through an orientation video. The video explains that if they provide incorrect information regarding, say, Social Security numbers or household composition, they can be charged with fraud. Penalties rise from a twelve-month eligibility ban (first infraction) to a twenty-four-month ban (second infraction) to a lifetime ban plus a fine of up to $250,000 and incarceration (third infraction). Immediately after noting the potential for "jail time," the video ends with an admonition from the narrator: "So, if you're going to apply for welfare, you have to be sure that you're not committing fraud."[4]

The story of privatization in Florida also parallels other states in its predictable narrative arc. In one policy area after another, conservative political leaders used crisis imagery and abstract claims of market superiority to outsource government operations. Program failures and financial scandals soon accumulated. Amid growing public outrage, state officials intervened to clean up the mess and issue calls for greater vigilance in the future. Having depleted state capacities through outsourcing, however, they usually found it difficult to do anything other than substitute a new contractual partner for the discredited provider they had just dismissed.

Beginning in the late 1990s, Florida Republicans passed a series of measures to outsource state services. These changes were aggressively promoted by Republican Governor Jeb Bush (1999–2006), who promised to reduce the size of government and improve conditions for Florida businesses. Two years into his first term, the *Tampa Tribune* concluded that "virtually every major initiative the governor has launched since his election has aimed to help business and the economy. Record tax cuts have benefited corporations and Floridians with stock portfolios. And the Legislature has passed bills giving the manufacturers of everything from escalators to jetliners financial protection from injured consumers who file lawsuits" (Wasson 2001).

Outsourcing emerged as the most ambitious element of Bush's pro-business agenda. Speaking at the state capitol in January 2003, Bush pointed to the government buildings around him and declared: "There would be no greater tribute to our maturity as a society than if we can make these buildings around us empty of workers—silent monuments to the time when government played a larger role than it deserved or could adequately fill" (A. Smith 2003). The Bush administration initiated 138 separate outsourcing projects during this period, sometimes abolishing whole state agencies (Cotterell 2006). Corporations were hired to run foster care and collect child support payments, operate prisons and identify felons on voter registration rolls, maintain public parks and fisheries, manage pay and benefits for state employees, license and monitor regulated professions such as engineering, and carry out a host of other state functions. Across the board, Bush "put the state's workforce on notice that the long-held notion of government service as a lifelong career is essentially dead in today's economy. State workers have been told they must compete with private companies for their jobs" (Wasson 2001).

Programs for the poor were targeted for a particularly thorough outsourcing effort that quickly led to charges of corruption and cronyism.[5] In 2006, the former head of the Department of Corrections and an aide admitted to taking more than $135,000 in kickbacks from for-profit prison vendors they hired (*Tampa Tribune* 2006b). In 2004, the head of the Florida Department of Children and Families (DCF) resigned after admitting that he and two top aides accepted gifts from companies before hiring them to run child welfare services (Ackerman and Jones 2004). The scope of corrupt contracting was further underscored by the special commission established to privatize casework and vocational-rehabilitation services for people with disabilities:

Six of the panel's 16 members [had] ties to the service providers who
[were] in a position to profit from the contracts the panel award[ed]. One
commissioner resigned when it was disclosed that a company he headed
sought $5.3 million in contracts throughout the state. When the privatiza-
tion plan was scaled back from a statewide effort to a handful of counties,
the commissioner was awarded two of the first three contracts, for a total
of $1.1 million in work. (C. Miller 2001)

It is hard to know whether a less corrupt process would have yielded the
promised savings and performance gains. In practice, however, neither came to
fruition. Two years after the privatization of disability services began in 1999,
the state found that the effort resulted in fewer clients being served and a decline in service effectiveness (C. Miller 2001). In 2006, a state audit found that
child welfare costs increased by 70 percent after privatization, and Florida children experienced an increased incidence of abuse (*Tampa Tribune* 2006a).

To promote entrepreneurial innovation, reformers emphasized the need to
limit state regulations and monitoring. Market competition, they argued, would
swiftly punish inappropriate or wasteful uses of state funds. Billing scandals
soon emerged. In 2005, for example, a state audit found that two prison vendors received $12.7 million in undeserved funds: "The money went for guards
who didn't exist and enabled Corrections Corp. of America and GEO Group to
misuse funds that are obligated to the welfare of inmates (chaplain and library
services, for example) and to avoid minimal training requirements for several
groups of prison employees. They even helped pay expenses of the agency policing their contracts" (*Tallahassee Democrat* 2005).

It was in this broader context that Florida passed the Workforce Innovation
Act of 2000, replacing its old TANF program, WAGES, with the more privatized, localized, and performance-driven WT program. The new law effectively
dismantled Florida's Department of Labor and stripped Florida DCF of control
over local operations. In their place, a statewide public-private partnership between Workforce Florida Inc. (WFI) and the Agency for Workforce Innovation
(AWI) was created to oversee local poverty governance. The twenty-four Regional Workforce Boards (RWBs) that held primary authority were required by
law to outsource service provision.

The reformers who pushed for these changes adopted the standard neoliberal tactic of substituting market models of efficiency and accountability for
more conventional criteria. Promises of efficiency emphasized the pressures of
vendor competition, while downplaying questions of institutional design. The

old system ran through a simple hierarchical relationship between state and local DCF offices. To make it more "efficient," reformers created a byzantine network of cross-sector collaborations. DCF would continue to receive federal TANF funds and assess client eligibility, but it would have only a contractual relationship with the state's public-private policy authority, WFI. WFI, in turn, would have a memorandum of understanding with AWI, the state entity charged with monitoring and incentivizing the local RWBs. The RWBs would then be responsible for negotiating their own separate contractual agreements with private service providers, who, in turn, would be held responsible for results through performance-based pay points tied to statewide benchmarks.

The superiority of the market model was embraced as an article of faith, rarely tempered by attention to organizational realities. As Senator Jim King, a Republican champion of welfare outsourcing, put it: "I have always thought that private business can do better at filling jobs than the state government can" (Parks 2000). The Democratic Senate Minority Leader, Tom Rossin, summed up the prevailing ethos by stating that "the Bush administration seems to be privatizing for privatization's sake. There seems to be an assumption that a [provider] outside of government can do it better automatically than the state doing it themselves" (Wasson 2001).

Our interviews with WT officials later in the decade confirmed the persistence of this belief. When describing daily operations, frontline workers would tick off a host of frustrating problems arising from onerous, profit-driven rules and from the need to coordinate across so many entities. But when asked about privatization in general, most would offer an almost-mythical contrast in which lean and nimble private providers outshine stagnant, inefficient state bureaucracies. Even the most critical workers in our interviews, who suggested that "privatization is really handing it to mercenaries," would use images of the "bad old days" of AFDC to legitimate the current system: "When it was the state, it wasn't handled right, and that's why it was privatized."

To workers in rural regions with small budgets, the routine conversion of TANF dollars into corporate profits seemed to be an especially inefficient use of public funds. The following exchange from a group interview highlights the opportunity costs that many of these frontline workers perceive.

Employee 1: There's a big push from corporate-level executives to bring in the money. Higher level executives get bonuses for meeting certain standards and the money goes either to them or the corporation instead of going to the individuals [who] really need that money to be able to succeed.

Employee 2: Absolutely.

Employee 3: [The money] doesn't come back to the region. [It] all goes back to the corporation [and] stockholders. So how does that help us? And I'm Republican, by gosh! Why should my tax dollars go toward that? What could ten thousand dollars more in this region do? A lot. We could benefit from [those] 10 or 20 thousand or 30 thousand [dollars]. We could put people in training. We can expand their opportunities and get them off of welfare, until they are self-sufficient. Why don't we have so many education opportunities for these people? We should be able to send everyone to college [who's] ready for it and train them up to 20 bucks an hour. That's a success story. But we don't have that opportunity [because] we don't have the money for it.

Reformers also approached questions of accountability through a market frame, stressing the bottom-line mentality of customer satisfaction. In the 1990s, Governor Lawton Chiles promoted this shift, downplaying the importance of transparency and citizen participation, while distributing hundreds of copies of *Reinventing Government* (Osborne and Gaebler 1992) to state employees. The Bush administration tilted further still, ignoring institutional dimensions of accountability while stressing how performance-centered markets hold providers accountable. Under the old system, a single entity, Florida DCF, could be held responsible for implementation outcomes at all levels. Under the new system, failures would emerge from a complex collaboration of organizations in which blame could easily be deflected from one to another.

Equally important, by devolving contracting authority to local RWBs, the new law created a sphere of unmonitored and unknowable contracting practices. Since 1967, Florida has had a strong system of "sunshine laws" requiring that state hearings and documents, including contracts, be open to the public. Unlike the DCF, however, local RWBs are not state entities. As a result, the terms of their private contracts with providers fall outside the sunshine laws: They cannot be accessed by citizens, advocacy groups, or even state officials.

In our research, we hoped to analyze how local contracts influenced WT outcomes. When we asked for contract information, however, senior officials at WFI and AWI reported that even they had no idea how pay points and agreements varied across the twenty-four regions. Indeed, one reported several cases in which inexperienced RWB members had been "taken to the cleaners" in the bargains they struck with veteran corporate negotiators. The terms of these contracts were discovered long after the fact, when AWI officials asked about low performance numbers and high expenditures, and were told that little could be changed in light of existing contracts.

In addition to producing weak contracts, the limited capacities of local RWBs translated into loose oversight. In designing the new system, reformers claimed that accountability would be achieved through performance systems that closely monitored program results and used them as a basis for pay points. Process oversight was subordinated to outcome analysis, and outcomes were measured primarily through the *self-reports* providers supplied. Providers had financial incentives to cook their numbers and confronted few barriers to spending funds in questionable ways. As a senior ACS manager told us in an interview: "There is always the incentive there to, uh, not *make* your numbers but to *make up* your numbers." The full scope of unreported problems cannot be known, but the most publicized scandals paint a damning portrait.[6]

In 2003, ACS reported that nearly 70 percent of businesses in Miami-Dade and Monroe counties were using its services, compared to a state average of 30 percent. An investigation revealed that ACS was copying entries from new-hire reports filed with the Florida Department of Revenue, and falsely claiming that the new jobs had been obtained through its services (Caputo 2004a). A second investigation focused on 219 cases in which ACS claimed that it had secured relatively high-paying jobs for WT clients. ACS was able to verify employment in only half the cases, and, in 57 percent of these, ACS had reported higher salaries than the workers were actually making (Caputo 2004a). A third audit, targeting a separate group of 335 cases in which ACS claimed that it had secured well-paying jobs for WT clients, again revealed that almost half the cases had paychecks at odds with ACS claims. The *Miami Herald* reported: "In some cases, ACS personnel filled out wage-information forms that were actually supposed to be completed by the employers. In one case, according to the audit, when the employer corrected the earnings information, ACS whited out the correction and resubmitted a false wage that was $5.40 an hour higher" (Caputo 2004b). Estimates suggest that these actions may have earned ACS up to $1.4 million in performance-based bonus payments that it did not deserve (Caputo 2004b).

As a governance fiasco of epic proportions, however, no scandal surpasses the events that unfolded after Pinellas County awarded a $15 million contract to Lockheed Martin IMS in 1999.[7] In the summer of 2000, Pinellas County administrator Rick Dodge received complaints about Lockheed, which boasted of having placed 893 of its clients in new jobs. When Dodge asked for details, Lockheed refused, citing "confidentiality concerns." When an audit was initiated, Lockheed was able to document only seven placements, including one at an Arby's restaurant and another at a topless bar called "Baby Dolls." In response, Dodge and a senior associate, Janet Gifford-Meyers, adopted a whistle-blowing strategy, contacting the state attorney's office and calling for a full-scale "forensic audit" of Lockheed operations.

Dodge and Gifford-Meyers's concerns were bolstered when another targeted inquiry found that Lockheed had double- and triple-billed the county for services. Yet the state refused to initiate a forensic audit and told the county that it would have to pay for it alone. When county officials took up this question, they were informed by the county attorney that a forensic audit would cost between $300,000 and $500,000; recovered funds would go to the state, not the county; and because the contract was poorly drafted, the county could be held liable for Lockheed's fraud. "What we are going to end up with," she warned, "is with a smoking gun that points at you."

Meanwhile, amid the charges made by Dodge and Gifford-Meyers, Lockheed unilaterally withdrew from its contract and suspended operations. In response, Pinellas officials stopped paying the company's outstanding invoices. As the standoff escalated, Lockheed sold its government services unit to ACS, which promptly sued Pinellas County for roughly $2 million in unpaid invoices—payments for Lockheed's earlier work that ACS counted as part of its new $825 million purchase. As Pinellas officials sought to avoid a costly court battle by making a $612,000 payment to ACS, the fates of the two whistle-blowers took a sharp turn for the worse.

In 2002, Rick Dodge was fired by Pinellas County for exercising "poor judgment." Dodge sued the county for wrongful termination, and, in 2006, the county settled out of court for $170,000. Janet Gifford-Meyers was not so fortunate. Throughout the scandal, she claimed that she was being harassed and threatened by Lockheed. When her body was found in a local state park in 2001, the death was ruled a suicide. Her husband sued Lockheed Martin for wrongful death, claiming that its officials and paid surrogates (including a local woman named "Momma Tee" Lassiter, whom Lockheed hired for $15,000) had driven Gifford-Meyers to kill herself through "intentional infliction of emotional distress [and] placement in a false light."[8] Lockheed Martin settled the lawsuit out of court for an undisclosed sum.

As scandals accumulated in the Florida WT program, broader frustrations with outsourcing emerged as well. Indeed, the Florida experience has paralleled the national pattern. As promised gains have failed to materialize, government officials have repeatedly been forced to expand state regulation, scale back outsourcing efforts, or shift to new providers (L. Brown and Jacobs 2008;

Vestal 2006). Virtually all of the reformers' promises—greater efficiency, accountability, savings, performance, and so on—depended on the same mechanism: competitive pressures that arise as multiple bidders vie for contracts. In practice, however, social service contracts have usually drawn only a handful of "high-quality bidders" and have often gone to sole bidders (Handler and Hasenfeld 2007: 201–5). During the extended periods of contracts, vendors enjoy long stretches of competition-free operation, and public sector capacities dwindle to the point where "de-privatization" becomes a costly, long-term proposition (AFSCME 2006). In the Florida WT program, providers have turned over with some frequency, not because new rounds of competition have yielded different victors, but because a few major corporate players have sold their contracts to one another in an ongoing search for the most profitable holdings.

Nationally, privatization has rarely produced the savings its advocates have promised (Vestal 2006; Progressive States Network 2007). In the Florida WT program, it has also led to a steady stream of costly fraud investigations and efforts to recover misspent funds. For these and other reasons, a number of RWBs began to question the state rule that required them to contract with private providers. Acting at their behest, state officials enacted legislation in June 2008 that, for the first time, made it possible for RWBs to "to be designated as a one-stop operator and direct provider of intake, assessment, eligibility determinations, or other direct provider services except training services." In August 2009, AWI reported that thirteen regions had elected to shift from contracts to direct provision. In telephone interviews we conducted with seven of these regions, executive directors said their decisions reflected a growing consensus that revenue-minded providers (1) maintained poorly trained, high-turnover staffs; (2) reported performance numbers plagued by errors and falsifications; (3) submitted vague bookkeeping and poorly documented expenses; (4) churned recipients off the welfare rolls to improve their performance numbers; and (5) engaged in excessive profit taking as a normal practice.

It is telling that, when given the chance, thirteen of the state's twenty-four RWBs elected to retreat from contracting. The limits of this retreat are, however, equally striking. Eleven regions chose to continue contracting with private providers, and among the other thirteen, a number have had difficulties extricating themselves from existing contracts. Even in the cases in which RWBs have switched entirely to direct provision, it should be noted that local provision continues to operate outside the public sector. By law, employers must make up 50 percent or more of the RWBs' members, and their semiprivate governing activities remain beyond the reach of Florida sunshine laws. After a decade of welfare privatization, the government capacities needed to take over local welfare operations no longer exist, and, outside labor unions, there is virtually no discussion of rebuilding them. The Florida WT program is moving forward with a mix of privatized governing arrangements. And as the challenges of direct provision become more apparent, it seems likely that contracting (the most viable alternative) will become attractive once again—amid hopes that new management strategies will make the next time different.

Servicing and Subsidizing Markets

As neoliberalism has brought new actors to welfare provision, it has also redefined what welfare programs do. Under the business model, employers and low-income families are approached as dual clienteles: they are coproducers of the job placements that stand at the center of the welfare mission. Services and subsidies for employers are the counterparts to "work first" policies that aim to bring discipline to the dependent poor. Together, they enact a neoliberal vision of welfare policy as a labor-market supplier. The contrast with traditional images of the welfare state is profound. Instead of offering a decommodified space of needs-based relief, welfare providers serve as disciplinary agents of commodification that serve the market.

On their websites, virtually all Florida RWBs advertise their efforts to make job-ready workers available and attractive to employers. JobsPlus states that its mission is to ensure that "every business has access to employees that meet their needs." Workforce Plus tells employers, "We are excited to assist you with your workforce needs through an aggressive and proactive [approach to ensuring] that our community has a well-prepared, educated, and adaptable workforce that meets the current and future needs of its employers." In another region, the welfare provider calls itself the Center for Business Excellence and bills itself as "The Area's #1 Resource for Business." It declares that its goal is "to help our business communities reduce recruitment costs" and "attain and maintain qualified employees at no additional cost."[9]

Employers who visit the Pasco-Hernando Region website discover that "our business is helping you make the most of yours," and, on the Brevard website, they learn that "by actively recruiting welfare-to-work recipients, you can expand your job applicant pool of entry-level workers." Low-income families seeking assistance receive a less solicitous message that stresses the work-first model of personal growth. At the Workforce Alliance site for the Chipola Regional Workforce Development Board, they are reminded that "welfare is temporary,

not an entitlement. The only dead-end job is welfare. The program seeks to provide jobs, which result in a better job, and, ultimately, a career." The Workforce
Plus website elaborates on how skillful self-commodification will pave the way
to personal success: "To stand out [in the applicant pool], you must have a flaw-
less, skillfully crafted marketing document [résumé]. Once you land a job, the
next step is to maximize your value as an employee."[10]

The messages conveyed on RWB websites fit well with the practices we found
in our field research. WT clients are subjected to a variety of tutelary interventions that seek to instill work commitments, teach employee compliance, and
describe the promising tomorrows that will flow from an entry-level job today.
Instead of offering clients educational and training programs to raise their wage
potential, one-stops direct clients to the low-wage hiring fairs they host for local
employers. In this sense, the one-stops operate as biased workforce intermediaries: They ask a great deal from clients while offering them little; they offer a
great deal to employers while asking little from them in return. Their goal is to
make people more suitable for existing jobs, not to make jobs more suitable for
people trying to raise children in difficult circumstances (Peck 2001). As one
frustrated case manager explained to us:

> We can tell [clients] to go work minimum wage at McDonalds, but that's
> not the point. They are not going to be able to live off that maybe if they
> have three other jobs, then yeah, then they can support themselves. [But]
> we're not going to be able to go to Red Lobster and say, "You need to pay
> your people $15 an hour so they can live." It's a business. They're there
> to make money, so they're not going to increase their wages that much.
> [And] a lot of our main purpose [at the one-stop center] is to draw these
> industries here. It's not that easy.

Although their personal views vary, most case managers describe rapid job
placement as the priority at their one-stop centers. In our statewide survey, we
asked, "Which goal *should be* given more importance at the agency where you
work: helping clients get jobs as quickly as possible or raising clients' skill levels
so they can get better jobs in the future?" While 41.1 percent of case managers
favored raising skills, only 12.5 percent favored work first. When asked what was
"given more importance *at the agency where you work*," 52.4 percent said work
first, while only 7.7 percent said raising skills.[11] As one case manager explained,
the primary mission is "trying to develop more jobs, more business for people,
more employees, more goods and services, bringing more tourists into the econ-

omy, and bringing that labor market information. [When we do our job,] the unemployment rate goes down which is better for the market, for the economy."

In addition to hosting hiring fairs where businesses can shop for employees, many one-stops conduct workshops to teach local employers how they can benefit from welfare programs. In Brevard County, for example, the RWB held a "learning event for business owners, executives, managers and HR professionals" titled "Success from Strengths: Growing Your Bottom Line through Employee Strengths." Through these and related events, one-stops function as state-sponsored adjuncts to local hiring operations. On the WorkNet Pinellas website, one employer states, "I feel like we're dealing with a professional staffing company. We consider WorkNet an extension of our recruiting team." This view is echoed by Wal-Mart: "WorkNet has exceeded our expectations by providing outstanding diligence and attention to detail in assisting us with meeting our hiring goals." A third employer praises WorkNet's "private interviewing rooms, telephones, copy machine, Internet access and [separate] employer services area," and goes on to state, "The accommodations that are provided by WorkNet are not only outstanding but are above any accommodations that are provided to us by other interviewing locations!"[12]

To celebrate the employers who hire their clients, some RWBs give out awards. And in an era of massive incarceration growth, correctional facilities often turn up among the winners. Workforce Plus, for example, gave its 2007–08 Employer of the Year Award to the Wakulla Correctional Institution. In accepting it, the warden of the facility stated, "The service you provided to Wakulla in the hiring of correctional officers is the best we ever witnessed, hiring 170 employees in less than four months has to be a record." That same year, Workforce Plus partnered with the corporate corrections contractor GEO Blackwater and awarded an Employer of the Quarter Award to the for-profit Corrections Corporation of America (CCA).[13]

Beyond their efforts to supply low-wage workers, welfare one-stops collaborate directly with business interests in a variety of other ways. At one local agency we visited, the program manager held up a large three-ring binder with "Wal-Mart" written on the side. She explained that she worked with Wal-Mart on so many different aspects of the program—job placements, work activities, employer workshops, purchasing goods and gift cards—that it was easier to keep all the papers in one place. Indeed, Wal-Mart's interests were served through the very act of distributing benefits to WT clients. To incentivize the completion of work-activity hours (which allow providers to make their pay points), case managers give clients gift cards as a reward each week. Like scrip at the company store, clients who document thirty or more hours of weekly work activity receive cash substitutes that can be spent only at a single business: a $25 card to Wal-Mart and a $10 card to Shell Oil. Over the month, the client's $240 WT check can be augmented by $140 in this way, meaning that 37 percent of the funds going to the client are channeled through two corporations that enjoy gains whenever the gift cards are redeemed.

Neoliberal efforts to incentivize welfare-to-work transitions also benefit employers in a more direct way. The Welfare-to-Work tax credit, created in 1996 and later folded into the broader Work Opportunity Tax Credit (WOTC), is a federal program designed to give private employers incentives to hire TANF recipients (Hamersma 2005). Under the program, employers can receive subsidies of up to $9,000, covering as much as 40 percent of a former TANF recipient's wages. In fiscal year 2008, employers received WOTC payments for over 691,000 "certified" U.S. employees (U.S. Department of Labor 2009). From 2000 to 2008, welfare-to-work payments alone cost the federal government approximately $650 million in lost tax revenues (U.S. Office of Management and Budget 2010). WOTC payments as a whole cost $3.7 billion during this period. Meanwhile, the most careful study of the tax credits, assembled by the Urban-Brookings Tax Policy Center, concludes that "no meaningful increase in the employment of the disadvantaged can be attributed to the programs" (Hamersma 2005: 4). Firms rarely change their hiring patterns in response to the tax credits; they usually just claim the tax credits as windfall gains for workers they would have hired anyway (Hamersma 2005).

In all these respects, neoliberalism has blurred the state-market boundary that once defined welfare programs. Yet proactive efforts to service employers and transform clients have not rendered older methods of labor regulation obsolete. They have deepened and elaborated on older strategies for controlling the accessibility, generosity, and stigma of public aid (Piven and Cloward 1971). In the WT program, benefits are kept extremely low and one-stop centers limit program entry in a variety of ways (see chapter 9). On the exit side of the program, sanctions for noncompliance provide a coercive way to force clients out into the local labor pool. Indeed, sanctioning patterns offer perhaps the clearest illustration of how the system's new disciplinary emphasis gets woven together with older strategies of administrative exclusion.

Prior to the welfare rights movement of the 1960s, local control allowed agencies to provide welfare in a manner calibrated to local labor market needs (Piven and Cloward 1971). This dynamic took its most overt forms in southern welfare agencies that served large numbers of African American agricultural workers. Local officials provided subsistence benefits in a highly seasonal manner, doling them out when the fields lay idle and shuttering their operations when hands were needed in the fields (Piven and Cloward 1971; Lieberman 1998). Today, of course, local providers cannot pursue the blunt, collective strategy of closing down their offices. Sanctions, however, provide an individualized tool that can be used in a similar manner, to push welfare clients out in waves that are pegged to seasonal variations in labor market needs.

To examine this possibility, we can take advantage of Florida's high level of dependence on the seasonal tourism industry, which brought 76.8 million visitors and $57 billion to the state in 2004.[14] If sanctioning is calibrated to seasonal changes in labor needs, sanction rates should rise during the months when employers need more hands on deck to serve the influx of visitors. As a first cut at this question, we can simply plot how monthly changes in state tourism revenues align with monthly changes in the risk of a WT client being sanctioned. To measure sanction risks in a way that controls for individual and local differences, we use hazard ratios generated by the multivariate model described in chapter 7 (see discussions of figures 7-4 and 7-5). Figure 8-1 plots these monthly hazard ratios against monthly tax revenues generated by the Florida tourism industry. At this high level of aggregation, we observe a remarkably tight relationship. The correlation between the two series is an astonishing r = .95.

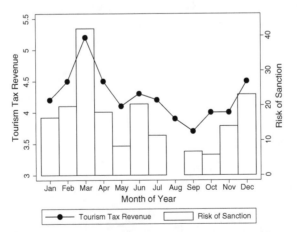

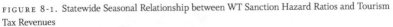

FIGURE 8-1. Statewide Seasonal Relationship between WT Sanction Hazard Ratios and Tourism Tax Revenues

Note: The "risk of sanction" is the percentage increase in the risk of sanction, compared to the baseline month (August). These values were calculated from monthly indicator variables used in the survival model analysis discussed in chapter 7 and reflected in figure 7-1. More details concerning this analysis are available in our online appendix.

By moving down to the county level, we can provide a more stringent multivariate test that conforms to the idea that devolution promotes local labor market calibration. A county-level analysis also allows us to provide a further test of the RCM's prediction that efforts to discipline labor participation become more intense when African Americans are more prevalent in the welfare caseload. To test these expectations, we apply a multivariate OLS regression analysis to panel time-series data spanning the twenty-four-month period from January 2002 through December 2003. All variables are measured at the county level, and county fixed effects are included to control for unobserved local differences, thus ensuring that our results only reflect variation over time within counties. The dependent variable consists of each county's reported sanction rate in each month of observation, where the sanction rate is measured as the percentage of the adult caseload that was sanctioned that month. The independent variables include our key predictors—monthly tourism revenues (as a percentage of county tax revenues) and the percentage of the county WT caseload that is black—as well as a number of other relevant control variables.[15]

Among our control variables, the most noteworthy result is for county unemployment, which provides a general indicator of how sanction rates respond to local labor availability. As expected, welfare recipients are sanctioned off the rolls at significantly higher rates when local employers confront tighter labor markets. The results for our key variables, illustrated in figure 8-2, are observed above and beyond this general responsiveness to local labor needs. Consistent

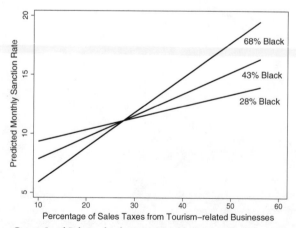

FIGURE 8-2. County-Level Relationship between Monthly Tourism Tax Revenues and Predicted Monthly Sanction Rates by Black Percent of the County WT Caseload

with our statewide analysis, we find a strong seasonal relationship. In the months when county tourism revenues expand, county sanction rates rise as well. In addition, we find the expected interaction with racial composition. Consistent with the predictions of the RCM, the significant seasonal relationship observed when blacks make up 28 percent of the caseload (the 10th percentile value in our sample) becomes far stronger as the black percentage rises to 43 percent (the median) and then 68 percent (the 90th percentile value). Here, as in other areas of our analysis, we find that disciplinary poverty governance operates to service local labor markets and pursues this agenda more vigorously when confronted with black policy targets.

The Business Model and Organizational Culture

Our analysis thus far has emphasized the material dimensions of marketization. To grasp the business model of governance, however, one must also come to grips with neoliberalism as a project of cultural transformation. Reformers in the 1990s applied discourses of pathology not just to the poor, but also to the bureaucracies that served them. The organizational cultures of welfare agencies were derided as "fundamentally flawed" (Winston et al. 2002). Paternalists argued that the problems of the underclass were fostered by permissive, paper-processing mentalities in AFDC offices (Mead 1992). To change the culture of welfare programs, neoliberals used contracts to move operations out of older state agencies and worked to "reinvent" government itself according to the principles that make successful corporations productive and dynamic (Diller 2000; Osborne and Gaebler 1992).

Did their efforts succeed in creating a marketized organizational culture in the Florida WT program? Does the business model function today as a dominant ideology, shaping the norms and worldviews of street-level workers? If one focuses on the "front stage" of organizational life, where public interactions and self-presentations play out (Goffman 1959), the answer would seem to be yes. As we have already seen, WT officials at all levels cite the business model as an organizing principle. Its rationality pervades official communications, from event announcements and website publications to core statements of organizational mission. A closer look inside the one-stop center, based on our field research, underscores the cultural primacy of the business model on the front stage of organizational life.

Consider, for example, the built spaces of one-stop centers, where WT workers interact with one another and their clients (Yanow 2006). Moving from room to room, one encounters a steady stream of interiors designed to imitate the trappings of the corporate world and stress market values and goals. In some of the best-funded urban locations, one-stops look and feel like successful businesses. Their carpeted waiting rooms contain fashionable furniture placed in conversational arrangements; their walls are lined with banks of up-to-date computers. These spaces are inviting, impressive, and carefully scripted around the business model. Flat-screen televisions show pictures of well-dressed women with briefcases, as they cycle through a variety of résumé tips and motivational exhortations. Posters extol the values of work and praise the business partnerships that are building a better community for all. Meeting spaces in the one-stops are adorned with titles such as the Excellence Room and the Opportunity Room.

Small, rural offices are rarely able to match the businesslike environments of the larger operations. But they participate in the same aesthetic on a reduced scale. The Opportunity Room looks a bit more beleaguered, and the tips for success appear on a white board instead of a flat-screen, but the message conveyed is largely the same: You (clients) are competing in the business world, and we (agency workers) are in the business of making you more competitive.

As the Opportunity Room suggests, strained efforts to impose market-friendly, business-sounding labels have become a defining feature of organizational culture under welfare reform. Indeed, the RWB that named its agency the Center for Business Excellence falls into the linguistic mainstream of the WT program. WT recipients are almost always referred to as customers or candidates (as in job candidates). Welfare case managers are called career counselors. A mother with a disabled child is classified as having a "work barrier," and nearly every relationship in the one-stop setting is described as a contract of some sort.

The business model, however, is more than just a project of renaming and reframing. It is a system of regulative norms for public interaction. Agency personnel at all levels are supposed to look and behave as if they are working in a professional, corporate environment. Case managers are expected to maintain professional distance when working with clients and remain focused on employment goals. Staff members who are seen as over-identifying with clients or getting too deeply involved with their problems risk being seen as unprofessional and "old school" (in the AFDC sense). Clients are expected to arrive as an employee would, dressed appropriately, on time, and free of personal encumbrances. As one senior state official explained, "We're supposed to be business-friendly. And I hate to tell you, that does not mean having a bunch of kids running around at the one-stop [when clients meet with their case managers]." In the neoliberal frame, the fact that children are a majority of WT clients is rendered irrelevant.

Steeped as they are in this environment, one might imagine that frontline workers internalize the business model and enact it with enthusiasm. The coherent ethos that pervades front-stage culture, however, is complicated by tensions that rise to the surface in the conversations that workers have with one another (and with interviewers) behind the scenes. In these "back-stage" settings, one finds that marketization has given rise to a culture of profound ambivalence. Many of the case managers we interviewed were deeply conflicted about the business model, extolling it one moment and lamenting it the next.

The focal point for this ambivalence, in many cases, is the business model's relentless focus on profitability. Our informants were somewhat divided on the question of whether nonprofits are as revenue driven as for-profits. Many argued that, because of their revenue needs, nonprofits focus just as much on contractual pay points, even though they lack shareholders. Others disagreed. Beliefs about for-profits were more uniform, however. As one official put it, "for-profit is about profits period, bottom line and then some."

Relentless attention to the bottom line underwrites a potent atmosphere of insecurity among case managers. Most know that they have been hired as low-skilled workers who can easily be replaced and that service contracts are traded as commodities according to the returns they generate. Putting these observations together, they draw the obvious conclusion:

> [The pay point] matters a lot. For me, it would be my job. If I don't make any pay points, and we lose the contract, well everyone's in trouble at that point. Let's say we don't get nothing for 6 months. That puts me more at risk. I mean, [the corporate investors] just don't get money and then they're not very interested in [continuing on]. Either they're going to switch me out [for another worker], or they're going to say this [region's] contract's not worth it.

These insecurities about job loss are compounded by resentments regarding the organizational disruptions that result from the buying and selling of service operations. Welfare operations get sold off when they generate weak revenues; they are acquired by investors who think they can make them more profitable. New owners typically sweep away settled routines and force frontline workers to adapt to new expectations and procedures. As one case manager put it, "you have a completely different company [saying] 'You need to be doing this, you need to be doing this, doing this, doing this.'" Turnover of this sort can be driven by either party to the service contract, the RWB or the provider, and the resulting disruptions can affect workers' long-term security as much as their work routines. As one case manager explained:

> [If outcomes are poor, the RWB] can say, "You know what, we're tired of [this provider]. We're going to renegotiate." And from [the provider's] standpoint, they could say, "We're not making good money on this. We don't want the contract anymore." Pretty much everyone [working] here has been through the [different] service providers, including me. You know, so we just go to the next group, the next group. [We have to worry about] profit. If we fail, the [RWB] fails, if the [RWB] fails, they lose money from the state and then we are all screwed, pretty much. When [the provider] goes away, we're stuck holding the bag. It's a very fluid business. I mean, what retirement plan can we have when we are bouncing from company to company every 2 years?

Thus, the same case managers who praise the business model for its innovation and focus also tend to see it as a source of organizational disruption and personal insecurity. The resulting ambivalence is deepened by more fundamental conflicts related to professional mission and identity.

Of all the actors in the WT program, case managers are positioned to experience most intimately the clash of social needs and market pressures. They work in organizations that focus on the financial bottom line and work-first placements. But they spend their days with clients whose problems are real and deep, who are anxious for their children, who long to escape poverty, and who have come to them for help. They want their difficult daily work to have a purpose and to mean something more than the numbers on a balance sheet. As a result, most continue to value traditional images of caseworkers as sympathetic counselors who provide much-needed social services and help people solve their problems. Beneath the dominant ethos of the business model runs a potent counterdiscourse rooted in experiences with clients' lives and values of social service and caregiving.

> They say that we're not, how would you say it a social service agency in a sense, like we're a business. But at the same time you're working with people who have needs, who have barriers, and bringing the two together

is very difficult. It's hard for me to sit with an individual there telling me that they've been evicted from their apartment, they don't have any place to live, they don't have any food, they don't have any clothes. And then here I am as a case manager: "You have to participate at 40 hours a week." You know, it's just kind of, it's crazy!

On one side, WT case managers derive important aspects of professional identity from the business model. They frequently contrast themselves with disparaged "government bureaucrats" and embrace the idea that they are engaged in an innovative business enterprise. As described earlier, they stress the important contributions they are making to the community by supporting local employers and promoting economic growth.[16] On the other side, these sources of positive professional identity are countered by aspects of the business model (profit maximization, inflexible work enforcement, and so on) that threaten to dehumanize the client-caseworker relationship. As client compliance becomes a means toward multiple ends, case managers are pushed toward a stance of indifference that many find hard to reconcile with their conceptions of human compassion.[17]

Many discuss the bottom-line mentality of the business model in regretful or hushed tones, as if sharing an unattractive insider's secret: "Gosh, it's all about the numbers [laughs]. Are you sure no one [at the one-stop] is going to hear this? OK, we have to meet the numbers. It's surviving by numbers, numbers, numbers." Some find it painful to think about the gap between their hopes of helping the needy and their daily experiences implementing TANF policy:

> The policymakers need to come and sit in our chairs for a while and see. Do they even understand the welfare program? There has to be another way. I was a Mom. I was at home, until things changed in my life. I was on welfare, so I know partially what these people are going through. I can remember feeling ashamed. Society makes it that way. Is that where we're going to be one day? There should always be a system to help people. I always hoped there would be because [pauses, sobs].

As this quotation suggests, marketization has not imposed a seamless governing mentality on frontline workers. It has produced an organizational culture in which case manager identities and commitments are shifting and contested. Case managers do not "buy in" to the neoliberal agenda, internalizing it as a hegemonic ideology and enacting it as their own free will (Ridzi 2009). They experience it, sometimes with pride and sometimes with dismay, as the organizing reality of their daily routines. Most feel torn by conflicting emotions when they reflect on the business model and its implications for the work they do. Their ambivalence raises the critical question of how such case managers can be relied on to carry out the work of disciplinary poverty governance—a question we will take up more directly in chapter 9.

Conclusion

In this chapter, we have taken an empirical approach to the neoliberal agenda of marketization, asking how it has actually proceeded on the ground. One advantage to this strategy is that it reveals the complexity of historical change and continuity in practice. In the neoliberal era, poverty governance has moved forward along familiar paths, even as it has been marketized in unprecedented ways. Older forms of labor regulation, such as administrative exclusion, coexist with new uses of welfare programs to subsidize and service labor markets. Traditional social work values persist in counterdiscourses, just beneath the surface of jaunty claims that the business model has swept them into the dustbin of discredited history. Old obsessions with welfare fraud are criminalized and turned into justifications for new police-style approaches to claimant processing and more muscular systems of surveillance and punishment.

Although historical precedents can be identified, some of the developments analyzed in this chapter suggest that a new rationality has, indeed, taken hold in poverty governance. Reliance on private providers, for example, is a long-standing tradition in American social policy (Katz 2002: 171–94). Public support for charitable relief efforts and social service organizations has often served as an alternative to building state capacities for social protection. But these forms of semiprivate provision should not be equated with an era in which welfare contracts are approached as lucrative revenue streams, bought and sold as corporate holdings. Welfare provision in the United States has been recast as a site of profitable investment, where nonprofits can generate organization-sustaining revenues and corporations can make good on their promises to bring shareholders increasing returns.

Public aid programs in the United States have always offered weak and partial protections from the market. Low benefit levels, administrative rules, and degrading rituals have long been used to push low-income people into labor markets (Piven and Cloward 1971). Our analysis underscores the continuing relevance of such practices—from seasonal patterns of sanctioning to deterrent finger-printing rituals and fraud-investigation threats. These practices persist, however, as part of a new relationship between welfare programs and labor markets. WT operations today are designed to serve employers by pushing clients into jobs, hosting hiring fairs, removing barriers to work, subsidizing wages, and teaching the importance of complying with work expectations. Labor is not decommodified at the one-stop; it is actively commodified through tutelary programs to "cultivate workers" (as one RWB website puts it) and through coercive approaches to work enforcement. Welfare agencies today are adjuncts to the labor market that specialize in women with precarious work attachments. They blur the boundary between state and market as they use public authorities and funds to service and subsidize employers.

Neoliberalism has also transformed the organizational culture of governance. At the one-stop center, roles, relationships, and physical spaces are all swept into an almost-Orwellian project of market-centered renaming and reframing. On the front stage of organizational life, where governance is enacted, the business model is pursued as an aspirational ideal and deployed as a powerful regulatory norm. Like all cultures, however, it contains internal contradictions and counterdiscourses that create tensions within its matrix of meanings and priorities.

The business model has its share of true believers, especially in the ranks of higher officialdom. But most case managers appraise it with a decidedly conflicted consciousness. They applaud it as an antidote to the failed culture of the AFDC program, and they value images of themselves as participants in an innovative and important business enterprise. Their enthusiasm is complicated, however, by their lived experiences of what the model means in practice. The business model, for them, is inseparable from job insecurity, disruptions of basic operations, and the conversion of sorely needed taxpayer dollars into shareholder profits. It is experienced by many as a willful denial of the desperate facts of clients' lives and the importance of compassion. As case managers struggle to find a deeper purpose in their work, they express values and identities that expose cracks in the edifice of the business model, revealing it to be far less than an unquestioned hegemonic ideology.

The hard edge of neoliberal reform is perhaps best illustrated by its bifurcated approach to waste, fraud, and abuse. The potential for clients to commit small-stakes fraud has become an organizing priority of the system. Cast as a criminal violation of contract, its specter drives costly investments in police-style processing tools and investigative units. The welfare application now doubles as an open-ended waiver of privacy rights, permitting state surveillance and information sharing. Discoveries of fraud, small and rare as they may be, can be pursued as felonies punishable by imprisonment. The contrast with service-provider fraud could hardly be greater.

Corrupt contract processes and fraudulent takings of taxpayer dollars have been recurrent themes of welfare privatization. Despite the vast sums involved, providers continue to enjoy the fruits of a mindset that treats red tape and regulation as the enemy of free-market efficiency, innovation, and productivity. They are rarely subjected to routine investigative procedures and, in multimillion-dollar cases of fraud, do little more than pay back their unearned revenues. Criminal prosecution is reserved for the poor families they serve.

This stunning contrast signals a deeper structural shift in poverty governance. Welfare for the poor is no longer just market conforming, in the negative sense of doing as little as possible to infringe on market relations (Noble 1997). Today, it is an affirmative enforcer of market participation that criminalizes and penalizes noncompliance among the poor. It is an active aide to employers that services and subsidizes low-wage hiring. It is a market in its own right, where corporations and their shareholders turn taxpayer dollars into profits with little fear of strenuous oversight or criminal investigation.

PERFORMANCE, PERVERSITY, AND PUNISHMENT

I N A HIGHLY FRAGMENTED SYSTEM OF POLICY IMPLEMENTATION, central authorities confront a difficult administrative challenge: how to en-sure that policy agendas will be pursued in a coherent and accountable manner. To meet this challenge, hierarchical government bureaucracies employ a variety of strategies. They carefully select and train frontline personnel; they establish action categories and clearance procedures to constrain decision making; they use budgets, inspections, and reporting requirements to stay abreast of what is happening on the ground; and so on (Kaufman 1960). In recent decades, neoliberal reformers disrupted this system. As we saw in chapters 7 and 8, they outsourced implementation to a diverse array of private providers that do not operate within a single organization. To encourage entrepreneurial innovation, they freed these providers from the constraints of governmental red tape, pro-cedural monitoring, and standards for hiring and training personnel. The old challenges of coherence and accountability were sharpened, and traditional ad-ministrative solutions were rendered less effective.

In this chapter, we explore how performance systems and the "new public management" have been deployed as neoliberal responses to this challenge. In poverty governance today, autonomy at the frontlines is disciplined by a market rationality that focuses relentlessly on the bottom line of results. The new tools for securing compliance tie benchmarks and outcome measures to financial in-centives and penalties, grounding governance in a market calculus designed to raise the odds that preferred paths will be freely chosen. Like the clients they serve, welfare officials in street-level organizations have been subjected to new techniques that strive to shape the ways they govern themselves. As we will see, these new strategies are plagued by contradictions and failures yet, at the same time, "succeed" in promoting a more disciplinary stance toward clients that penalizes the most vulnerable segments of the poor.

The new public management (NPM) has been aptly described as a reform movement that seeks "to replace traditional rule-based, authority-driven pro-cesses with market-based, competition-driven tactics" (Kettl 2005: 3). Under the NPM, central authorities promote innovation by multiplying the number of points where officials can choose divergent paths. Policy authority is rolled out to lower-level jurisdictions and transferred to nonprofit and for-profit providers through contractual arrangements (Heinrich 2000; Dias and Maynard-Moody 2006). In "one-stop" welfare offices, local program managers and casework-ers are given greater discretion over how to process and handle their clients (Hasenfeld, Ghose, and Larson 2004; Brodkin 1997).

As positions of discretionary authority have proliferated, so too have efforts to discipline the ways that actors perform in this role. "The beginning of the twenty-first century," Donald Moynihan (2008: 3) writes, "finds us in an era of governance by performance management." Indeed, performance systems now serve as the core technology for bringing coherence and accountability to a frag-mented system of poverty governance. By establishing outcome benchmarks focused on work promotion, higher-level officials define the goals of service provision and the terms of its evaluation. Through measurement matrices and sophisticated information systems, they make frontline activities more legible and susceptible to influence (Scott 1998). By tying financial rewards and pen-alties to outcomes, they incent preferred behaviors and bring lagging service providers to heel. Under welfare reform, performance measures guide resource allocations at all levels of the system, from federal decisions about how to dis-tribute funds to state TANF programs to local decisions about whether to renew or terminate service contracts (Ridzi 2004; Ewalt and Jennings 2004).

Proponents of performance management rarely conceptualize or analyze it as a disciplinary system. Typically, they present it as a way to promote efficiency and effectiveness, ground policy choices in objective evidence, and reconcile policy experimentation with public accountability (Talbot 2005). The implicit promise is that local actors will be freed to go their own ways and then, later, will be judged by their performance and given the information they need to improve. The reality, however, involves a more complex interplay of structure and agency (Moynihan 2008; Radin 2006). The focusing effects of outcome benchmarks, the pressures of competition, the prospects of incurring rewards or penalties, the awareness that one is being closely monitored: These features of performance management do more than just make agents accountable; they reshape agency itself.

In this chapter, we present an empirical critique of performance systems and the NPM. We begin by examining organizational behavior. The NPM, we show, does function to cultivate particular habits of mind (Foucault [1975] 1997). But it does so in ways that often lead to self-defeating and goal-displacing dynamics at the frontlines. Unlike many critiques of performance management, we do not treat perverse organizational responses as corruptions of or deviations from the NPM. Rather, we argue that they are predictable products of contradictions that lie at the center of the NPM itself. Echoing Foucault (1980), we suggest that the disciplinary power of the NPM is deep and far-reaching yet also fractured, inconsistent, and incomplete.

Our second goal in this chapter is to clarify, from an organizational perspective, how efforts to discipline service providers shape efforts to discipline welfare recipients. Under welfare reform, sanctions for noncompliance function as the ultimate paternalist tool for supervisory efforts to reshape client behavior. In chapters 7 and 8, we showed how sanction patterns respond to local political and economic conditions, often in highly racialized ways. Like most previous studies, our analyses paid little attention to how sanctioning may be influenced by performance management or other aspects of organizational structure and process (see, Wu et al. 2006; Pavetti, Derr, and Hesketh 2003; Kalil, Seefeldt, and Wang 2002). Sanction decisions, however, are always made in the context of organizational routines, by actors who occupy specific organizational positions. To understand them, one must analyze how efforts to discipline clients are shaped by the disciplinary pressures that organizations are forced to adapt to and navigate.

Taking up this challenge, we present a mixed-methods study of how discipline operates on "both sides of the desk" in the Florida WT program. Using administrative data, we establish a clear pattern linking performance pressures on providers to sanctions imposed on clients. Turning to field research, we explain this relationship and clarify its underlying mechanisms. Our analysis casts doubt on rational-actor stories suggesting that case managers sanction clients strategically to boost their performance numbers. Instead, we show how performance pressures combine with other organizational conditions to encourage case managers to sanction. Here, as in chapter 7, we find that sanction decisions are more than just individual (case manager) responses to individual (client) misbehaviors. To explain them, we must understand how the work of welfare provision is organized and managed, why it operates as it does, and how organizational structures, routines, and priorities shape disciplinary action.

Performance Pressures and Organizational Behavior: Perversity in the Field

In the Florida WT program, local devolution and privatization emerged alongside one of the nation's leading systems of performance management. Each year, a state board negotiates with each Regional Workforce Board (RWB) to establish a region-specific set of performance goals. Goal-adjusted performance measures are then used to determine state-level evaluations of the regions and RWB evaluations of service providers. Provider "pay points" are tied directly to statewide performance goals, which local contracts often specify in distinctive ways.

Performance in the WT program is tracked on a monthly basis and focused squarely on goals related to work promotion.[1] Results are reported at regular intervals in a competitive format via "the red and green report"—so called because it uses colors to indicate the rankings of the twenty-four regions: red for the bottom six, green for the top six, and white for the twelve in between.

Performance on the red and green report is taken very seriously at all levels of the WT program. Green scores can qualify a region for additional funding to undertake program improvements and allow a region to enter competitions for resources allocated by WFI. For service providers, red scores can mean the difference between contract renewal and termination. Between these extremes, providers typically lose pay points as a result of weak performance rankings and can draw unwanted scrutiny from the state board if their performance rankings fall.

In principle, the NPM suggests that local organizations should respond to this system by pursuing innovations that advance statewide goals and improve the programs available to clients. Devolution should provide local actors with the *freedoms* they need to experiment with promising new approaches. Performance feedback should provide them with the *evidence* they need to learn from their own experiments and to identify best practices in other regions. Performance-based competition should provide them with *incentives* to make use of this information and to adopt program improvements that work.

Previous studies suggest a variety of reasons why organizations may actually deviate from this script in "rationally perverse" ways. Performance indicators present organizations with ambiguous cues that, in practice, get "selected, interpreted, and used by actors in different ways consistent with their institutional interests" (Moynihan 2008: 9). Managers may fail to make positive use of performance indicators because they lack authority to make change, do not have access to learning forums, or cannot identify effective strategies for reforming ingrained organizational routines and cultures (Moynihan 2006, 2008). At the same time, performance "tunnel vision" can lead managers to innovate in perverse ways that subvert important program goals. Performance pressures can divert attention from important-but-unmeasured values and activities (Radin 2006). And in an effort to boost their numbers, welfare providers may engage in "creaming" practices that direct "services to those already close to being 'job-ready' at the expense of those with barriers to employment" (Considine 2003: 71).

Our field research confirms that reformers succeeded in establishing performance as a focal point and organizing principle for WT personnel. Regional officials and program managers expect to be held accountable for their outcomes. They carefully scrutinize performance reports and keep a close eye on other regions. Most express a strong desire to improve performance through evidence-based revisions of practice. In reflecting on their work, local officials routinely place performance numbers at the center of the "business model" described in chapter 8. In a system where performance is exchanged for payments, performance management becomes inseparable from, and is ultimately a form of, profit management.

Bolstering this logic, state officials repeatedly emphasize the need for regions to "make their bogey" (meet performance goals). In response, regional officials affirm that performance measures guide their decisions in a wide variety of ways. As one local manager explained, "We're at the bottom of the chain, and we look up to [the state level to] see what's important. And the performance measures are how we know. When you tell me I need to do participation rate, I know what my priorities are. And that's where we spend our time." Another local official summarized: "This whole process with the Welfare Transition program, it's a number thing. It's about the numbers. Your participation rate, your employment rate."

Performance anxiety is, in this sense, a broad and deep feature of organizational culture in the WT program that has far-reaching consequences for policy implementation. The consequences, however, deviate considerably from the optimistic predictions of the NPM. Indeed, our interviews point to deep contradictions in the NPM that tend to subvert the dynamics of organizational learning and program innovation promised by the model.

Consider first the double-edged nature of performance competition and its relation to trust. In theory, competition is supposed to encourage regional managers to learn from one another's experiments. Yet it also encourages managers to view other regions as competitors who have a stake in outperforming them. Our site visits make clear that the latter dynamic tends to undermine the former. Policy learning and diffusion require a modicum of trust, and this trust can be undermined by highly competitive performance systems. Echoing others we spoke with, one local manager stated unequivocally that regions try to maintain a competitive edge by guarding their best innovations as "trade secrets" and, in the same interview, asked us not to tell other regions about new techniques being tried at her one-stop. Another explained how high-stakes evaluations undermine learning by fostering suspicions that "other regions" are cheating: "They can't tell you their 'best practices' because their practice is cheating [to win the] competitive game." In these and other ways, competition works at cross-purposes with policy learning. It encourages local actors to distrust the numbers that other regions produce, the best practices they recommend, and the wisdom of sharing their own positive innovations.

Policy learning also founders on a second dynamic that is rooted in discursive tensions between devolution and performance management. In principle, these two aspects of the NPM are supposed to work hand in hand to promote the diffusion of best practices. Yet there is a rhetorical tension between the two. Performance reports and efforts to publicize best practices function as parts of a broader discourse suggesting that "what worked there can work here too." By contrast, the discourse that justifies state-to-local devolution prizes locally tailored solutions and trumpets the idea that localities have radically different needs, goals, populations, and capacities. Not surprisingly, these two ideas clash in the consciousness of the local manager. When presented with successful innovations from other regions, local officials cite a litany of characteristics that distinguish the region of origin from their own. Resource differences are also sometimes cited, as in the case of one official who stated flatly: "There are best practices that there is no way we can implement or staff." The deeper tension, however, is between a discourse that denigrates "one size fits all" ideas and celebrates local uniqueness, on one side, and a system that treats localities as comparable and seeks to generalize innovations across them, on the other. One local official spoke for many when he deployed the discourse of local differences to challenge the wisdom of having regions compete on the basis of performance: "Philosophically, to me it makes more sense to compare us against us. Don't compare us against Miami. Don't compare us against Orlando. Compare us against us."

In addition to these dynamics, three additional perversities flow from tensions within the NPM between decentralized management and centralized performance evaluation. Under devolution, local actors are supposed to exercise discretion in responding to performance pressures—to draw on local knowledge to select the most effective and efficient program strategies. But program effectiveness and efficiency are not the only ways that strategies differ. From an organizational perspective, some paths of innovation are easier to pursue than others.

One such "easy path," well known to students of performance management, is to engage in creative counting of activities (Radin 2006). In the WT program, serious reforms designed to deal with problems of poverty and work are (not surprisingly) often viewed as difficult to achieve, and their performance effects are usually seen as distant and uncertain. It is far easier to change how one classifies existing activities and counts measured behaviors. As a result, as one local official told us forthrightly, "people game the numbers all the time." In describing efforts to meet the required participation rate, another regional official explained: "You have to do all sorts of things to fill the participation hours. We've got a client who we found out was taking her pastor to church on Sunday. We went out and asked her pastor to sign on saying this was community service. The trick is to find out what people are already doing and find a way to count it as work or community service. This is how you have to do it."

The search for easier organizational paths also underlies a related dynamic that we have not seen noted and will call "stream-creaming." Previous studies of creaming have suggested that when performance standards are high, organizations may cope by ignoring the "hard the serve" and focusing on clients who are easier to lift above a measurement threshold (Bell and Orr 2002; Considine 2003; Dias and Maynard-Moody 2006). In an era of service integration and multiprogram one-stop centers, however, providers often hold contracts related to several programs at once. Under this arrangement, which has emerged most strongly—though not exclusively—in states where TANF programs are integrated into workforce systems, profitability in each stream depends on meeting contract "pay points" tied to performance. (As one manager put it, "If we make [the performance standard,] we get paid; then if we don't, we get zero.") Thus, the profitability of the operation as a whole can be increased by raising efforts across the board, by creaming clients in each program, *or* by strategically focusing on programs that offer "softer" pay-point targets. The latter is what we mean by stream-creaming.

When state officials raise benchmarks in a program, they hope that organizations will work to improve their performance in that program. But when providers are contracted for multiple program streams, they may have incentives to do the opposite—that is, to reduce their efforts in the program that now has tougher benchmarks and shift their energies to programs where pay points and profits seem easier to obtain. In discussing higher performance benchmarks recently put in place for the WT program, one local manager told us, "If they are going to make our profit closely tied to something that is so hard to fully obtain, there will be problems." Asked to elaborate, he explained that the provider would abandon efforts to meet unrealistic goals and use its resources to meet pay points in another program. In addition, the company would seek new program streams with more profitable targets. "[My employer] is committed to this welfare industry but they need to make a profit as well. We have been trying to diversify our services and clientele. For instance, we are now working with ex-offenders and things like that. We provide the support system for ex-offenders who are coming out of jail."

Finally, when local actors respond to performance pressures, they also confront "easy versus hard" paths when deciding whether to improve services to the existing clientele or, alternatively, select a client pool that will make it easier to make their "bogey." Our interviews suggest that the latter path is usually seen as easier. Accordingly, creative efforts to innovate are often directed toward reshaping the clientele rather than serving them more effectively.

In this regard, it is instructive to consider the reforms that emerged in what we will call "Region A" in 2005. Early that year, Region A officials attended a statewide meeting where their low performance numbers were publicly criticized. In response, they decided to overhaul key features of the local operation. Acting on the assumption that their low numbers resulted from having too many clients who were "not serious enough," Region A officials chose a path of action designed to trim the caseload down to an easier-to-serve core of clients. The relevant changes went into effect around the time of June 2005 and included the following:

1. Intake and orientation procedures were revamped so that applicants would need to attend daily classes for at least one week *before* having their application for benefits submitted. Forty hours of class attendance was required, and applicants who missed a class or showed up inappropriately dressed were required to start over the following week.
2. Intake meetings with new applicants were redesigned to emphasize the significant time investments demanded by program requirements, the limited amount of assistance available for meeting these requirements, and the fact that these requirements could be avoided if applicants chose to pursue only Medicaid and Food Stamp benefits. As one case manager responsible for intake explained, "Doing the overview presentation, what I kinda tell them is that, if you're in a situation right now where transportation is a hindrance for you, you may want to reconsider getting your cash assistance open because you're going to be required to participate in this program on a daily basis."

3. The region instituted a more frequent and intensive quality assurance system for monitoring caseworkers' handling of sanctions and work participation.

4. The region moved to a new system for "curing" sanctions. In the past, a sanctioned client could reenter the caseload and reinstate benefits simply by contacting her caseworker and beginning to document work hours again. Under the new system, only one local staff member (known among the staff as the "sanction queen") was given authority to sign off on the return of a sanctioned client, and this staff member was made available to clients on only one day each week, for two hours. Sanctioned clients who missed this window would have to wait another week to return.

Reflecting on these changes, one Region A case manager explained:

> [We have] what we call, I guess, an upfront process so that, before they even receive their cash assistance, we can identify who is serious about the program. [Some say,] "I've had enough. I don't want to do this. I'm going to go out and find a job on my own." And for whatever reason they decide not to get the cash assistance. So with that new process we're hoping that our caseloads continue to decrease in size. [We want clients] who are going to utilize the services that we have here and [are] really, seriously looking for a job.

Staff from Region A consistently reported that these program innovations had major effects on the region's caseload and operations. Figure 9-1 presents results from an analysis of administrative data that corroborates this perception. Between January 2003 and June 2005, the caseload of Region A tracked closely with caseloads around the state. Both trends rise and fall in a seasonal pattern, with Region A showing slightly higher peaks and troughs than the state average. In the months immediately prior to June 2005, the two trend lines lie right on top of each other. Immediately after this date, however, the caseload in Region A falls precipitously. Indeed, despite the fact that caseloads were falling across the state during this period, Region A's caseload falls so quickly that it produces a substantial gap in relation to the state average. Moreover, while Region A's caseload had previously been more responsive to seasonal ebbs and flows, it now becomes less responsive than caseloads in other regions of the state. From June 2005 to July 2006, Region A's caseload fell by an astonishing 53 percent.

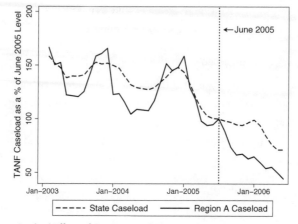

FIGURE 9-1. Caseload Effects of Organizational Change in Region A

Note: All values are expressed as a proportion of the June 2005 caseload. Entries for "State Caseload" are based on the twenty-three workforce regions in Florida other than Region A.

As a disciplinary regime, then, the performance ethos is powerful yet incomplete. It is powerful in the sense that it shapes the thinking of local officials, focuses organizational behavior, and motivates efforts to innovate at the front lines. It is incomplete, however, because local organizations retain substantial discretion in the ways they respond to performance information and pressure. In the WT program, performance is the name of the game for local service providers. But organizations typically adapt in perverse ways, and internal contradictions embedded in the NPM work systematically against policy learning and program improvement.

Performance Pressure and Sanctioning: A Statistical Analysis of Administrative Data

The operational shifts observed in Region A suggest that performance pressures can motivate responses that severely limit access to aid for low-income families. Extending this observation, we turn now to a mode of limiting aid that has more explicit disciplinary content. Do local providers respond to performance pressures by imposing sanctions on WT clients at higher rates? Circumstantial evidence is suggested by two facts noted in chapter 6: Florida has one of the strongest performance systems in the country, and it sanctions clients at an unusually high rate. Unfortunately, without consistent indicators of performance pressures across the states, we cannot conduct a rigorous test of this relationship at the state level.

An alternative approach is to specify a series of "observable implications" that we should see in WT administrative data if performance pressures drive sanction rates upward. Based on our evidence that performance anxieties are pervasive in the WT program, it makes sense to begin with the effects of "chronic" pressures—that is, pressures felt throughout the regions on a more or less continual basis. Chronic pressures, by definition, do not vary within the current system. Thus, evidence must come from comparative indicators: changes associated with the onset of this system and differences in the ways organizations respond to the resulting pressures.

In July 2000, Florida replaced the old WAGES program with the WT program, a more performance-driven model emphasizing stronger monitoring, feedback, and pressures to meet measured goals.[2] If providers respond to chronic performance pressures by sanctioning at higher rates, we should observe an increase in statewide sanction rates after July 2000. Figure 9-2 tracks the average sanction rate for Florida workforce regions from January 2000 to April 2004 (based on a three-month moving average of the percentage of the adult caseload receiving a sanction). The trend line indicates a seasonal pattern to sanctioning, which complicates interpretation because rates were on the rise just prior to the inauguration of the WT program. On the whole, though, the trend line is consistent with our expectation. The statewide sanction rate rises significantly after July 2000 (denoted by the vertical line in the figure) and, under the WT program, never falls again to its lower rate under WAGES. The average sanction rate from January to June 2000 was 9.02 percent. Taking the seasonal pattern into account, we find that the average sanction rate for the same six-month period (January-June) for years 2001–03 was 11.8 percent, a percentage increase of roughly 31 percent.

If chronic performance pressures lead to higher sanction rates, we should also find a second pattern: Organizations that are more sensitive to pay-point incentives should generate higher sanction rates. To test for this pattern, we can exploit the mix of nonprofit and for-profit providers operating in the WT program. In theory, the key difference between the two should be the "nondistribution constraint"— the inability of nonprofit organizations to distribute profits to managers and shareholders. Some scholars argue that both types of organizations are sensitive to revenue concerns (Weisbrod 1998), and, as we saw in chapter 8, our informants were divided on the question of whether nonprofits

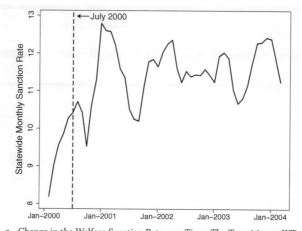

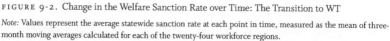

FIGURE 9-2. Change in the Welfare Sanction Rate over Time: The Transition to WT

Note: Values represent the average statewide sanction rate at each point in time, measured as the mean of three-month moving averages calculated for each of the twenty-four workforce regions.

are less revenue centered. All else equal, though, prevailing theories predict that for-profit managers will stress performance incentives and pay points to a greater degree; nonprofit managers, freed from shareholder pressures, will be somewhat less focused on cost minimization and profit enhancement (Gilman 2001; Heinrich 2000). The expectation for our case is clear: under the strong performance pressures of the WT program, for-profit organizations will sanction higher rates than nonprofit organizations.

To test this expectation, we use a sample consisting of all adults who participated in the WT program for at least one month during the period from November 2003 to April 2004. Our outcome variable indicates if a client was sanctioned during this period (1) or not (0). Our key predictor equals 1 for the sixteen regions where one-stop centers were operated by for-profit firms and 0 for the eight regions with nonprofit organizations. Our analysis also controls for a number of variables suggested by the literature on sanctioning, including client characteristics and differences in local context (see chapter 7).[3] Our results indicate that even after controlling for these conventional factors, WT clients were significantly more likely to be sanctioned if they participated in a region with a for-profit provider. The odds of receiving a sanction are estimated to be 25 percent higher for such clients, relative to similar clients served by nonprofit providers.

Although performance pressures are ubiquitous in the WT program, more precise tests are possible if we examine how local sanction patterns respond to episodic changes in performance feedback over time. Because chronic performance anxieties run so high in the WT program (producing a "ceiling effect"), periodic changes in performance numbers are unlikely to produce large spikes in sanctioning rates. As we have seen, however, regional officials say they pay close attention to performance reports and are eager to respond in ways that might improve their numbers. Accordingly, additional evidence of performance-pressure effects can be obtained by testing for smaller-scale "episodic" responses to negative performance reports.[4]

The simplest expectation is that a region's sanction rate will increase in the period that follows a decline in its performance numbers (because negative performance feedback will put providers under greater pressure, as in the story of Region A). Going further, we may also look for episodic differences in the types of clients who are sanctioned. Because the WT system penalizes regions that are less successful in moving clients into the workforce, we should find stronger effects for clients who are seen as "harder to serve" or lacking work motivation. Finally, because providers in politically conservative locales tend to rely more heavily on sanctions to motivate clients (see chapter 7), we should find that negative performance feedback leads to larger increases in sanction rates in more conservative regions.

To test these expectations, we employ a panel dataset consisting of aggregate monthly observations for each of Florida's twenty-four Workforce Board regions. This dataset consists of thirty monthly observations for each region, spanning the period from October 2001 to March 2004.[5] We measure regional performance based on the average monthly regional ranking (1–24) across the three key measures used by the state board to monitor regional performance in the WT program—the entered employment rate, the welfare return rate, and the entered wage rate.[6] We sum the rankings so that higher scores indicate *stronger* pressures (declining performance).

The outcome variable for these analyses is the regional sanction rate, which we define as the percentage of each region's monthly caseload that received a sanction in a given month. The control variables include a variety of characteristics of the adult caseload, including racial/ethnic composition, average age, the work participation rate, family structure, family size, TANF dependency, and the overall size of the monthly adult caseload. Finally, each analysis includes a full set of regional and monthly fixed effects. The former control for all time-invariant factors that vary across regions, thus providing control for unmeasured differences in regional contexts that may affect client outcomes, while the latter control for time-varying variables that do not differ across regions, such as changes in state-level policies that affect all regions.

The results of our analyses are consistent with all three of our expectations

regarding episodic effects.[7] For each one-unit increase in our ranking-based measure of performance pressure, we find that the regional sanction rate increases
by an average of about .13.[8] In addition, we find that providers in conservative
regions are more likely to turn to sanctions as a response to poor performance
feedback. Indeed, we find no discernable episodic effect on sanction rates in the
twelve most liberal workforce regions. In the twelve most conservative regions,
the effect is significant and roughly ten times what we observe in the twelve
liberal regions. In conservative regions, a one-unit increase in our measure of
performance pressure leads to an immediate increase in the sanction rate of
approximately .18. After six months, the cumulative effect is modestly larger,
estimated to be .24.

Our third expectation regarding episodic increases in performance pressures is that they should increase sanction rates to a greater degree for clients
who are viewed as harder to serve and/or lacking motivation. Combining this
expectation with the logic of the Racial Classification Model (RCM), we expect
sanction rates to increase more for black clients than for white clients.[9] Extending it further, we expect to find larger effects on sanction rates for clients with
lower education levels, who are more likely than their more educated counterparts to have multiple barriers to work (Danziger, Kalil, and Anderson 2000).

Our results support both expectations. When regions receive negative performance feedback, sanction rates go up for clients of all types, but the increases are
significantly larger among clients who are black and/or less educated. The effect
on clients with less than twelve years of education is approximately 35 percent
larger than the effect among clients with twelve or more years of education.[10]
The effect for black clients is 50 percent larger than for white clients.

Connecting these separate expectations, and building on the conditional
propositions of the RCM, one might also make a prediction that parallels the interaction of race and ideology observed in chapter 7: Falling performance rankings will have their greatest effects on sanction rates when clients are disadvantaged by race and/or education *and* participate in a politically conservative
region. Here again, we find results consistent with our expectations. In liberal
regions, we find that the relationship between performance feedback and sanction rates does not vary significantly across client subgroups. In conservative
regions, however, we find that sanction rates increase in the wake of negative
performance feedback in a pattern that disproportionately targets harder-to-
serve clients. Specifically, they rise to a significantly greater degree for black
clients and clients with low education levels.

Finally, as our discussion of Region A illustrated, organizations can employ a variety of strategies beyond sanctions to limit and shape their caseloads. Regional officials may respond to falling performance rankings by adopting restrictive measures unrelated to the sanction rate. The case closure rate—calculated as the percentage of open cases each month that are closed for reasons other than sanctions or earnings—provides a way to capture the sum total of such efforts.[11] If local TANF offices respond to declining performance by shedding clients, this response should be manifested not only in the sanction rate, but also in the rate at which clients are pushed off for other administrative reasons.

Indeed, our analysis of case closure rates corroborates our analysis of sanction rates.[12] Episodes of negative performance feedback are followed by significant increases in case closure rates across all workforce regions, with our analysis suggesting that for each one-unit increase in our measure of performance pressure, a region's case closure rate is expected to increase by .7 percent. As in our analysis of sanction rates, we find no discernible effects on case closures in the most liberal regions. In the most conservative regions, the effect is four times as large and statistically significant: For each unit increase in our performance measure, the case closure rate increases by .012. These effects are smaller than for the sanction rate, but the consistency of findings across two dependent variables should bolster our confidence in the results.

In sum, our statistical findings consistently match what we would expect to observe if performance pressures motivate service providers to push clients off the rolls more frequently. Under the strong performance system implemented in 2000, chronic performance pressures raised sanction rates across the state. Sanction rates are slightly but significantly higher among the for-profit providers we would expect to be especially attuned to the profit implications of performance-based pay points. Episodic declines in performance rankings appear to heighten performance pressures in ways that lead to increases in sanction and case-closure rates. These effects also vary across client subgroups and regions in the ways we would expect if performance pressures have a real impact on sanctioning. While these effects are often modest, their consistency offers impressive evidence of a meaningful relationship.

From Performance Pressures to Sanctioning:
A Field Perspective on Mechanisms

With this evidence in hand, we can turn to the question of *how* performance pressures influence sanction rates. The most logical candidate for a causal mechanism in this context, and the one most clearly suggested by the literature, is the practice of "creaming" (Bell and Orr 2002). In response to performance pressures, this view holds, frontline workers use sanctions strategically to rid themselves of low-performing clients, leaving only the "cream" clients who generate positive numbers. In addition to being well established, this hypothesis fits well with the "perversely rational" behaviors we found in our analysis of organizational responses.

Thus, when we started our research on case manager discretion and sanctioning, we expected to find a creaming dynamic. Our field research, however, failed to cooperate with this expectation. Today, we refer to the strategic creaming account as the "causal story that failed."

Why? To begin with, our interviews make it clear that few case managers approach their clients with such cold calculation. As we saw in chapter 8, most case managers hold ambivalent feelings toward the business model. They value it and draw a positive sense of identity from it, but they also resist it as a dehumanizing force that threatens their commitments to a more caring and responsive vision of social service. These conflicted sentiments form the backdrop for case managers' views of performance systems and sanctions. Virtually all case managers support sanctions in principle because they believe there should be consequences for noncompliance. As one put it, "I think realistically, you have to have teeth in the program to get people to participate." In practice, though, many worry that sanctions punish clients who are, in effect, set up to fail. The clients who confront the toughest life problems, they argue, are rarely given the supports and services they need to meet tough program requirements. Many echoed the case manager who lamented, "Florida has a punitive system that gets increasingly harsh the more problems a [client] has."

Performance tends to be viewed from an equally conflicted perspective, especially when case managers consider it alongside their desires to provide a humane and supportive resource for clients.

> The way we're able to [stay in business and] help people is by making our measurements on our red and green reports and getting paid, so that we can therefore in return help with childcare and support services. So the more we make those measurements and those goals, the more we can help candidates. But the more we focus on those [performance goals], the less we're focusing on the candidates. So, it's a catch-22.

As we progressed with our fieldwork, we found it less and less plausible to accept the view that case managers are narrow performance maximizers who intentionally sanction clients to improve their numbers. The creaming account, however, was contradicted in a more fundamental way by a second discovery in the field. Throughout our interviews, we found strong and widespread adherence to one basic belief: In the WT program, high sanction rates *lower* a region's performance numbers. Indeed, virtually no one we interviewed believed that sanctions would have a positive effect on their performance rankings. Thus, even if case managers did operate as single-minded performance maximizers, their beliefs about performance measures would make it highly irrational to sanction larger numbers of clients as a creaming strategy.

Regional officials worried about high sanction rates because they expect them to hurt performance and invite unwanted attention. As one put it, "Our region doesn't want to have a sanction rate that's too high. High numbers (of any kind) draw attention to the region, so it had better be something positive. So we wouldn't want to be seen as overly punitive in a way that might not be within the rules." Case managers appeared to have internalized this message, telling us that "if sanctions get high, they hinder [our numbers]" and adding that supervisors "want you to maintain your sanctions as low as possible." The clear message from supervisors is couched not just in terms of performance, but in terms of the business model itself. As one explained: "This is a private company, and our goal is to get them employed, not sanctioned."[13]

In sum, our field research demolished the simplest explanation for the statistical findings presented in the previous section, leaving us with a considerable puzzle. Fortunately, our transcripts and field notes also pointed to an alternative and less direct explanation. To explain how performance pressures raise sanction rates, one must adopt a more organizational perspective. The key mechanisms can be found in a conjunction of four factors: (1) the distinctive ways that the WT program organizes case management, (2) the specific performance pressures experienced by case managers, (3) the limited number of tools available to WT case managers, and (4) case managers' beliefs and frustrations regarding client noncompliance.

Our explanation begins with the organization of WT casework as a highly routinized operation focused on performance-related tasks. Caseworkers typically describe their workdays as a series of step-by-step responses to system needs rather than as a proactive endeavor. The following exchange among senior officials underscores this point.

Regional Official A: You don't hire a "people person" anymore for a career manager position. You hire a clerical computer person. You can teach them the social work stuff easily. The job's all about time, accuracy, and files now. There's a person [client] down there somewhere. But the technical stuff is what matters.

State Official: What you're telling me is the [information] systems are driving the [case management] process.

Several Regional Officials: Oh yes. Oh yes!

Regional Official B: You don't get any credit [in the performance measures] for hand holding. You don't get any credit for mentoring.

Regional Official C: If you talk to any case manager here, they will tell you they're not a case manager; they're a technician. They spend about 10 percent of their time on their clients. Their time is about being a technician, and that's the way the program is written. They're doing what they have to do under this system.

WT case management is reactive and clerical. It focuses mainly on documenting client activity hours and entering results into the One-Stop Service Tracking (OSST) system. Indeed, many officials argued that the data-entry fields of OSST function, in daily practice, as the real policy on the ground. As one put it, "The policy [on the books] doesn't always match up with the [OSST] system. People on the front lines see the computer screens as the policy. Whatever can or can't be done in a straightforward way on the system, it's assumed that that's the policy."

Case managers typically begin their day by logging on to the information system so they can address the slew of new alerts that arrives each morning. The alerts focus on two kinds of actions: documenting work participation hours for clients and pursuing sanction procedures when documentation is lacking. From this point forward, the daily round consists mostly of efforts to do one or the other, punctuated by face-to-face meetings with clients that often focus on the same two issues. Case managers spend most of the day either seeking documentation for work-related activities or taking next steps in the sanction process such as sending out a "pre-penalty" warning letter, requesting a sanction, or working to bring a sanctioned client back into compliance. In short, performance and sanctioning are two sides of a single coin in the work life of the case manager, and, together, they stand at the center of the job.

These objective realities of the job are reflected in the subjective focus of frontline workers. Case managers worry about performance almost continually. As one put it, "It's just weird, I mean it really is. And I don't know how to explain how, um, you know, we all run around and we're like, 'where are you at now with your [participation numbers]?' 'Oh, I'm at like 20 percent.' 'Oh man!' So we're all just stressed!" The stress felt by case managers can be traced partly to a belief noted in chapter 8: Case managers expect performance-based pay points to matter greatly for their job security and trajectory. Few expect to be "fired" if their numbers drop. But they are keenly aware that performance equals profit, and declining profits could lead their employer to downsize the staff or sell the operation to another company whose retention of old employees is uncertain. At a less absolute level, most expect that if they produce weak numbers, they will be subjected to greater supervision in a way that will make their work more stressful and harder to do. One case manager explained, "We [case managers] get our own sanctions. [Laughs] So, um, you know, that's a big stress. Um, and they also tell us, 'yeah, the entered employment; um, how many jobs are you getting?' I mean, that's just things that are hit every day, 50 percent [work participation], 50 percent."

In describing these pressures, case managers make it clear that they do not see sanctioning as a *desirable* response. As one explained, "No career manager wants to sanction. You go through all these papers to try to get in touch with the person. It's a struggle. You try to help them get everything in to keep them out of a sanction, but a lot of times you can't." Sanctions are valued by some case managers as sticks to motivate compliance and as a way to "stop [clients] from wasting their own time [in a time-limited program]." On the other hand, case managers believe that sanctions hurt their performance numbers and tend to be skeptical that sanctions deter bad behavior. Many agree with the case manager who told us that "[a sanction] is not a deterrent at all. It's used like a punishment." Most often, case managers reject lofty justifications for sanctions in favor of a more mundane view: "To be honest, I'm not always sure what sanctions are good for. Sanctions are just a reality of the program. They don't really deter or gain more attention. They're just how the program works."

Indeed, sanctions *are* how the program works. As one senior official explained, "sanctions are the most important process we have in terms of case management and in terms of producing results." The primacy of the sanction as a policy tool emerges, in a sense, by default. Case managers have few alternative tools at their disposal. They are limited in what they can do to raise their numbers, and they are even more limited in their abilities to address the real-life problems of their clients. Most caseworkers have no training as social workers; they have few options for matching clients to services; and they are essentially powerless to change clients' opportunities and life conditions. Buffeted by performance pressures and lacking the tools to respond to client needs, case managers experienced their workdays as a series of frustrations and disappointments. The following quotations illustrate.

> Never mind that Deborah can't read, and she's got a 6th grade education, but you want [her to] go out and get a job at ten bucks an hour. Or, my candidate, who has a substance abuse problem, you know, he keeps drinking on the job, that's why he can't *keep* his job, but [he's] got to go out there and get a job, you know. [So] I think we're more frustrated about meeting our participation rate every single month—that [50] percent. It's a big frustration because you're like "I want to make my 50 percent. I don't want to be evaluated at the end of the month and told, 'Oh, you didn't make 50 percent.'" What do you do?
>
> We try the best not to sanction clients, try to help them overcome barriers. But if we follow regulations and procedures—if they [clients] don't do their part—we have to go by what the program says [and impose that sanction]. The program regulations need to be looked at immediately [at the] highest level and [they need to] give us the tools to help clients to a better outcome.

Frustrated and lacking effective tools, case managers must find ways to reconcile competing demands. A small number square this circle by shifting part of the client's burden onto themselves. They put in long hours to establish whatever documented activities are needed to satisfy performance goals and avoid a sanction. With little time to spare at the office, they often spend hours at the end of the workday trying to locate clients and secure documentation. As one explained, "My level of sanction is so low. If I were to go by policy [alone], all of [my] caseload would be sanctioned. I go way and beyond [the policy]: a lot of communication, a lot of calling, trying to find where they're at. 'Hey, this is what's going on. If you don't come in, your benefits are going to be stopped.'" Going further, some case managers in this group make use of "creative counting" strategies as a way to soften the program rules confronted by clients. Here again, we see how the disciplinary power of performance management occasions its own resistance (Foucault 1980). But it is a subversion that comes at a substantial personal cost. Case managers in this group report that they are exhausted, burned out, and disappointed that their job is so often about protecting clients from the program itself.

For most WT case managers, performance pressures are a more controlling organizational reality, shaping their use of discretion. Ultimately, most believe that it is the client alone who is responsible for documenting work activities, and it is the client who must, in some way, be prodded to do so. The problem is that, aside from the threat of sanctions, case managers have few tools for motivating clients. In principle, incentives for good behavior, such as child-care vouchers or transportation assistance, offer an alternative disciplinary tool for shaping clients' calculations regarding desirable behavior. In practice, however, appeals to these incentives often amount to little more than an implicit threat of sanction. Most benefits for program participants are already available to the client. So the discussion is, at root, about the possibility of a current benefit—or a future transitional benefit—being terminated through a sanction. Thus, as one official explained, sanctions are usually the most effective "tool for helping clients see the benefits of sticking with the program in order to get transitional benefits."

Although they usually want to avoid imposing a sanction, case managers quickly find themselves turning to the *threat* of a sanction as a way to cajole clients into participating at higher rates and turning in documentation. When such threats fail, as they often do, they find themselves initiating "pre-penalty" actions as a way to signal that they "mean business" and that the client had better do what is required. At this point, organized sanction procedures are set in motion. The computer alerts and requests for action kick in and the caseworker's discretion diminishes. If the client now fails to comply, the case manager confronts strong pressures to move the sanction process forward in a "timely manner." As one explained:

> If you have a customer who turns in 15 [hours] instead of the 20, at that point in time you can elect to start the penalty process or you can elect to call them and say "Okay, you know what, you have 20 due. It could have just been an oversight or whatever. Can you bring in the other 5 today, by 5:00 p.m.?" So you have a little flexibility to work it. *But once you start that [pre-penalty], that 8–10 process, there's no way to work around that.* It's going to pretty much take its course. Okay, you place the [pre-penalty] on the customer's case; you give them the pre-penalty call. Try and find out, okay, why have you failed to participate? Um, they have the 10 days to comply. [If there's] failure to comply, it will lead to a sanction.

This, then, is the first mechanism that explains how performance pressures increase sanction rates. It is a story of intentional tactics producing unintended outcomes.[14] With few tools at their disposal, caseworkers turn to threats in the hope that compliance will ensue, performance numbers will improve, and a sanction will be averted. Once set on this path, though, they must (however reluctantly) put one foot in front of the other. In a short time, they find themselves imposing a sanction that, in the abstract, they see as a hindrance to high performance.

There is also a second mechanism at work, and it is a dynamic that one might expect few case managers to reveal. In a surprising number of instances, case managers report that they sanction clients out of frustration. Performance pressures contribute to this dynamic in two ways. First, as noted above, performance pressures combine with limited tools to produce high levels of frustration at the front lines. Second, the performance system is structured so that evaluations of the case manager depend on client behavior. When clients fail to turn in documents on time, for example, their actions lower the case manager's performance numbers and invite unwanted scrutiny from supervisors. Not surprisingly, clients tend to become the focal point for case managers' frustrations in such instances. (And it is worth recalling here the extent to which case managers believe that their jobs depend on performance numbers.)

In the WT program, the noncompliant client is not just behaving in a way that *concerns* the case manager; she is doing something *to* the case manager. As one case manager explained, "The stress is, okay, well *I'm* caring about this, but the customer doesn't care. So then after a while, you still do what you got to do because you need your job, and you got to make your [measured] hours." Another reported:

> When it comes to, you know, the problem cases, we get frustrated. I think some people say, "Yeah, technically I could give her another day [to get her documents in], but you know what, I'm gonna slam it [a sanction] on her." You know? [Laughs] It's that whole accountability thing. Because *we* have to be accountable, so I think when you get a customer [who] doesn't feel that they have to be *as* accountable, you can get frustrated.

This frustration-sanction dynamic was prevalent enough to be openly discussed at statewide training sessions. In explaining the role of sanctions, one trainer began by observing that "some people want to penalize because they're angry with a client. That's not the point." In a private interview afterward, a state-level official elaborated: "There [is] no training about case management or emotional issues. Anger management is a big issue. Case managers snap and then sanction because they're mad."

In sum, then, the linkages between performance pressures and sanctioning do not run through the strategic rationality of individual case managers seeking to maximize their numbers. They are more deeply embedded in the organization of case management itself. Case managers are positioned as the ultimate repository for the performance pressures that rain down on the front lines. Yet they are given few tools to respond. Lacking alternatives, they turn to the most basic threat they can wield—the sanction—as a way to motivate client compliance. Predictably, the threat leads to a first procedural step, and what was at first intended as saber rattling turns into a sanction. At the same time, many case managers become frustrated with clients and perceive an injustice in the fact they are being held accountable while the client is not. In such circumstances, it is not hard to see why they occasionally "snap" and levee a sanction that, under other circumstances, they would prefer not to impose.

Conclusion

In poverty governance today, performance systems and the NPM are shrouded by free-market images of autonomy, innovation, and efficiency. They are rarely seen or investigated as disciplinary regimes, yet this is precisely what they are. Indeed, the technologies of discipline that govern clients and case managers have strong parallels. Both rest on incentives for right behavior and penalties for noncompliance; both aim to reshape the motivations of targets so that they will pursue preferred ends as self-regulating subjects; and neither controls behavior completely enough to forestall subversion. Just as welfare clients resist and evade the supervisory regimes of welfare-to-work programs (Gilliom 2001), so too do service providers subvert the goals of performance management. The ubiquity of resistance, however, should not be confused with a weakness of disciplinary power (Foucault 1980). Performance pressures have profound effects on consciousness and behavior at the front lines, and these effects matter greatly for the disciplinary penalties that are meted out to the poor.

In this sense, our analysis has important implications for how scholars understand street-level discretion. Images of case managers acting on personal whim have been a staple of anxieties regarding welfare reform, even from its inception. Critics on the right have worried that liberal or lazy frontline workers might not really implement the demanding new supervisory regime. Critics on the left have worried that tough new rules and tools would give case managers carte blanche to treat clients in arbitrary and unjust ways. Field studies of implementation have reinforced these anxieties at times by making it clear that frontline discretion is powerful and endemic to policy implementation. It cannot be eradicated by supervision or procedure.

Our findings do not contradict this view or the studies that have advocated it (Lipsky 1980; Brodkin 1997; Maynard-Moody and Musheno 2003). Rather, they underscore the perils of taking this lesson while failing to appreciate its counterpart in the leading scholarship: the organizational forces that systematically shape the use of frontline discretion. As scholars such as Lipsky (1980) and Brodkin (2007) have repeatedly argued, frontline workers may be weakly constrained by rules, but they are rarely free to act as they wish. Their uses of discretion are not "ad hoc, unsystematic, or incomprehensible" (M. Feldman 1992: 163), nor are they mere reflections of individual preference (Baumgartner 1992: 129; Mashaw 1983: 213). Organizational routines, tools, norms, incentives, information systems, and categories of understanding function as mechanisms of social control that shape the use of discretion in predictable ways.

Our analysis in this chapter underscores the limits of discretion in the work lives of local program managers and caseworkers. In the WT program, case managers hold *broad* discretion, in the sense that they are authorized to make a wide variety of decisions affecting the client. But they do not hold *deep* discretion if by "deep" one means an individual liberty to treat clients as one would like. WT case managers work under tremendous performance pressure and have strong incentives to attend to this pressure. To initiate any sort of action, they must use computer systems that, by design, ensure that their uses of discretion will be tracked. As a result, case managers make their choices as actors who know they are being observed and evaluated.

Our interviews suggest that welfare reform has initiated a tougher regime of social control, not just for welfare clients, but also for their case managers. Indeed, the high rates of sanctioning in the WT program flow from the power of this organizational regime more than from any expectations case managers have about how sanctions affect clients or performance numbers. Strong performance pressures function as a form of coercive power that drives and directs action and as a form of productive power that shapes subjective understandings, perceptions, and choices at the front lines.

To be sure, our analysis also reveals a substantial amount of discretion in street-level organizations. We see it, for example, in the case managers who shift burdens onto themselves in an effort to protect clients, who act on their personal frustrations by sanctioning in cases where they otherwise would not, and who use threats and impositions of sanctions as a way to exert greater control over client behavior. We see it also in the ways that local program managers pursue strategic but perverse organizational maneuvers in response to performance pressures.

Yet a closer look at these examples also serves to underscore the dependence of individual agency on organizational forces. In Foucault's (1980) terms, one might say that as disciplinary power instigates resistance, it also shapes the mentalities of resistance and the terrains that resistance must traverse. The frustrations that influence case managers' sanction decisions are rooted in the organization of WT casework and the pressures of competitive performance systems. Case managers turn to sanction threats for precisely the reasons emphasized by Lipsky (1980, 1984): because bureaucratic processes push them to use their discretion in ways that lead to rationing, silencing, and disentitlement. "Burden shifting" case managers, who work to protect their clients, swim against the organizational tide. But their small numbers and stories testify to the difficulties and costs of doing so and to the forces that make it difficult to maintain such a strategy over the long haul. The perverse organizational responses we observed are facilitated by managerial discretion, to be sure. But as we have seen, they are, for the most part, predictable outcomes of the structures and processes in which officials operate.

In this regard, our analysis also raises troubling questions about the NPM and the sharp turn toward performance systems in recent years. We are hardly the first to point out that performance indicators can give rise to perverse organizational responses. But our analysis suggests that such problems may come in a broader variety of forms than previous studies have suggested. Equally important, we find that these problems flow from contradictions that are deeply embedded in the NPM itself—tensions among core principles that are supposed to fit together seamlessly and efficiently. At the same time, our analysis also underscores that a narrow focus on the strategic rationality of individuals is likely to understate the scope of perversities engendered by performance pressures. To understand why case managers impose sanctions that they expect to harm their strategic interests, one must look to broader organizational dynamics and consider how performance pressures affect emotions as well as interests.

The new public management suggests to many reformers that they can have their cake and eat it too: centralized control of outcomes *and* local autonomy; generalization of best practices *and* diverse solutions tailored to local needs; private provision *and* public purpose; competition between regions *and* collaboration among regions. It sounds too good to be true, and it is. Reformers would be better served by an open acknowledgment that features of the new public management lie in tension with one another and tend to work at cross-purposes. When officials are placed in a competitive performance system that promotes conformity, we should not expect the benefits of organizational diversity to emerge. The same can be said for locally tailored problem solving. When these values are paramount, performance pressures may need to be eased, at least for a time, to facilitate their achievement. Alternatively, if reformers wish to pursue outcome-focused goals through strong performance systems, they should recognize that their pursuit is likely to come at the cost of some valuable forms of diversity and innovation.

Finally, by employing an organizational lens, our analysis has provided some important correctives for the literature on welfare sanctions. First, statistical analyses of sanctions that focus narrowly on individual traits create a somewhat misleading view of their origins. Because sanctioning is an organized practice, sanctions emerge as products of organizational forces. To ignore these forces, as most studies have, is to promote systematic misunderstandings of what sanctions are and why they vary across times, places, and client subgroups as they do.

Second, performance pressures influence sanctioning in ways that go beyond the typical narrative of rational actors who sacrifice substantive program goals in favor of instrumental performance interests. When performance pressures rise, local providers respond by sanctioning at higher rates—a reaction that they actually expect to *hurt* performance. Performance-driven sanctioning is not a rationally chosen strategy. It emerges as an unintended byproduct of organizational forces. It occurs because frontline workers are under great stress, possess few tools, are pressured to control performance-related client behaviors, and get frustrated when client behaviors put their own performance at risk.

Last, our analysis suggests that performance-driven sanctioning follows a conditional pattern that fits comfortably into the findings presented in earlier chapters. When performance indicators go south, politics matters: ideologically conservative regions respond with higher sanction rates, while liberal regions show no change. Cash motives matter too: In a system where high stakes attach to performance pay points, for-profits sanction at systematically higher rates than nonprofits. Power and group stigma matter too: When regional performance declines, the clients most disadvantaged by racial classifications and educational factors bear the heaviest burdens of increased sanctioning. In these ways, sanctions are not just products of organizations; they are also expressions of broader dynamics related to power, culture, profit, and ideology.

CASEWORKER DISCRETION AND
DECISIONS TO DISCIPLINE

T HIS CHAPTER COMPLETES OUR JOURNEY DOWN THROUGH THE LEVELS
    of poverty governance by focusing directly on case managers' relation-
ships with clients and decisions about when to impose sanctions. The policies
and pressures that shape poverty governance eventually funnel down to a tip
where the individual case manager must interpret and implement the priorities
of the system. TANF case managers are responsible for evaluating client cases,
distributing supports and services, and applying penalties (Watkins-Hayes
2009). For poor people who seek aid from the TANF program, they are primary
the face of decision-making authority (Soss 2000). Thus, to understand poverty governance as a concrete practice, we must look beyond the environmental
and organizational forces that structure disciplinary action (see chapters 7–9)
and directly examine the dynamics of human agency and choice in caseworker-
client relationships.

We begin by clarifying how the caseworker's role has changed in recent
years. Case managers occupy a role that blends conventional features of the
street-level bureaucrat with a more therapeutic role. To be sure, their jobs bear
little resemblance to that of a psychologist or social work professional: They do
not possess resources, expertise, or powers of diagnosis and action on anything
like that scale. Case managers get little training and have few tools at their disposal. They use their discretion mainly to ration time and resources, offer small
favors, control their caseloads, and make decisions about whom to penalize or
"cut some slack."

The therapeutic dimensions of their position bear a closer relationship to the
mentor or sponsor roles found in recovery programs that treat chemical depen-
dencies. Case managers today act as experienced guides in the client's journey
from pathology (welfare dependency) to normalcy (the neoliberal paternalist vision of the worker-citizen). As low-wage workers who have often known
poverty and welfare participation firsthand, they serve as role models who can
relate to the struggles of their charges. They are positioned, in the paternalist
ideal, as experienced parental authority figures. They are "elders" who know
enough to be sympathetic yet strict, who call clients out on their self-delusions
and evasions of responsibility, who are wise to the gambits of those who would

play them for fools. It is their job, as they see it, to size up a client's character and story and to exercise judgment in dispensing benefits and punishments.

In the client-caseworker relationship, the official status of the street-level bureaucrat is but one of the many identities in play (Watkins-Hayes 2009). When case managers approach clients, they do so as more than just ambivalent representatives of the "business model." They are more than just agents of the state and more than just organizational actors. Their conflicted mentalities, and the strategies they use to govern, are equally rooted in social identities that come from outside the welfare system. When case managers arrive at work, they do not check their personal histories and social statuses at the door. To the contrary, they experience their work and forge their connections with clients through particular identities—as a Christian black woman, as a Latino father, as a white woman who has risen from the degraded ranks of welfare receipt herself, and so on. Case managers, positioned as experienced guides, build their relationships with clients at the intersections of their personal histories. The cultural resources they deploy as they work to persuade and transform clients are supplied by race, class, gender, religion, sexual identity, parenthood, rural/ urban experience, and other aspects of social selfhood.

These dynamics, we argue, play a central role in the production of racially biased disciplinary practices. The root of racial inequity in the Welfare Transition (WT) program is not that white, professional civil servants lack the "cultural competence" needed to understand their low-income, nonwhite clients. Indeed, according to our statewide survey, most WT case managers are not white, and very few have advanced degrees or professional qualifications. The staffing practices of private welfare providers have little to do with civil service requirements or social work training. With case management reduced to a deskilled, low-wage position, providers frequently recruit staff from the local pool of low-skilled labor and from the ranks of their own welfare recipients. As a result, case management takes place in the context of what Cathy Cohen (1999) calls "advanced marginalization"—a situation in which some members of a marginalized group are elevated to positions in dominant institutions where they are called on to serve and discipline the most disadvantaged and unincorporated members of their group.

Building on this analysis, the second half of the chapter explores how individual case managers make sanction decisions (a process question) and analyzes the sanction patterns that result (an outcome question). Based on our field research, we suggest that sanction decisions follow a "logic of appropriateness" that depends on assessments of persons as much as behaviors (March and Olsen 1989, 2004). In principle, sanctions are supposed to be triggered by objective behavioral events. In practice, behaviors and events, and the explanations clients give for them, are always ambiguous. They must be interpreted through the case manager's perception of the person. Is a client really being delayed by factors beyond her control, or is she merely trying to game the system? Should a failure to turn in documentation be treated as a one-time mistake, signifying nothing, or as evidence that a "problem client" needs to be sent a strong message?

It is in the nebulous realm of such judgments that client race enters into case managers' decisions about when to use disciplinary tools. The influence of client race rarely takes the crude form of white case managers consciously discriminating on the basis of prejudice. As suggested by the Racial Classification Model (RCM), the roots of racial bias can be traced to more subtle and conditional dynamics that are not restricted to white case managers. Drawing on survey-experimental and administrative data, we show how client race and discrediting personal markers interact to influence case manager sanction decisions. As frontline workers use their discretion, their choices and actions are not always biased by racial classifications. But when clients of color have markers that appear to be consistent with negative racial stereotypes, they are targeted for disciplinary action in ways that white clients are not.

Clarifying the Case Manager's Role

From the 1910s to the 1960s, welfare caseworkers devoted much of their time to monitoring families on relief (Piven and Cloward 1971). Their intrusions into the lives of poor women and children flowed from their mandate to enforce means-tested eligibility rules and "morals tests" focused on family environments and virtuous behavior (Abramovitz 1988). The early Mother's Pensions were offered only to women who maintained a "suitable home," and this standard was carried forward when the Social Security Board drafted its model state law for the Aid to Dependent Children (ADC) program in the 1930s: Aid was to be offered only to "any dependent child who is living in a suitable family home" (Gordon 1994: 276). Throughout this period, case managers were charged with tasks such as carrying out home inspections, gathering character evaluations from neighbors and clergy, and enforcing policies such as the "man in the house" rule (Bell 1965).

Morals tests served as mechanisms for denying aid to the "undeserving poor," controlling sexual behaviors, and regulating gender and race relations

(Gordon 1994). By pushing women off the rolls, and ensuring that their benefits could not be shared with unemployed men, they also served as a means of work enforcement (Piven and Cloward 1988). For caseworkers, however, this labor-regulating function was only a secondary effect. Their job was not to enforce work requirements. It was to enforce standards of deservingness by certifying that needs were genuine, homes suitable, and behaviors morally acceptable.

This era of case management came to an end in the 1960s, when welfare rights victories led to new procedural protections in Aid to Families with Dependent Children (AFDC) administration (M. Davis 1995). Extending this development, the federal government moved in the early 1970s to have states separate the provision of social services and income support (Sosin 1986; Hasenfeld 2000). As a result, casework in the AFDC program became a more routinized, clerical activity focused on eligibility determinations. Caseworkers evaluated many aspects of clients' lives to decide whether technical eligibility rules had been met, but they no longer managed family cases in the hands-on ways that their predecessors had. Most activities of this sort were moved to separate child welfare units and to officials who pursued cases of child abuse and neglect (Roberts 2002).

The rise of neoliberal paternalism signaled a new shift in the nature of casework, marked by the passage of federal welfare reform in 1996 (Lurie 2006). The prime directives for TANF case managers today are to convey and enforce work expectations and to advance and enable transitions to employment. Efforts to promote family and child well-being are downplayed in this frame, but they are not entirely abandoned. Under neoliberal paternalism, they are assimilated into efforts to promote work based on the idea that "work first" will put clients on the most reliable path toward achieving a self-sufficient, stable, and healthy family.

Thus, case managers today initiate their relationships with new clients by screening them for work readiness and delivering an "orientation" to describe work expectations and penalties for noncompliance. They then develop "individual responsibility plans"—or "contracts of mutual responsibility"—to specify the steps that each client will take in order to move from welfare to a job. These rites of passage establish a relationship in which the case manager's primary tasks are to facilitate, monitor, and enforce the completion of required work activities.

In celebratory portrayals of the new paternalism, case managers are described as being deeply involved in their clients' development, as "authority figures as well as helpmates" (Mead 2004a: 158). In the Florida WT program, this ethos is expressed by the neoliberal relabeling of caseworkers as "career counselors" (see chapter 8). The label evokes images of a well-trained professional who draws on diverse resources to advise and assist entrepreneurial job seekers. In practice, however, few aspects of case management fit this template. To understand why, one must begin with three defining conditions of WT case management: time pressures, tool and resource deficits, and performance-focused monitoring for quality assurance (QA).

Time is, in many respects, the most precious resource for the street-level bureaucrat (Lipsky 1980). As case managers struggle to complete their tasks in the hours available, opportunities to think patiently and carefully about clients' situations are exceedingly rare. The more pressing question is how to tame the tide of demands closing in: the slew of new alerts from the One-Stop Service Tracking (OSST) system, due dates for documenting work activities, the completion of pre-penalty letters and sanction forms, client phone calls and requests, and so on. Demands on the case manager's time come from all directions, but some are more negotiable than others. Because the work required by information systems and supervisors must be done, the most feasible approach to reducing time demands is to defer or deflect client requests. As one case manager explained:

> There isn't enough time in a day to do everything that we need to do. It's supposed to be 40 hours a week, and I'd say [I usually work] 50, 50 or more. And unfortunately, because of the way that the program is structured, the penalties and the sanctions and the hours are a priority. You're not necessarily going to have time to review all of your phone calls [from clients]. But you know, you have to get into your system and work your to-dos, to sanction people, to close cases and open them.

In addition to lacking the time needed to "really counsel," case managers lack the palette of tools and resources needed to approach clients' cases in personally tailored ways. The funding needed to furnish such tools is in short supply, and the goal of maintaining profitability pushes toward a limited number of low-cost tools that focus on enforcing program requirements. This dynamic was best captured by a case manager who referred to herself as "Ms. Cookie Cutter" because of the one-size-fits-all approach she must implement in the Florida WT program.

> This program is structured the way that it is and the bottom line, I guess, is money. You're required to fulfill so many things within that contract

that you have. [So] it's like it is a cookie cutter approach to people who are individuals [who] have different needs, who have different barriers, and they're forcing us to put them in the same type of process. Even though they've implemented all these new quote-unquote programs, they're cookie cutter programs. You're requiring everyone to come in and do the same thing and follow the same process from beginning to end, and it's not conducive [to client success] at all. [There is] such a huge emphasis placed on employment, employment, employment. I disagree. If you don't have a high school diploma, your primary focus needs to be getting your high school diploma, you know, versus going out and getting a job. It's like putting a band-aid over a bullet wound.

Constrained in this manner, case managers are pressed ever-forward by the knowledge that their actions are being tracked by information systems and QA managers. As one case manager explained, "We have a QA person, who can, you know, anytime have access to your caseload. She reviews it and if there is a problem, she will let you know. And then we go ahead and do [what she says]. Immediately." In one region we studied, a new for-profit provider sought to boost efficiency by implementing a "time management" approach to QA. Case managers had to enter all their activities into a database in half-hour increments. As one described it, "Every time I'm working on a case, I'll write in what I did for the case. I think [the information is] actually going up to [the for-profit owner] because they are a time-management company. They want to see how we are managing our time. [But] to take the extra time to document everything it adds up over the course of the day." Whatever its effects on efficiency may be, a key feature of QA management is that it converts organizational goals into matters of "personal responsibility" for frontline workers. As one QA manager told us:

We also have what we call "case manager goals." Each one has particular goals they must achieve monthly or try to come close to [in order to] meet and exceed standards. [The goal] is personal responsibility—making sure that they're doing their job correctly. But also, it pushes them to get the information timely into the system. [Their actions as case managers affect] just about everything that helps your performance regional-wide.

Working at the intersection of these forces, career counselors bear little resemblance to professional therapists. As one put it, "We're not really given the time to really counsel. I mean, they call us career managers, but really, you're tracking hours. 'Hey, did you get a job yet?'" WT case managers are, at the end of the day, harried street-level bureaucrats who must focus on clearing their to-do lists, rationing their resources, and controlling the potential for clients to disrupt their routines. To do so, they practice many of the time-honored tactics identified in classic studies of street-level bureaucracy, such as limiting access and classifying clients in ways that do not call for time-intensive procedures (Lipsky 1980, 1984; Brodkin 1986). In the era of neoliberal paternalism, however, their action repertoire also includes new tactics.

Under the business model of service provision, the relationship between client and case manager is rooted in an employment metaphor: The client has signed a "contract" to do a job and should approach the program as if it were a job. This aspect of neoliberal discourse provides the case manager with a resource for deflecting client demands. Consider, for example, how the following case manager responds to new applicants who say they lack access to transportation and need help to fulfill their work-activity requirements.

> [I tell them] if you're in a situation right now where transportation is a hindrance for you, you may want to reconsider getting your cash assistance open because you're going to be required to participate in this program on a daily basis. What I tell them too is: If you want in this program, what would you do in terms of getting to and from your job? How would you find a job? Okay, if you weren't in this program, what would you do about daycare, if you were not in this program?

Here, as elsewhere, neoliberal discourse blurs the boundary between welfare participation and the labor market. As welfare is recast as an employment relationship, the individual's obstacles to success in the market are converted into obstacles in the WT program—problems that clients must address if they want to remain eligible for aid. For many case managers, this framing is experienced as a double-edged sword. It offers a way to deflect and limit client demands, but it also undermines the idea that they are professional counselors who tend to the needs of their clients and help them overcome real barriers to labor market success.

> [Welfare in Florida] is no longer a social service; it is a business. I find it to be the difference between herding cattle and herding sheep. A cattle herder is just running people through, not taking time to look after them.

A shepherd takes care of the sheep, tends after them, cares for them. It is not my nature to herd cattle and now I have to learn to do that.

Following this metaphor, we might say that sanctions provide a "prod" for case managers who must find a way to "herd their cattle." In explaining this dynamic, one case manager also touched on how sanctions can promote the paternalist goal of instilling self-discipline:

[Sanctions] are a method, I could say, of controlling [or] maintaining some type of hold on the person in the program. You've got to have some type of hold. Their life situation hasn't taught them probably the skills necessary to determine what they should be looking for. [The sanction] changes the mind set of [the client to] what it is to be employed.

In this sense, case managers see sanctions as a tool for maintaining control over clients. In another sense, however, sanctions often remind case managers that they *lack* control over the ways their clients get treated—that their control over client outcomes is limited by the organization's control over them. As one explained, "There may be times where I may think that maybe they didn't really deserve that sanction or whatever, but it's a process. You may have a customer who has faithfully participated in a program then you run across a week where they haven't turned something in, [and] you can't give them any slack. You have to start that penalty process on them." At the extreme, case managers tell stories of imposing sanctions in cases that disturb them months later. One, for example, recalled a client who had entered the pre-penalty phase for failing to turn in work documentation. At the last minute, her mother called to say she had been "severely burned" and was in the hospital.

I told her, you know what, we have two days before her case is going to be sanctioned. The mother's like, well she needs to keep her child care because she can't take care of her [kids], you know, being in the hospital. At that time I kind of explained to her that if she's not working, not participating in the program, she wouldn't qualify for the child care anyway. The child care is continued upon you participating and getting all your hours of participation in the program. The outcome of that was that the sanction process had to proceed. Her case was sanctioned and her case was closed. Because here we have a systematic thing again: we can't just leave sanctions open. We can't say, oh, okay, we'll wait for you to bring [the documentation] in. The process has to take its course. [It was] maybe four or five months that she was off the cash assistance [and then she had to] start the whole [application] process from the very beginning. [In the end,] the case never really reopened, so I don't know what happened.

Identities, Experiences, and the Recovery Model

These changes in the case manager role have proceeded alongside others that have brought therapeutic dynamics to the fore. Three developments have converged to make the case manager into a more therapeutic role and to make social identities more central to its fulfillment.

The first is closely related to what Cathy Cohen (1999) calls "advanced marginalization," a process by which some members of a marginal group are incorporated into dominant institutions and, thus, are placed in new positions vis-à-vis other members of their own group. As these group members navigate their new opportunities, they "confront incentives to promote and prioritize those issues and members thought to 'enhance' the public image of the group, while controlling and making invisible those issues and members perceived to threaten the status of the community" (Cohen 1999: 27). As they are incorporated into dominant institutions, these group members also enter positions that make them responsible for managing the problems and populations associated with the most marginal segments of their own groups. Thus, Cohen (1999: 27) observes, advanced marginalization "not only allows for limited mobility on the part of some marginal group members, but also transfers much of the direct management of other, less privileged marginal group members to individuals who share the same group identity."

The second development can be traced to discourses in recent decades that have "medicalized" welfare dependency as a treatable pathology akin to addiction (Schram 2000). Welfare programs, in this frame, follow a "recovery model" that is closely aligned with the twelve-step programs employed by Alcoholics Anonymous (AA) and other programs for drug addicts, criminals, and social service populations (D. Brown 1991; Cressey 1955; Grant 1965; Sigurdson 1969; Silverman 1982). To find the strength to overcome addiction, such models suggest that individuals must take personal responsibility for their situations, be willing to undergo a spiritual transformation, and enter relationships of mutual trust, support, and responsibility with group members who have traveled a greater distance down the path to recovery (AA 1953). Through the lens of the recovery model, welfare recipients are cast as disordered subjects who require a transformative program to cure their pathologies and help them gain control over their lives. Case managers are positioned as knowledgeable guides whose experiences allow them to empathize with clients' struggles yet also apply a firm hand in requiring personal responsibility and moving clients along the reformative path.

The third development is the transformation of casework into a deskilled position. The contracted providers who hire case managers today are not required to consider markers of skill such as civil service credentials and social work training. And with much of casework focused on documentation and data entry, they have few incentives to forgo low-wage workers in favor of hiring professionals. As a result, the legitimacy and credibility of the case manager (beyond her or his formal policy authority) has become disconnected from any credential or claim to diagnostic and prescriptive expertise. Life experience is the trait that fills this vacuum. Drawing on their own struggles and identities, case managers lay claim to a kind of wisdom that, for many, is more profound than professional expertise and more deserving of client attention.

At the intersection of these three developments, relationships between clients and case managers proceed on a complex terrain of identities and experiences. Relative to earlier eras, case managers today are more likely to share defining elements of personal history and social identity with their clients. The resulting dynamics matter greatly for the practice of case management, as Celeste Watkins-Hayes (2009: 189) shows in a perceptive analysis of professional identities in two welfare offices: "A personal history of poverty," she observes, "provides a set of tools and experiences that caseworkers can draw upon in their interactions with clients and can be used to set tones of benevolence, malevolence, or something in between, depending on the worker." Some minority caseworkers adopt a politics of racial respectability and uplift that leads them to be especially tough on clients who share their racial background. Others practice different forms of "racialized professionalism," drawing on community knowledge and shared personal experiences to work more effectively with clients from their own racial group. Watkins-Hayes (2009: 212) concludes:

> [My field research has] revealed the unique complications faced and the resources wielded by some minority street-level bureaucrats of color. For those who actively engage in what I call racialized professionalism, perceived group interests help to shape how they interpret and operational-

ize their roles as policy implementers. Yet, we must not assume that a singular racial agenda characterizes the views and actions of these bureaucrats, as they clearly make choices about whether and how to inject their social group memberships into the bureaucratic context.

Our interviews underscore this emphasis on the ways that intersecting identities provide a foundation for contemporary case management. Gender and experiences of motherhood figure prominently in WT case managers' accounts of how they "connect" with clients and seek to gain their trust and cooperation. Appeals to shared Christian identities and values also play an important role. Given their centrality for our analysis, however, we focus here on dynamics related to race, poverty, and experiences with welfare receipt.

WT case managers routinely stress how their own backgrounds matter for their relationships with clients. Communication is a common theme in these accounts. A black male case manager, for example, explained that "information is shared among people with commonalities. The less in common you have with individuals, the less information you receive, you know?" Beyond information, case managers emphasize how experiences with poverty and racial marginality give them "perspective and wisdom" in understanding clients' situations. The complex lessons drawn from such experiences are well illustrated by a black female case manager, who describes how her personal history helps her understand her black clients' frustrations but also leads her to emphasize that they will have to work extra hard because nothing comes easily for racial minorities.

> I've picked apples. I've worked in the mill cutting cabbage. So, I know how it feels to get in the car and drive somewhere and see wealthy areas and houses, when you are with all of your sisters crammed into one room. So I think that helps me relate to the clients. I can [also tell my clients from experience that] being a black woman puts you in a position where you have to work a little harder. You have to try harder because we are in America and that is just how America is.

At the case manager's desk, shared racial identities can also generate tensions related to questions of group loyalty and special treatment. Consider, for example, the following narrative told by a black female case manager. The ambiguity of the story (does the client expect a special favor, or is her plea for help being misread as an appeal to racial solidarity?) serves only to underscore the various ways that racial identities may shape expectations and interpretations.

[Laughs] Being black and working in this organization, it is a struggle with me and my own race. I feel like, well, minorities feel like that we're supposed to give them more of a leeway. Most of the black people that come in here, it's always a game behind it. They will expect you to bend a little bit for them. Like I had a client [who] told me, "You are supposed to understand me. Why are you not helping me out? You can do this for me," and she wanted me to give her more than what I should have given her in supportive services. And I looked at her and asked her, "So I'm supposed to understand you because we're the same race?" She said, "No, that's not what I'm saying," but I say, "Yes, that is what you are saying."

People of color have become more prevalent in the ranks of case managers and, for good and for ill, are often thought to have a greater ability to relate to minority clients. The counterpart to this view, less often expressed in interviews, is a lingering suspicion that white case managers have privileged pasts and, as a result, "just don't get it." Recalling a recent experience with job placement managers, a black male case manager observed that the "people who were in those positions were white and, just because I had opportunities to get to know them, I knew that their experiences did not allow them to see that all people had something to bring to the table." A white female case manager who worried greatly about this issue described it as a form of "prejudice" and argued that it was equally prevalent among her minority clients and coworkers.

When I moved here I expected the white people to be prejudiced, but what I found was that I was the one being judged because I was young and white. [People at the one-stop] started calling me preppy little white girl and really picking on me because they think you're born with a silver spoon in your mouth. Believe me I wasn't. I think I'm prejudiced against [subject to prejudice for being white] just as much as any other case manager would be from the other races.

As this quotation suggests, identity markers such as age, race, and gender can matter as much for workplace relations as for interactions with clients. For some case managers, the politics that arise from intersecting identities define a central facet of the work experience. Reflecting on dynamics at his own one-stop, one black case manager explained:

Organizations have difficulty in dealing with differences in race and sex and gender. In the old days of business, the women were secretaries and nurses, the men were supposed to be business leaders and managers, the blacks were supposed to be subservient and just smile. There are still some of those biases that come through [here]. There are individuals who cannot overcome race and gender differences, not just clients and case managers but professionals.

In all these respects, case managers experience their identities as salient features of their work lives and dealings with clients. For an increasing number, however, the aspect of personal background that matters most is more specific: the experience of having sat on the other side of the desk as a welfare recipient. In an era of deskilled case management, private providers often view caseworker positions as suitable entry-level jobs for welfare clients who have demonstrated their ability to exercise personal responsibility and prevent their family obligations from interfering with work activities. Indeed, a woman who has pulled herself out of welfare and into a full-time job offers an especially attractive candidate for a case manager position because of her added value as a role model, experienced guide, and credible authority for clients.

Like other recent studies (Ridzi 2009; Watkins-Hayes 2009; Oberfield 2008), our interviews revealed that a sizeable percentage of case managers, roughly a third, had previously received welfare themselves. Some were actually put on the path toward their jobs by the work activities they had to complete as WT recipients. Case managers often struggle to find enough "countable" work activities for clients to complete, and one-stop centers are often short-staffed. For providers, the labor of WT recipients is essentially cost-free because it is already "paid for" by program benefits. For all these reasons, small numbers of recipients are often brought into the office to fulfill their work requirements by doing work such as copying or filing. While these experiences may not improve a client's prospects on the labor market in general, they do increase the odds that a client will be identified as a good candidate for a job that comes open at the one-stop. Reflecting on this transition, two case managers underscored how their earlier experiences as clients continued to shape their current relationships with clients and coworkers.

I was on TANF for a month and a half and I saw how we as clients were treated. I just hated the way we were treated. It was, "You do what we want you to do and that's it." Career managers talking to you nasty. Everyone talking to you nasty. And we were just treated so harsh, and I did not like that. So once I went back to the school system, I got a phone call because I had done some community service [as a WT work requirement], and they offered me a job. That [experience] affects me a lot. Just that one month experience of how I was treated. I would never want to treat anyone else the same way. Right here in [this region], I now work with my former case manager but it is not hard, not really, because when I was receiving TANF, I voiced my own opinions and I let that person know how I felt. So when I got employed that person already knew who I was, so you know. [Laughs]

I think my experience makes it easier to deal with clients because I've been on cash assistance before and I didn't stay on cash assistance. Some of [my coworkers] have made some comments that I did not take too kindly to. Especially when we are in, like, staff meetings, and they will [say], "I was a single mother and I did all right." But maybe they did not have the exact same circumstances as some of the customers. You may have been a single mother but you had some child-support payments coming in and maybe they did not have to deal with criminal records and things like that. I think they are insensitive.

For some case managers, personal experiences of material hardship and welfare receipt provide a basis for more empathetic relationships with clients. As one explained, "I tell them, 'I've been there before and I know where you are coming from.' I know they have to walk a little ways to the bus and I know what they are going through but they can get out of it eventually." In some cases, welfare experiences combine with shared racial identities to forge powerful feelings of obligation to serve a particular subset of clients. As a Latina case manager explained:

I was a single mom before I met my husband, who just happens to be a migrant worker. We were migrants for a few years, and I know what it's like to be on the other side of the desk. I used to be on cash assistance. Now I'm a mom and a grandmother, and I want to see [the clients] succeed. I do really want to help the Spanish clients because I do speak the language and I have worked in the Latino community for twenty-five years.

Virtually all of the case managers we interviewed emphasized that they serve as role models for their clients. Among former recipients, this dynamic took on a stronger form, as case managers extrapolated general lessons from their own personal stories. In many cases, these lessons stress moral commitment and personal responsibility: "I used to receive cash, and, like I didn't receive it for long because I didn't want anything for free, so I got a job right away." For some, the personal storyline of responsibility and perseverance becomes a normative standard for evaluating current clients, who often appear to fail by comparison.

> Being previously on the other side of the desk definitely makes it easier to relate to the clients. But on the other hand, when they come in and sit down and say, "I'm divorced and I don't get child support and I can't afford child care or I don't have a good car," and they're using that as an excuse that angers me more than maybe your usual caseworker because I know it's really hard but I know you just have to get out there and do it and not use it as an excuse. Because I myself got out there and did it myself, and within a month I was reemployed, and I had some pretty big barriers. In terms of housing, I had to find my own place. I had to get enough money to get my own place and child-care assistance. So I get angered with clients who play the victim role. It's okay to have barriers but don't use them as an excuse. Overcome them.

As "recovered" welfare recipients, case managers frequently deploy their own stories as motivational object lessons for clients. They use their tales at various times to raise a client's hopes for success, to shame a client for not working hard enough, to suggest that there is no alternative to the path of work, and to convey a stigma-relieving empathy for the client's plight. The following reflections by two case managers illustrate such uses of personal narrative.

> I'll tell my clients that I received cash and I used to be here. But I got it in my mind that I didn't want to be here anymore and I didn't want to get in trouble, so I got a job. So I'll tell them, even if they don't want to go to school, they need to get a job. So I'll use my background as a welfare recipient for that. I think it motivates some people. [I know] what it's like, exactly. I've been there and done that and I know it's not easy but it's something you have to do.

I try to go the extra mile and share with them some of my life experiences. I tell them I've been on the other side of the desk and I know how
it is. My husband was really sick, and I was laid off with [another city],
and so I was on the other side of the desk. So I just encourage them and
tell them that I went to work with three kids and that you can do it. I've
had customers come back and congratulate me and I've had them cry-
ing just talking about their lives. Individually they are all important, and
I just want to help people. I always address my customers as Mr. and
Mrs. and show them respect because sometimes life throws us curves.

Decision Making, Appropriateness, and Race

As this discussion suggests, client-caseworker interactions are often deeply personal and tend to be shaped by social identities in far-reaching ways. In this
sense, case managers should be seen as embedded not only in organizations,
but also in social contexts where appraisals of personal identity and behavior
are highly salient. In this section, we explain how this social context matters for
case manager decisions about how to handle client cases. In particular, we focus on how efforts to make "appropriate" case decisions are guided by the ways
that case managers "size up" clients as persons. By unpacking this process, we
lay the groundwork for our subsequent analysis of how client racial characteristics influence sanction decisions.

When making decisions regarding client cases, case managers may be concerned with a variety of potential consequences: effects on family well-being,
effects on performance numbers, and so on. In the main, however, when case
managers describe their decisions in actual cases, they tend to emphasize this
means-ends "logic of consequences" far less than a "logic of appropriateness"
(March and Olsen 1989, 2004). By "appropriate," we mean decisions that con-
form not only to formal rules and official expectations, but also to "mutual,
and often tacit, understandings of what is true, reasonable, natural, right, and
good" (March and Olsen 2004: 4). Following a logic of appropriateness, they
implicitly ask: "What kind of a situation does this case present? What is my role
in the program, in the organization, in the community, and in relation to this
particular client? And what is a person such as I supposed to do in a situation
such as this?"

Efforts to answer such questions would be straightforward if rules, norms,
identities, and values all lined up neatly in a single direction, and if cases fell
unambiguously into one action category or another. Unfortunately, in the real

world of poverty governance, neither condition is met very often. To identify the "right" action at a given moment, frontline workers must search for case-specific cues that offer guidance. In this process, few factors are as decisive as the case manager's assessment of the client as a person. As Maynard-Moody and Musheno (2003: 78) explain, "street-level workers want to get a sense of who citizen-clients are, get a fix on people, to decide how to handle them. In figuring out who a person is, they may also put a fix on people, assigning them to a social identity or group belonging that carries with it significant meaning and consequence." When describing how they size up a case and decide what to do, case managers almost always stress the importance of sizing up the person. Judgments about whether to believe a story or treat this week's problem as an acceptable aberration ultimately hinge on beliefs about whether the individual in question is a straight shooter, trying hard, or playing games.

Case managers tend to see efforts to assess the person as not just necessary, but desirable. Successful welfare relationships and outcomes, they argue, ultimately depend on whether "the person's going to come through" and is "really serious about getting a job," as one case manager put it. She and most other case managers contend that "it starts with the customer." Thus, when case managers receive a new client, they treat efforts to evaluate the person as a high priority and pursue this task through a search for markers that may offer some indication of character and motivation.

> The first time when I meet with a client, the first thing I'll do is that I'll look on the screen that we utilize for sanctions. So I'll do research and see how many sanctions they have had in the past or any, and that will give you a feeling if the client is going to participate. That is the first clue there. [And] clients that are routinely [returning to] the program from the start, you know they will be unwilling to participate and will be someone [who] will always push the limits of the program.

Once the client's case is established, perceptions of the person underwrite case managers' commonsense decisions about when to give a client some extra time to turn in documentation, grant a good-cause exemption, or impose a sanction. In general discussions of their work, case managers often assert that moral evaluations do not matter for their decisions to impose sanctions. When discussing specific cases, however, their accounts pivot time and again on moral assessments of what specific clients did, whether they were exerting sufficient effort, and whether they appeared to be trustworthy in explaining their actions.

The matter-of-fact report that a sanction was imposed because of a missed work assignment is followed by the more impassioned judgment that "you failed to meet your employment responsibility here. We were working to put you there so you could learn, and you failed. That to me is more than just [work-activity] hours; it's commitment—which is the whole purpose of the program."

Thus, while sanctions are nominally applied to categories of behavior, decisions to impose sanctions hinge, to a significant degree, on the ways that case managers categorize people. Efforts to size up the person precede and guide decisions about whether to believe a hard-luck story, treat a client's misstep as willful, let this one slide or send a message. In making these sorts of judgments, case managers draw on "gut feelings" that reflect not just professional experiences and worksite norms, but also their implicit beliefs about how people from particular groups tend to think and act. It is here that one finds the opening for racial classifications to enter as unacknowledged and perhaps even unwanted influences on case managers' interpretations of what particular actions, explanations, and markers suggest.

The RCM suggests that race will be more likely to structure policy choice when it is a salient feature of a policy context and when group reputations indicate policy-relevant differences. As we have already seen in this chapter, race is a highly salient feature of case managers' daily relations with coworkers and clients. Our research also suggests that significant numbers of case managers perceive racial-group differences that are directly relevant to the goals of welfare-to-work programs.

As one would expect, case managers almost never expressed crude racial stereotypes or prejudices in our interviews. Yet it was common for case managers to note differences in program outcomes across racial groups and to cite "cultural differences" as one of the factors that explained the patterns. The tenor of such comments is well illustrated by the following exchange with a Latina case manager.

> With the Afro-Americans and whites I do see differences in terms of them gaining employment. The white clients tend to get the jobs that pay the higher wages. [Q: Why do you think that is?] I don't know, I guess that here the mentality still exists where they [blacks] look back and think that even if [jobs do] exist they will not be capable of finding better employment. So they stick to, you know, the fast-food [jobs] because they don't think they are capable of doing better. I've definitely seen this. I think that people should work harder and believe that they are capable

of succeeding. But they [blacks] are still stuck in that mentality that, you know, they don't have a lot of faith in their abilities.

Based on case managers' references to "cultural differences" in our interviews, we included a question in our statewide survey that asked, "On the whole, do you think that cultural differences between social groups play a role in explaining why some clients are more likely than others to achieve self-sufficiency?" Of the 109 case managers who responded, 84.4 percent answered yes, while only 15.6 percent answered no. Although the RCM emphasizes how implicit racial biases can influence policy choices by actors who do not overtly embrace racial stereotypes, it is also instructive to consider case managers' explicit expressions of a stereotype-consistent belief. To do so, we can turn to a question that asked case managers whether they believed that "lack of motivation and a willingness to work hard" is a major reason, a minor reason, or not a reason at all "for the economic and social problems that black people face today." In response, a 57.5 percent majority of case managers identified "lack of motivation and a willingness to work hard" as either a major or a minor contributing cause for these problems, while 42.5 percent deemed it not a reason at all. When the same question was asked about Latinos and Latinas, 45 percent identified this factor as a major or minor reason, while 55 percent deemed it not a reason at all.

Client Race and Sanction Decisions: An Empirical Test

If efforts to size up the client play a key role in frontline decision making, and if race is a salient feature of welfare interactions, it stands to reason that clients' racial characteristics might influence the ways case managers use their discretion to sanction. What if two clients, one white and one black, were identical in every way except race? And what if they also had some kind of characteristic that fit the negative stereotype of minority welfare recipients? Would case managers be equally likely to sanction the two recipients? In this section, we present empirical tests of this question, focusing on the RCM's prediction that racial disparities will be more likely to emerge when policy targets possess discrediting traits that are policy-relevant and aligned with group reputations. Extending the work of Devah Pager (2007), we test the potential for stereotype-consistent markers to provide "expectancy confirmation" regarding group members (Darley and Gross 1983) and, as a result, generate stronger racial biases in policy treatment.

Our empirical analysis employs two types of data. First, we draw on two experiments that we embedded in our statewide survey of case managers. Each presented respondents with a realistic rule-violation vignette in which key client characteristics were randomly assigned. Case managers were then asked whether they favored imposing a sanction in the case.[1] By using survey-experiments, we gain the advantages of causal inference associated with random assignment while remaining close to the phenomenon of study: decisions made by actual case managers (Kinder and Palfrey 1993). Despite these strengths, however, the use of hypothetical vignettes and the limitations of our survey sample both counsel some humility regarding these data.[2] Accordingly, we tri-angulate our findings with administrative data from the Florida WT program. While these data offer a weaker basis for causal inference, they have the benefit of reflecting decisions made on actual cases under normal working conditions.

Our statewide survey included two 2x2 experiments, each of which described a hypothetical TANF client who had arguably fallen out of compliance with pro-gram rules. For the racial dimension of the design, each vignette makes use of a procedure developed by Bertrand and Mullainathan (2003), who showed that by randomly assigning "black-sounding" and "white-sounding" names to a set of identical résumés, they could influence the rates at which employers contacted a fictitious job seeker. Adapting this procedure, we randomly assigned the cli-ent in vignette 1 a Latino-sounding name or a white-sounding name. Similarly, we assigned the client in vignette 2 a black-sounding name or a white-sounding name.[3]

The second dimension of the 2x2 design manipulates client markers that are commonly associated with (a) images of undeserving welfare clients and (b) negative stereotypes of minority racial/ethnic groups. To select these client traits, we drew on our field interviews, which revealed substantial caseworker attention to two client "types": the young mother of multiple children and the repeat recipient who has been sanctioned in the past.[4] The vignettes are pre-sented below with our experimental manipulations bracketed.[5]

Vignette 1: [Emily O'Brien/Sonya Perez] is a twenty-eight-year-old single mother with [one child aged seven/four children who is currently in her fourth month of pregnancy]. She entered the Welfare Transition program six months ago, after leaving her job as a cashier at a neighborhood gro-cery store where she had worked for nine months. [Emily/Sonya] was recently reported for being absent for a week from her assignment for community service work experience. Immediately after hearing that

[Emily/Sonya] had not shown up for a week of work, [Emily's/Sonya's] caseworker mailed a Notice of Failure to Participate (Form 2290) and phoned her to ask why she had missed her assignment. [Emily/Sonya] was not home when the caseworker called. However, when she responded to the 2290 three days later, she said she no longer trusted the person who was looking after her [child/children], and she did not want to go back to work until she found a new child-care provider. [Emily/Sonya] returned to work the next day.

Vignette 2: [Emily O'Brien/Lakisha Williams] is a twenty-six-year-old single mother with two children. She has been in the Welfare Transition program for five months. [Emily/Lakisha] was recently reported for failing to show up for a job interview that had been scheduled for her with a local housecleaning service. Immediately after hearing about the missed interview, [Emily's/Lakisha's] caseworker mailed a Notice of Failure to Participate (2290) and phoned her to ask why she had not shown up. [Emily/Lakisha] said she had skipped the interview because she had heard that a better position might open up next month with a home health agency. [She had been sanctioned two months earlier for failure to complete her hours for digital divide, a computer skills class.]

The two experiments offer a more and a less likely case for finding effects. Vignette 1 identifies the client as white or Latino, a contrast associated with smaller stereotype differences than the black-white client contrast used in vignette 2. In addition, vignette 1 focuses on child-care instability, which is a "normal" rather than "deviant" problem for women moving into employment (Loprest 2002). Likewise, although we expect the attribution of numerous children here to cue negative stereotypes related to sexuality and reproduction, this feature of the vignette may also indicate that a comparatively sympathetic group (children) will suffer hardship as a result of the sanction. As a result, one might expect this cue to produce ambivalence about sanctioning the family. The marker in vignette 2 is far less equivocal. By stating that the client has previously drawn a sanction, we simultaneously provide case managers with two pieces of information that may cue negative perceptions: The client is a repeat recipient and also has a record of at least one previous failure to comply with welfare-to-work rules.

Finally, the two narratives themselves differ in relation to sanction procedures. Although the client in vignette 1 was not at home when the case manager called, she responded to the Notice of Failure to Participate (2290) within the permissible ten-day period and then reestablished compliance by returning to work the next day. According to WT sanction rules, the pre-penalty phase for this client should end when compliance is reestablished by a return to work. In other words, based solely on the vignette, one cannot say that the appropriate response is to sanction the client.[6] By contrast, the client's reason for not complying with her welfare contract in vignette 2 clearly fails to meet the requirements for a good-cause exemption.

Thus, the two vignettes allow us to test the RCM in quite different cases. Following each vignette, respondents were asked to indicate on a four-point scale whether they strongly favored, somewhat favored, somewhat opposed, or strongly opposed imposing a sanction in the situation described. Baseline responses confirm that the two vignettes present divergent cases: 34 percent of case managers favored a sanction in vignette 1; 79 percent did in vignette 2. At the same time, these results confirm that case managers' judgments are not uniform or dictated in lockstep by program rules. Despite the fact that WT program rules seem to suggest otherwise, 34 percent of case managers favored a sanction in vignette 1. Likewise, 21 percent opted not to sanction the client in vignette 2, despite a clear violation of the rules.

Because case managers assigned to the different experimental conditions may vary in ways that affect their sanction decisions, we use multivariate models to control for respondent differences and, thus, to better isolate the effects of client traits. In addition to measures indicating the respondent's experimental condition, our logistic regression models include measures of selected case manager characteristics that studies of welfare casework suggest may affect a case manager's willingness to impose sanctions: years of work experience, religiosity, education level, partisan identification, marital status, and racial identity (see Gooden 2003; Dias Johnson and Maynard-Moody 2007; and Watkins-Hayes 2009).

The results of our analysis indicate that almost none of these covariates exert a statistically discernible influence on sanction decisions.[7] Perhaps most notably, black and Latino or Latina case managers did not respond to these experiments in any way that set them apart, statistically, from white case managers. The only case manager characteristic associated with a significant difference was work experience. Case managers with more than two years of welfare services experience emerge in both experiments as less likely to impose sanctions. Several factors may explain this result. Case managers with more years of experience, for example, are more likely to have been trained in an earlier era of welfare provision that placed less emphasis on sanctioning (AFDC prior to

1996, or the Florida WAGES program between 1996 and 2000). Alternatively, if case managers learn over time that sanctions negatively affect clients or performance ratings, then greater experience may lead to greater reluctance to impose sanctions. Another possibility is that experienced case managers become more adept at working with clients and, hence, resort to sanctions less quickly than novice case managers. Our data do not allow us to arbitrate among these alternatives.[8]

The key findings from our analysis, regarding the effects of the experimental conditions, are striking for their consistency. In vignette 1, we find that when case managers are presented with a white client, their sanction decisions are not influenced in any discernible way by information that the client has multiple children as opposed to one child. For the client described as having only one child, we find statistically borderline evidence that a sanction is more likely if the client is Latina than if she is white ($p = .067$). Most important, we find that, consistent with the RCM's predictions, a Latina woman with multiple children is significantly more likely to be sanctioned than a white woman with one child or multiple children.

The results for vignette 2 tell a similar story, only in stronger form. Here, we find no discernible differences in the odds of a new sanction for a white woman with no prior sanction, a black woman with no prior sanction, and a white woman who has a prior sanction. Sanction decisions are, from a statistical perspective, invariant across these conditions. Compared to all these hypothetical clients, however, a black woman with a prior sanction on her record is substantially and, in statistical terms, significantly more likely to receive a sanction.[9]

To make these results more concrete, we can calculate the predicted probability of a "typical" case manager imposing a sanction in each experimental condition. Holding our measures of case manager characteristics constant at their median values, we estimate the probability that a sanction will be favored for each type of client in each vignette. Figure 10-1 presents the results. For vignette 1, we find that the predicted probability of receiving a sanction rises steadily from a low of .14 for a white woman with one child, to .21 for a white woman who is pregnant and has multiple children, to .39 for a Latina woman with one child, to a high of .47 for a Latina mother who is pregnant and has multiple children. For vignette 2, we find that the mention of a prior sanction has no effect on the predicted probability of a white client being sanctioned (.67 versus .66). By contrast, when black clients are identified as having a prior sanction on their record, their predicted probability of being sanctioned rises from .75 to .97.

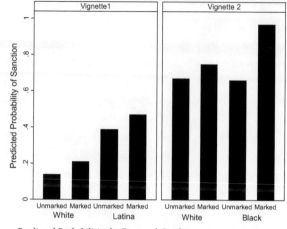

FIGURE 10-1. Predicted Probabilities by Race and Condition

Note: Each panel of figure 10-1 contains predicted probabilities of sanction for each experimental condition, holding all other variables at their median value, based on the regression results presented in table A10-3, found in the online appendix.

The consistency of the key finding across these experiments, that minority clients are disproportionately penalized when they possess discrediting markers, is striking. Nevertheless, one must bear in mind that the results are based on hypothetical scenarios. When case managers responded to the vignettes, they were not confronted with a real person; they did not have a detailed case file; they did not have to worry about effects on performance numbers; and they did not have to consider real material hardships that might result. To get closer to these real-world conditions, we must turn to administrative data generated by the Florida WT program itself. In so doing, we lose a major advantage of the experiment— certainty that clients with different characteristics have equivalent cases—and must instead rely on imperfect statistical controls to capture differences. In return, however, we gain the ability to triangulate our experimental results with data that bear a closer relationship to the real world of administrative practice.

Using WT administrative data, we can attempt to replicate the experimental vignettes as closely as possible within an event history model of sanction initiation. To do so for vignette 1, we restrict our sample to all new applicants to the WT program between January 2001 and December 2002 who were single parents, female, and Latina or white. Using a Cox Proportional Hazard Model, we then estimate the odds of being sanctioned for clients who are Latina with one child, Latina with four children, white with one child, and white with four children. For our replication of vignette 2, we restrict our sample to all clients who were single parents, female, and black or white, who entered the WT program from January 2001 through December 2002, and who returned for a second WT spell during this same observation period. To control for the possibility that clients who received an earlier sanction differ in unobserved ways that make them more likely to receive a sanction in the second participation spell (a "selection effect"), we use a Weibull Selection Model for this analysis. In addition to our primary variables of interest, both models include a number of variables to control for individual-level client differences and for relevant community-level characteristics.[10]

In our replication of vignette 1, we find no evidence that Latina clients are sanctioned at a higher rate than white clients. This is true regardless of whether we examine the direct effect of ethnicity or the effect of ethnicity in conjunction with the client's number of children. Thus, our first analysis of WT administrative data yields results that are inconsistent with our experimental findings regarding the penalization of Lataina women with multiple children.

By contrast, our replication of vignette 2 provides stronger corroborating evidence. To begin with, we find that black clients are significantly more likely to be sanctioned than white clients, regardless of their sanction history. In addition, we find that client race and sanction history have an interactive effect in these data that mirrors our experimental results. Indeed, if we begin with the baseline risk of sanction for a white client who has no prior sanction, we find that the positive effect of making this client black is estimated to be *significantly greater than* the effect of giving the white client a prior sanction. Among white clients, the possession of a prior sanction has no statistically discernible effect on the odds of being sanctioned in the second participation spell ($p = .63$). By contrast, black clients who have no prior sanction are approximately 14 percent more likely than their white counterparts to be sanctioned ($p > .05$). For black clients with a prior sanction on their record, this 14 percent greater risk is doubled. That is, black clients with a prior sanction are 28 percent more likely to receive a sanction during the second spell than are white clients with no prior sanction ($p > .01$). In sum, even though black clients with no prior sanction are *already* at a higher risk of being sanctioned in the second spell (relative to their white counterparts), the addition of a prior sanction increases the risk of sanction for black clients to a significantly greater degree than for white clients.[11]

Conclusion

Case managers are organizational actors. As they carry out their "transformative moral work" with clients, their efforts are structured in a variety of ways by the tools, cultures, and routines supplied by their organizations (Hasenfeld 1992). As a result, much of their behavior can be explained by their organizational position (Lipsky 1980). In the WT program, the case manager's job is to document client behavior, enforce expectations, and, if necessary, penalize noncompliance. Working under time and resource constraints, and the watchful eyes of QA managers, they implement a "cookie cutter" regimen focused on work activities. As they make use of their discretion, they are often motivated by nothing grander than the goals of completing their to-do lists, rationing what they have to offer, keeping their caseloads under control, and "putting out the fires" that threaten to engulf their routines (Lipsky 1980).

It would be a mistake, however, to conceive of case managers as nothing more than organizational actors—as officials who, in principle, could be anyone. Frontline interactions play out on a landscape that is defined, in significant ways, by the social identities of case managers and clients. Case managers draw on shared identities and experiences to forge connections with clients, persuade and motivate them, size them up, and make decisions regarding their cases. They draw on their own personal histories to find meaning and purpose in their work, and to interpret and judge the stories that clients tell. As case managers deploy their discretion, they act from a standpoint that is as much social as organizational.

When scholars overlook these social dynamics, they miss an important part of what is new about poverty governance today. Over the past two decades, case management has been recast as a deskilled, low-wage position. At the same time, it has become more accessible to select members of marginalized groups, including individuals drawn from the ranks of welfare recipients. As a result, case managers today are increasingly likely to share community backgrounds and social characteristics with their clients.

There is much to applaud in this rise of shared identities. It represents a weakening of occupational exclusion and, in many cases, a strengthening of local knowledge in casework relationships. All else equal, we should expect it to reduce problems of "cultural competence" that result when caseworkers are unable to relate to their clients' experiences and worldviews. The dynamics that emerge in place of these problems, however, are less straightforward, and often less salutary, than advocates of "representative" bureaucratic staffing might hope (Selden 1997). Like Celeste Watkins-Hayes (2009), we find that shared racial identities and experiences of poverty and welfare reframe casework relationships in a variety of ways, including some that are troubling. Like Watkins-Hayes (2009) as well, we find that the complex dynamics that result cannot be reduced to a simple contrast of opposing storylines: case managers who punish their clients for failing to work as hard as they did "versus" case managers who are more perceptive and attentive because of their greater empathy.

The problem with this contrast is that it is framed by the temptation to distinguish case managers as "good" or "bad" people. A better starting point for analysis is to ask how shared identities and experiences get woven into client-caseworker *relationships*. For this perspective, we can begin to appreciate how the social identities of clients and case managers create possibilities, frame interpretations, supply rhetorical resources, and organize cooperation and conflict. In welfare programs today, client-caseworker relationships are rooted in a "recovery model" that places a premium on the case manager's status as an experienced guide and authority for the client's journey. As we have seen, the recovery model plays out in different ways depending on the identities of the actors involved. Conversely, the identity dynamics that play out in welfare offices depend greatly on the recovery model as a frame of governance.

A relational perspective on identity is essential, not just for understanding how frontline interactions work, but also for explaining the outcomes they produce. In this chapter, we have focused on how and why race matters for case managers' sanction decisions. Although no single study can be decisive, our results offer the strongest evidence to date that case manager choices regarding penalties tend to be biased in systematic ways by client race.

In the daily work of governance, attempts to "size up the individual" play a key role in case manager's efforts to interpret clients' behaviors, evaluate their stories, and arrive at appropriate decisions. From the first meeting onward, case managers inspect clients and their records for clues that might point to problems or indicate "what's really going on." When a client falls short in some way, events and explanations are almost always ambiguous. They must be interpreted in light of what the case manager believes to be true about the client. Did this hardworking woman get sidetracked by circumstances beyond her control, or is she just a "pro" trying to game the system and evade responsibility yet again? The art of case management lies, to a large degree, in the ways that frontline workers navigate countless questions of this sort.

Judgments of the person are inevitable in this process, and, by softening program rules at the edges, they can play a positive role in promoting humane responses to individual cases (Jewell 2007). The problem is that they also provide an entry point for social biases. As a mountain of social cognition research attests, interpretations of individual traits and behaviors can be influenced by race in a variety of ways that are unconscious, and even unwanted, but nevertheless powerful (Winter 2008; Quillian 2008). As case managers try to size up their clients based on limited information, they do so in a policy setting where race is highly salient. Indeed, our evidence suggests that race matters greatly for the meanings case managers attach to particular markers and cues and, as a result, exerts a significant influence on their decisions to impose sanctions.

Our findings are not well explained by the familiar narrative of racism in which white case managers, driven by prejudice, consciously discriminate against minority clients. To be sure, the contemporary system is not free of such dynamics. As a general explanation, however, this narrative strikes us as lacking in several respects. First, by focusing narrowly on the agency of dominant group members, it offers a white-centered explanation that is hard to square with the growing racial diversity of case managers. It tells us little about how or why case managers of color resemble their white counterparts in generating racial disparities. Second, in emphasizing racial animus and intentionality, this account understates the scope of the problem. It wrongly implies that actors will be unlikely to produce racial disparities if they feel no racial animus and deplore discrimination. Third, it provides few resources for thinking about *when* a given case manager will become more likely to treat clients in a racially biased way. The bluntness of its narrative creates a blind spot, obscuring how specific combinations of racial cues and discrediting markers can influence administrative treatment in contingent ways.

On this score, several pieces of evidence merit special note. In our interviews, group-cultural explanations for client outcomes were proffered by case managers of all racial and ethnic backgrounds. In our statewide survey, we find no statistical difference in the rates at which white and nonwhite case managers cite "cultural differences" to explain racial/ethnic disparities in program outcomes and point to "lack of motivation and a willingness to work hard" as a reason for the problems that black and Latino people face today. In our experiments, we find that white and nonwhite case managers are, statistically speaking, equally likely to impose sanctions and equally likely to be influenced by manipulations of race/ethnicity and client traits.

Thus, our evidence offers little support for explanations that emphasize the race of the case manager. By contrast, it offers powerful support for the RCM and related models that emphasize the implicit and contingent effects of client race. White clients in our experiments suffer no discernible effects when linked to characteristics that hold negative meanings in the welfare-to-work context. As advocates of administrative consistency might hope, case managers produce a stable pattern of responses, regardless of discrediting client attributes, *when clients are white.* Minority clients enjoy no such immunity. Their odds of being sanctioned rise in the presence of discrediting markers even when the details of their case do not change a bit.

Consistent with the RCM and our findings in earlier chapters, our analysis suggests that white-Latina sanction disparities arise in comparatively small and inconsistent ways. Contingent biases emerge in the experimental findings but are not corroborated by the administrative data. By contrast, we find consistent evidence of sizable black-white disparities. The presence of a discrediting marker (a prior sanction) raises the odds of being sanctioned only for black clients, and, in the administrative data, it does so even though black clients are already more likely to be sanctioned than whites.

The upshot of our analysis is that race matters for client treatment in subtle and contingent ways (Schram 2005). Racial identities are highly salient in welfare settings and tend to frame casework relationships. In frontline interactions, interpretations and strategies depend greatly on the ways that case manager and client identities fit together. When it comes to sanction decisions, however, the race of the client appears to matter more than (and irrespective of) the race of the case manager. Black clients carry the greatest disadvantages, but they are not positioned as objects of unwavering discrimination. Instead, they possess a precarious kind of equality that can be easily undone by a discrediting, stereotype-consistent marker. Regardless of whether they favor racial equality in principle, frontline officials tend to respond to such markers in ways that reliably contribute to institutional patterns of racial inequity.

DOES NEOLIBERAL PATERNALISM
MATTER FOR THE POOR?

I N THE PRECEDING CHAPTERS, WE HAVE SOUGHT TO CLARIFY THE origins and operations of poverty governance in the United States today. Moving from the national level down to the local front lines, we have explored how the paternalist turn toward direction and supervision has intersected with the neoliberal shift toward decentralized, privatized, and performance-driven strategies. Our analysis has uncovered remarkable consistencies in governance across levels of the system and underscored the persistent power of race as an influence on policy design and implementation. The troubling portrait that has emerged raises many questions, but none is more important than the one we take up in this final empirical chapter: How has the rise of neoliberal paternalism mattered for the lives of poor women, men, and children in the United States?

The campaign to remake poverty governance attacked the existing regime on many fronts. Critics derided the prevailing approaches to crime and welfare as too soft and permissive to bring social order and self-sufficiency to poor people's lives. Entitlements sustained an endless cycle of poverty by discouraging work and rewarding irresponsible choices (Murray 1984). By failing to enforce social obligations, welfare made the poor into second-class citizens, ensuring that they would not merit the respect of their fellow citizens or be able to shoulder the burdens of civic and political participation (Mead 1986, 1992). Reformers promised that the new regime would do better. Tougher criminal laws would bring peace and progress to poor communities. Welfare reform would place the poor on a work-based path out of poverty and allow them to flourish as self-sufficient, responsible members of society. Poverty would decline; social and economic well-being would improve; the poor would become full and equal citizens, earning the esteem of others as they became competent participants in public life.

In the years that followed, disciplinary poverty governance was declared a stunning success. As welfare rolls declined and work levels rose, reform advocates returned to declare that the new regime was visibly producing beneficial results. As early as the summer of 1997, President Bill Clinton was ready to conclude, "The debate is over. We now know that welfare reform works"

(W. Miller 1998: 28). Media stories on welfare reform were overwhelmingly positive (Schram and Soss 2001), and prominent journalists such as Michael Kelly (1999: A21) declared, "It's official: the reform of the welfare system is a great triumph of social policy." The leading theorist of paternalism, Lawrence Mead (2002: 140), touted it as nothing less than a "triumph for democracy." Ron Haskins (2006), a key architect of reform in 1996, summarized its effects ten years later by stating: "Poor mothers scored a victory for themselves and their children, showing that given adequate motivation and support from work-based government programs, they can join the American mainstream, set an example for their children and communities, and pull themselves and their children out of poverty."

In this chapter, we take a critical look at the evidence for such appraisals. Incarceration rates have spiraled upward in recent decades and, since the mid-1990s, welfare caseloads have plummeted. Poverty governance has changed dramatically, yet there is little evidence that disciplinary approaches have led the poor out of poverty or hastened their civic incorporation. To the contrary, as we will see, neoliberal paternalism has produced a system that is less responsive to the poor, even in times of dire need, and more likely to enhance their civic marginality.

We begin with an analysis of governmental responsiveness, showing how the TANF program is organized to withhold support and deter claims, even under conditions that produce severe need. Increasingly, poor women (and especially poor women of color) find resistance at the doors of the welfare office and easy entry at the gates of the prison. We then turn to effects on the social and economic well-being of poor Americans. The evidence, we suggest, offers little reason to celebrate neoliberal paternalism as a victory for the poor. Finally, we assess neoliberal paternalism as a project of civic and political incorporation. Reformers claimed that tough new policies would move the poor into the ranks of respected and engaged citizens. We show that nothing of the sort has occurred. Paternalist welfare policies do not advance civic and political incorporation or strengthen American democracy; they do the opposite.

The Dynamics of Declining Access

In chapters 8 and 9, we explored a variety of ways that welfare providers work to limit program entry and speed recipients out into the labor market. Efforts to service low-wage employers have become integral to welfare operations under the Temporary Assistance for Needy Families (TANF) program. Performance pressures reinforce the drive to limit clienteles and close welfare cases. These developments contribute to what is arguably the most widely discussed effect of welfare reform: the massive decline of caseloads. From its high point in 1993 to the end of 2008, the number of welfare recipients in the United States dropped by about 72 percent (U.S. Department of Health and Human Services 2009).

Champions of reform typically cite this development as evidence of success: Transitions to work have reduced the need for dependence on public aid. Data on program coverage, however, cast considerable doubt on this interpretation. The percentage of income-eligible families receiving TANF declined from 84 percent to 40 percent between 1995 and 2005, and almost certainly declined further during the recession that began in late 2007 (U.S. Government Accountability Office 2010a). Government estimates indicate that 87 percent of the caseload decline during this period was due to fewer poor, eligible families participating in the TANF program, as opposed to rising family incomes (U.S. Government Accountability Office 2010b). If caseload decline had been restricted to people whose successes made them ineligible, 3.3 million additional families would have been receiving TANF support, and 800,000 children would have been lifted above the half-the-poverty-line standard of extreme poverty (U.S. Government Accountability Office 2010b). Instead, the percentage of "disconnected" low-income mothers (neither working nor receiving welfare) doubled between 1990 and 2005, rising as high as 25 percent by some definitions (Blank and Kovak 2008). The meaning of TANF caseload decline is, in this respect, fairly straightforward: Income support has been withdrawn from poor women and children who continue to need it.

A striking feature of this development has been its patterning across the nation. Between 1993 and 2001 (when trends began to flatten out), *every* state in the United States experienced significant caseload reductions. Clearly, national developments were central to the change. Yet the welfare rolls did not drop equally in all states. Caseload declines between 1993 and 2001 varied significantly, with states such as Florida, Idaho, and Wyoming experiencing declines in excess of 75 percent, and states such as Minnesota, New Mexico, and Rhode Island experiencing declines of less than 40 percent.[1] This variation suggests that state-specific forces may have played a significant role in shaping the caseload purge and weakening access for poor, eligible families.

TANF caseload declines have been analyzed in a wide variety of ways and well summarized elsewhere (see reviews by Blank 2002, 2009; Grogger, Karoly, and Klerman 2002). For our purposes, two key features of the literature stand out. First, there is strong agreement that welfare reform explains a significant portion of the decline, above and beyond the effects of economic expansion and work incentives such as the Earned Income Tax Credit (EITC). Second, there is little clarity on which specific features of "welfare reform" have been responsible. After 1996, states built their TANF programs by adopting bundles of policy elements. Rather than breaking down these bundles, most caseload studies have simply compared trends before and after the date when each state implemented its package as a whole. In addition to limiting our knowledge of specific policy effects, this approach may distort overall conclusions if the effects of some reforms cancel out others.

The analyses of policy choice presented in this book suggest that a more precise investigation is needed.[2] To pursue this task, we return to the disciplinary policy choices that we examined (as political outcomes) in chapters 4 and 5, and analyze their effects on state caseload trends from 1980 through 2003. The outcome variable for our analysis is the welfare recipient rate, calculated as the number of Aid to Families with Dependent Children (AFDC) and TANF cases per 100 state residents. For the period up to August 1996, our key predictor measures the cumulative number of restrictive AFDC waivers implemented in each state, based on waivers that (1) limited exemptions for work requirements; (2) introduced time limits for welfare receipt; (3) strengthened sanctions for violations of program rules; (4) introduced a family cap on benefits for children born during a welfare spell; or (5) strengthened work requirements. We also include a separate dummy variable for waivers that increased the earnings disregard for AFDC clients in order to strengthen work incentives.

To test the impact of relevant TANF reforms, we employ the six-point neoliberal-paternalism scale introduced in chapter 5. The scale indicates how many of the following reforms each state adopted: strong work requirements, short time limits, a family cap, strong sanctions, and second-order devolution (see chapter 5 for details). We assume that the effects of these reforms began on the date of TANF implementation in each state, which ranged from September 1996 to July 1997.[3] In addition to our policy variables, we control for various social, economic, and political determinants of caseload dynamics suggested by past studies (Blank 1997, 2001; Fording 2001; Ziliak et al. 2000).[4] Finally, our model includes state and year fixed effects, which control for state-specific trends in caseload levels, as well as the effects of national forces affecting caseload dynamics across all the states.

Consistent with most recent studies, we find that the expanding economy of the 1990s played a significant role in caseload decline. Falling unemployment rates and rising real per capita incomes, which were observed in all states

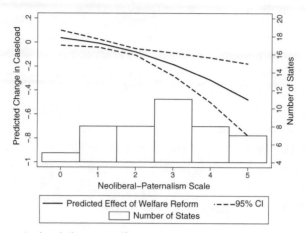

FIGURE 11-1. Predicted Change in Welfare Caseload Due to Welfare Reform, by Type of TANF Regime

through most of the 1990s, contributed significantly to declining rates of welfare receipt. Beyond these effects, however, we find strong evidence that disciplinary policy choices mattered for caseload decline. Steady declines in the real value of AFDC/TANF benefits (analyzed in chapter 4) were associated with significant caseload reductions, and we find a similar depressive effect for the restrictive AFDC waivers that states adopted in the years up to 1996.[5] By far, however, the largest effects observed here are associated with the adoption of strong neoliberal-paternalist reforms under the TANF program.

To illustrate, figure 11-1 shows how the predicted effects of TANF implementation vary across the values of our neoliberal-paternalist scale. Remarkably, we find that, in states with the least disciplinary policy regimes, TANF implementation had no discernible effect on caseload levels. Moving from left to right on the scale, the effect becomes statistically significant (at a value of 2) and increases in substantive impact. For the fifteen states at the high end of the scale (with values of 4 or 5), we estimate that TANF implementation led to a reduction of roughly .40 in the number of participating families per 100 state residents. In 1995, the year prior to TANF implementation, the average caseload size in this subset of states was 1.54. Thus, we find that the tough new TANF policies in these states led to a decrease in welfare caseloads of roughly 26 percent.

This figure almost surely underestimates the total impact of neoliberal-paternalist reforms because it fails to account for administrative strategies that produce "bureaucratic disentitlement" at the front lines (Lipsky 1984; Brodkin

1986). Written state TANF rules do not capture local efforts to regulate access, such as the ones illustrated by the story of Region A in chapter 9. At welfare offices, local providers "stiffen the front door" in a variety of ways. Intake workers emphasize the large number of work-activity hours required and the meager income returns they produce. In some locales, applications go unprocessed for one to two weeks as applicants complete daily orientation sessions that set goals and define obligations. Procedural complexity, confusion, and delay combine with excessive procedural demands to present applicants with high barriers to program entry (Brodkin, Fuqua, and Waxman 2005).

Indeed, there is good reason to believe that, as welfare reform has progressed, the importance of administrative strategies has risen relative to the impact of written policies. Brodkin and Majmundar (2010), for example, argue that as welfare programs have been restricted to ever-more deeply disadvantaged claimants, formal policies have become less effective and "administrative means of caseload reduction [have] become increasingly important." Consistent with this view, the authors find that procedural reasons accounted for a higher percentage of TANF program exits in 2002 than in 1999: "Proceduralism [became] more strongly associated with caseload decline *after* the initial period of sharp reductions" in the late 1990s.

Because good measures of procedural exclusion do not exist at the national level, we cannot extend our cross-state analysis of governance effects to this domain. By returning to our data from the Florida Welfare Transition (WT) program, however, we can pursue a more focused inquiry. Welfare caseloads rise and fall through a complex interplay of entry and exit dynamics. Poor women with weak labor-market prospects often cycle between welfare and low-wage work, as they are churned off the welfare rolls and then find that kin support and employment do not provide a sustainable income package (Edin and Lein 1997). As a result, procedures that reduce caseloads by increasing exits can have magnified effects if they make program leavers less likely to return.

To explore this dynamic, we analyze a sample consisting of all first-time clients who entered the WT program in January 2001 or later and who exited their first spell by December 2002. For each case, we analyze the number of months between the client's exit and her return for a second spell using an event history model of TANF reentry.[6] Our predictors include a variety of individual-level and county-level characteristics potentially related to welfare reentry, as well as two indicators of local implementation stringency.[7]

The first focuses on the paradigmatic tool of discipline under neoliberal paternalism: sanctions for noncompliance. Given the centrality of this tool in the

WT program, we include the county sanction rate for all TANF clients, averaged over the entire 2001–03 period. More muscular uses of sanctioning may
deter reentry in at least three ways. First, sanctioned clients may have direct,
personal experiences that leave them feeling unwanted and disrespected or con-
vince them that the WT program is not a viable option for support. Second, to
reenter the program, clients must "cure" their earlier sanction. In some locales,
this procedure is trivial, but, as the story of the "sanction queen" illustrated in
chapter 9, some locales erect special barriers to reentry for sanctioned clients.
Third, local providers that sanction at higher rates may produce an ecological
effect, cultivating social networks of poor people who reinforce one another's
beliefs that it is not worth it to return to the program. For all these reasons, we
expect clients to return for a second spell less frequently in counties with higher
sanction rates.

Our second measure offers a more indirect, but also more holistic, indicator of procedural stringency. Throughout this book, we have seen that conservative jurisdictions tend to adopt more disciplinary approaches to poverty
governance—not just in selecting policies but also in implementing them.
Welfare providers in more conservative Florida counties sanction WT clients at
higher rates (chapter 7), and, once exits due to sanctions and earnings are set
aside, they are far more likely to respond to performance pressures by closing
cases for procedural reasons (chapter 9). Building on this evidence, we supplement our sanction measure in the current analysis with the index of local political ideology employed in earlier chapters.

The results for our individual-level variables comport with earlier studies
showing that reentry rates are highest among the most economically vulnerable clients.[8] The results for our contextual variables are of more central interest. Here, we find no effects associated with county differences in population
size, unemployment rate, and poverty rate. The only contextual variables that
emerge as significant influences on reentry are our indicators of implementation stringency. To make their combined effects easier to interpret, we can consider two hypothetical clients who are identical in every respect, except that
one lives in the "most stringent" county (with a sanction rate and conservatism
score at the 95th percentile of each county distribution) while the other lives
in the "least stringent" county (where each value falls at the 5th percentile of
the county distribution). Our results indicate that, at any point after exiting
the first spell, the client living in the least stringent county has a 40 percent
greater likelihood of returning to TANF than the client in the most stringent
county.

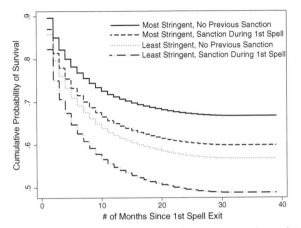

FIGURE 11-2. Predicted Cumulative Survivor Function for TANF Reentry, by Local Implementation Stringency and Client Sanction History

The relevant dynamics can be seen with greater specificity in figure 11-2, which plots the predicted cumulative survival rates for four hypothetical groups: clients residing in the "most" and "least" stringent implementation environments (as defined above) and, for each environment, clients who exited due to a sanction and clients who exited for some other reason. At each month after exit (along the horizontal axis), the cumulative survival rate indicates the proportion of clients that we predict would *not* have returned to TANF.

Consistent with prior research (Cherlin et al. 2002), the estimates suggest that sanctioned clients have a 27 percent greater likelihood of returning to TANF after an exit. Sanctioned clients are less likely than other program leavers to have what is needed to support themselves in the market and, as a result, experience disruptions in income that lead to greater suffering and pressures to return to welfare.[9] Within this general dynamic, the results clearly show the access effects of implementation environments. Among nonsanctioned clients, the percentage of clients returning to TANF within twenty-four months of the first exit is 25 percent greater in the least stringent county than in the most stringent county. The disparity is similar for sanctioned clients, though the absolute rates of return are higher in each environment. Thus, regardless of whether the individual experiences a sanction, we find that program reentry is significantly depressed in locales that are more conservative and sanction more frequently.

With this analysis in hand, we can return to caseload dynamics at the national level. Our analysis so far suggests that new policies and procedures have made the TANF program unresponsive to poor people's needs, organizing its operations to deter and minimize welfare participation. This proposition was put to the test in dramatic fashion in 2007, when the United States fell into the greatest economic crisis it had experienced since the Great Depression. Consistent with our analysis, the TANF program proved highly resistant to meeting the growing needs of the poor. As the ranks of beneficiaries swelled in other programs, the paltry change in TANF caseloads stood out (DeParle 2009). Despite the large pool of income-eligible families who were *already* not receiving benefits (U.S. General Accountability Office 2010b), the TANF program stood its low-caseload ground. Between the start of the recession (December 2007) and the last month for which we have data (December 2009), state TANF caseloads increased by just 12.4 percent.

Across the nation, however, program responsiveness varied considerably during this twenty-four-month period. A few states, like Oregon, Utah, and Washington, experienced caseload increases in excess of 37 percent, while ten states actually experienced further declines in their caseloads.[10] In the absence of good procedural measures at the state level, we cannot tie this variation directly to differences in governing practices. Nevertheless, state responses in the face of growing need provide an opportunity to extend our earlier analyses of how the characteristics of jurisdictions shape the dynamics of welfare provision. To do so, we estimate a multivariate regression model predicting the percentage change in each state's TANF caseload during the twenty-four-month period. The independent variables for this analysis include (1) change in the state unemployment rate, (2) full Democratic control of state government, (3) the percentage of families receiving TANF headed by black adult, (4) the budget shortfall as a proportion of the FY2009 General Fund in each state, (5) a measure of the TANF strictness in 2008 based on the number of the three possible policies adopted (immediate full-family sanctions, time limits less than sixty months, and a family cap), and (6) the maximum benefit level for a family of three (with no income) in 2008.

Our results indicate that TANF caseload change during the Great Recession was influenced by three variables: growth in the state unemployment rate, partisan control of state government, and the racial composition of the TANF caseload. One way to gauge the magnitude of each effect is to compare the predicted caseload change that would have occurred in two "otherwise-identical" hypothetical states: one with a low value on the variable (5th percentile) and one with a high value (95th percentile). Figure 11-3 presents the results of this procedure.

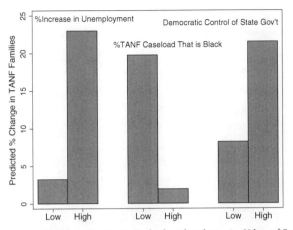

FIGURE 11-3. Predicted Change in TANF Caseload, under Alternative Values of State Socioeconomic and Political Variables

Note: The bars represent the predicted percentage change in the number of TANF families, based on our regression results, at "low" and "high" values of each variable represented in the figure. In calculating each predicted value, we held all other variables constant at their mean values.

In an otherwise typical state that saw little increase in its unemployment rate (1.7 percent), we predict that the TANF caseload would have increased by about 3.2 percent.[11] In an identical state with a large surge in unemployment (7 percent), we predict a caseload increase of 22 percent—a difference of 19 percentage points. The results also suggest that state politics mattered a great deal for TANF responsiveness during the recession. In a typical state where Republicans controlled either the governor's office or at least one chamber of the legislature, we predict that TANF caseloads would have increased by about 8 percent. If, in this same state, the Democrats controlled the governor's office and both chambers of the legislature, we predict a caseload increase of 21 percent.

For race, we predict that an otherwise typical state with a low percentage of TANF families headed by a black adult (1.7 percent) would have experienced a caseload increase of 20 percent. If this same state had a high value on this variable, (79 percent), our analysis predicts virtually no change in the TANF caseload at all—only 2 percent. Thus, the Great Recession has provided yet another illustration of how state welfare programs adopt a tougher stance in the presence of greater numbers of African Americans. In fact, we find that the "blackness" of a state's TANF population had an effect on caseload growth during the recession (an eighteen-point gap) that is roughly equivalent to changes in the unemployment rate (a nineteen-point gap).[12]

The upshot of our analysis is that, under neoliberal paternalism, state welfare programs are far less responsive to the needs of poor women and children; their intransigence persists even under conditions of dire need; and it grows deeper when conservatives hold sway and African Americans become more prominent among policy targets. The stiffening front doors of welfare offices find their counterpart, of course, in the expanding reach of the state's "right hand" of social control: incarceration, probation, and parole (Wacquant 2009). Although men continue to make up the vast majority of Americans under correctional control, neoliberal paternalism has produced a dramatic transfer of poor women from welfare caseloads to prison populations.

From 1995 to 2005, as TANF caseloads fell by 60 percent, the number of women prisoners in the United States rose by 57 percent. Since the 1980s, the female prison population has been growing at twice the rate for males. Roughly 82 percent of incarcerated women are behind bars for nonviolent offenses, and 75 percent were responsible for children prior to entry (Haney 2004). About 40 percent of these women are incarcerated for drug felonies that, in many states, bar them from receiving TANF assistance after they exit (P. Allard 2002). And just as women of color have been most affected by welfare contraction, they have also been most affected by carceral expansion. In 2008, imprisonment rates were 50 percent higher for Latina women, and 200 percent higher for black women, than for white women in the United States (Sabol, West, and Cooper 2009).

In prisons, these women increasingly find an emphasis on work that parallels the direction of the TANF program. After federal restrictions on prison labor were lifted in 1979, prison work programs expanded to cover over 50 percent of inmates (Atkinson and Rostad 2003). At least thirty-seven states have passed laws allowing private companies to employ prisoners, and roughly 25 percent of federal inmates work for employers through Federal Prison Industries. As Lynn Haney (2004, 2010) notes, these prison work programs are framed much like welfare-to-work programs, as efforts that benefit the inmate and the employer in equal measures. The Joint Venture Program in California, for example, promises that inmate labor will give businesses a "competitive edge" while, at the same time, instilling a "work ethic in idle prisoners" (California Department of Corrections 1994). Like the imbalances in welfare services described in chapter 8, however, prison labor clearly benefits employers at the expense of the poor. Business profits from prison industries run into the billions of dollars, while estimates suggest that inmates' average take-home pay (after "room and board" deductions) is around 18 cents an hour (Lafer 1999).

Social and Economic Effects of Neoliberal Paternalism

To many champions of the disciplinary turn, changes in welfare and prison entry rates are less important than the broader social and economic effects observed in poor communities. The tough new stance in poverty governance is ultimately a means to an end. It is designed to break the cycle of dependency and dysfunction, and place the poor on a work-based path to self-sufficiency. There are, of course, large scholarly literatures that explore the social and economic effects of welfare reform and rising incarceration (see, Blank 2002, 2009; Grogger and Karoly 2005; Handler and Hasenfeld 2007; Western 2006; Harris and Miller 2003; Alexander 2010). We will not attempt the impossible task of summarizing this literature in this section. Instead, we focus more narrowly on the policy changes that lie at the heart of neoliberal paternalism and the social and economic effects that speak directly to the promises of reformers.

Our negative assessment of disciplinary governance is least controversial on the carceral side of neoliberal paternalism. Empirical research has overwhelmingly shown that the era of mass incarceration has been destructive for poor individuals, families, and communities (Western 2006; Harris and Miller 2003; Chesney-Lind and Mauer 2003). The hardships of prison and the symbolic branding of a felony record combine to significantly reduce individuals' lifelong prospects for employment and earnings (Western 2006). Individuals who are marked as ex-felons are subjected to stark discrimination in the labor market, especially if they are African American (Pager 2007). Negative effects on marriage and family formation are equally substantial (Western 2006), and evidence suggests that the people who are sent to the toughest prisons return with more criminogenic social networks and attitudes (Lerman 2009). Moreover, when prisoners return to poor communities, they tend to do so with very high rates of mental illness and chronic disease (Western 2006).

To grasp the disaster that has unfolded, one must consider how incarceration effects ripple out through families and social networks in poor communities. The tears in the social fabric that arise when individuals are removed to prison often deepen when ex-offenders return home (Chesney-Lind and Mauer 2003). At both points in the cycle, incarceration acts as a destabilizing force in the families and communities that have the fewest resources to cope (Clear 2009). Moreover, the spatial and social concentration of these effects is stunning. By the age of fourteen, 25 percent of black children will see their father sent to prison, compared to just 4 percent of white children (Western 2008). In poor minority neighborhoods, concentrated rates of imprisonment and reentry multiply the burdens of residential segregation and depressed labor markets. Todd Clear (2009: 5) summarizes the research as follows: "Concentrated incarceration in those impoverished communities has broken families, weakened the social control capacities of parents, eroded economic strength, soured attitudes toward society, and distorted politics; even, after reaching a certain level, it has increased rather than decreased crime."

In short, the effects of mass incarceration on economic inequality and social marginality in the United States have been nothing short of calamitous. Two of the leading scholars in this area, Bruce Western and Becky Pettit (2002: 42–43), conclude:

> The expansion of imprisonment represents a more massive intrusion of government into the lives of the poor than any employment or welfare program. [Insofar as it] undermines economic opportunities [and adds] to the stigma of residence in high-crime neighborhoods the criminal justice system is now a newly significant part of a uniquely American system of social inequality. Under these conditions, the punitive trend in criminal justice policy may be tougher on the poor than it is on crime.

By comparison, the more controversial part of our critique concerns the disciplinary turn in welfare provision. Widely hailed as a success, welfare reform has been strengthened over the past decade and touted as a model for other target populations, including reentering prisoners. Champions such as Mead (2005) and Haskins (2006) argue that disciplinary governance has moved poor women into jobs and toward self-sufficiency. Mead (2004b: 672) goes so far as to argue that welfare reform, "along with the economy, was the chief force that moderated trends toward inequality in the 1990s, because it drove up work and earnings at the bottom of society."

In the political debates that led up to welfare reform in the 1990s, liberals often made dire predictions about how the new law would affect the poor. In the years that have followed, the image of naysayers' advancing misguided "predictions of doom" has become a standard trope in conservative celebrations of welfare reform (Haskins 2006) and liberal capitulations to the new order (Jencks 2005). Caseloads are down, work rates are up, and the predicted avalanche of hardship and deep poverty has not happened. To say the least, this is a low standard of success. Proponents rely on an equally low bar when they emphasize comparisons to the AFDC program, which failed the poor both as a source of income support and as a path toward stable, family-supporting jobs. We adopt a higher standard of success based on what reformers promised to deliver and what citizens expect from a massive governmental effort directed at the poor. Have the disciplinary features of the TANF program lifted poor women and children out of poverty and improved the social and economic conditions of their lives?

We can begin with the mirage of success created by caseload declines. If the dwindling welfare rolls had signified that fewer people actually needed assistance, they would indeed be good news. But they did not. Here, it is important to remember that, to meet the restrictive poverty guidelines for TANF eligibility, a family must be living under fairly dismal economic conditions. If such families had continued to receive the aid they needed, the caseload decline between 1995 and 2005 would not have been 57 percent; it would have been 7.4 percent.[13] The remaining 49.6 percent reflected a withdrawal of aid from families in need that emerged from the most basic incentives of the system. As the policy center CLASP (2009) recently put it: "The work participation requirement has focused states on minimizing numbers who are receiving welfare and not working. There is no penalty for failure to serve needy families."

The best-case scenario for poor families should have emerged where a celebrated TANF program operated in a thriving economy. The W-2 program in Wisconsin, for example, has been hailed as the most successful TANF program in the country (Mead 2004a), and in the late 1990s it pushed clients toward jobs in an unusually strong economy.[14] How did these exiting clients fare? A study by the state's Legislative Audit Bureau found that program leavers in 1999 earned an average of just $8,306 during their first year out (with 81 percent below the poverty line) and an average of only $11,577 in their fourth year out (with 73 percent below the poverty line); their most common job placement was with a temporary help service (Schultze 2005). A more in-depth study has recently described the resulting hardships for women and children in rich detail, concluding that the W-2 program is little more than a "downward mobility machine churning workers to the bottom of the labor market" (Collins and Mayer 2010: 123). But with caseloads disappearing and work rates up, the W-2 program has repeatedly won federal accolades and high-performance bonuses, and its officials have been consulted by reformers around the globe who hope to recreate the "Wisconsin Miracle" (Mead 2004a).

Nationally, as TANF programs have pushed poor women out of welfare and into jobs, their work hours and earnings, almost by definition, have risen (Grogger and Karoly 2005). But the amount of work these women are able to find is often exaggerated. Even during the strong economy of the years surrounding 2000, Grogger and Karoly (2005: 38) found that "only about 40 percent [were] employed in each of their first four quarters after leaving welfare. Only 13 percent work[ed] full-time for the entire year." Indeed, as noted earlier, the number of "disconnected" low-income single mothers (neither working nor receiving welfare) has doubled since 1990 and is now as high as 25 percent by some definitions (Blank and Kovak 2008).

When they do find work, these women overwhelmingly enter jobs that offer very low wages, unstable hours, few if any benefits, and little opportunity for advancement (Morgen, Acker, and Weigt 2010). In essence, the welfare poor have moved into a world of precarious work that leaves them just as poor. Relative to AFDC, the TANF program has moved clients off the rolls and into work more quickly, but the earnings of leavers have been so low that Cancian et al. (2002) find that they have been outweighed by benefit losses (resulting in a net income loss). As Grogger and Karoly (2005: 39) summarize the available research: "Leavers have about the same household income after leaving welfare, on average, as they had while they were on welfare. The sources of income are different, with earnings accounting for a larger proportion and transfer payments a smaller one, but the total level of income is about the same."

The root of the problem lies in a governing approach that forcefully pushes the poor toward low-wage work while asking nothing in return from the employers it services (see chapter 8). "The primary reason those who work remain poor," Handler and Hasenfeld (2007: 31) rightly note, "is the deterioration of working conditions in the low-wage sector." Reformers focused narrowly on changing poor people's behaviors. They did nothing to change the employer behaviors that have brought welfare leavers pay rates averaging $5.67 to $8.42 an hour and annual earnings averaging $8,000 to $15,144 (CLASP 2001). At the same time, as Collins and Mayer (2010: 158) point out, "welfare reformers profoundly misread the barriers to work faced by mothers of young children living in poverty. They did not address the incompatibility between the terms and conditions of low-wage employment—its uncertain hours, its shift work, its lack of leave and benefits—and women's social reproductive responsibilities."

The central issue has been underscored time and again by ethnographic studies of working single mothers (Morgen, Ackerman, and Weigt 2010; Collins and Mayer 2010; Dodson 2010). In Randy Albelda's (2001) pithy formulation, significant numbers of poor mothers are not job-ready, but the deeper problem is that virtually no low-wage jobs are mother-ready. Beyond their insufficient wages, these jobs simply do not provide the accommodations that full-time parents need. Collins and Mayer (2010: 84) conclude: "By far the largest factor leading the women in our study to turn to welfare was their inability to balance work and care for their families." When poor mothers are pushed from welfare to work, they return to the same no-win situation that brought them to the TANF program in the first place. A dogged commitment to the job means that "you're stealing from your kids to provide for them," while efforts to meet the obligations of motherhood put jobs at risk (Collins and Mayer 2010: 97).[15] The following account by Shakira offers but a small glimpse into the dilemmas and burdens that define daily life for such women (Collins and Mayer 2010: 99; see also Dodson 2010).

> When my son was born, his lungs were underdeveloped. So when he gets sick, he gets wheezy. One time he wasn't talking right and he got really flushed, so they called me and I had to leave work to take him to the instant care. She [her boss] had an attitude about it, but I still went. My son comes first. You know Zack, he's already had so many problems since he was a baby, and he gets sick a lot. I mean, he almost died when I had him. So for me to leave him—I feel like I'm going to freak out. I have anxiety. So they [her welfare caseworkers] made me go see a psychiatrist.

Under the banner of personal responsibility, the structural tensions between low-wage work and family obligations are transformed, for Shakira, into a psychiatric problem of coping effectively. As it rides roughshod over the realities of contemporary social and economic relations, the work-first philosophy also fails poor women by depriving them of the skills and credentials they need to attain better jobs in the future. The emphasis on immediate work placement has pushed poor women into dead-end jobs and away from education and training. Dave, Reichman, and Corman (2008), for example, find that the TANF program has led to 20 to 25 percent declines in both high school and college enrollment. Indeed, the TANF program undercuts education, not only by pushing work first, but also by imposing explicit limits on how long recipients can use education and training to fulfill their work participation requirements. Although the limits vary across the states, the broad trend has been toward a contraction of the educational opportunities that provide the most reliable road out of poverty (Shaw et al. 2006).

In these ways and others, work-centered, disciplinary poverty governance has failed to improve the lives of poor mothers in general. Its implications for the most deeply disadvantaged have been worse. The TANF program today serves large numbers of women who struggle with significant mental and physical health issues and who carry the long-term burdens of sexual abuse and domestic violence. For many of these women, employment alone will never result in "self-sufficiency." Indeed, the broader population of poor people in the United States is characterized, in large numbers, by limitations that cannot be overcome by jobs alone. As Handler and Hasenfeld (2007: 51) explain:

> Many of the poor would not benefit from a full-employment economy be-cause they experience major barriers to employment—disability, family care responsibilities, age, and very limited education and skills. In 1999, less than half (42 percent) of poor individuals worked at all. Of those who did not work, 24 percent were disabled, 27 percent were retired, 23 per-cent had family and care responsibilities, 15 percent were older than 64, 17.5 percent had only a grade school education or less, and 23 percent were immigrants with limited skills.

Domestic violence offers a particularly stark illustration of how the relent-less push toward work imposes costs on those who already suffer the greatest hardships. Nationwide, studies suggest that 60 to 75 percent of women in the TANF program have experienced physical abuse in their lifetimes (Tolman and Raphael 2000). Historically, welfare programs have offered a way to escape dependence on an abusive male breadwinner (Gordon 1994; Soss 2000). This option has been restricted by the inaccessibility of TANF benefits. But even when women enter the program, the performance-driven focus on work results in little attention to the lingering effects and persistent dangers arising from domestic violence. Studies find that case managers rarely screen for domestic violence and have few resources available for dealing with the problems that re-sult (Lindhorst, Meyers, and Casey 2008; Lindhorst and Padgett 2005). When women are pushed into low-wage jobs that prove unsustainable, and have dif-ficlty returning to the TANF program, they are left with few options other than returning to an abusive partner. Even within the program itself, TANF rules often make poor women more vulnerable to abuse. Collins and Mayer (2010: 121) provide a telling illustration from their interview with Delia.

> This man almost killed me one time—and in front of my son. He threat-ened to kill me again—in front of a lot of people this time. So I really felt like in my heart that he was serious. I let my [case] worker know that I was scared to leave the house. I mean it got so bad that I would not even

go to the store—I would pay little kids around the neighborhood to go to the store for me. So, I am not doing no activities in that neighborhood. You know I am not going to die at the hands of this man because y'all want me to come and sit in a class for two hours and then go clean up somebody's bathrooms. And I tried to ask them to put me somewhere else on the other side of town. Nobody could do that. You know what I'm saying? None of them could put me nowhere else. I was just sanctioned.

Just as the TANF program converted Shakira's social dilemmas (of care and work) into an individual psychiatric problem, it converted Delia's social vulnerability (to abuse) into an individual case of noncompliance meriting a sanction. Sanctions, of course, are supposed to promote social and economic advancement by instilling discipline and moving clients along the path to employment. Empirical research, however, suggests that sanctions rarely have positive effects (Meyers et al. 2006). Most studies find that the most disadvantaged clients, who face significant barriers to work, are the most likely to be sanctioned, and that sanctions tend to exacerbate their problems (Meyers et al. 2006; Cherlin et al. 2002; Wu et al. 2006). These findings fit the general pattern of negative or null effects associated with the most disciplinary TANF tools, such as time limits and work requirements, in contrast to the more positive effects of extending child care and other work supports (Looney 2005; Grogger 2003).

Given the centrality of sanctions to neoliberal paternalism, and to the Florida WT program, it is instructive to take a closer look at how this tool affects an important measure of well-being among program leavers: earnings. To assess this relationship, we estimate regression models of client earnings, using individual-level panel data for a period that spans more than two years for each client. We observe client earnings for all single, female adult clients who entered WT for a first spell as early as January 2001 and exited prior to the third quarter of 2002.[16] Each client is observed across three periods: (1) each of the four quarters prior to WT entry, (2) the period of WT enrollment, and (3) each of four quarters after exit.[17] Our outcome measure is inflation-adjusted quarterly earnings, and the predictors in each model include several client characteristics,[18] county fixed effects, and indicators for each quarter of observation. Finally, each model includes a variable indicating whether a client exited due to a sanction and a series of interaction terms between this variable and each of the quarterly indicator variables. The logic of the analysis is straightforward. The sanction variable allows us to observe the difference in earnings between sanctioned and nonsanctioned clients, while the interactions allow us to see

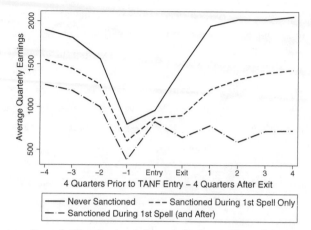

FIGURE 11-4. Quarterly Client Earnings before and after First TANF Spell, by Sanction Status

how this "earnings gap" changes across the periods before and after the first TANF spell.

We estimated two versions of this model, defining the "nonsanctioned" group in each case as clients who were not sanctioned in any spell in the observation period. In the first model, we compare this group to clients who were sanctioned during the first spell but not a second time in the four quarters after exiting. In the second, we compare this group to clients who were sanctioned in the first spell and in at least one other spell in the four quarters after exit.[19]

Figure 11-4 presents our main results as predicted quarterly earnings for each group. These results indicate disparities that exist *after* controlling for individual-level differences, such as race and education level (see note 18). And because we include county fixed effects, they can be interpreted as average differences between clients who reside in the same county—and, thus, are exposed to the same local economies and WT sanctioning practices.

Because sanctioned and nonsanctioned clients differ in ways we cannot observe, the results reveal a clear hierarchy of earnings across the groups during the quarters prior to WT entry. The clients who would never be sanctioned had higher earnings than clients who would receive a single sanction, who had higher earnings than clients who would receive multiple sanctions. This same ordering reappears in the post-TANF quarters, but the earnings gaps in each case expand considerably. Prior to WT entry, once-sanctioned clients earned approximately $300 per quarter less than nonsanctioned clients; after exit, this gap rises to over $500 per quarter. The results for clients who received multiple sanctions are similar but on a larger scale. Prior to entry, this group earned approximately $600 per quarter less than clients in the nonsanctioned group; after exit, this gap doubles to more than $1,200 per quarter.

To gauge the substantive meaning of these results, one must look more closely at the best-case scenario of never-sanctioned clients. As shown in figure 11-4, these clients had very low earnings prior to entering the program, approximately $1,900 per quarter ($633 per month). For this group of "most successful" clients, passage through the WT program results in an increase of only 8.4 percent in real earnings over a period that spans more than two years. By the fourth quarter after exit, the average quarterly earnings for the never-sanctioned group is only $2,160 ($720 per month), a figure that remains far below the poverty line for any family size.

For sanctioned clients, the results are even worse. Passage through the WT program results in earnings that, in absolute terms, are even lower than the insufficient earnings they had one year prior to entering their first TANF spell. Clients who were sanctioned only once experienced a decrease of 7.4 percent, despite the fact that these clients "learned their lesson" and were never sanctioned again. The erosion of earnings among clients sanctioned more than once is especially dramatic. By the fourth quarter after exit, these clients were earning an average of $700 ($233 per month). Compared to the fourth quarter prior to entering WT, this represents an average decrease in real earnings of 42 percent. Clearly, the large pre-participation earnings gap between this group and the others indicates that these heads of households face significant work barriers. The TANF experience does nothing to improve their position relative to the other groups and pushes them toward lower earnings than they made previously. For these clients, the welfare one-stop truly is a "downward mobility machine" (Collins and Mayer 2010).

Citizenship and Civic Incorporation

To assess the consequences of neoliberal paternalism, one must also take stock of how it has positioned the poor as citizens and participants in the polity. Citizenship, of course, has been central to the history of the modern welfare state (Marshall 1964; Esping-Andersen 1990; Lieberman 2005; Somers 2008). Welfare programs for poor families have, at various times, served as tools for supporting the civic contributions of Republican Mothers, "Americanizing" immigrant families, teaching virtues, regulating moral behaviors, and empowering the poor as democratic participants (Gordon 1994; Cruikshank 1999; Ward

2005). Welfare programs serve as an important site of citizenship in their own right and as an active force positioning the poor in relation to other citizens and the state (Soss 2000; Soss and Schram 2008).

In recent years, a growing literature has begun to investigate how public policies matter for the meaning and practice of citizenship and, more broadly, for the vitality and functioning of democracy (Mettler and Soss 2004). A substantial body of research now suggests that policy regimes can, indeed, strengthen democratic citizenship. In addition to giving citizens reasons to participate and resources for doing so, policies can foster engagement through the messages they convey (Campbell 2007b; Schneider and Ingram 1997). In welfare programs, for example, citizens have unusually direct, personal encounters with state authority, on issues that matter greatly to them (Soss 2000). Positive experiences in these encounters can affirm that citizens are full and equal members; they can demonstrate to citizens that their concerns are legitimate, their voices are effective, and their government is responsive (Mettler 2005).

Thus, when Deborah Stone (2008: 245) states that "done right, government help strengthens democracy," she is not just expressing the hopes of social citizenship theorists (Marshall 1964; Pateman 2005; Olson 2006). Research suggests that social policies "done right" strengthen democracy by positioning citizens as bearers of shared rights, as participants in decision making, and as active subjects who are supported in efforts to direct their own lives. Policies that draw citizens together under "universal" social supports tend to raise levels of social trust and convey to beneficiaries that they enjoy full civic standing (Kumlin and Rothstein 2005; Mettler 2005). Such policies can also serve as powerful wellsprings for political participation. Seniors in the Social Security program, for example, have higher levels of political engagement because they receive resources that facilitate participation, are mobilized by program-related interest groups, and have clear incentives to mobilize in defense of benefits (Campbell 2003).

Suzanne Mettler's (2005) study of the G.I. Bill points to an even broader array of incorporating mechanisms. The G.I. Bill raised levels of engagement among World War II veterans because it affirmed their civic membership, built civic commitments, lifted education levels, and supplied recipients with positive experiences of government "marked by fairness and ease of accessibility" (Mettler 2005: 85). The importance of this last factor is underscored by studies showing that when citizens see program procedures as fair and believe that authorities are responsive to rules and requests, they develop more positive views of government and become more willing to express their needs and grievances (Soss 2000; Kumlin 2004).

As an approach to civic incorporation, neoliberal paternalism entails a sharp rejection of this line of thinking. Democratic citizenship may be deepened for some people by programs that offer secure and adequate benefits, equalize rights and standing, and structure authority relations according to democratic values. But the poor are different. Their dysfunctional behaviors and social pathologies render this approach ineffective or, worse, counterproductive.

Lawrence Mead (1986, 2005), for example, argues that social disorder and weak self-discipline have left the poor unable to shoulder the burdens of civic obligations. Their low rates of work and civic participation flow from a common origin: They lack the self-discipline needed to order their affairs, bring behaviors in line with intentions, make productive societal contributions, "merit the esteem of others [and make] a community of equal citizens imaginable" (Mead 1997b: 229). In this context, civic and political incorporation are ill served by "permissive" rights-oriented programs that assume recipients can act on their self-interest, pursue opportunities, and participate as equals in decision making.

The great achievement of welfare reform, for Mead (2005), is that it sets forth an obligation-centered "operational definition of citizenship" and enforces it through directive and supervisory methods (Mead 1986, 1997a). Bypassing liberal-democratic values (privacy, rights, and participation), it seeks to "make citizens first" by using state authority to impose work and penalize noncompliance (Mead 2005). By ensuring that civic obligations are met, Mead argues that state authorities can make the poor more respectable to their fellow citizens and instill them with the self-discipline needed to function as full participants in the community.

The civic consequences of this disciplinary turn can be evaluated along multiple dimensions. One key measure of the quality of citizenship enjoyed by the poor is the manner in which governing institutions respond to changes in their needs and claims (Nelson 1984; Hasenfeld 1985; Soss 2000). As we have already seen in this chapter, the rise of neoliberal paternalism has been marked by a sharp contraction in responsiveness. Administratively and culturally, the TANF program has adopted a deterrent stance, while criminal policies have drawn the poor into more punitive and custodial strategies of state management (Wacquant 2009).

Under neoliberal paternalism, correctional and welfare institutions have also been reorganized as more authoritarian settings for state-citizen interactions. For poor people, experiences in these settings bring practical meaning to abstract political concepts such as rights and obligations, power and authority, voice and civic standing. Thus, it matters greatly that the balance of interactions between the state and the poor has shifted to the controlling terrains of prison, probation, and parole. It matters as well that corrections and welfare provision have both been restructured to emphasize directive authority, surveillance, and compliance.

The past few decades have witnessed the rise of the supermax prison and broader moves toward restricted-activity warehousing. They have been marked by the pruning of rehabilitation and leave programs, a growing tendency to transfer prisoners to distant and remote locations, and new limits on prisoner voice (the Prison Litigation Reform Act of 1996). These and related changes have increased the isolation and vulnerability of people sentenced to prison, at a time when prisons have become more central to poor people's relationships to government (Johnson 2002; Feeley and Swearingen 2004; Katzenstein 2005; Wacquant 2009).

As earlier chapters demonstrate in detail, welfare programs have undergone a similar shift toward authoritarian relations that emphasize client compliance and subordination to state power. To facilitate the construction of competent worker-citizens, the new regime curtails recipients' formal rights as *both* workers and citizens. In the neoliberal frame, welfare benefits have been recast as "wages" paid in exchange for work activity hours. Yet TANF recipients do not qualify as the equals of other workers and, thus, have ambiguous standing in relation to minimum wage laws and anti-discrimination statutes; they do not share in workers' rights to bargain collectively; they are stripped of the constitutional right to choose the conditions of their own labor (Collins and Mayer 2010: 131–46; C. Goldberg 2007). At the same time, the TANF program has erased the entitlement to aid and, in many places, has imposed new restrictions on due process rights, acceptable grounds for grievances, and access to fair hearings (Mink 1998). In return for their meager aid, clients also give up substantial rights to privacy that other citizens enjoy under the Fourth Amendment (Gustafson 2009). Their state records can be searched and matched across information systems, often in concert with criminal investigations, and in some states their homes can be visited and searched by program officials (Gustafson 2009).

Beyond these formal erosions of civic standing, one must also consider the lived experiences of civic position that poor women endure in the TANF program today. Entry into the program is marked by stigmatizing rituals that underscore their suspect status and obligations to authorities. In many states, applicants are subjected to police-style processing, fingerprinted and photographed to facilitate surveillance. They are told of strict penalties for fraud and forced to sign Individual Responsibility Plans that enumerate obligations while stressing the absence of entitlement rights. To comply with child support enforcement and paternity establishment, they are required to divulge details regarding their sexual histories—alongside details about their home lives that facilitate monitoring of assets, income sources, and benefit usage.

Once past the application phase, TANF clients are positioned as vulnerable subordinates dependent on case manager authority. They are pushed from one activity to another, without opportunities to set agendas and goals or participate in the direction of their case. They are summoned again and again to produce documents that verify their compliance, under the threat of a sanction should they stray. The significant constraints on case manager discretion discussed in earlier chapters are rarely visible to clients. The case manager is experienced as a directive authority that holds great powers for good or ill. As one client explained to Joe Soss (2000: 134), "Your life is in their hands. Your kid's life is in that worker's hands. If that worker don't like you, if you don't smile at that worker she can do anything she wants to."

Indeed, case managers and clients often converge in striking ways as they describe relationships that center on paternalist power relations and the rote processing of documents. In chapter 10, we noted the WT case manager who described her job as "herding cattle": "A cattle herder is just running people through, not taking time to look after them. A shepherd takes care of the sheep, tends after them, cares for them. It is not my nature to herd cattle and now I have to learn to do that." A welfare client interviewed by Soss (2000) reached for the same metaphor, among other illuminating comparisons, to convey her feelings of subordination and frustration: "It's like you're in a cattle prod. It's like you're in a big mill. I felt like a number, or like I was in a prison system. Like I said, it feels like you're in a cattle prod. They're the cowboys and you're a cow. [T]hese people are like 'just be quiet and follow your line.'"

The emphasis on silencing in this statement was a common theme in the interviews Soss (2000) conducted with welfare clients. As subordinates in disciplinary relationships, clients explained that "you learn to be quiet and take whatever is dished out." The women made great efforts to present themselves in ways they expected case managers to like and reward. And although it was not uncommon for clients to fail in their efforts to stay quiet, most reported that they actively worked to avoid speaking up or raising complaints. The reasons they gave for disciplining themselves in this manner focused consistently on two themes: Speaking up would be futile (it would not affect decisions), and it would be risky (it could antagonize the case manager and, thus, result in benefit losses or punitive actions). One client interviewed by Soss (2000) offered a particularly concise statement of both lessons and their implications for political voice.

> Futility: You just have to wait and see what they do to you. That's how I feel. Sometimes I do want to say something. But I just leave it at that. Because I feel like I'll get treated the way I've been getting treated anyway. So it wouldn't matter if I said something or not. Whatever they want to do, they're going to do regardless, whether I say something or not. They've got the power, so you have to listen to what they say.
> Vulnerability: I figure if I say something back, they know a way of getting me cut off. And then I wouldn't have anything for me and my kids, just because I said something. That's their power, right there. That's the power. That's why nobody complains.

Advocates of neoliberal paternalism might argue that these dynamics are acceptable because they ultimately promote the broader civic incorporation of the poor. Two branches of this argument merit particular attention. First, by demanding competence and visibly enforcing work, advocates argued that the TANF program would raise public respect for the poor, increase public willingness to aid the poor, and neutralize the corrosive effects of racial stereotypes (Soss and Schram 2007). Second, by bringing discipline to the poor and integrating them into work, advocates claimed that the TANF program would give the poor the competence needed to shoulder the burdens of civic participation. It would curb the passive "culture of complaint" about marginality and move the poor toward forms of civic and political engagement that would place them on equal terms with their fellow citizens (Mead 1992, 2005).

The first expectation has been sharply contradicted by research on public attitude trends before and after welfare reform in the mid-1990s.[20] Disciplinary poverty governance has been popular, but it has not generated more positive public perceptions of poor people or welfare recipients. Work-centered reform did not reduce the association of public aid with dependency or the association of poverty with lack of effort. In the wake of welfare reform, Americans did not become more willing to spend on the poor, on blacks, or on welfare. Public opposition to reducing inequality and raising living standards for the poor actually increased. Welfare continued to elicit high levels of public opposition, and welfare opponents did not become any more supportive of anti-poverty efforts in general. The strong relationship between anti-black stereotypes and attitudes toward poverty and welfare did not diminish in any discernible way.

Only an observer schooled in the twisted logic of civic arguments for welfare reform could find these results surprising. Paternalists claimed that disciplinary poverty governance would lead citizens to view the poor as equals by, in essence, treating the poor as more suspect and less competent than themselves. Nothing of the sort has come to pass.

Empirical research has been equally unkind to the prediction that paternalist reforms would turn the poor into more active participants in civic and political life. In his interviews with welfare recipients in the 1990s, Soss (2000) found that individuals tend to draw lessons from their program experiences about the nature of government and the efficacy of political action. More positive experiences with program authorities led to more positive views of government and political engagement; more negative ones had the opposite effect. Further research has corroborated this "spillover effect," suggesting that authoritarian experiences with welfare and criminal justice systems undermine social trust, political participation, and faith in government (Lawless and Fox 2001; Kumlin 2004). Analyses of large survey samples confirm that these effects remain discernible after controlling for traits that distinguish welfare clients from other poor people (Campbell 2003) and that civic and political withdrawal deepen as individuals accumulate experiences with means-tested welfare programs (Mettler and Stonecash 2008).

Responding to these studies, Lawrence Mead (2004b: 672) has countered that he is "not persuaded because they do not control for selection effects." Thus, the apparent negative effects of paternalist designs may "reflect the people who enter programs rather than what the program does" (Mead 2001b: 676). More recent research, however, has made this claim difficult to maintain. Analyzing data from the longitudinal Fragile Families study, Bruch, Ferree, and Soss (2010) are able to control for many of the previously unobserved differences emphasized by Mead (substance usage, domestic violence, levels of material hardship, criminal convictions, and living apart from one's child). In addition, their analysis accounts for state-level differences in TANF policy regimes and institutional features that shape electoral access. Even with these stronger controls, Bruch, Ferree, and Soss (2010) find that experiences with state TANF programs have significant and substantial negative effects on rates of civic engagement and rates of political engagement among the poor.

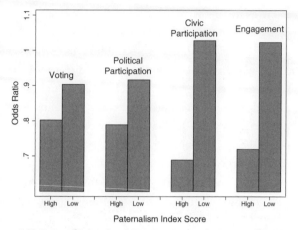

FIGURE 11-5. Odds Ratios of Political and Civic Participation by Receipt of TANF in States with High and Low Paternalism Index Scores

Moreover, using an index of TANF paternalism similar to the one we employ in chapter 5, the authors investigate how effects on civic and political engagement vary across states with different TANF regimes. If experiences with authority relations in TANF programs influence civic and political engagement, then the effects of program participation should vary across states with more versus less paternalist TANF designs. Figure 11-5 presents their key findings as odds ratios for two client groups—those who participated in a high-paternalism program and those who participated in a low-paternalism program—relative to a baseline group of respondents who did not participate in a TANF program at all. Odds ratios above 1.0 indicate a positive program effect relative to the baseline group; ratios below this level indicate a negative effect. Four outcomes are examined: voting, all reported forms of political participation, all reported forms of civic participation, and an overall measure of the individual's degree of civic and political engagements (see Bruch, Ferree, and Soss 2010 for details).

The results are unequivocal. Across all four outcomes, the effects of welfare participation depend on the degree of paternalism in a state's TANF program. Experiences in TANF programs that are more paternalist than the national average significantly lower odds of all forms of civic and political engagement. By contrast, experiences in TANF programs that are less paternalist than the national average have no statistically discernible civic and political effects. Thus, contrary to paternalists' claims, directive and supervisory welfare programs do not seem to hasten civic and political incorporation. In more moderate forms, these programs appear to have no effect on the profound civic and political marginality of the poor. In stronger forms, they actively enhance this marginality, pushing the poor further outside civic and political life.

Further evidence of this dynamic is supplied by an analysis of panel data from the Youth Development Study, which followed a group of Minnesota public school students from ninth grade onward, surveying the same individuals repeatedly over the years that followed 1988 (Swartz et al. 2010). Although the Minnesota sample may limit generalization, it allows for a particularly sharp test of political effects. For example, to neutralize biases from self-reports of electoral participation, which can vary across groups, Swartz and her colleagues (2010) base their analysis on voting records validated by the state of Minnesota. In addition, to better isolate the effects of welfare experiences, the authors predict post-program voting in the 2000 election while controlling for pre-program voting in the 1994 election. Their results strongly confirm the earlier studies.

> [The] 1994 voters [were] 10 times more likely to vote in 2000 [than] those who did not vote in 1994. Even net of this strong control, however, 1996 welfare recipients remained 61 percent less likely to vote than non-recipients in the 2000 election. [W]e interpret the persistent effects of welfare experience on later voting as resulting from the institutional structure and cultural meanings associated with this form of government assistance, including means-tested criteria, caseworker discretion, surveillance, and stigma associated with welfare receipt that teach young adult recipients that they lack power and influence in their interactions with government.

The conclusions of these welfare studies are reinforced by analyses that address the carceral side of paternalist poverty governance. Mass incarceration, of course, has limited civic participation among the poor through the direct effects of felony disenfranchisement laws (Manza and Uggen 2006) and through the indirect effects of social and economic marginalization (Western 2006). Recent research by Vesla Weaver and Amy Lerman (2010) demonstrates that these depressive effects are strengthened considerably by dynamics that mirror the consequences of welfare paternalism. Analyzing two national datasets, they find that criminal justice contacts have large, negative effects on turning out to vote, participating in civic groups, and trusting the government. These negative effects deepen as encounters with the criminal justice system grow more numerous and/or severe, and they cannot be explained by differences in criminality or socioeconomic status.

In sum, the existing empirical research strongly suggests that disciplinary poverty governance has failed to promote civic and political incorporation for the poor. Indeed, it appears to have deepened their marginality. In this regard, it is crucial to note that more positive results for the poor seem to flow from the same kinds of policy designs that produce such results in the broader citizenry. Indeed, even means-tested, targeted aid programs that link rights to obligations appear capable of drawing the poor into civic life if they adopt more democratic design elements.

In the United States, the best example is the Head Start program for poor children, a holdover from the War on Poverty's ethos of "maximum feasible participation" that stresses parental volunteering and participation in self-governance through center-based policy councils. Client descriptions of Head Start turn the silencing dynamics of welfare paternalism on their head. Mothers involved with the program emphasize that "when you go to orientation, they say, 'we need you to help,'" and that they value "the opportunity to go to a meeting where you are making decisions" (Soss 2000). They express confidence that someone will "listen when you express your opinion" and say that Head Start leaves them feeling "pumped up in a way" (L. White 2002). Analyzing the Fragile Families dataset, Bruch, Ferree, and Soss (2010) provide statistical support for these conclusions. Experiences with the Head Start program significantly raise overall levels of civic and political engagement. As Deborah Stone (2008: 259) summarizes, "In Head Start, mothers grow into their citizenship roles as they [participate in making decisions and] realize that not only are they helping others, but others are counting on them."

In sum, there is no reason why policies cannot be designed to reduce the civic marginality of the poor. Neoliberal paternalism, however, diminishes poor people's citizenship by subordinating it to the authoritarian pursuit of discipline. Women in welfare programs are no longer supported as mother-citizens, and they are subject to coercion under ambiguous and limited legal protections as worker-citizens (Collins and Mayer 2010). Disciplinary poverty governance has brought the poor none of the esteem promised by paternalist reformers. Instead, it has pushed them further toward the margins as participants in civic and political life.

Conclusion

As welfare caseloads have declined and work levels have risen, conventional wisdom has coalesced around the idea that disciplinary poverty governance has been good for the country, good for poverty reduction efforts, and good for the poor themselves. This chapter has presented a critical appraisal that is sharply at odds with the prevailing view. Now that we have considered the evidence, it is worth taking a moment to reflect on why so many thoughtful observers have converged on a conclusion so different from our own.

First, most positive assessments proceed by treating welfare reform in isolation, severing it from the broader disciplinary turn in poverty governance. Yet as we have seen throughout this book, penal and welfare operations have been transformed, and operate today, as two sides of a single political development. The state's shifting emphasis, from welfare to carceral control, and the criminalization of welfare itself stand at the center of poverty governance today (Wacquant 2009). Because it is their conjunction that affects lives in poor communities, it makes little sense to analyze the effects of welfare reform as if they were not part of a broader governing regime.

Second, most assessments of welfare reform have occurred within the frame established by the political campaign to abolish AFDC (Schram and Soss 2001). The elevation of "long-term dependency" to the status of a critical social problem made the declining caseloads and rising work rates that ensued into powerful signifiers of policy success. This conclusion has been bolstered by repeated references to the overheated "predictions of doom" that liberal opponents made during the final struggle over reform in 1996. Poor women with children moved from welfare to work, and the sky did not fall. Or perhaps we should say, "the sky did not fall further," because life conditions for poor, female-headed families prior to welfare reform were nothing short of terrible. By emphasizing how work has been reinstated without making these conditions dramatically worse, reformers have obscured the fact that they have not delivered on their promises. Declining caseloads are framed as signs of declining need, when they actually reflect restricted access. Higher work rates are interpreted as steps toward self-sufficiency, as if we lacked evidence that these are dead-end jobs that provide inadequate wages, fail to accommodate family obligations, and offer vanishingly small prospects for advancement. Bold promises of civic and political incorporation are left standing, untroubled by serious empirical scrutiny.

Third, healthy debate has been stifled by the symbolic contrast between AFDC, a program cast as "making people dependent on welfare handouts," and TANF, a program cast as "rewarding people who work hard and play by the rules by helping them achieve independence." Critics of the TANF program are dismissed as defenders of the failed AFDC program who, for obvious reasons, should not be taken seriously. The consequences for liberal poverty researchers, who (with good reason) want to be taken seriously, have been profound. Technical discussions of marginal changes flourish in this environment, turning small regression coefficients into reasons for optimism or pessimism at the edges of the system. But those who question whether the system itself is wise or just, who argue that the disciplinary agenda has failed the poor, risk losing their seats at the table of "reasonable" discourse. As a result, welfare's reformers continue to trumpet their success and leverage it for further policy advances, while skeptical researchers police themselves in an effort to remain relevant and protect their ability to promote marginal improvements that seem more politically feasible. To do otherwise is to risk being seen as an out-of-touch liberal who thinks handouts are better than jobs, who rejects the idea that everyone should do their fair share, who thinks people should have rights without obligations, who is nostalgic for a policy that, by all reasonable criteria, failed.

To be sure, some changes in welfare provision have benefited the poor in important ways over the past two decades. The lives of the working poor would be far worse if expansions of child care, health care, and wage supplements had not occurred. But advocates for the poor sought these supports long before the rise of neoliberal paternalism, and they do not lie at the heart of the disciplinary turn in governance that is the focus of our inquiry. The analysis presented in this chapter has been more focused, emphasizing effects that have flowed from the distinctive policy developments we explored as outcomes in earlier chapters.

Surveying the evidence, we conclude that disciplinary poverty governance has failed to deliver on its promises and is failing poor Americans today. Its carceral emphasis is destabilizing poor communities, exacerbating civic marginality, and undermining the social and economic prospects of millions of people born into poverty. Its work-first philosophy is regimenting poor mothers into dead-end jobs that are not "mother-ready," while undercutting their access to educational and training opportunities that could improve their position in the labor market. Its cultural and organizational emphasis on combating dependency has made the TANF program unresponsive to poor people's needs, even in the hardest economic times. Its heavy reliance on sanctions has reduced earnings for the most disadvantaged, while failing to bring more than paltry increases to the below-poverty earnings of clients who "play by the rules" and never get sanctioned. Its governing mentality of compliance to directive and supervisory authorities has deepened the civic and political marginality of the poor. The title of this chapter asks whether the rise of neoliberal paternalism has mattered for the poor. Yes, unfortunately, it has mattered a great deal.

12

CONCLUSION

DISCIPLINARY POVERTY GOVERNANCE EMERGED IN THE LATE TWENTIETH century as a political response to new social and economic insecurities. The insecurities were mental as well as material, a tapestry of unstable life conditions and unsettling anxieties that arose as the familiar order of American life gave way. Disruptive movements upended laws and norms as they challenged the terms of social control surrounding gender, race, and sexuality. The iconic nuclear family buckled as women flooded the workplace and conventions related to marriage and reproduction underwent rapid change. Industrial jobs evaporated, taking their family-supporting wages and paths to advancement with them. Employers moved to reduce costs, increase flexibility, weaken collective bargaining, and undercut regulations. Low-skilled American workers were left adrift in an unreliable pool of low-wage, high-turnover, service-sector jobs.

As these developments reshaped the structural foundations of poverty, they laid the groundwork for a sea change in the politics of poverty governance. From the 1960s on, conservatives brandished the troubled lives of the poor as evidence of liberal failure and as a wedge issue to divide the Democratic coalition. Pathological images of poor, minority neighborhoods became a repository for diffuse public anxieties, personified by the lazy and licentious welfare queen and the violent, drug-dealing gangbanger. A new "underclass" was discovered, and its problems were folded into a broad narrative of declining morality and authority. Blame was laid squarely at the feet of liberals, whose "permissive" policies had coddled criminals and failed to enforce social obligations. To restore personal responsibility and social order, state authority would have to be deployed in a more disciplined and disciplinary manner—one that emphasized the bottom lines of efficient performance and effective results.

The preceding chapters have analyzed this disciplinary turn in some detail, seeking to clarify its origins, operations, and consequences. Our approach has been distinctive in two respects. First, we have asked how efforts to govern the poor proceed across levels of scale that are intimately related in practice but rarely drawn into a common frame of analysis. Most studies of policy and politics focus on (and speak to scholarship regarding) a particular institution or stage of the policy process. Instead, we have built our study around the substantive problem of governing the poor, asking how consistencies, variations, elaborations, and contradictions arise as authorities pursue this project in different institutional settings.

Second, because poverty governance is multifaceted, we have sought to avoid the distortions and blind spots that arise when scholars rely heavily on a single form of evidence or method of analysis. As we shifted our attention across different sites and dimensions of governance, new questions arose and we followed them toward different analytic strategies and empirical sources. As early statistical findings emerged, they raised questions that could be answered only in the field; and as our interviews accumulated, they signaled new directions for revising and extending our statistical work. Wherever possible, we asked how different forms of evidence fit together—to corroborate or cast doubt on a conclusion, suggest discrepancies in need of investigation, or suggest plausible explanations for earlier findings.

Thus, for both substantive and methodological reasons, variety has been a hallmark of the preceding chapters. Although poverty governance has remained at center stage, we have pursued this topic in an unusually wide range of locales using an uncommon diversity of methods. In this final chapter, we assemble our key themes and findings to draw some conclusions about neoliberal paternalism in American poverty governance. Building on this critical analysis, we conclude with an agenda for developing a more just, caring, and democratic approach.

Key Themes and Findings

Efforts to reform and regulate the poor are very old, and our study has uncovered a great deal of historical continuity. The idea of getting tough with the poor for their own good is hardly new, and welfare provision has always been responsive, in one form or another, to market needs and ideologies. Now, as in the past, poverty governance serves a complex dual agenda of civic incorporation and social control, rooted in prevailing constructions of social group differences. It extends the long tradition of American reliance on nongovernmental organizations as well as the old and troubled relationship between American federalism and social inequality.

Our effort to specify change amid this continuity builds most directly on the scholarship of Frances Fox Piven and Richard Cloward (1971) and Loïc Wacquant (2009). To clarify our conclusions, it is helpful to engage these works directly. Our empirical findings provide the strongest evidence to date that the dynamics identified in *Regulating the Poor* (1971) persist as vital elements of poverty governance today. Welfare programs for the poor continue to operate, as Piven and Cloward argue, as derivative institutions shaped by pressures that arise from the polity and market. Our evidence confirms that they continue to enforce work through the principle of less eligibility, pushing the poor into the least attractive jobs by keeping benefits low, making them inaccessible, and surrounding them with stigma.

The disciplinary turn was driven by political mobilization and, in states and localities, took on different forms depending on who controlled political institutions. Labor market conditions were equally important. From the 1970s to the 1990s, benefit cutbacks and restrictive Aid to Families with Dependent Children (AFDC) waivers were pursued most vigorously in states where benefit levels encroached on wages for low-skilled workers. Moreover, as Piven and Cloward's analysis suggests, policy devolution facilitated the calibration of welfare practices to local political pressures and labor market needs. Patterns of sanctioning in the Florida Welfare Transition (WT) program, for example, have been highly responsive to local unemployment rates and seasonal demands for cheap labor to service the tourism industry.

Based on these and other findings, we conclude that Wacquant (2009: 290) overstates the case when he suggests that the regulatory dynamics emphasized by Piven and Cloward have been "rendered obsolete by the neoliberal remaking of the state." At the same time, our study supports key themes in Wacquant's broader analysis. Mass incarceration, penal logics, and policing (in a broad sense) have become defining elements of poverty governance. The state's carceral "right hand" has risen in importance; welfare discourses and procedures are increasingly criminalized; and welfare and criminal justice operations now function as integrated elements of a single system for managing marginal populations. As Wacquant rightly argues, an adequate analysis of poverty governance today must draw welfare and criminal justice operations into a shared analytic frame.

Indeed, our study has yielded substantial evidence for Wacquant's core claims regarding the integration of these two systems and the centrality of race for contemporary poverty governance. Between the 1970s and 1990s, rising incarceration rates and welfare cutbacks in the states were driven by virtually identical forces. After 1996, state policy choices produced a tight triadic relationship linking larger black population rates, more disciplinary and localized Temporary Assistance for Needy Families (TANF) regimes, and more aggressive correctional control. Welfare fraud was drawn into the orbit of draconian criminal penalties, and sanctions restructured welfare participation around a (racially biased) logic of violation and penalty. In Florida, we find that larger racial disparities in arrest rates and welfare sanction rates tend to emerge from the same local communities.

In these respects, our study aligns closely with Wacquant's. Our analysis, however, has also yielded important differences. Arguing that the neoliberal state "sheds economic responsibility," Wacquant (2009: 19) seeks to explain how the rollback of social protections "necessitates the grandeur of the penal state." In the preceding chapters, we have offered arguments and evidence that make a contrary point. Neoliberalism has expanded and recast the state's economic responsibilities. It has blurred the boundary between state and market, restructured the state around market principles, and placed the state in service of market actors. The empirical materials presented in chapters 8 and 9, for example, do not suggest a withdrawal of the state from the market. They show in concrete ways how state and market operations have become integrated and how state authority is used affirmatively to meet market needs.

Our rejection of this "rollback" narrative has also led us to emphasize, more than Wacquant does, the dynamics that have emerged as poverty governance has been *rolled out* to diverse locales and organizations. Wacquant's interpretation of national developments is insightful, but it pays little attention to one of the most defining features of contemporary poverty governance: the remarkable variation of policies and practices across jurisdictions, institutions, and circumstances. Our point is not just that Wacquant's analysis fits empirical reality more in some places than others. Rollout and variation are essential to the operation of neoliberal paternalism, and they play a critical role in explaining the racial dynamics of disciplinary governance. American federalism functions today as a powerful mechanism for the production of racial disparities. Under first-order devolution, states with larger black populations have adopted the most disciplinary polices, and, as a result, African Americans have been subjected to the most disciplinary regimes. Similarly, second-order devolution has paved the way for a complex interplay of political conservatism and racial bias in welfare sanctioning—a dynamic that does not appear in states that have retained more centralized control. These and related patterns underscore the contingency of racial dynamics in poverty governance today and highlight how decentralized governing structures play a critical mediating role.

Contrary to Wacquant, we have also presented an empirical case for the argument that (a) poverty governance operates today as a productive project of discipline and (b) this project applies to governing officials as much as the poor themselves. We also differ from Wacquant in our view of what discipline entails and how it relates to the contemporary uses of punishment. Wacquant places punishment at the center of his account and theorizes its disciplinary functions for the poor. In contrast, we advance a theoretical and empirical case for two points. First, poverty governance today operates as a productive project of discipline that deploys a wide variety of tools to incentivize, structure, and cultivate mentalities of self-rule. Many of these policy tools—such as tax credits, classes, transitional work supports, benchmarks, and performance bonuses—do not follow a penal logic. Second, this disciplinary project has targeted the governing officials of poverty management as much as the poor themselves.

At all levels of the system, negative powers of punishment, restriction, and coercion are complemented by productive powers that "incite, reinforce, control, monitor, optimize, and organize the forces under it"—forms of power "bent on generating forces, making them grow, and ordering them, rather than impeding them, making them submit or destroying them" (Foucault 1990: 136). At each link in the governing chain, we have seen how superior authorities give lower-level actors new freedoms to choose, while working diligently to structure and incentivize the choices that result. From federal funding schemes to local performance systems, poverty governance today is an effort to shape the mentalities and calculations of policy officials so that, under conditions of apparent autonomy, they can be relied on to carry out the work of disciplining the poor.

In poverty governance today, actions that roll back access to decommodifying welfare protections are assimilated into a more ambitious and transformative practical rationality. Welfare operations have become affirmative sites of commodification, actively cultivating labor pools for employers as they strive to construct more competent and compliant worker-citizens. Such Foucauldian dynamics are downplayed by Wacquant, who emphasizes the contraction of welfare programs and argues that incarceration is mostly about punishing and containing (rather than transforming) the poor. With prison rehabilitation in decline and supermax warehousing on the rise, he is surely right up to a point. But on this score, we ultimately part ways.

Despite rising incarceration rates and falling welfare rolls, poor women remain far more likely to enter a welfare program than a prison. The reverse is true for poor men. But most men under correctional supervision do not live in prison; they live under the directive and supervisory ministrations of probation and parole. Increasingly, parole offices, "reentry" programs, alternative custodial institutions, and recovery houses for drug felons are adopting work-centered, reformative programs similar to the regime illuminated by our field research in the Florida WT program (Fairbanks 2009; Haney 2010; Mead 2007). Beyond the correctional system itself, discourses of criminality and victimization have functioned as productive forces in the polity at large, reconstructing mentalities of American citizenship and normative visions of governance (Garland 2002; J. Simon 2007).

Neoliberal paternalism defines the operations of American poverty governance today, both as a mentality of rule (specifying who is to be governed, why, how, and for what purposes) and as a regime of practice (organizing the exercise of authority around specific technologies and institutional arrangements). Under this practical rationality, citizen rights have been subordinated to contractual responsibilities, and diverse notions of civic virtue and contribution have been collapsed into the foundational obligation to work. State operations have been redesigned—through privatization, devolution, and performance systems—to follow market principles and serve as an opportunity for profitable investment. As state authorities have been deployed to direct, supervise, and transform the poor, state resources have been marshaled to service labor markets, subsidize employers, enhance profits, and absorb wage and benefit costs.

Few developments illustrate this contrast as starkly as the criminalized policing of small-stakes recipient fraud in a privatized system that facilitates corporate fraud and profiteering on a vast scale. Such contrasts, however, emerge from a deeper symbiotic relationship between neoliberalism and paternalism. Throughout the preceding chapters, we have seen how neoliberal and paternalist modes of governance converge on a shared disciplinary agenda, track one another across time and space, and bolster one another in a relationship of mutual support. Decisions to pursue second-order devolution emerge most often in states that adopt the most stringent rules for TANF clients. Privatization and sanctioning proceed hand in hand, as for-profit providers penalize TANF clients at significantly higher rates. Competitive performance pressures discipline case managers and subject welfare clients to higher rates of disciplinary penalty. Champions of devolution, privatization, and performance management typically promote them as politically neutral reforms: They are merely ways to enhance efficiency, effectiveness, and responsiveness. In poverty governance, however, these reforms are far from neutral; they are integral parts of a regime that disciplines the poor and services labor markets and corporations.

Our field research also underscores how neoliberalism and paternalism have intersected to recast the organizational culture of welfare provision. On websites and in the physical spaces of one-stop centers, in rituals of contract and insistent invocations of performance and personal responsibility, the "business model" and the paternalist ethos are cemented as guides to organizational sense making and operational mission. Our fieldwork reveals that the power of this discourse is far from complete. In conflicted and sometimes anguished reflections on their work, case managers embrace the business model even as they criticize it for depriving them of resources, putting performance numbers ahead of human development, and subordinating client needs to behavioral compliance. They deride the social services model as a failed "old school" mentality, while drawing on it as a valued source of professional identity. In their daily work, they find ample reasons to worry that sanctions are counterproductive. Yet they continue to impose them, just as they carry out other aspects of their disciplinary mission. They do so not because they have internalized neoliberal paternalism as a hegemonic worldview, but because their work lives have been organized around its logics and goals. Ambivalence aside, this is "just how the program works," as one case manager put it. It is the low-wage, deskilled job they have been hired to do, and their uses of discretion run primarily within its confines.

Looking across time and space, our study has also shed light on the key forces that have driven the disciplinary turn and shaped its variations. Since the 1970s, three factors have emerged with remarkable consistency to shape the contours of poverty governance: prevailing partisan and ideological orientations, labor market conditions, and racial constructions and compositions of target populations. Changes in labor markets and partisan competition created intense pressures for national reform, which were fueled by deeply racialized images and arguments regarding the urban underclass. From the 1970s to the 1990s, the same three factors shaped state-level patterns of rising incarceration, welfare benefit cutbacks, and restrictive AFDC waiver adoptions. As states rushed to create disciplinary TANF regimes in the late 1990s, amid the bipartisan "national consensus" on welfare reform, differences in labor markets and partisan control briefly ceased to matter; the racial identities of target groups emerged as a singularly powerful predictor of the policy choices that stood at the heart of a thoroughly racialized project.

Beyond this exceptional moment, however, the same three factors emerged time and again as wellsprings of state and local governance. All emerged as significant predictors of state decisions to pursue second-order devolution. Their interplay shaped differences in sanction rates across Florida counties and mediated the tendency for performance pressures to induce higher rates of sanctioning. Even in our analysis of TANF (non)responsiveness during the recession that began in late 2007, we find that the same three factors identify the states that did the least to extend aid to the increasingly desperate families in low-income communities.

Among these factors, race has played an especially central role in our analysis. In chapter 3, we showed how racial discourses and stereotypes underwrote the mobilization of public support for welfare reform. Building on this analysis, we drew on theories of implicit racism and social cognition to develop the Racial Classification Model (RCM) of policy choice, a concise framework for thinking about when and how racialized identities can be expected to influence policy selection and implementation. In poverty governance today, de jure discrimination is outlawed and discredited, egalitarian racial norms are more widely embraced, and racial minorities are increasingly incorporated into the ranks of governing authorities. As a result, racism in poverty governance emerges in contingent and subtle ways that cannot be reduced to conscious white prejudice and discrimination—or eradicated by their absence.

The RCM offers a way to specify how race operates to shape policy trajectories on this new terrain. Across a remarkable range of settings and levels of governance, we find consistent empirical support for its predictions. In some cases, such as state choices to adopt disciplinary TANF rules, racial effects have been fairly straightforward. The more impressive evidence of how race works in poverty governance today has come from tests of the RCM's conditional propositions regarding factors that should mediate racial effects: the presence of a discrediting marker on a client's record, the uneven dispersion of racial groups across political subunits, the ideological orientations of local implementation environments in a context of second-order devolution, variations in the stereotype gaps associated with different racial/ethnic groups, converging benefit and wage levels that make racialized anxieties over work disincentives more salient, and so on. In places where we have not found simple disparities, racial patterns of policy choice and implementation have emerged under precisely the conditions predicted by the RCM.

Our field research has helped to clarify the processes involved, showing how poorly they fit with classic images of middle-class whites intentionally discriminating against poor, minority clients. Most WT case managers are women; only a minority identify as white; and many are former welfare recipients themselves. Yet as we have seen, these case managers work in a policy setting where race provides a salient cultural frame for interactions with clients. As they apply a logic of appropriateness to the events that unfold at their desks (asking what is permissible, reasonable, and right to do in a case such as this), they must assign meaning to a client's action—treating it as a fluke, an unavoidable mishap, or an intentional act of noncompliance and deceit. To do so, they must get a sense of the person behind the act. But as they try to "get a fix on people to decide how to handle them they may also put a fix on people, assigning them to a social identity that carries with it significant meaning and consequence" (Maynard-Moody and Musheno 2003: 78). In poverty governance, racial identities matter greatly in this process, especially when they are cued by stereotype-consistent, discrediting markers. Amid the great changes that have occurred in U.S. race relations, cultural constructions of blackness remain a potent force in American poverty governance. They played a key role in the rise of neoliberal paternalism for all poor people, regardless of individual racial identification, and they have shaped policy choice and implementation in ways that have focused the most disciplinary tools and practices on African Americans.

Reimagining Poverty Governance

The preceding chapters provide a variety of reasons why people who value justice, care, and democracy should reject the neoliberal-paternalist approach to poverty governance. Racial inequity is endemic to the normal operations of the system, predictable in its patterning at all levels. Privatization has not made service provision more efficient, effective, or responsive; it has produced a scandalous record of corruption and service failure, enriching corporations and shareholders at the expense of citizens. Competitive performance systems have encouraged providers to cook their books, restrict access to aid, and sanction at higher rates, while doing little to stimulate or diffuse innovations that benefit the poor. Decentralization has abetted inequality and created obstacles to public accountability. Paternalist corrections and welfare policies have deepened the civic and political marginality of the poor. Ex-prisoners and welfare leavers have been pushed into low-wage, dead-end jobs that fail to accommodate family needs and force them to cobble together precarious survival strategies well below the poverty line.

In these respects and others, our study lays bare the urgent need to ask how poverty governance might be reimagined to promote a more inclusive and just society. In taking up this task, we do not aim to provide a detailed blueprint for policy designs and program rules. Positive modes of poverty governance can take many forms, and the lessons of our study cannot resolve debates over the finer points of organization. Having taken a long and careful look at the operations of disciplinary poverty governance, we seek to make a broader contribution to public discourse by connecting an explicit base of political values to a set of policy priorities and institutional principles that can provide an orienting vision for reform efforts.

We begin from the premise that poverty is not primarily a problem of low income; it is, more fundamentally, a condition of marginality and deprivation in which people are denied the capabilities they need to lead the kinds of lives they have reason to value and to participate effectively in the defining relations and institutions of their community (Sen 1999). If poverty is conceptualized in this manner, three value sets loom large as guides to what a more positive form of poverty governance would look like. First, it would serve *democracy* by enhancing people's abilities to participate in decisions that shape their lives, check arbitrary uses of authority, and reconfigure the terms of their relations to one another (Shapiro 1999; Hayward 2000). Second, it would serve *social justice* by expanding capabilities for self-development and self-determination: capacities to learn, grow, accumulate skills and put them to use, on one side, and capacities to participate in defining the direction and conditions of one's actions, on the other (Young 2000). Third, it would value the ethic and practice of *care*—acknowledging the necessity and societal contributions of care work, enhancing people's abilities to give and receive care, and ensuring that they can do so without being marginalized in social, economic, or political relations (Tronto 1993; Glenn 2000; Fineman 2004; Stone 2008).

Efforts to achieve these goals must begin from a basic insight underscored by our study. Poverty governance is a practice, not just a policy. It is an ongoing human transaction shaped, inevitably, by the social, political, and economic relations in which it is embedded. It fails low-income Americans today not just because of its misguided policy designs, but because it serves a labor market that is exploitative and unaccommodating; it is the creature of hierarchical political relations that meet only the most anemic definitions of democracy; it is rooted in persistent racial stigmas and dynamics of marginalization; it operates in a gender system that forces poor women to meet new breadwinning expectations while continuing to bear the primary costs of social reproduction. The lesson for reformers is that we cannot develop a more just and humane form of governance simply by devising a more clever design for "poverty policy" narrowly conceived. Such efforts must proceed side by side with reform agendas designed to democratize American politics, restructure jobs, and undercut the mechanisms that perpetuate social inequalities. Bad poverty policies can be bad in any environment; good poverty policies can only be as good as the societal relations they serve.

What would better poverty policies look like? As a starting point, they must undo the failures of the current system. Stability and development in lower-income communities will be thwarted at every turn so long as we maintain the policies—draconian criminal penalties, the war on drugs, violation-centered parole, and so on—that cycle vast numbers of poor men and women through U.S. prisons each year. Similarly, welfare programs must be reorganized so that criminalized questions of compliance and violation do not stand at their center. Legal protections must ensure that recipients are not forced to give up their rights as workers and citizens in exchange for aid. Reformers must repeal coercive work-first rules that impede education, undercut skill development, and push the poor away from sustainable paths of labor-market advancement. Casework relationships must be freed from their debilitating and demoralizing focus on efforts to monitor, document, and penalize behavior.

With the demise of this disciplinary system, public investments should shift toward more active forms of labor-market engagement and individual investment that, together, can enhance the economic capabilities of low-income adults. In recent decades, the "market conditioning" policies of government have worked to increase economic inequality and abet the long-term, structural decline of family-supporting jobs for lower-skilled Americans (Kelly 2009; Soss, Hacker, and Mettler 2007). No policy directed at the poor can seriously reduce poverty unless government takes a more proactive approach to creating good jobs, setting stronger wage and benefit floors, constructing ladders for advancement, and ensuring rights to collective bargaining. Equally important, as Collins and Mayer (2010: 162) emphasize, new policies "must be based on the recognition that *poor women with children are already working,* and wage work must be compatible with the care work they must provide." In the context of such efforts, meaningful progress can be made by expanding public supports that have already grown in recent decades. For lower-income Americans, sustainable labor market incorporation will depend on government policies that ensure reliable access to child care, health care, transportation, and wage supports.

Beyond these efforts, policymakers must respond to the inevitable limitations of poverty policies that are designed narrowly around wage work. The severe recession that began in late 2007 underscored the tragic lesson that has unfolded in deindustrialized urban centers for decades: U.S. social policies offer woefully inadequate protections "when work disappears" (W. Wilson 1997). Inability to work, however, is not just a problem of job availability. It is a more basic and persistent source of poverty in the United States. Work-based safety nets, even in stronger forms, will do little to protect the considerable numbers of Americans who are effectively shut out of work by their struggles with physical and mental illness, experiences of domestic and sexual abuse, and responsibilities to care for spouses, children, and parents with high levels of need. Under the current regime, such people typically fall into the chasm that lies between the work-based safety net and the strict eligibility criteria of U.S. disability programs. Prisons have become our largest mental institutions, and the ranks of people "disconnected" from both welfare supports and work continues to grow. To reverse this travesty, we must recognize not only the centrality of wage work for anti-poverty efforts but also its limitations.

If some of these ideas about *what* should be done sound less than novel, it is because so many thoughtful poverty scholars and advocates have arrived at similar conclusions. Our study's more distinctive contributions focus on *how* poverty governance should be organized and pursued. How can practices of governance and experiences of program participation be restructured to reduce the harms of neoliberal paternalism? How can we build capabilities through an inclusive process of enablement that serves the goals of justice, care, and democracy?

At the ground level, reforms must shift governance from an authoritarian model of discipline to a model that democratizes and expands opportunities for poor people to experience themselves as effective, contributing agents. To do so, poverty programs do not need to bestow unconditional rights without any corresponding obligations. Full citizenship entails both, and aid recipients, above all, must be assisted as citizens. The goal of reform should be to change the kinds of obligations and the terms of power relations that define welfare participation. The TANF program embraces personal responsibility only in the cramped sense of telling the poor that they will be held accountable for failing to do as they are told. Instead, we should work to deepen the capabilities of clients by giving them meaningful responsibilities as participants who take part in shaping program conditions, defining needs, prioritizing investments, providing mutual care and support, and setting pathways of personal development. As we have seen, low-income parents tend to embrace such participatory expectations in the Head Start program, describing them as valued opportunities, and evidence suggests that this model has positive effects on both civic incorporation and economic advancement.

Theoretical and empirical supports for this approach, which seeks to establish a virtuous cycle of enablement, have been developed by a variety of scholars, such as Thomas Kane (1987), Joel Handler (1992), Kevin Olson (2006), and Deborah Stone (2008). Its institutional requirements and rationales have also been specified in some detail by students of empowered participatory governance (Fung and Wright 2003; Fung 2004). There is no need to review the minutiae of its organization here. Two basic points, however, merit emphasis. First, paternalism fails, in part, because it reinforces some of the most debilitating and repetitive experiences associated with poverty: feeling that your fate rests in other people's hands, experiencing yourself as an object rather than an agent of authority, realizing that others do not trust you with the reins of control and that the available responses have been defined as compliance or failure. Experiences of shared control and effective participation allow people to build the capabilities and feelings of efficacy needed for full civic and economic incorporation (Stone 2008).

Second, no such model can succeed if it ignores the participatory disadvantages of the poor and assumes (unrealistically) that they need only be notified of opportunities for input. Resources must be used to inform and recruit engagement; participation must be embedded in the core technologies of service provision; rules must allow clients to have a visible impact on decisions they have reason to value; collective processes of self-governance, in the welfare office as in the democratic polity, must be secured as both a right and an obligation of citizenship.

As this discussion suggests, we do not endorse efforts to eliminate discretionary choice in administrative settings. Discretion in street-level bureaucracies can be used for good or ill, and efforts to eradicate it are often counterproductive—both for the quality of administration and for efforts to incorporate the poor, who have little ability to influence policy at earlier stages of legislative design and administrative specification. The problems and inequities revealed by our study have little to do with individual abuses of street-level authority. They are the predictable consequences of the structures, routines, incentives, and senses of mission that shape and discipline the use of discretion. Reformers should strive not to tie the hands of frontline workers, but to restructure decision making around mutual engagement and interdependence, ensuring that power is shared on terms that are subject to renegotiation (Handler 1992; Hayward 2000).

This goal, in turn, cannot be achieved in a system where case management is treated as a deskilled, low-wage position focused on rote procedures. If case managers are to work effectively and collaboratively with clients, their discretion must be protected and structured to promote these efforts, and, equally important, they must be given the training, skills, and resources needed to work effectively in this mode. Leading students of public management, such as Feldman and Khademian (2000, 2007), have recently begun to conceptualize "effective managers" as leaders who develop the skill sets and strategies needed to advance and benefit from inclusive forms of participatory collaboration. Their analysis of senior managers should be extended as a vision of how case managers ought to be enabled and positioned alongside clients.

The implication of this argument is that the poor can benefit from some forms of policy control being kept close to the ground in local settings. As we have seen, however, policy devolution has played a key role in producing racial inequities under the present system. In this sense, our analysis underlines the importance of national protections for the poor, but we do not believe it precludes a more progressive vision of how federalism might be put to use. The starting point should be a division of labor that shields the poor from pressures that drive states and localities toward the low road of poverty governance: threats of business disinvestment, fears of becoming a welfare magnet, pressures to service local employers and institutionalize local moralities as practices of behavioral regulation (Peterson 1995; Lowi 1998; Donahue 1999). The most basic protections—such as those related to income, health, and working conditions—should be guaranteed by national benefit standards, procedural rights, and "floors" that states and localities can move beyond but not fall below (Freeman and Rogers 2007).

Within these structural constraints, policy experimentation and democratic governance can be promoted in lower jurisdictions through a set of institutional arrangements that Archon Fung (2004) terms "accountable autonomy." Rather than imposing a single policy from above or incentivizing subunit choices in a quasi-market system, Fung (2004) shows how central authorities can play an affirmative role in promoting more inclusive, just, and democratic forms of local governance. In addition to setting floors and protecting rights, central authorities support local actors by informing them about problems and options and providing resources designed to reduce the marginalization of disadvantaged (non)participants. As local actors define and pursue their priorities, central authorities evaluate processes for problems related to domination, corruption, and faction—and monitor outcomes for evidence that might guide improvements. Not surprisingly, Fung (2004) finds that such arrangements are easiest to implement in more advantaged communities, where citizens tend to fare well already. *Relative* gains in the quality of governance, however, tend to be largest in disadvantaged neighborhoods, where market-centered and top-down approaches have routinely proved inadequate and unresponsive.

By rejecting the neoliberal market model, the accountable autonomy framework makes it possible to imagine more productive uses of performance feedback. Perversity and failure are by no means necessary outcomes of efforts to inform governance with an ongoing stream of evidence. The problems identified in our study flowed from the neoliberal ways that such evidence was being used: to pressure, incentivize, and penalize lower-level actors; to cultivate a bottom-line mentality that focuses on outcomes to the exclusion of processes; to make agents of governance into competitors; and so on. Local operations can benefit greatly from a system that provides them with regular feedback about how they are doing, so long as "how they are doing" is defined to include assessments of process and the dimensions of feedback are well conceived. Indeed, students of public management have already suggested a variety of concrete ways that performance measures might be used more effectively to promote racial justice (Gooden 2003), deepen civic and political engagement (Wichowsky and Moynihan 2008), and provide resources for policy learning and improvement (Moynihan 2008).

Finally, there is the question of whether poverty governance should be pursued as a site of cross-sector collaboration or as the sole province of government. For reasons discussed earlier in detail (chapter 8), we do not believe that just and democratic forms of poverty governance can be achieved in a regime where services for the poor are traded as revenue-generating commodities and subordinated to the profit motives of corporations and their shareholders. The same may be said for aggressive systems of pay points and performance pressures that virtually force nonprofits to adopt the bottom-line mentalities of their for-profit counterparts. Freed from the neoliberal project, however, we believe that nonprofit community organizations can be vital collaborators in poverty governance. Strong civil society organizations can support a deeper and more inclusive form of democracy for the disadvantaged in a variety of ways (Cohen and Rogers 2003; Skocpol 2003). They have the potential to bring important capacities and forms of knowledge to service provision (Salamon 1995), to serve as intermediaries creating mutually beneficial alignments of worker and employer needs (Dresser and Rogers 2003), and to strengthen advocacy for the poor at multiple levels of governance (Marwell 2007; Berry and Arons 2003). There is a long history of civil sector involvement in American poverty governance (Katz 2002). Its lessons combine with recent experience to suggest that neoliberal paternalism has subverted nonprofit involvements that, under different conditions, have considerable potential to play a more positive role (Fabricant and Fisher 2001; Sandfort 2010).

In outlining these ideas, we harbor no illusions about the barriers presented by the current configuration of power in American politics (Hacker and Pierson

2010; Jacobs and King 2009; Winters and Page 2009; Bartels 2008). Major shifts in poverty governance do not come to fruition within the political confines that mark their inception. They are created in convulsive political moments, such as the 1930s and 1960s, when normal politics is disrupted and people challenge authority from below (Piven 2006). Or they are forged over time, as in the contemporary case, by actors who marry power and strategic innovation to a long-term vision that, at its origins, appears to fail the test of political feasibility (Pierson and Skocpol 2007; Teles 2008). Disciplinary poverty governance was created through political mobilization and struggle, and nothing less will be needed to replace it with something better. To live up to the values of justice, care, and democracy, Americans must turn the neoliberal themes of ownership and personal responsibility on their head. We must take ownership of our complicity in the present system and assume personal responsibility for changing it.

NOTES

CHAPTER ONE

1. The term *social control* refers broadly to the means by which collectives secure adherence to ideational and behavioral norms and curtail disruptive forms of deviance (see, e.g., Piven 1981; Gordon 1990).

CHAPTER TWO

1. A number of factors beyond welfare reform contributed to AFDC/TANF caseload declines after 1994, especially the strong economy of the late 1990s and expansions of the Earned Income Tax Credit. Most scholars today, however, agree that the new welfare policies drove caseloads down and, when the Great Recession hit in 2007, kept them at very low levels (Grogger and Karoly 2005; Brodkin and Majmundar 2010).

CHAPTER THREE

1. Among the favored strategies was "counterscheduling," a maneuver in which Clinton would purposely deliver criticism or an inflammatory centrist speech to a left-of-center group. Coverage of the event, combined with the group's public expression of outrage afterward, was expected to send a signal to the broader electorate that Clinton would not be a kept man if he gained control of the White House (Williams 2003: 221).

2. A few months before the passage of the Personal Responsibility and Work Opportunity Reconciliation Act in 1996, David Ellwood, a prominent poverty scholar and liberal reform advocate within the Clinton administration, described this dynamic as follows: "The president's famous promise to 'end welfare as we know it' was the most potent sound bite on welfare [during the 1992 election]. It came up so often that we referred to it as EWAKI. Yet while implying that welfare is a massive failure and conveying seriousness of purpose about reform, EWAKI only vaguely suggests that we can replace the current system with something better. Even more destructive was the phrase 'two years and you're off.' Our pollsters told us that 'two' was the single most memorable number of the 1992 campaign. The problem, of course, is that 'two years and you're off' seems to imply no help at all after two years. That is never what was intended. Nonetheless, this phrase gave real impetus to plans now before Congress and in the states that call for time limits followed by nothing—no welfare, no jobs, no support—even if the person is willing to work and genuinely cannot find any job. In my view, these measures are appalling" (Ellwood 1996).

3. To preserve comparability across the full-time series, all responses indicating attention to poverty or attention to welfare are included for each year shown in figure 3-1. No attention is paid to more detailed coding categories appearing in particular years within the series.

4. In 1982, 11.9 percent of ANES respondents viewed welfare as a problem. Other polling data from the 1992–96 period corroborate this spike in public attention. The Harris Interactive Poll, which limited respondents to "the two most important issues for the government to address" (as opposed to the four issues allowed by the ANES at this time) saw a dramatic increase in respondents choosing welfare— from a low of 2 percent in January 1993 to a high of 16 percent in February 1995 (Bowman 2003).

5. The administration was diverted in part by a pitched political battle over its national health-

care plan (Skocpol 1996; Hacker 1997). But the delay was also a product of internal polls showing that welfare policy had not yet become a top public priority and uncertainty about what kind of reform bill to propose. Many in the administration did not care very deeply about the issue (Ellwood 1996), but those who did faced internal disputes about whether welfare reform should be treated as an instance of "talking right and governing left" or as an opportunity to make a fundamental break with "old" Democratic commitments to entitlements for the poor (Heclo 2001: 189–90).

6. David Ellwood (1996), a key Clinton advisor on welfare policy, would comment in May 1996, "I doubt most Americans are even aware that we introduced a welfare reform bill."

7. At its high point in 1996, only 26.6 percent of surveyed Americans listed "welfare" as a major national problem. By contrast, in August 1996, as the political events reached their climax, 44 percent of the public said they did not know enough about welfare reform to say whether President Clinton did the right or wrong thing by signing it (R. Weaver 2000: 338).

8. It should be noted, however, that additional specification tests indicated no significant differences across subgroups of women defined by employment status, family income, education, or marital status.

9. We employ a standard difference measure created by subtracting respondents' placements of "most whites" from their placements of "most blacks" on a seven-point scale running from "hardworking" to "lazy." Respondents with positive values (black greater than white) are coded as expressing the stereotype of black laziness.

10. The full set of statistical results that serve as the basis for the estimates presented in figures 3-3, 3-4, and 3-5 are presented in our online appendix: http://www.discipliningthepoor.com.

11. The conclusion that the anti-welfare campaign activated racial stereotypes and concerns over welfare "in tandem" is corroborated by results using a second measurement approach. Using the respondent's 1992 perceptions of laziness (black score minus white score) as a baseline, we identified all respondents whose score increased between 1992 and 1996—regardless of where they fell on the scale. Using the same procedure described in the text, we find that the predicted probability of activation in this group is .37. This estimate is significantly greater than the predicted probability for the "Absent" group as well as the "Expressed" group.

12. For example, when an NBC News Poll in 1995 asked a national sample of Americans whom they thought of when they heard about "someone on welfare," more than twice as many respondents named "black women" as any other group (NBC News Poll 1995).

13. *Intersectionality* refers to the idea that plural social categories create more than just identity alternatives (e.g., experiencing social identity in one context as a woman and in another as a Jew) and more than just additive effects (as when the consequences of being a woman augment the separate consequences of being a Jew). Intersectionality suggests that social categories intersect in a multiplicative way to produce specific social identities and social locations (such as that of a Jewish woman). Dimensions of identity become meaningful *in combination*. Thus, to be a poor black woman in the United States is to occupy an identity that can be distinguished from being poor and white, from being black and middle class, and from being a woman who is white or wealthy.

14. Thus, for the laziness stereotype, the NSPP asked: "Where would you rate whites in general on a scale of 1 to 7, where 1 indicates hard working, 7 means lazy, and 4 indicates most whites are not closer to one end or the other." For the sexuality stereotype, it asked: "Where would you rate white women on a scale of 1 to 7, where 1 indicates sexually responsible, 7 means sexually irresponsible, and 4 indicates most white women are not closer to one end or the other."

CHAPTER FOUR

1. Our definition of southern states is based on the Census Bureau's definition, which classifies sixteen states as part of the southern region of the United States.

2. Detailed statistical results for all of the analyses presented in this chapter are available in the online appendix.

3. U.S. Census Bureau Historical Poverty Tables, table 1, http://www.census.gov/hhes/www/poverty/data/historical/people.html.

4. Even if one considers the added value of the Food Stamp benefit, which was protected by yearly cost of living adjustments, the combined real worth of the AFDC-FS package declined by 13 percent over the 1970–95 period.

5. Prior to 1975, retail wages offer the best available measure of wages for low-skilled workers. The results described in the preceding paragraph rely on this measure to ensure that our historical comparisons are not distorted by inconsistencies in measurement. After 1975, however, changes in federal data reporting make it possible to construct a superior measure of wages for low-skilled workers based on the retail sector and the most relevant segments of the service and agricultural sectors. In this paragraph and the discussions that follow, all references to "wages for low-skilled workers," as opposed to retail wages, refer to this measure.

6. The ratio would be far higher, of course, if we counted the value of Medicaid benefits, which AFDC recipients automatically qualified for during this period. We do not do so, however, because it is difficult to place a monetary value on Medicaid services and the value of these services is likely to vary substantially across welfare families.

7. To ensure that our results are not spurious, our multivariate model includes a number of control variables inspired by the large literature on state welfare generosity. Most important, we test for the effects of benefit competition among neighboring states by controlling for the average benefit level in neighboring states. We also control for changes in the partisan control of state government, the ideological orientation of a state's citizens, changes in the per capita income and state tax revenue, the federal reimbursement rate for the costs of AFDC, and the size of the AFDC caseload. By controlling for all of these factors, in addition to including dummy variables for states and years, our model thus provides a rich specification of alternative explanations for benefit reductions. We estimate the model for the forty-eight continental states, 1976–95.

8. The dependent variable in our analysis of benefit decline is an ordinal variable representing actual changes made by policymakers to the statutory (i.e., nominal) benefit level (-1 = decrease, 0 = no change, 1 = increase) (see Volden 2002). Because this measure acknowledges only benefit changes resulting from legislative actions (rather than inactions), it provides a measure of intentional decisions that is more appropriate for testing the RCM's predictions.

9. Given the large literature on "welfare magnet" fears and the potential for interstate benefit competition to produce a "race to the bottom," a nonfinding in this analysis merits special note. We find no evidence that benefit competition had any effect on AFDC benefit decisions, as the effect of the average neighbor benefit was in the wrong direction (positive) and statistically insignificant.

10. The cross-sectional correlation between the percentage of the AFDC population that is black and the percentage of the state population that is black is .95 (for 1976, the first year for which we have data on the racial composition of the AFDC caseload). Based on this relationship, we expect that the black population percentage will serve as a reasonable proxy for the racial composition of the GA caseload.

11. We control for the state poverty rate and state citizen ideology.

12. For discussions of the reasons for disaggregating state incarceration trends by race, see Yates and Fording (2005) and Western (2006). Our dependent variables in these analyses are measures of imprisonment growth created by (a) computing a race-specific imprisonment rate (number of black [white] prisoners per 100,000 black [white] state residents and then (b) computing annual changes in the race-specific imprisonment rates. By using annual change in the imprison-

ment rate, rather than the overall number, our measure is roughly equivalent to the prison admission rate adjusted for the prison release rate, both of which play key roles in state carceral control.

13. Following Yates and Fording (2005), these additional control variables include the annual growth in state tax revenues, the level of representation of blacks and women in state politics, the presence or absence of determinate sentencing laws, the presence or absence of a court order to reduce prison overcrowding, the race-specific unemployment rate, the race-specific poverty rate, and an indicator for state election years. Finally, we include indicator variables for each year of the analysis, which effectively control for the impacts that any national-level developments may have had on state imprisonment growth.

14. Specifically, for each of the variables in the figure, we multiply the coefficient from the regression by the average change in that variable during the period of our analysis. The regression results used to produce this figure, along with the average historical changes in all the variables, are presented in the online appendix.

CHAPTER FIVE

1. For a detailed historical analysis of the developments described in this section, see Teles 1996.

2. JOBS refers to the Job Opportunities and Basic Skills Training *program* created as part of the Family Support Act of 1988. JOBS was designed to provide recipients with job training and education or, alternatively, to promote faster movement into paid employment.

3. Event history analyses explain variation in the amount of time that elapses between a given starting point (in our case, January 1992) and an event of some kind (in our case, adoption of one of the specified AFDC waivers). Although there are a variety of models appropriate for event history data (Box-Steffensmeier and Jones 1997), we rely on the Cox proportional hazards model. One important advantage of this method is that it makes no assumptions about how the passage of time itself affected state waiver adoptions (i.e., the shape of the baseline hazard rate). Because our theoretical concerns do not focus on differences in effects across waiver types, we pool the observations for our seven types of waivers and treat them collectively as repeated events data—rather than estimating our model separately for each type of waiver. This approach raises two concerns: differences in the baseline hazard rate across the different waiver types and error correlations within units (i.e., states) across different waiver types. To deal with these potential problems, we (1) estimated a stratified Cox model, which allowed the baseline hazard to vary across waiver types; and (2) estimated robust standard errors that accounted for error clustering within states (Therneau and Grambsch 2000). Based on these analyses, we determined that stratification was unnecessary. Thus, the final results reported here are based on a simple Cox model.

4. These variables include state population size and a measure of a state's historical propensity for welfare policy innovation constructed by Gray (1973).

5. The predicted survival rates are calculated for a hypothetical "average state" created by holding all other independent variables constant at their mean value. Detailed results for all of the statistical analyses summarized in this chapter (including this analysis) are presented in our online appendix.

6. On the salience and consideration of these policy choices, see Soss et al. 2001; Fellowes and Rowe 2004. The first three measures described in this paragraph are identical to those analyzed in Soss et al. 2001, with one exception: We analyze the adoption of "full-family sanctions" here as a dichotomous choice rather than as the highest value on a three-point sanction scale. The final two measures are taken from Fellowes and Rowe 2004. We reverse the direction of their "Flexibility"

measure to produce a measure of work requirement rigidity that runs in the same (disciplinary) direction as our other four dependent variables.

7. For all analyses reported below, however, we find no significant differences when we replace this measure with our conventional indicator of partisan control.

8. PRWORA barred legal immigrants who arrived after the law's passage from receiving Medicaid, Food Stamps, Supplemental Security Income, and TANF benefits, lifting this ban only after the establishment of citizenship. The law directed states to choose whether to offer federally funded Medicaid and TANF benefits to "preenactment" noncitizen immigrants; Food Stamps were made available to these immigrants only if they were over age 65, under age 18, or subsequently became disabled. The Congressional Budget Office (1996: 27) estimated that almost half of the $54 billion savings initially attributed to the welfare reform bill could be traced directly to such restrictions on immigrant use of welfare.

9. In 2000, 30 percent of surveyed Americans said they thought most blacks were "lazy," while the parallel percentages for questions about Latinos and whites were 18 percent and 7 percent, respectively (Fox 2004). In the National Survey on Poverty Policy conducted by one of the authors in 2002 and described in chapter 3, 42 percent of surveyed Americans said they thought most black women were "sexually irresponsible," while the parallel percentages for questions about Latino women and white women were 30 percent and 20 percent, respectively

10. With the exception of the year-of-waiver measure, all variables are based on state-level data for 1996.

11. For each of our dichotomous outcomes, we conducted a separate logistic regression analysis. For the two outcomes measured as continuous scales, we conducted separate ordinary least squares regression analyses.

12. We find no significant effects associated with rates of unemployment or rates of births to unmarried women. We find only a single instance of effects for party competition (lowering the odds of a full-family sanction), for class-based electoral bias (raising the odds of a family cap), and for the earlier adoption of an AFDC waiver (raising the odds of a full-family sanction). We find two significant effects for per capita tax revenues, but they are inconsistent: a positive effect on family cap adoption and a negative effect on eligibility restrictions.

13. Some have questioned whether these racial results might be a spurious reflection of "southern distinctiveness." We do not include a separate indicator of southern location in our models because we prefer to rely on more precise indicators of the ways that southern states may differ from others (e.g., lower tax revenues and more conservative ideological orientations). Nevertheless, to assess whether the unmeasured traits of southern states might be creating an appearance of racial bias, we performed two additional kinds of analyses. First, we simply added a southern dummy variable to our models to capture unmeasured regional differences. Across all five models, our results for the black percentage of the caseload remain unchanged when this variable is added. Second, we took the more radical step of simply omitting all southern states from analysis. Because this approach leaves only between thirty-seven and thirty-nine states for analysis, it makes statistical significance far harder to obtain. Nevertheless, the coefficients for the black percentage of the caseload remain significant in the expected direction in four of the five models. In the fifth, family cap, the coefficient is in the right direction but fails to reach significance. These specification tests provide strong evidence that racial effects were neither limited to the south nor created as a spurious reflection of unmeasured southern differences.

14. In addition, or alternatively, local officials themselves may be more likely to believe that they serve different clienteles and, hence, need greater freedom to deploy policy tools in ways that differ from other local jurisdictions. The dynamics we describe here could have racialized devolution choices through either top-down or bottom-up dynamics.

15. For models that test of a variety of alternative explanations (including southern distinctiveness, county proliferation, and heterogeneity in county ideological orientations and citizens' preferences for public aid), see Soss, Fording, and Schram 2008.

16. To limit the influence of extreme cases, the four states with a score of 5 have been combined with states having a value of 4. Thus, a value of 4 indicates "4 or 5."

17. Once again, we limited the influence of extreme cases by combining the top two values of the scale. The two states with values of 6 were combined with the five states having a value of 5. Thus, a value of 5 indicates "5 or 6."

CHAPTER SIX

1. On this methodological distinction, see Yin 2003 and Ragin 2000. Selecting an "extreme" case for analysis, as we have done here, has a long and influential history in the study of policy implementation (as in the social sciences more generally). For example, when Herbert Kaufman (1960) wanted to understand how central administrators attain compliance from frontline workers who cannot be directly controlled, he did not study an agency where this problem might be found in modest form. Rather, he selected one of the most fragmented and far-flung bureaucracies, the Forestry Service, to observe the relevant dilemmas and responses in their clearest forms. Similarly, when Martha Derthick (1990) sought to understand the general political dynamics underlying bureaucratic failure in the United States, she did not select an average bureaucracy that might be expected to fail for any number of reasons. She chose instead to study of one of the most highly regarded and well-functioning bureaucracies in the United States, the Social Security Administration, to isolate the challenges that emerged from political context and observe them in bolder relief.

2. The Workforce Investment Act of 1998 was passed by Congress one year after welfare reform was implemented and serves displaced and unemployed workers.

3. As we discuss in later chapters, a Florida law passed in 2008 removed the ban that prevented RWBs from directly managing one-stop centers. Roughly half of the state's RWBs elected to take over service provision rather than continue contracting. Thus, while the Florida system remains decentralized, privatized, and performance driven, it now includes a mix of contract-based service provision and direct service provision by public-private boards.

4. To explore the later developments described in note 3, we also conducted follow-up telephone interviews with executive directors of seven of the twenty-four regional boards in September 2009.

CHAPTER SEVEN

1. A number of WT cases are missing data on the age of TANF children (7 percent of cases) and for the education level of TANF adults (25 percent of adults). Yet, a comparison of sanction rates of missing and nonmissing cases finds the difference to be trivial (38 percent for nonmissing cases, 37.2 percent for missing cases). Accordingly, we do not have reason to believe that the omission of these cases leads to any bias in our statistical estimates. As a further validity check, we have estimated our models with education and child age omitted from the analysis. Despite the specification bias introduced by dropping these variables, the substantive conclusions reported in this section do not change at all. After removing the cases with missing data, our total sample includes over 74,000 individuals, over 28,000 sanctions observations, and approximately 200,000 person-month observations.

2. Each client in each of the twenty-four cohorts is followed for a maximum of twelve consecutive months or until a sanction is imposed (whichever comes first). Thus, the entire period of analysis extends from January 2001 (first cohort enters) to December 2003 (twelfth month of spell for last cohort). Clients who exit for reasons other than a sanction, or who are not sanctioned by the

twelfth month of the spell, are treated as right-censored. The sample for our analysis is restricted to each client's first TANF spell during this period and to U.S. citizens. A spell is defined as continuous months of TANF receipt. As a result of this definition and missing data for a small percentage of cases, our total sample includes 60,045 individuals; this results in 169,438 person-month observations. Detailed variable definitions and statistical results for all of the analyses summarized in this chapter are presented in our online appendix.

3. Because our EHA examines sanction dynamics over time, we include two controls related to this dimension of analysis. First, to control for seasonal patterns in sanctioning rates, we include a dummy variable for each calendar month. Second, to capture the possibility that sanction risks vary across the participation spell, we measure the number of months of program participation accumulated by each client at each monthly observation.

4. We restrict our attention to white, black, and Latino welfare recipients due to the fact that sample sizes are too small to analyze other racial and ethnic groups at the county level.

5. Supplementary analyses confirm that the relationships shown in figure 7-2 are robust across time periods and regions in the United States. The most consistent measures for this analysis can be found in the General Social Survey (GSS), although switching to the GSS forces us to rely on a simpler measure of ideological self-identification. The results for all years from 1990 to 2006 are consistent with the analyses presented in figure 7-2. We also estimated the relationship separately for each of the four census regions. For blacks, the relationship is relatively stable and statistically significant in each of the four census regions. For Latinos, the relationship is statistically significant in the South and West regions at the .05 level, and close to significance in the Northeast and North Central regions.

6. The relationships shown in figure 7-3 cannot be estimated with NES data for the state of Florida alone because the sample size is simply too small (N = 58). By pooling the samples from the three states with the largest Latino populations (California, Florida, and Texas), we are able to achieve a suitable sample size.

7. Although we continue to use EHA, we estimate the model as a multilevel model in this instance. The multilevel model is arguably better suited to correct for violations of statistical assumptions that may bias our results due to the simultaneous use of data measured at two levels of analysis (in our case, individual-level and county-level data). These biases are most acute when one is estimating interactive (i.e., conditional) relationships between independent variables measured at different levels of analysis, or what are sometimes referred to as "cross-level interactions" (Steenbergen and Jones 2002). Since we rely heavily on cross-level interactions in this analysis, we utilize multilevel modeling procedures.

8. Once again, we base our predictions on a hypothetical "typical" client, defined as a U.S.-born thirty-one-year-old single woman with two children (aged five to twelve years), less than twelve years of education, and an average level of wage income in the quarter preceding the current month, who resides in an average county (reflecting mean values on all of the contextual variables).

9. This explanation might also explain why we see this pattern in Florida, but we fail to see it in the national data (as we report below). Florida's WT program is especially tough—not only does the WT program rely on the most severe type of sanction, but sanctions are enforced in Florida at a rate that is very high compared to other states. Thus, to the extent that this phenomenon of "self-sanctioning" is important, it is possible that we will observe it (to a significant degree) only in the most punitive states.

10. An alternative explanation for these results is that it is not ideology but rather the size of the minority population that mediates the effect of client race on sanctioning. To explore this possibility, we tested for interactions between racial/ethnic status of client and the black and Latino percentage of the county population (i.e., *Black*Black percent* and *Latino*Latino percent*). Neither

term was statistically significant. In addition, to validate results based on our ideological index, we reran our models with the Republican share of presidential votes as a proxy for local ideology. This procedure produced highly consistent results.

11. Because welfare benefits do not vary greatly across counties, the BWR we employed at the state level is less useful at the county level. In its place, we focus on variation in the relative prevalence of benefits and wages as sources of income in each county.

12. After accounting for missing data, our analysis is based on sixty-three Florida counties. Among our control variables, we find significant effects on black-white sanction disparities only for county population size (positive) and for the white arrest rate (negative). These results suggest that the tendency for black WT clients to be sanctioned more often than their white counterparts is greater in more urban counties and in counties that arrest whites at lower rates.

13. In our main analysis, we rely on separate measures of black and white arrest rates to facilitate interactive tests of the RCM and make our interaction term easier to interpret. Our simpler specification is identical to this model with two exceptions: It omits interaction terms and substitutes black-white arrest disparities for our separate measures of white and black arrest rates. The results confirm that counties that produce larger black-white arrest disparities tend to produce larger black-white sanction disparities in the WT program.

14. Nationwide, 66 percent of black TANF families participated in state programs with full-family sanctions in 2001, as compared to 56 percent of white TANF families.

15. Implementing officials may be more or less likely to impose a sanction depending on the severity of the penalty involved. To limit this potential source of bias, we restrict our comparison here to states that have full-family sanctions similar to what we have analyzed in Florida.

16. Our national-level analysis relies on a slightly larger set of control variables at the individual level, due to the availability of more detailed data in the federal dataset. Specifically, we are able to add variables for public housing, Social Security, and Supplemental Security Income receipt among TANF clients. At the county level, we rely on a slightly smaller set of control variables (we do not control for the county poverty rate, the size of the TANF caseload, and the local wage rate).

17. We define a "typical" client as a U.S.-born thirty-one-year-old single woman with two children (aged five to twelve years), less than twelve years of education, and an average level of wage income in the quarter preceding the current month, who resides in an average county (reflecting mean values on all of the contextual variables).

CHAPTER EIGHT

1. Our use of this term is meant to evoke Kent Weaver's (2000) insightful analysis of the "dual clientele trap" in welfare politics: the difficulties that arise for legislators who want to get tough with adult welfare recipients (and see electoral benefits to doing so) but also worry about bringing harm to the sympathetic children of adult recipients (and see electoral risks to doing so). Welfare reformers in the 1990s overcame this trap by focusing narrowly on adult behavior (Weaver 2000) and by reframing self-sufficient employment as a necessary foundation for responsible motherhood and child well-being (Korteweg 2003; Collins and Mayer 2010). Building on this account, we suggest that the old dual clientele trap was not replaced by a single clientele model. A new pairing of clienteles has emerged, with the low-income family's need for work attachment set alongside the low-wage employer's need for workers.

2. Such states include Arizona, California, Connecticut, Illinois, Massachusetts, New York, Pennsylvania, and Texas.

3. One of the most notorious tragedies was the case of a fourteen-year-old Houston boy, Devante Johnson, who died of kidney cancer after his health insurance was dropped, even though his mother tried repeatedly to obtain the coverage that he was eligible for (see Walters 2007).

4. Video available at "Penalties for Welfare Fraud in Florida," accessed February 9, 2011, http://www.ehow.com/video_2200179_penalties-welfare-fraud-florida.html.

5. Although we maintain our focus on poverty governance, the pattern of corruption and failure in Florida's privatization push was hardly limited to this sphere. In 2002, for example, Florida privatized the management of state employee payroll, benefit, and application processing by awarding a seven-year, $278 million contract to Convergys, a private contractor that had recently donated $1 million to the Florida Republican Party. Four years later, the contract with Convergys was widely condemned for failing to generate the promised savings and for replacing a reliable public system with one plagued by routine payment delays, benefit errors, and allegations of mishandled information (*Tampa Tribune* 2006b; James 2006).

6. We focus here on problems related to the oversight of ongoing operations. It should be noted, however, that the WT program also had its share of scandals related to the awarding of contracts, similar to those we described earlier in other areas of poverty governance. In Hillsborough County in 2003, for example, it was discovered that a subsidiary of ACS had offered the RWB a gift of $53,000 one month before it was slated to award a $4.7 million contract. Amid a wave of negative press, the members of the RWB voted to decline the gift, noting what one board member called its "public relations aspect." Shortly thereafter, ACS was awarded the contract and became the region's sole WT provider (see Nguyen 2003; Brannon 2003).

7. The events described in the following four paragraphs have been documented by a variety of news media. See, for example, Greene 2003; Moncada 2003; Sandler 2004a, 2004b, 2004c; Tan 2004; Van Sant 2006.

8. According to the *St. Petersburg Times* (Tan 2004), depositions under oath indicated that "Lassiter ordered copies of [Dodge and Gifford-Meyers's] personnel files, according to pleadings and depositions in the federal case. A Lockheed employee saw Lassiter in the Lockheed office copying inflammatory fliers assailing the character of Gifford-Meyers and Dodge. Lassiter left a message on Gifford-Meyers voice mail: 'I am going to see how you squirm next week. . . . After next week, I doubt you'll even be here; you'll probably be history 'cause I'm after your job.' Another witness said Lassiter called Gifford-Meyers and said, 'I know where you live. And you have a little boy, don't you?' Meyers gave his wife a bulletproof vest, and she asked to have a sheriff's deputy at public meetings she attended." Although Lassiter denied taking these actions, she would later write that she regretted buying into what she now thought were "lies from the pit of hell" and allowing herself to be "used as a mere prostitute by Lockheed Martin."

9. The Center for Business Excellence (CBE) website goes on to clarify how its composition as a RWB promotes its business-centered mission: "The CBE is led by a private-sector majority Board of Directors and is comprised of executives from a broad spectrum of professions, businesses and industry. The Board assures that CBE efforts support local business needs." The Center for Business Excellence, accessed February 9, 2011, http://www.centerforbusinessexcellence.net/; see also JobsPlus Veterans Services, accessed February 9, 20100, http://vets.jobsplusonestop.com/services/; Workforce Plus, accessed February 9, 2011, http://www.wfplus.org/index.php/jobseeker/jobs/.

10. See Career Central, accessed May 20, 2010, http://www.careercentral.jobs/employers/employers/; Brevard Workforce, accessed February 9, 2011, http://www.brevardjoblink.org/home/pages/EmployersResourcesRecruitmentPage.cfm; Chipola Regional Workforce Development Board, Inc., accessed May 20, 2010, http://www.onestopahead.com/onestop/welfare/index.php, and http://www.wfplus.org/JobseekerServices/JobseekerToolkit/tabid/5482/language/en-US/Default.aspx.

11. A balanced approach was personally favored by 46.4 percent of case managers; it was identified by 39.9 percent as the approach taken at their own one-stop center.

12. See Brevard Workforce, accessed February 9, 2011, http://www.brevardjoblink.org/; WorkNet Pinellas, accessed February 9, 2011, http://www.worknetpinellas.org.

13. See Workforce Plus, "Opportunities at Every Turn," accessed February 9, 2011, http://www.wfplus.org/documents/WORKFORCE_plus_Annual_Report_2007-2008.pdf.

14. See State of Florida.com, accessed February 9, 2011, http://www.stateofflorida.com/Portal/DesktopDefault.aspx?tabid=95.

15. To ensure that are results are representative of the statewide WT program, we weight county observations by WT caseload size. Our model controls for several characteristics of the county TANF caseload, including the percentage of the caseload that is female, Latino, and a U.S. citizen; the average age and education level of TANF adults; average quarterly earnings of TANF adults; and the county unemployment rate. Detailed data descriptions and statistical results for this analysis, as well as the analysis underlying figure 8-1, are presented in our online appendix.

16. This sense of professional identity resonates with Maynard-Moody and Musheno's (2003) claim that street-level bureaucrats often see themselves as "citizen agents" acting on behalf of the community. But in this rendering, the community is reduced to its market relations, and the agents construe themselves as acting in and for the local economy.

17. Our analysis here has close ties to Celeste Watkins-Hayes's (2009) argument that "efficiency engineering" and "social work" identities exist side by side among welfare case managers, and that both identities are legitimized by organizational and policy cues. We largely agree, but with two caveats. In the WT program, the business model provides the dominant and normalized discourse, accepted even if complicated by those who embrace a social work ethic. In addition, the business model is about more than just engineering efficiency. It is a normative commitment to market rationality, and it promotes a substantive vision of what governing officials should accomplish. Its commitments focus not on efficiency per se, but on the importance of adopting market principles, behaving as market actors, serving market needs, and transforming clients into marketable workers.

CHAPTER NINE

1. During the period of our study, the red and green reports included three WT-specific items: the "entered employment rate" among program leavers, the "employment wage rate" based on leavers' average initial wage, and the "welfare return rate" based on the percentage of clients who left for employment but later returned to WT.

2. With the onset of the WT program in July 2000, Florida implemented a new information system focused on tracking performance information, One-Stop Service Tracking (OSST), as well as stronger procedures for monitoring, disseminating, and rewarding/penalizing performance. The sanction rates shown for the prior WAGES program in figure 9-2 cover a comparatively short time span. Unfortunately, no comparable data are available for sanction rates in Florida prior to January 2000.

3. Detailed variable definitions and statistical results for all of the analyses summarized in this chapter are presented in our online appendix.

4. Unfortunately, because we have been unable to obtain longitudinal data on local one-stop operators, we are unable to test an episodic variant of our organizations hypothesis—that is, whether for-profits and nonprofits vary in the ways they respond to declining performance feedback over time.

5. This time period reflects the maximum amount of time for which we are able to obtain data for regional performance rankings, regional sanction rates, and the characteristics of TANF clients.

6. We use the regional ranking, rather than the actual performance measures themselves, because performance incentives are largely based on the region's performance relative to other regions

in the state. We measure average regional ranking cumulatively within each fiscal year (i.e., the region's average performance ranking from the first month of the fiscal year (July) through the most recent month) because performance incentives are based on a region's performance across the entire fiscal year. Specifically, we measure regional performance as the monthly *change* in the average ranking. This reflects our belief that local TANF administrators are likely to be most responsive to the short-term trajectory of the region's performance ranking, rather than the overall ranking itself. Finally, our measure of performance feedback is lagged two to three months to account for the lapse of time between the end of the month, the publication of the monthly performance reports by the state (which are not available until the following month), and the communication of the regional response by regional managers to frontline personnel.

7. Complete details concerning the research design and variables used in these analyses, along with the full set of results, are presented in our online appendix.

8. Because we include a lagged dependent variable in our models, this estimate represents only the immediate effect of performance feedback, with the effect distributed over time through the lagged dependent variable. Even so, this effect is statistically discernible but modest. After six months, the cumulative effect stands at .17.

9. Although our individual-level data permitted an analysis of Latino sanction rates in chapter 7, the uneven dispersion of the Latino caseload across the state limits the number of regions for which we can perform an equivalent panel analysis of sanction rates. For this reason, we compare the effects of performance measurement across black and white clients only.

10. Limited data on client education levels force us to restrict the time period for this analysis to twenty-three months.

11. In the analysis that follows, our dependent variable is the natural log of the case closure rate, as published in Florida's official regional caseload reports.

12. We are unable to test for differences across client subgroups with case closure data because, for nonsanction exits, our individual level data (which we use to build our control variables for racial and educational subgroups) do not allow us to distinguish between clients who leave TANF due to earnings and clients who exit for other reasons. However, such data are available to us at the regional level for the entire caseload.

13. Confidence that sanctions hurt performance should not be confused with clarity about how, precisely, the two relate. At numerous meetings, we observed regional staff disagreeing about how sanctions factor into performance calculations and asking state-level officials for clarification. When asked for *details* about how sanctions affect specific performance measures, case managers frequently laughed and said that they honestly were not quite sure.

14. To be sure, sanction imposition can be seen as an intended feature of the system. Our point here is that, from the case manager's perspective, the sanction is not an intended or desired outcome.

CHAPTER TEN

1. For full details on survey procedures, response rates, and respondent characteristics, see Schram et al. 2009.

2. Florida officials estimated that 200 to 250 case managers worked in the state's WT program. Thus, our overall sample of 144 case managers suggests a response rate somewhere between 58 and 72 percent. In the analyses that follow, 137 caseworkers responded to vignette 1 and 131 to vignette 2. For more details and a demographic profile of our sample, see Schram et al. 2009.

3. To guard against confounding effects that might arise from the use of a specific name, we randomly assigned one of three names for each group in each vignette. White-sounding names included Sarah Walsh, Emily O'Brien, and Meredith McCarthy; black-sounding names included

Lakisha Williams, Aisha Jackson, and Tanisha Johnson; and Latina-sounding names included Sonya Perez, Maria Rodriguez, and Luisa Alvarez. To test for name-specific effects, we analyzed responses within each "race condition" to search for significant differences associated with each name. We found no significant differences and, hence, treat all racial name cues as equivalent.

4. The two vignettes, which were initially developed based on interviews with case managers and observations at WT sanction training sessions, were refined through consultation with Agency for Workforce Innovation (AWI) staff responsible for sanction training. The entire survey, including the experiment, was then pilot tested with AWI staff members who had prior experience as case managers but no longer worked in this role and, hence, were not part of the population sampled for our survey.

5. The two vignettes were presented near the beginning of the survey, in order to minimize the amount of bias potentially introduced by subsequent questions on sanctioning practices. We tested for order effects—specifically, whether sanctioning decisions in vignette 1 predict sanctioning decisions in vignette 2—and found no evidence of such effects.

6. In addition, the vignette introduces the possibility that a good-cause exemption might apply in this case because the mother provided some evidence of her child-care problem. The cue is ambiguous, however, because the WT program precludes good-cause exemptions in cases where clients fail to provide sufficient documentary evidence of their child-care problem and in cases where the child or children are too old to qualify a client for Florida's child-care exemption policy.

7. Detailed variable descriptions and full statistical results for this analysis, as well as for all subsequent analyses summarized in this chapter, are presented in our online appendix.

8. In alternate specifications of our models, we find no significant interactions between case manager experience and client race. Thus, the effects of case manager experience should be seen as independent of the racial patterns presented below.

9. We tested our models including interactions that combine the race of the caseworker with the race of the client to see if the results were better explainable in terms of intergroup hostility between caseworkers and clients rather than the logic of the RCM. The interaction terms proved insignificant, suggesting the results are not reflective of intergroup differences between the caseworkers and the clients and that the RCM offers a better explanation.

10. For full model specifications and results, see our online appendix.

11. We tested in the administrative data whether Latina clients with a prior sanction were more likely than white clients to be sanctioned again and found this not to be the case.

CHAPTER ELEVEN

1. State caseload data were obtained from public reports available from the Administration of Children and Families (http://www.acf.hhs.gov/programs/ofa/data-reports/index.htm).

2. The few studies that have examined the caseload effects of such policies suggest that they have, indeed, had an impact. For example, random-assignment studies revealed that strong work requirements led to modest declines in program participation, but the declines were larger for job search–focused programs than for programs that emphasized skill enhancement (Grogger, Karoly, and Klerman 2002). A majority of studies also found that sanctions have had a negative effect on participation (e.g., Council of Economic Advisers 1999). Beyond these results, however, the literature offers little insight into the effects of policies such as time limits, family caps, and second-order devolution.

3. For states in which TANF was implemented mid-year, we multiply the index score by the proportion of the year that TANF was in place.

4. Our control variables include a lag of the dependent variable, the unemployment rate, per capita income, the minimum wage in a state, the AFDC/TANF benefit for a family of three, and

a measure of state government ideology. Due to stationarity problems, we first-difference our data prior to estimation (Ziliak et al. 2000). Detailed variable definitions and full statistical results for all the analyses summarized in this chapter are presented in our online appendix.

5. We find no significant effect for our separate indicator of waivers used to increase the earnings disregard.

6. Specifically, we use a Cox Proportional Hazards Model, where our dependent variable is the "hazard" (i.e., risk) of returning for a second TANF spell. All clients who did not return by August 2003 are considered right-censored, meaning that data on reentry for these clients is unavailable for our analysis.

7. At the individual level, we control for education, race (black, Latino, other), citizenship status, gender, age, marital status, earnings, whether the first spell ended in a sanction, and the number of children and the age of the youngest child in the TANF family. At the county level, we control for population, unemployment, and the county poverty rate, in addition to our measures of implementation stringency.

8. Specifically, reentry is more likely for clients who are black, female, and single; clients with lower earnings; clients who received a sanction during the first spell; and clients with more children. There were two exceptions to this pattern: Reentry rates were lower for clients who lacked at least some college education and for clients who were not U.S. citizens.

9. Interestingly, we find some variation in this result across groups. The effect of a first-spell sanction matters most for Latino clients, as well as for clients with more than twelve years of education. For these subgroups, the experience of a first-spell sanction increases their risk of return by 48 percent and 35 percent, respectively.

10. The data used to calculate these caseload changes, as well as the caseload data used in the analysis that follows, is available from the Administration for Children and Families (http://www .acf.hhs.gov). Because of the importance of state-sponsored program (SSP) caseloads, our caseload measure includes SSP cases.

11. To generate these predictions, we set all other independent variables at their mean values.

12. In a further analysis, we applied the same model to the rates at which states drew on supplemental TANF funds that federal law makes available for hard economic times, as indicated by data on the TANF Contingency Fund and the TANF Emergency Fund reported by the Center for Law and Social Policy, as of May 2010 (http://www.clasp.org/resources_and_publications/publication? id=0758&list=publications). By the end of 2009, the average state had claimed only about 42 percent of its maximum allocation of these funds. Analyzing cross-state variation, we find a highly political pattern of resource usage. The average take-down rate was just 32 percent in the thirty-four states where Republicans controlled the governor's office or one chamber of the legislature. In the sixteen states where Democrats had full control of state government, the average take-down rate was 64 percent, fully twice as large.

13. We calculate this figure by subtracting the 87 percent of caseload decline that the U.S. General Accountability Office (2010) attributes to the TANF program's receding coverage of income-eligible families.

14. Wisconsin Department of Workforce Development, Office of Economic Advisors, "Wisconsin Economic Indicators," accessed February 12, 2001, http://dwd.wisconsin.gov/oea/wi_econ_ indicators.htm.

15. For reasons of space, we do not take up the voluminous literature on welfare reform's effects on children. The major conclusions of this research can be summarized briefly. Prior to welfare reform, the children of poor single mothers fared very poorly in both the short and long term. There was limited room for welfare reform to make these outcomes worse, and the evidence suggests it has done little to make them better. The positive effects of moving mothers into work have

generally been meager and restricted to young children—and even in this group, occur only under the minority of circumstances where mothers find job that pay higher incomes and do not impose fluctuating schedules. Effects on adolescent outcomes have tended be negative but also quite small. In the main, the turn to disciplinary governance for poor mothers has meant only a continuation of poor outcomes and life prospects for their children (Bassuk, Brown, and Buckner 1996; Grogger and Karoly 2005: 199–226; Johnson, Kalil, and Dunifon 2010).

16. We restrict our sample to clients who entered during the first month of a quarter (January, April, July, or October) and who exited during the last month of a quarter (March, June, September, or December). This ensures that we have accurate earnings data for each client during each quarter, thus minimizing measurement error.

17. Upon exiting, clients may or may not return to TANF in our sample.

18. The variables include the client's race, education level, citizenship status, age, gender, the number of children in the family, as well the age of the youngest child.

19. Clients in the never-sanctioned group comprised 56 percent of all first-spell clients during our observation period. Approximately 31 percent of first-spell clients were sanctioned during the first spell, but not afterward. Clients sanctioned during the first spell and at least once more afterward comprised 6.2 percent of all first-spell clients. Our analysis excludes clients who were not sanctioned during the first spell, but who were sanctioned during a subsequent spell, as this did not seem to be an interesting comparison group for our purposes. This group comprised 6.9 percent of all first-spell clients during our observation period.

20. Empirical evidence for the various developments described in this paragraph can be found in Soss and Schram (2007) and Dyck and Hussey (2008).

REFERENCES

AA (Alcoholics Anonymous). 1953. *Twelve Steps and Twelve Traditions*. New York: AA.

Abramovitz, Mimi. 1988. *Regulating the Lives of Women: Welfare Policy from Colonial Times to the Present*. Boston: South End Press.

ACF (Administration for Children and Families). 1999. *Report to Congress: Analysis of the Impact on Welfare Recidivism of PRWORA Child Support Arrears Distribution Policy Changes*. Washington, DC: U.S. Department of Health and Human Services, Administration for Children and Families. http://www.acf.hhs.gov/programs/cse/pubs/1999/reports/distribution/.

Ackerman, Sherri, and Allison North Jones. 2004. "DCF Chief Resigns, Citing Turmoil." *Tampa Tribune*, August 31.

ACS. 2009. "Public Sector." Accessed February 13, 2001. http://www.acs-inc.com/public-sector .aspx.

Adkisson, Richard V., and James T. Peach. 2000. "Devolution and Recentralization of Welfare Administration: Implications for New Federalism." *Policy Studies Review* 17 (1): 160–78.

AFSCME (American Federation of State, County, and Municipal Employees, AFL-CIO). 2006. *Government for Sale: An Examination of the Contracting Out of State and Local Government Services*. 8th ed. Accessed February 13, 2001. http://www.afscme.org/docs/GovernmentSale.pdf.

Akard, Patrick J. 1992. "Corporate Mobilization and Political Power: The Transformation of U.S. Economic Policy in the 1970s." *American Sociological Review* 57 (5): 597–615.

Albelda, Randy. 2001. "Fallacies of Welfare-to-Work Policies." *Annals of the American Academy of Political and Social Science* 577: 66–78.

Alexander, Michelle. 2010. *The New Jim Crow: Mass Incarceration in the Age of Colorblindness*. New York: New Press.

Allard, Patricia. 2002. *Life Sentences: Denying Welfare Benefits to Women Convicted of Drug Offenses*. Washington, DC: Sentencing Project.

Allard, Scott. 2009. *Out of Reach: Place, Poverty, and the New American Welfare State*. New Haven, CT: Yale University Press.

Allport, Gordon W. 1954. *The Nature of Prejudice*. New York: Doubleday.

APSA Task Force. 2004. "American Democracy in an Age of Rising Inequality." *Perspectives on Politics* 2 (4): 651–66.

AP-Yahoo. 2008. Associated Press-Yahoo News Poll conducted by Jon Krosnick, Morris P. Fiorina, and Paul M. Sniderman. Palo Alto, CA: Stanford University Institute for Research in the Social Sciences.

Armey, Richard. 1995. *The Freedom Revolution: The New Republican House Majority Leader Tells Why Big Government Failed, Why Freedom Works, and How We Will Rebuild America*. New York: Regnery.

Atkinson, Rob, and Knut A. Rostad. 2003. "Can Inmates Become an Integral Part of the U.S. Workforce?" Paper prepared for the Reentry Roundtable, The Employment Dimensions of Prisoner Reentry: Understanding the Nexus between Prisoner Reentry and Work, New York, NY, May 19–20. http://www.urban.org/url.cfm?ID=410854.

Austin, Curtis. 2005. *Workforce Investment Act Reauthorization: Hearing before the Subcommittee on*

Employment, Safety and Training of the Senate Committee on Health, Education, Labor and Pensions, 108th Cong. (June 18, 2003) (testimony of Curtis C. Austin, President, Workforce Florida, Inc.).

Avant, Deborah D. 2005. *The Market for Force: The Consequences of Privatizing Security*. New York: Cambridge University Press.

Avery, James M., and Mark Peffley. 2005. "Voter Registration Requirements, Voter Turnout, and Welfare Eligibility Policy: Class Bias Matters." *State Politics & Policy Quarterly* 5 (1): 47–67.

AWI (Agency for Workforce Innovation). 2004a. *FG 03-037: Work Penalties & Pre-penalty Counseling*. http://www.floridajobs.org/pdg/guidancepapers/037wrkpenaltyprepenaltywtrevo12104.rtf.

———. 2004b. Noncompliance and Sanctions Policy. http://www.floridajobs.org/PDG/wt/sanctionsSWTTrainingSpring041105.ppt.

Bachrach, Peter, and Morton Baratz. 1962. "Two Faces of Power." *American Political Science Review* 56 (4): 947–52.

Barber, Jennifer S., Susan A. Murphy, William G. Axinn, and Jerry Maples. 2000. "Discrete-Time Multilevel Hazard Analysis." *Sociological Methodology* 30:201–35.

Barnett, Michael, and Raymond Duvall. 2005. "Power in International Politics." *International Organization* 59:39–75.

Bartels, Larry. 2008. *Unequal Democracy: The Political Economy of the New Gilded Age*. Princeton, NJ: Princeton University Press.

Bassuk, Ellen, Angela Brown, and John C. Buckner. 1996. "Single Mothers and Welfare." *Scientific American* 275:60–67.

Baum, Dan. 1997. *Smoke and Mirrors: The War on Drugs and the Politics of Failure*. New York: Little, Brown.

Baumgartner, M. P. 1992. "The Myth of Discretion." In *The Uses of Discretion*, edited by Keith Hawkins, 129–62. Oxford: Clarendon Press.

Bell, Stephen H., and Larry L. Orr. 2002. "Screening (and Creaming?) Applicants to Job Training Programs: The AFDC Homemaker–Home Health Aide Demonstrations." *Labour Economics* 9 (2): 279–301.

Bell, Winifred. 1965. *Aid to Families with Dependent Children*. New York: Columbia University Press.

Bell, Stephen H., and Larry L. Orr. 2000. "Screening (and Creaming?) Applicants to Job Training Programs: The AFDC Homemaker–Home Health Aide Demonstrations." *Labour Economics* 9 (2): 279–301.

Bendick, Marc, Jr. 1989. "Privatizing the Delivery of Social Welfare Services: An Idea to Be Taken Seriously." In *Privatization and the Welfare State*, edited by Sheila Kamerman and Alfred J. Kahn, 97–120. Princeton, NJ: Princeton University Press.

Berg, Allison. 2002. *Mothering the Race: Women's Narratives on Reproduction, 1890–1930*. Chicago: University of Illinois Press.

Berrick, Jill Duerr. 1995. *Faces of Poverty: Portraits of Women and Children on Welfare*. New York: Oxford University Press.

Berry, Jeffrey M. 1999. *The New Liberalism: The Rising Power of Citizen Groups*. Washington, DC: Brookings Institution Press.

Berry, Jeffrey M., with David F. Arons. 2003. *A Voice for Nonprofits*. Washington, DC: Brookings Institution Press.

Berry, William D., Evan Ringquist, Richard Fording, and Russell Hanson. 1998. "Measuring Citizen and Government Ideology in the American States, 1960–93." *American Journal of Political Science* 42 (1): 327–48.

Bertrand, Marianne, and Sendhil Mullainathan. 2003. "Are Emily and Greg More Employable than

Lakisha and Jamal? A Field Experiment on Labor Market Discrimination." NBER Working Paper No. 9873, National Bureau of Economic Research, Cambridge, MA.

Besharov, Douglas J. 1995. "A Monster of His Own Creation." *Washington Post*. November 2.

Bevir, Mark, ed. 2007. *The Encyclopedia of Governance*. 2 vols. London: Sage.

Blalock, Hubert M. 1967. *Toward a Theory of Minority Group Relations*. New York: Wiley.

Blank, Rebecca. 1997. "What Causes Public Assistance Caseloads to Grow?" NBER Working Paper No. 6343, National Bureau of Economic Research, Cambridge, MA.

———. 2001. "Declining Caseloads/Increased Work: What Can We Conclude about the Effects of Welfare Reform?" *Economic Policy Review* (September): 25–36.

———. 2002. "Evaluating Welfare Reform in the United States." NBER Working Paper No. 8983, National Bureau of Economic Research, Cambridge, MA.

———. 2009. "What We Know, What We Don't Know, and What We Need to Know about Welfare Reform." In *Welfare Reform and Its Long-Term Consequences for America's Poor*, edited by James P. Ziliak, 22–58. New York: Cambridge University Press.

Blank, Rebecca, and Brian Kovak. 2008. "The Growing Problem of Disconnected Single Mothers." Working Paper Series No. 07-28, National Poverty Center, Ann Arbor, MI.

Bloch, Marc. 1953. *The Historian's Craft*. New York: Vintage

Bloeser, Andrew J., and Michelle Brophy-Baermann. 2009. "Ending Welfare as We Didn't Know It: The Story of Welfare Privatization in California, New York, Texas and Wisconsin." Paper prepared for the Annual Meeting of the American Political Science Association, Toronto, Ontario, Canada, September 3–6.

Bloom, Dan, and Donald Winstead. 2002. "Sanctions and Welfare Reform." Welfare Reform and Beyond Initiative Policy Brief No. 12, Brookings Institution, Washington, DC. http://www.mdrc.org/publications/191/policybrief.html.

Blumer, Herbert. 1971. "Social Problems as Collective Behavior." *Social Problems* 18 (3): 298–306.

Bobo, Lawrence D., and Michael Massagli. 2001. "Stereotyping and Urban Inequality." In *Urban Inequality: Evidence from Four Cities*, edited by Alice O'Connor, Charles Tilly, and Lawrence Bobo, 89–162. New York: Russell Sage Foundation.

Bonilla-Silva, Eduardo. 1997. "Rethinking Racism: Toward a Structural Interpretation." *American Sociological Review* 62 (June): 465–80.

Born, Catherine, Pamela Caudill, and Melinda Cordero. 1999. *Life After Welfare: A Look at Sanctioned Families*. Baltimore: University of Maryland, School of Social Work.

Botsko, Christopher, Kathleen Snyder, and Jacob Leos-Urbel. 2001. *Recent Changes in Florida Welfare and Work, Child Care, and Child Welfare Systems*. Washington, DC: Urban Institute.

Bourdieu, Pierre. 1990. *In Other Words: Essays Towards a Reflexive Sociology*. Translated by M. Adamson. Stanford, CA: Stanford University Press.

———. 1998. *Practical Reason: On the Theory of Action*. Stanford, CA: Stanford University Press.

Bowman, Kathryn. 2003. "Attitudes about Welfare Reform" AEI Studies in Public Opinion. Washington, DC: American Enterprise Institute.

Box-Steffensmeier, Janet M., and Bradford S. Jones. 1997. "Time Is of the Essence: Event History Models in Political Science." *American Journal of Political Science* 41 (4): 1414–61.

Brannon, Rob. 2003. "Goodwill Protests Loss to Rival Bidder: The Tampa Bay Workforce Alliance Picks Another Agency to Run Its Programs, Prompting a 'Sorry Episode.'" *St. Petersburg Times*, August 28. http://www.sptimes.com/2003/08/28/news_pf/Hillsborough/Goodwill_protests_los.shtml.

Brewer, Marilynn. 1999. "Perpetrators of Prejudice: The Psychology of Prejudice: Ingroup Love and Outgroup Hate?" *Journal of Social Issues* 55 (3): 429–44.

Brodkin, Evelyn Z. 1986. *The False Promise of Administrative Reform: Implementing Quality Control in Welfare*. Philadelphia: Temple University Press.

———. 1997. "Inside the Welfare Contract." *Social Service Review* 71 (1): 1–33.

———. 2007. "Bureaucracy Redux." *Journal of Public Administration Research and Theory* 17 (1): 1–17.

———. 2008. "Accountability in Street-Level Bureaucracies: Issues in the Analysis of Organizational Practice." *International Journal of Public Administration* 31 (3): 317–36.

Brodkin, Evelyn Z., Carolyn Fuqua, and Elaine Waxman. 2005. *Accessing the Safety Net: Administrative Barriers to Public Benefits in Metropolitan Chicago*. Chicago: Sargent Shriver National Center on Poverty Law and Legal Assistance Foundation of Metropolitan Chicago.

Brodkin, Evelyn Z., and Malay Majmundar. 2010. "Administrative Exclusion: Organizations and the Hidden Costs of Welfare Claiming." *Journal of Public Administration Research and Theory* 20 (4): 827–48.

Brophy-Baermann, Michelle, and Andrew Bloeser. 2006. "Stealthy Wealth: The Untold Story of Welfare Privatization." *Harvard International Journal of Press/Politics* 11 (3): 89–112.

Brown, David J. 1991. "The Professional Ex-: An Alternative for Exiting the Deviant Career." *Sociological Quarterly* 32 (2): 219–30.

Brown, Ed, and Jon Cloke. 2005. "Neoliberal Reform, Governance and Corruption in Central America: Exploring the Nicaraguan Case." *Political Geography* 245:601–30.

Brown, Lawrence D., and Lawrence R. Jacobs. 2008. *Private Abuse of the Public Interest: Market Myths and Policy Muddles*. Chicago: University of Chicago Press.

Brown, Michael K., Martin Carnoy, Elliott Currie, Troy Duster, David B. Oppenheimer, Marjorie M. Schultz, and David Wellman. 2003. *Whitewashing Race: The Myth of a Color-Blind Society*. Berkeley: University of California Press.

Brown, Robert D. 1995. "Party Cleavages and Welfare Effort in the American States." *American Political Science Review* 89 (1): 23–33.

Brown, Wendy. 2003. "Neo-liberalism and the End of Liberal Democracy." *Theory and Event* 7 (1). http://muse.jhu.edu/login?uri=/journals/theory_and_event/v007/7.1brown.html.

———. 2006. "American Nightmare: Neoliberalism, Neoconservatism, and De-democratization." *Political Theory* 34 (6): 690–714.

Brubaker, Roger. 2004. *Ethnicity without Groups*. Cambridge, MA: Harvard University Press.

Bruch, Sarah, Myra Max Ferree, and Joe Soss. 2010. "From Policy to Polity: Democracy, Paternalism, and the Incorporation of Disadvantaged Citizens." *American Sociological Review* 75 (2): 205–26.

Burtless, Gary. 1986. "Public Spending for the Poor: Trends, Prospects, and Economic Limits." In *Fighting Poverty: What Works and What Doesn't*, edited by Sheldon H. Danziger and Daniel H. Weinberg, 18–49. Cambridge, MA: Harvard University Press.

California Department of Corrections. 1994. "Joint Venture Employers." Joint Venture Program. June.

California State Auditor. 2003. *Statewide Fingerprinting Imaging System*. California State Auditor, Bureau of State Audits Report No. 2001–015.

Campbell, Andrea Louise. 2003. *How Policies Make Citizens: Senior Political Activism and the American Welfare State*. Princeton, NJ: Princeton University Press.

———. 2007a. "Parties, Electoral Participation, and Shifting Voting Blocs." In *The Transformation of American Politics: Activist Government and the Rise of Conservatism*, edited by Paul Pierson and Theda Skocpol, 68–102. Princeton, NJ: Princeton University Press.

———. 2007b. "Universalism, Targeting and Participation." In *Remaking America: Democracy and*

Public Policy in an Age of Inequality, edited by Joe Soss, Jacob Hacker, and Suzanne Mettler, 121–40. New York: Russell Sage Foundation.

Cancian, Maria, Robert Haveman, Daniel R. Meyer, and Barbara Wolfe. 2002. "Before and After TANF: The Economic Well-Being of Women Leaving Welfare." *Social Service Review* 76 (4): 603–41.

Caputo, Marc. 2004a. "Jobs Firm Probed for Fraud." *Miami Herald*, January 28.

———. 2004b. "Labor Records Sloppy." *Miami Herald*, January 31.

Carmines, Edward G., and James A. Stimson. 1989. *Issue Evolution: Race and the Transformation of American Politics*. Princeton, NJ: Princeton University Press.

Council of Economic Advisers. 1999. *The Effect of Welfare Policy and the Economic Expansion on Welfare Caseloads: An Update*. Washington, DC: Council of Economic Advisers.

Cherlin, Andrew J., Karen Bogen, James M. Quane, and Linda Burton. 2002. "Operating within the Rules: Welfare Recipients' Experiences with Sanctions and Case Closings for Noncompliance." *Social Service Review* 76:387–405.

Chesney-Lind, Meda. 1995. *The Female Offender*. Thousand Oaks, CA: Sage.

Chesney-Lind, Meda, and Marc Mauer, eds. 2003. *Invisible Punishment: The Collateral Consequences of Mass Imprisonment*. New York: New Press.

CLASP (Center for Law and Social Policy). 2009. *Looking Ahead to TANF Reauthorization*. Washington, DC: CLASP.

Clawson, Rosalee A., and Rakuya Trice. 2000. "Poverty As We Know It: Media Portrayals of the Poor." *Public Opinion Quarterly* 64:53–64.

Clear, Todd R. 2009. *Imprisoning Communities: How Mass Incarceration Makes Disadvantaged Neighborhoods Worse*. New York: Oxford University Press.

Cohen, Adam. 1998. "When Wall Street Runs Welfare." *Time*, March 23. http://www.time.com/time/magazine/article/0,9171,988010,00.html.

Cohen, Cathy. 1999. *The Boundaries of Blackness: AIDS and the Breakdown of Black Politics*. Chicago: University of Chicago Press.

Cohen, Joshua, and Joel Rogers. 2003. "Power and Reason." In *Deepening Democracy: Institutional Innovations in Empowered Participatory Governance*, edited by Archon Fung and Erik Olin Wright, 237–58. New York: Verso.

Collins, Jane, and Victoria Mayer. 2010. *Both Hands Tied: Welfare Reform and the Race to the Bottom of the Low-Wage Labor Market*. Chicago: University of Chicago Press.

Collins, Patricia Hill. 1991. *Black Feminist Thought: Knowledge, Consciousness and the Politics of Empowerment*. New York: Routledge.

Congressional Budget Office. 1996. *Federal Budgetary Implications of the Personal Responsibility and Work Opportunity Reconciliation Act of 1996*. Washington, DC: Congressional Budget Office.

Conlan, Timothy J. 1998. *From New Federalism to Devolution: Twenty-five Years of Intergovernmental Reform*. Washington, DC: Brookings Institution Press.

Considine, Mark. 2003. "Governance and Competition: The Role of Nonprofit Organizations in the Delivery of Public Services." *Australian Journal of Political Science* 38 (1): 63–77.

Conway, M. Margaret. 1986. "PACs and Congressional Elections in the 1980s." In *Interest Group Politics*, edited by Adam Cigler and Burdett Loomis, 70–90. Washington, DC: CQ Press.

Cooper, Michael. 2002. "Disputed Pacts for Welfare Will Just Die." *New York Times*, October 4.

Cotterell, Bill. 2006. "Audit: No Proof Privatization Saves Money." *Tallahassee Democrat*, December 11.

Crenshaw, Kimberle. 1991. "Mapping the Margins: Intersectionality, Identity Politics, and Violence against Women of Color." *Stanford Law Review* 43 (6): 1241–99.

Crenson, Matthew A. 1998. *Building the Invisible Orphanage: A Prehistory of the American Welfare State*. Cambridge, MA: Harvard University Press.

Crenson, Matthew, and Benjamin Ginsberg. 2002. *Downsizing Democracy: How America Sidelined Its Citizens and Privatized Its Public*. Baltimore: Johns Hopkins University Press.

Cressey, Donald. 1955. "Changing Criminals: The Application of the Theory of Differential Association." *American Journal of Sociology* 61 (2): 116–20.

Cruikshank, Barbara. 1999. *The Will to Empower: Democratic Citizens and Other Subjects*. Ithaca, NY: Cornell University Press.

Danziger, Sandra K., Ariel Kalil, and Nathaniel J. Anderson. 2000. "Human Capital, Physical Health, and Mental Health of Welfare Recipients: Co-occurrence and Correlates." *Journal of Social Issues* 56 (4): 635–54.

Danziger, Sheldon H., and Robert H. Haveman. 2001. "Introduction: The Evolution of Poverty and Antipoverty Policy." In *Understanding Poverty*, edited by Sheldon H. Danziger and Robert H. Haveman, 1–24. New York: Russell Sage Foundation.

Darity, William, Jr., and Samuel Myers Jr. 1998. *Persistent Disparity: Race and Economic Inequality in the United States since 1945*. Northhampton, MA: Edward Elger.

Darley, John M., and Paget H. Gross. 1983. "A Hypothesis-Confirming Bias in Labeling Effects." *Journal of Personality and Social Psychology* 44:20–33.

Dave, Dhaval, Nancy Reichman, and Hope Corman. 2008. "Effects of Welfare Reform on Educational Acquisition of Young Adult Women." NBER Working Paper No. 14466, National Bureau of Economic Research, Cambridge, MA.

Davis, Angela. 1983. *Women, Race, and Class*. New York: Vintage.

Davis, Martha. 1995. *Brutal Need: Lawyers and the Welfare Rights Movement, 1960–1973*. New Haven, CT: Yale University Press.

DeAgostino, Martin. 2005. "Privatization Moving Too Fast, State Union Says: AFSCME Cites Other States' Problems in Welfare Initiatives as a Warning." *South Bend Tribune*, October 21.

Dean, Mitchell. 1999. *Governmentality: Power and Rule in Modern Society*. Thousand Oaks, CA: Sage.

DeParle, Jason. 1996. "Mugged by Reality." *New York Times Magazine*, May 8.

———. 1999. "The Silence of the Liberals: Liberals Need to Be More Active in Welfare Reform." *Washington Monthly* 51 (April): 12.

———. 2004. "Dream Deferred: The Most Inspired Employee in America's Most Lauded Welfare Agency Can Barely Do His Job." *Washington Monthly*, September.

———. 2009. "Welfare Aid Isn't Growing as Economy Drops Off." *New York Times*, February 2.

DeParle, Jason, and Robert M. Gebeloff. 2010. "Living on Nothing but Food Stamps." *New York Times*, January 2.

DeParle, Jason, and Steven A. Holmes. 2000. "A War on Poverty Subtly Linked to Race." *New York Times*, December 26.

Derthick, Martha. 1990. *Agency Under Stress: The Social Security Administration in American Government*. Washington, DC: Brookings Institution Press.

Devine, Patricia G. 1989. "Stereotypes and Prejudice: Their Automatic and Controlled Components." *Journal of Personality and Social Psychology* 56:5–18.

Devine, Patricia G., and Sarah M. Baker. 1991. "Measurement of Racial Stereotype Subtyping." *Personality and Social Psychology Bulletin* 17:44–50.

Diamond, Sara. 1995. *Roads to Dominion: Right-Wing Movements and Political Power in the United States*. New York: Guilford Press.

Dias, Janice Johnson, and Steven Maynard-Moody. 2007. "For-Profit Welfare: Contracts, Conflicts, and the Performance Paradox." *Journal of Public Administration Research and Theory* 17:189–211.

Diller, Matthew. 2000. "The Revolution in Welfare Administration: Rules, Discretion, and Entrepreneurial Government." *New York University Law Review* 75 (5): 1121–1220.

DiPrete, Thomas A., and Gregory M. Eirich. 2006. "Cumulative Advantage as a Mechanism for Inequality: A Review of Theoretical and Empirical Developments." *Annual Review of Sociology* 32: 271–97.

Dodson, Lisa. 2010. *The Moral Underground: How Ordinary People Subvert an Unfair Economy.* New York: New Press.

Domke, David. 2001. "Racial Cues and Political Ideology." *Communication Research* 28 (6): 772–801.

Donahue, John D. 1989. The *Privatization Decision: Public Ends, Private Means.* New York: Basic.

———. 1999. *Hazardous Crosscurrents: Confronting Inequality in an Era of Devolution.* New York: Century Foundation.

Dresser, Laura, and Joel Rogers. 2003. "Part of the Solution: Emerging Workforce Intermediaries in the United States." In *Governing Work and Welfare in a New Economy: European and American Experiments*, edited by Jonathan Zeitlin and David Trubeck, 266–91. New York: Oxford University Press.

Duguid, Stephen. 2000. *Can Prisons Work? The Prisoner as Object and Subject in Modern Corrections.* Toronto: University of Toronto Press.

Dworkin, Gerald. 1971. "Paternalism." In *Morality and the Law*, edited by Richard Wasserstrom, 107–26. Belmont, CA: Wadsworth.

Dyck, Joshua J., and Laura S. Hussey. 2008. "The End of Welfare as We Know It? Durable Attitudes in a Changing Information Environment." *Public Opinion Quarterly* 72: 589–618.

Dye, Thomas R. 1990. *American Federalism: Competition among Governments.* Lexington, MA: Lexington.

Eberhardt, Jennifer L., Paul G. Davies, Valerie J. Purdie-Vaughns, and Sheri Lynn Johnson. 2006. "Looking Deathworthy: Perceived Stereotypicality of Black Defendants Predicts Capital Sentencing Outcomes." *Psychological Science* 17 (5): 383–86.

Edin, Kathryn, and Laura Lein. 1997. *Making Ends Meet: How Single Mothers Survive Welfare and Low-Wage Work.* New York: Russell Sage Foundation.

Edsall, Thomas Byrne, with Mary D. Edsall. 1991. *Chain Reaction: The Impact of Race, Rights, and Taxes on American Politics.* New York: Knopf.

Ehrenreich, Barbara. 1987. "The New Right Attack on Social Welfare." In *The Mean Season: The Attack on the Welfare State*, by Frances Fox Piven, Richard A. Cloward, Barbara Ehrenreich, and Fred Block, 161–93. New York: Pantheon.

———. 1997. "Spinning the Poor into Gold: How Corporations Seek to Profit from Welfare Reform." *Harper's* 294 (1767): 44–52.

Eichhorst, Werner, Otto Kaufman, and Regina Konle-Seidl. 2008. *Bringing the Jobless into Work? Experiences with Activation Schemes in Europe and the US.* Berlin: Springer.

Ellwood, David. 1988. *Poor Support: Poverty in the American Family.* New York: Basic Books.

———. 1996. "Welfare Reform as I Knew It." *American Prospect*, May-June.

Esping-Andersen, Gosta. 1985. *Politics Against Markets: The Social Democratic Road to Power.* Princeton, NJ: Princeton University Press.

———. 1990. *Three Worlds of Welfare Capitalism.* Princeton, NJ: Princeton University Press.

Ewalt, Jo Ann, and Edward T. Jennings Jr. 2004. "Administration, Governance, and Policy Tools in Welfare Implementation." *Public Administration Review* 64 (4): 449–62.

Fabricant, Michael B., and Robert Fisher 2001. *Settlement Houses Under Seige.* New York: Columbia University Press.

Fagnoni, Cynthia. 2007. *Unemployment Insurance: Receipt of Benefits Has Declined, with Continued*

Disparities for Low-Wage and Part-Time Workers. Report GAO-07-1243T. Washington, DC: U.S. General Accounting Office. http://www.gao.gov/new.items/d071243t.pdf.

Fairbanks, Robert P. 2009. *How It Works: Recovering Citizens in Post-welfare Philadelphia.* Chicago: University of Chicago Press.

Federico, Christopher M., and Jim Sidanius. 2002. "Sophistication and the Antecedents of Whites' Racial Policy Attitudes: Racism, Ideology, and Affirmative Action in America." *Public Opinion Quarterly* 66 (2): 145–76.

Feeley, Malcolm M., and Van Swearingen. 2004. "The Prison Conditions Cases and the Bureaucratization of Incarceration." *Pace Law Review* 24 (2): 433–76.

Feldman, Leonard C. 2006. *Citizens without Shelter: Homelessness, Democracy, and Political Exclusion.* Ithaca, NY: Cornell University Press.

Feldman, Martha S. 1989. *Order Without Design: Information Production and Policy Making.* Stanford, CA: Stanford University Press.

———. 1992. "Social Limits to Discretion: An Organizational View." In *The Uses of Discretion,* edited by Keith Hawkins, 163–84. Oxford: Clarendon Press.

Feldman, Martha, and Anne Khademian. 2000. "Management for Inclusion: Balancing Control with Participation." *International Public Management Journal* 3 (2): 149–68.

———. 2007. "The Role of the Public Manager in Inclusion: Creating Communities of Participation." *Governance* 20 (2): 305–24.

Fellowes, Matthew, and Gretchen Rowe. 2004. "Politics and the New American Welfare States." *American Journal of Political Science* 48 (2): 362–73.

Ferguson, Ronald F. 1996. "Shifting Challenges: Fifty Years of Economic Change toward Black-White Earnings Inequality." In *An American Dilemma Revisited,* edited by O. Clayton Jr., 76–111. New York: Russell Sage Foundation.

Ferguson, Thomas, and Joel Rogers. 1986. *Right Turn: The Decline of the Democrats and the Future of American Politics.* New York: Hill and Wang.

Fineman, Martha. 2004. *The Autonomy Myth: A Theory of Dependency.* New York: New Press.

Fiorina, Morris P. 2004. *Culture War? The Myth of a Polarized America.* New York: Longman.

Fla. Stat. § 414.065. 2009. Noncompliance with Work Requirements.

Fla. Stat. § 445.024. 2009. Work Requirements.

Florida Department of Children and Families. 2009. *Open-Closed TANF Data Report.* http://www .dcf.state.fl.us/ess/agencyforms.shtml#data.

Fording, Richard C. 1997. "The Conditional Effect of Violence as a Political Tactic: Mass Insurgency, Welfare Generosity, and Electoral Context in the American States." *American Journal of Political Science* 41: 1–29.

———. 2001. "The Political Response to Black Insurgency: A Critical Test of Competing Theories of the State." *American Political Science Review* 95 (1): 115–31.

Fording, Richard C., Joe Soss, and Sanford F. Schram. 2007. "Devolution, Discretion, and the Effect of Local Political Values on TANF Sanctioning." *Social Service Review* 81 (2): 285–316.

Foucault, Michel. (1975) 1997. *Discipline and Punish: The Birth of the Prison.* New York: Vintage.

———. 1980. "Power and Strategies." In *Power/Knowledge—Selected Interviews and Other Writings, 1972–1977,* edited by Colin Gordon, 134–45. Brighton: Harvester Press.

———. (1980) 1990. *The History of Sexuality.* Vol. 1, *An Introduction.* New York: Vintage.

———. 1991. "Governmentality." Translated by R. Braidotti and revised by C. Gordon. In *The Foucault Effect: Studies in Governmentality,* edited by G. Burchell, C. Gordon, and P. Miller, 87–104. Chicago: University of Chicago Press.

Fox, Cybelle. 2004. "The Changing Color of Welfare? How Whites' Attitudes toward Latinos Influence Support for Welfare." *American Journal of Sociology* 110 (3): 580–625.

Fraser, Nancy, and Linda Gordon. 1994. "A Genealogy of 'Dependency': Tracing a Keyword of the US Welfare State." *Signs* 19 (Winter): 309–36.

Free, Lloyd, and Hadley Cantril. 1967. *The Political Beliefs of Americans: A Study of Public Opinion.* New York: Simon and Schuster.

Freeman, Richard B., and Joel Rogers. 2007. "The Promise of Progressive Federalism." In *Remaking America: Democracy and Public Policy in an Age of Inequality,* edited by Joe Soss, Jacob Hacker and Suzanne Mettler, 205–27. New York: Russell Sage Foundation.

Friedman, Milton. (1962) 2002. *Capitalism and Freedom.* Chicago: University of Chicago Press.

Frymer, Paul. 1999. *Uneasy Alliances: Race and Party Competition in America.* Princeton, NJ: Princeton University Press.

———. 2007. *Black and Blue: African Americans, the Labor Movement, and the Decline of the Democratic Party.* Princeton, NJ: Princeton University Press.

Fung, Archon. 2004. *Empowered Participation: Reinventing Urban Democracy.* Princeton, NJ: Princeton University Press.

Fung, Archon, and Erik Olin Wright, eds. 2003. *Deepening Democracy: Institutional Innovations in Empowered Participatory Governance.* New York: Verso.

Gabbidon, Shawn, and Helen Taylor Green. 2005. *Race and Crime.* Pacific Palisades, CA: Sage.

Gainsborough, Juliet F. 2003. "To Devolve or Not to Devolve? Welfare Reform in the States." *Policy Studies Journal* 31 (4): 603–23.

Galbraith, John Kenneth. 1952. *American Capitalism: The Concept of Countervailing Power.* Boston: Houghton Mifflin.

Gallagher, L. Jerome, Cori E. Uccello, Alicia B. Pierce, and Erin B. Reidy. 1999. *State General Assistance Programs 1998.* Washington, DC: Urban Institute. http://www.urban.org/UploadedPDF/ga_main.pdf.

Gans, Herbert J. 1972. "The Positive Functions of Poverty." *American Journal of Sociology* 78 (2): 275–89.

Garland, David. 1990. *Punishment and Modern Society: A Study in Social Theory.* Chicago: University of Chicago Press.

———. 2002. *The Culture of Control: Crime and Social Order in Contemporary Society.* Chicago: University of Chicago Press.

Genovese, Eugene. 1974. *Roll, Jordan, Roll: The World the Slaves Made.* New York: Random House.

Gigerenzer, Gerd. 2002. *Calculated Risks: How to Know When Numbers Deceive You.* New York: Simon and Shuster.

Gilbert, Neil. 2002. *Transformation of the Welfare State: The Silent Surrender of Public Responsibility.* New York: Oxford University Press.

Gilder, George. 1981. *Wealth and Poverty.* New York: Basic.

Gilens, Martin. 1999. *Why Americans Hate Welfare: Race, Media, and the Politics of Antipoverty Policy.* Chicago: University of Chicago Press.

———. 2003. "How the Poor Became Black: The Racialization of Poverty in the Mass Media." In *Race and the Politics of Welfare Reform,* edited by Sanford F. Schram, Joe Soss, and Richard C. Fording, 101–30. Ann Arbor: University of Michigan Press.

Gilliam, Franklin D., Jr., and Shanto Iyengar. 2000. "Prime Suspects: The Impact of Local Television News on the Viewing Public." *American Journal of Political Science* 44 (3): 560–73.

Gilliom, John. 2001. *Overseers of the Poor: Resistance, Surveillance, and the Limits of Privacy.* Chicago: University of Chicago Press.

Gilman, Michelle Estrin. 2001. "Legal Accountability in an Era of Privatized Welfare." *California Law Review* 89 (3): 569–642.

Glaser, James M. 1994. "Back to the Black Belt: Racial Environment and White Racial Attitudes in the South." *Journal of Politics* 56 (1): 21–41.

Glazer, Nathan. 1995. "Making Work Work: Welfare Reform in the 1990s." In *The Work Alternative: Welfare Reform and the Realities of the Job Market*, edited by D. S. Nightingale and R. H. Haveman, 17–32. Washington, DC: Urban Institute Press.

Glenn, Evelyn Nakano. 2000. "Creating a Caring Society." *Contemporary Sociology* 29 (1): 84–94.

Goffman, Erving. 1959. *The Presentation of Self in Everyday Life*. New York: Doubleday Anchor Books.

Goggin, Malcolm, James Lester, Laurence O'Toole, and Ann Bowman. 1990. *Implementation Theory and Practice: Toward a Third Generation*. Glenview, IL: Scott Foresman.

Goldberg, Chad Allen. 2007. *Citizens and Paupers: Relief, Rights, and Race, from the Freedmen's Bureau to Workfare*. Chicago: University of Chicago Press.

Goldberg, David Theo. 2008. *The Threat of Race: Reflections on Racial Neoliberalism*. New York: Wiley-Blackwell.

Goldberg, Heidi, and Laura Schott. 2000. *A Compliance-Oriented Approach to Sanctions in State and County TANF Programs*. Washington, DC: Center on Budget and Policy Priorities.

Goldfield, Michael. 1997. *The Color of Politics*. New York: New Press.

———. 1989. *The Decline of Organized Labor in the United States*. Chicago: University of Chicago Press.

Gooden, Susan Tinsley. 2003. "Contemporary Approaches to Enduring Challenges: Using Performance Measurement to Promote Racial Equality under TANF." In *Race and the Politics of Welfare Reform*, edited by Sanford F. Schram, Joe Soss, and Richard C. Fording, 254–78. Ann Arbor: University of Michigan Press.

Gordon, Linda. 1990. "Family Violence, Feminism, and Social Control." In *Women, Welfare, and the State*, edited by Linda Gordon, 37–64. Madison: University of Wisconsin Press.

———. 1994. *Pitied but Not Entitled: Single Mothers and the History of Welfare 1890–1935*. New York: Free Press.

———. 2002. *The Arizona Orphan Abduction*. Cambridge, MA: Harvard University Press.

Grant, J. Douglas. 1965. "Strategies for New Careers Development." In *New Careers for the Poor: The Nonprofessional in Human Services*, edited by Arthur Pearl and Frank Reissmann, 209–38. New York: Free Press.

Gray, Virginia. 1973. "Innovation in the States: A Diffusion Study." *American Political Science Review* 67:1174–85.

Greene, Lisa. 2003. "Agency Must Return $785,000 to State." *St. Petersburg Times*, March 3.

Grogger, Jeffrey. 2003. "The Effects of Time Limits, the EITC, and Other Policy Changes on Welfare Use, Work, and Income among Female-Headed Families." *Review of Economics and Statistics*. 85 (2): 394–408.

Grogger, Jeffrey, and Lynn A. Karoly. 2005. *Welfare Reform: Effects of a Decade of Change*. Cambridge, MA: Harvard University Press.

Grogger, Jeffrey, Lynn Karoly, and Jacob A. Klerman. 2002. "Consequences of Welfare Reform: A Research Synthesis." RAND Working Paper DRU-2676-DHHS, RAND Corp., Santa Monica, CA.

Guetzkow, Joshua. 2006. "Common Cause? A Cultural Analysis of the Links Between Welfare and Criminal Justice Policies, 1960–1996." Working Paper No. 30, Center on Institutions and Governance, University of California–Berkeley.

Guetzkow, Josh, and Bruce Western. 2007. "The Political Consequences of Mass Imprisonment." In *Remaking America: Democracy and Public Policy in an Age of Inequality*, edited by Joe Soss, Jacob S. Hacker, and Suzanne Mettler, 228–42. New York: Russell Sage Foundation.

Gustafson, Kaaryn. 2009. "The Criminalization of Poverty." *Journal of Criminal Law and Criminology* 99 (3): 643–711.

Hacker, Jacob S. 1997. *The Road to Nowhere: The Genesis of President Clinton's Plan for Health Security.* Princeton, NJ: Princeton University Press.

———. 2002. *The Divided Welfare State: The Battle over Public and Private Social Benefits in the United States.* New York: Cambridge University Press.

———. 2004. "Privatizing Risk without Privatizing the Welfare State: The Hidden Politics of Social Policy Retrenchment in the United States." *American Political Science Review* 98 (May): 243–60.

———. 2006. *The Great Risk Shift: The Assault on American Jobs, Families, Health Care and Retirement—and How You Can Fight Back.* New York: Oxford University Press.

Hacker, Jacob, and Paul Pierson. 2005. *Off Center: The Republican Revolution and the Erosion of American Democracy.* New Haven, CT: Yale University Press.

———. 2010. *Winner-Take-All Politics: How Washington Made the Rich Richer—and Turned Its Back on the Middle Class.* New York: Simon and Schuster.

Hamersma, Sarah. 2005. *The Work Opportunity and Welfare-to-Work Tax Credits.* Brief No. 15. Tax Policy Issues and Options Series. Washington, DC: Urban Institute.

Hancock, Ange-Marie. 2004. *The Politics of Disgust: The Public Identity of the Welfare Queen.* New York: New York University Press.

———. 2007. "When Multiplication Doesn't Equal Quick Addition: Examining Intersectionality as a Research Paradigm." *Perspectives on Politics* 5:63–79.

Handler, Joel F. 1992. "Discretion: Power, Quiescence, and Trust." In *The Uses of Discretion*, edited by Keith Hawkins, 331–60. Oxford: Clarendon Press.

———. 1995. *The Poverty of Welfare Reform.* New Haven, CT: Yale University Press.

Handler, Joel F., and Yeheskel Hasenfeld. 1991. *The Moral Construction of Poverty.* Newbury Park, CA: Sage.

———. 2007. *Blame Welfare, Ignore Poverty and Inequality.* New York: Cambridge University Press.

Haney, Lynne A. 2004. "Introduction: Gender, Welfare, and States of Punishment." *Social Politics* 11 (3): 333–62.

———. 2010. *Offending Women: Power, Punishment, and the Regulation of Desire.* Berkeley, CA: University of California Press.

Harrington, Michael. 1962. *The Other America: Poverty in the United States.* New York: Macmillan.

Harris, David, and Ann Chih Lin, eds. 2008. *The Colors of Poverty: Why Racial and Ethnic Disparities Persist.* New York: Russell Sage Foundation.

Harris, Othello, and R. Robin Miller, eds. 2003. *Impacts of Incarceration on the African American Family.* New Brunswick, NJ: Transaction.

Harvey, David. 2005. *A Brief History of Neoliberalism.* New York: Oxford University Press.

Hasenfeld, Yeheskel. 1985. "Citizens' Encounters with Welfare State Bureaucracies." *Social Service Review* 59 (December): 622–35.

———. 1992. "The Nature of Human Service Organizations." In *Human Services as Complex Organizations*, edited by Yeheskel Hasenfeld, 3–23. Newbury Park, CA: Sage.

———. 2000. "Organizational Forms as Moral Practices: The Case of Welfare Departments." *Social Service Review* 74:329–51.

———. 2010. "The Attributes of Human Service Organizations." In *Human Services as Complex Organizations*, 2nd ed., edited by Yeheskel Hasenfeld, 9–32. Newbury Park, CA: Sage.

Hasenfeld, Yeheskel, Toorjo Ghose, and Kandyce Larson. 2004. "The Logic of Sanctioning Welfare Recipients: An Empirical Assessment." *Social Service Review* 78 (2): 304–19.

Haskins, Ron. 2006. "Welfare Check." *Wall Street Journal*, July 27.

Hay, Colin. 2006. "What's Globalization Got to Do with It? Economic Interdependence and the Future of European Welfare States." *Government and Opposition* 41: 1–22.

Hayek, Friedrich A. 1960. *The Constitution of Liberty*. Chicago: University of Chicago Press.

Hayward, Clarissa Rile. 2000. *De-Facing Power*. New York: Cambridge University Press.

Heclo, Hugh. 1994. "Poverty Politics." In *Confronting Poverty: Prescriptions for Change*, edited by Sheldon H. Danziger, Gary D. Sandefur, and Daniel H. Weinberg, 396–437. New York: Russell Sage Foundation.

———. 1995. "The Social Question. In *Poverty, Inequality, and the Future of Social Policy*, edited by K. McFate, R. Lawson, and W. J. Wilson, 665–91. New York: Russell Sage.

———. 2001. "The Politics of Welfare Reform." In *The New World of Welfare*, edited by Rebecca M. Blank and Ronald R. Haskins, 169–200. Washington, DC: Brookings Institution Press.

Heinrich, Carolyn J. 2000. "Organizational Form and Performance: An Empirical Investigation of Nonprofit and For-Profit Job-Training Service Providers." *Journal of Policy Analysis and Management* 19 (2): 233–61.

Henry, P. J., and David O. Sears. 2002. "The Symbolic Racism 2000 Scale." *Political Psychology* 23: 253–83.

Herd, Pamela. 2008. "The Fourth Way: Big States, Big Business, and the Evolution of the Earned Income Tax Credit." Paper presented at the annual meeting of the American Sociological Association Annual Meeting, Boston, MA, July 31.

Hero, Rodney E. 1998. *Faces of Inequality: Social Diversity in American Politics*. New York: Oxford University Press.

Herzfeld, Michael. 1992. *The Social Production of Indifference: The Symbolic Roots of Western Bureaucracy*. Chicago: University of Chicago Press.

Hochschild, Jennifer L. 1995. *Facing Up to the American Dream: Race, Class, and the Soul of the Nation*. Princeton, NJ: Princeton University Press.

Hodge, Graeme A. 2000. *Privatization: An International Review of Performance*. Boulder, CO: Westview Press.

Hodgson, Godfrey. 1989. *The World Turned Right Side Up: A History of the Conservative Ascendancy in America*. Boston: Houghton Mifflin.

Hogg, Michael A., and Dominic Abrams. 1988. *Social Identification: A Social Psychology of Intergroup Relations and Group Processes*. London: Routledge.

———. 1998. "Editorial: Group Processes and Intergroup Relations." *Group Processes and Intergroup Relations* 1 (1): 5–6.

Holmes, Leslie. 2006. *Rotten States? Corruption, Post-communism, and Neoliberalism*. Durham, NC: Duke University Press.

Holzer, Harry J. 1999. "Will Employers Hire Welfare Recipients? Recent Survey Evidence from Michigan." *Journal of Policy Analysis and Management* 18 (3): 449–72.

Holzer, Harry J., and Michael A. Stoll. 2003. "Employer Demand for Welfare Recipients by Race." *Journal of Labor Economics* 21 (1): 210–41.

Howard, Christopher. 1997. *The Hidden Welfare State: Tax Expenditures and Social Policy in the United States*. Princeton, NJ: Princeton University Press.

———. 1999. "Field Essay: American Welfare State or States?" *Political Research Quarterly* 52 (2): 421–42.

Hrebiniak, Lawrence G., and William F. Joyce. 1985. "Organizational Adaptation: Strategic Choice and Environmental Determinism." *Administrative Science Quarterly* 30: 336–49.

Hunter, Susan, and Richard W. Waterman. 1996. *Enforcing the Law: The Case of the Clean Water Acts*. Armonk, NY: M. E. Sharpe.

Hurwitz, Jon, and Mark Peffley. 1997. "Public Perceptions of Race and Crime: The Role of Racial Stereotypes." *American Journal of Political Science* 41 (2): 375–401.

Jackman, Mary. 1994. *The Velvet Glove: Paternalism and Conflict in Gender, Class, and Race Relations.* Berkeley: University of California Press.

Jacobs, David, and Ronald E. Helms. 1996. "Toward a Political Model of Incarceration: A Time-Series Examination of Multiple Explanations for Prison Admission Rates." *American Journal of Sociology* 102 (2): 323–57.

Jacobs, Lawrence, and Desmond King, eds. 2009. *The Unsustainable American State.* New York: Oxford University Press.

Jacobs, Lawrence R., and Theda Skocpol, eds. 2005. *Inequality and American Democracy: What We Know and What We Need to Learn.* New York: Russell Sage Foundation.

Jacoby, William A., and Saundra K. Schneider. 2003. "A Culture of Dependence? The Relationship Between Public Assistance and Public Opinion." *British Journal of Political Science* 33: 213–31.

———. 2005. "Elite Discourse and American Public Opinion: The Case of Welfare Spending." *Political Research Quarterly* 58 (3): 367–79.

James, Joni. 2004. "Free Market Fever." *St. Petersburg Times*, February 22.

———. 2006. "Did the Savings Balance the Cost?" *St. Petersburg Times*, December 30.

Jargowsky, Paul A. 1996. "Take the Money and Run: Economic Segregation in U.S. Metropolitan Areas." *American Sociological Review* 61:984–98.

———. 1997. *Poverty and Place: Ghettos, Barrios, and the American City.* New York: Russell Sage Foundation.

Jencks, Christopher. 2005. "What Happened to Welfare?" *New York Review of Books*, December 15.

Jencks, Christopher, and Paul Peterson, eds. 1991. *The Urban Underclass.* Washington, DC: Brookings Institution Press.

Jenkins, Richard. 1997. *Rethinking Ethnicity: Arguments and Explorations.* London: Sage.

Jessop, Bob. 2000. "From the KWNS to the SWPR." In *Rethinking Social Policy*, edited by G. Lewis, S. Gewirtz, and J. Clarke, 171–84. London: Sage.

Jewell, Christopher J. 2007. *Agents of the State: How Caseworkers Respond to Need in the United States, Germany, and Sweden.* New York: Plagrave Macmillan.

Johnson, Monica Kirkpatrick, and Margaret Mooney Marini. 1998. "Bridging the Racial Divide in the United States: The Effect of Gender." *Social Psychology Quarterly* 61 (3): 247–58.

Johnson, Robert. 2002. *Hard Time: Understanding and Reforming the Prison.* Belmont, CA: Wadsworth.

Johnson, Rucker C., Ariel Kalil, and Rachel E. Dunifon, with Barbara Ray. 2010. *Mothers' Work and Children's Lives: Low-Income Families after Welfare Reform.* Kalamazoo, MI: W. E. Upjohn Institute.

Jones, Bryan D. 2001. *Politics and the Architecture of Choice.* Chicago: University of Chicago Press.

Jordan-Zachery, Julia S. 2009. *Black Women, Cultural Images and Social Policy.* New York: Routledge.

Kalil, Ariel, Kristin S. Seefeldt, and Hui-chen Wang. 2002. "Sanctions and Material Hardship under TANF." *Social Service Review* 76 (4): 643–62.

Kane, Thomas J. 1987. "Giving Back Control: Long-Term Poverty and Motivation." *Social Service Review* 61 (3): 405–19.

Kang, Susan. 2009. "Forcing Prison Labor: International Labor Standards, Human Rights and the Privatization of Prison Labor in the Contemporary United States." *New Political Science* 31 (2): 137–61.

Katz, Michael B. 1990. *The Undeserving Poor: From the War on Poverty to the War on Welfare.* New York: Pantheon.

———. 1997. *Improving Poor People: The Welfare State, the "Underclass," and Urban Schools as History*. Princeton, NJ: Princeton University Press.

———. 2002. *The Price of Citizenship: Redefining the American Welfare State*. Philadelphia: University of Pennsylvania Press.

Katz, Daniel, and Robert L. Kahn. 1966. *The Social Psychology of Organizations*. New York: Wiley.

Katz, Michael B. 1996. *In the Shadow of the Poorhouse: A Social History of Welfare in America*. New York: Basic Books.

Katz, Michael B., and Lorrin R. Thomas. 1998. "The Invention of 'Welfare' in America." *Journal of Policy History* 10 (December): 399–418.

Katzenstein, May Fainsod. 2005. "Rights without Citizenship: Activist Politics and Prison Reform in the United States." In *Routing the Opposition: Social Movements, Public Policy, and Democracy*, edited by David S. Meyer, Valerie Jenness, and Helen M. Ingram, 236–58. Minneapolis: University of Minnesota Press.

Katznelson, Ira. 2005. *When Affirmative Action Was White: An Untold History of Racial Inequality in Twentieth-Century America*. Reprint ed. New York: W. W. Norton.

Kaufman, Herbert. 1960. *The Forest Ranger: A Study in Administrative Behavior*. Baltimore: Johns Hopkins University Press.

Kautt, Paula. 2009. "Heuristic Influences over Offense Seriousness Calculations: A Multilevel Investigation of Racial Disparity under Sentencing Guidelines." *Punishment and Society* 11 (2): 191–218.

Keech, William R. (1968) 1981. *The Impact of Negro Voting: The Role of the Vote in the Quest for Equality*. Chicago: Rand McNally.

Keiser, Lael R., Peter Mueser, and Seung-Whan Choi. 2004. "Race, Bureaucratic Discretion, and the Implementation of Welfare Reform." *Journal of Political Science* 48 (2): 314–27.

Keiser, Lael R., and Joe Soss. 1998. "With Good Cause: Bureaucratic Discretion and the Politics of Child Support Enforcement." *American Journal of Political Science* 42 (4): 1133–56.

Kellstedt, Paul M. 2003. *The Mass Media and the Dynamics of American Racial Attitudes*. New York: Cambridge University Press.

Kelly, Michael. 1999. "Assessing Welfare Reform." *Washington Post*, August 4.

Kelly, Nathan J. 2009. *The Politics of Income Inequality in the United States*. New York: Cambridge University Press.

Kershner, Vlae. 1991. "Wilson Plan Puts Welfare in Spotlight Across U.S., Other States Move to Trim Benefits." *San Francisco Chronicle*, December 16.

Kerwin, Cornelius M. 1994. *Rulemaking: How Government Agencies Write Laws and Make Policy*. Washington, DC: CQ Press.

Kettl, Donald F. 2002. *The Transformation of Governance: Public Administration for Twenty-first Century America*. Baltimore: Johns Hopkins University Press.

———. 2005. *The Global Public Management Revolution: A Report on the Transformation of Governance*. 2nd ed. Washington, DC: Brookings Institution Press.

Key, V. O., Jr. 1949. *Southern Politics in State and Nation*. New York: Knopf.

Khademian, Anne M. 2002. *Working with Culture: The Way the Job Gets Done in Public Programs*. Washington, DC: CQ Press.

Kinder, Donald R., and Thomas Palfrey, eds. 1993. *Experimental Foundations of Political Science*. Ann Arbor: University of Michigan Press.

Kinder, Donald, and Lynn Sanders. 1996. *Divided by Color: Racial Politics and Democratic Ideals*. Chicago: University of Chicago Press.

King, Desmond S., and Rogers M. Smith. 2005. "Racial Orders and Political Development." *American Political Science Review* 99 (1): 75–92.

King, Gary, Robert Keohane, and Sidney Verba. 1994. *Designing Social Inquiry*. Princeton, NJ: Princeton University Press.

Kingdon, John. 2003. *Agendas, Alternatives and Public Policies*. New York: Longman.

Klein, Naomi. 2007. *Shock Doctrine: The Rise of Disaster Capitalism*. New York: Metropolitan.

Kohler-Hausmann, Julilly. 2007. "The Crime of Survival: Fraud Prosecutions, Community Surveillance and the Original 'Welfare Queen'" *Journal of Social History* 41 (2): 329–54.

Koralek, Robin. 2000. "South Carolina Family Independence Program Process Evaluation." Prepared for South Carolina Department of Social Services. Washington, DC: Urban Institute.

Korteweg, Anna. 2003. "Welfare Reform and the Subject of the Working Mother: 'Get a Job, a Better Job, Then a Career.'" *Theory and Society* 32 (4): 445–80.

Krinsky, Jonathan. 2007. "The Urban Politics of Workfare." *Urban Affairs Review* 42 (6): 771–98.

Kumlin, Staffan. 2004. *The Personal and the Political: How Personal Welfare State Experiences Affect Political Trust and Ideology*. London: Palgrave Macmillan.

Kumlin, Staffan, and Bo Rothstein. 2005. "Making and Breaking Social Capital: The Impact of Welfare-State Institutions." *Comparative Political Studies* 38: 339–65.

Kusmer, Ken. 2007. "Outsourcing Plan Hits Key Milestone with State Workers' Switch." *Associated Press Financial Wire*, March 17.

Lafer, Gordon. 1999. "Captive Labor: America's Prisoners as Corporate Workforce." *American Prospect* 10:46.

Lakoff, George. 1987. *Women, Fire, and Dangerous Things*. Chicago: University of Chicago Press.

Lawless, Jennifer L., and Richard L. Fox. 2001. "Political Participation of the Urban Poor." *Social Problems* 48: 362–85.

Le Grand, Julian. 2003. *Motivation, Agency, and Public Policy: Of Knights and Knaves, Pawns and Queens*. New York: Oxford University Press.

Leighley, Jan E., and Arnold Vedlitz.1999. "Race, Ethnicity and Political Participation: Competing Models and Contrasting Explanations." *Journal of Politics* 61: 1092–1114.

Lemke, Thomas. 2001. "The Birth of Bio-Politics: Michel Foucault's Lecture at the College de France on Neo-Liberal Governmentality." *Economy and Society* 30 (2): 190–207.

Lerman, Amy. E. 2009. "Bowling Alone (with My Own Ball and Chain): The Effects of Incarceration and the Dark Side of Social Capital." QMSS Seminar, Columbia University, New York, NY, February 25.

Lieberman, Robert C. 1998. *Shifting the Color Line: Race and the American Welfare State*. Cambridge, MA: Harvard University Press.

———. 2005. *Shaping Race Policy: The United States in Comparative Perspective*. Princeton, NJ: Princeton University Press.

Lin, Ann Chih, and David R. Harris, eds. 2008. *The Colors of Poverty: Why Racial and Ethnic Disparities Persist*. New York: Sage Foundation.

Lindhorst, Taryn, Ronald J. Mancoske, and Alice A. Kemp. 2000. "Is Welfare Reform Working? A Study of the Effects of Sanctions on Families Receiving TANF." *Journal of Sociology and Social Welfare* 27 (4): 185–201.

Lindhorst, Taryn, Marcia Meyers, and Erin Casey. 2008. "Screening for Domestic Violence in Public Welfare Offices: An Analysis of Case Manager and Client Interactions." *Violence Against Women* 14 (5): 5–28.

Lindhorst, Taryn, and Julianna D. Padgett. 2005. "Disjunctures for Women and Frontline Workers: Implementation of the Family Violence Option." *Social Service Review* 79 (3): 405–29.

Lineberry, Robert L. 1977. *American Public Policy: What Government Does and What Difference It Makes*. New York: Harper and Row.

Lipsitz, George. 1998. *The Possessive Investment in Whiteness: How White People Profit from Identity Politics.* Philadelphia: Temple University Press.

Lipsky, Michael. 1980. *Street-Level Bureaucracy: Dilemmas of the Individual in Public Services.* New York: Russell Sage Foundation.

———. 1984. "Bureaucratic Disentitlement in Social Welfare Programs." *Social Service Review* 58 (1): 3–27.

Lipton, Eric. 2001. "Hevesi Accuses Mayor of Cover-Up in Corruption Case." *New York Times*, August 28.

Looney, Adam. 2005. "The Effects of Welfare Reform and Related Policies on Single Mothers' Welfare Use and Employment." Finance and Economics Discussion Series 2005–45, Board of Governors of the Federal Reserve System, Washington, DC.

Loprest, Pamela J. 2002. "Making the Transition from Welfare to Work: Successes by Continuing Concerns." In *Welfare Reform: The Next Act*, edited by A. Weil and K. Finegold, 17–31. Washington, DC: Urban Institute Press.

Loury, Glenn C. 2002. *The Anatomy of Racial Inequality.* Cambridge, MA: Harvard University Press.

Lowi, Theodore. 1998. "Think Globally, Lose Locally." *Boston Review* 23 (2). http://bostonreview.net/BR23.2/lowi.html.

Luker, Kristin. 1996. *Dubious Conceptions: The Politics of Teenage Pregnancy.* Cambridge, MA: Harvard University Press.

Lurie, Irene. 2006. *At the Frontlines of the Welfare System: A Perspective on the Decline in Welfare Caseloads.* Albany: State University of New York Press.

Manza, Jeff, and Christopher Uggen. 2006. *Locked Out: Felon Disenfranchisement and American Democracy.* New York: Oxford University Press.

March, James G. 1994. *A Primer on Decision Making: How Decisions Happen.* New York: Free Press.

March, James G., and Johan P. Olsen. 1989. *Rediscovering Institutions: The Organizational Basis of Politics.* New York: Free Press/Macmillan.

———. 2004. "The Logic of Appropriateness." Working Paper No. 9, ARENA-Centre for European Studies, University of Oslo, Norway.

Marshall, T. H. 1964. *Class, Citizenship, and Social Development.* Garden City, NJ: Doubleday.

Martin, Cathie Jo. 1994. "Business and the New Economic Activism: The Growth of Corporate Lobbies in the Sixties." *Polity* 27 (1): 49–76.

———. 2004. "Reinventing Welfare Regimes." *World Politics* 57 (1): 39–69.

Martin, Joanne. 1992. *Cultures in Organizations: Three Perspectives.* New York: Oxford University Press.

Marwell, Nicole P. 2007. *Bargaining for Brooklyn: Community Organizations in the Entrepreneurial City.* Chicago: University of Chicago Press.

Mashaw, Jerry L. 1983. *Bureaucratic Justice.* New Haven, CT: Yale University Press.

Massey, Douglas S. 2007. *Categorically Unequal: The American Stratification System.* New York: Russell Sage Foundation.

———. 2009. "Globalization and Inequality: Explaining American Exceptionalism." *European Sociological Review* 25 (1): 9–23.

Massey, Douglas, and Mary Denton. 1993. *American Apartheid: Segregation and the Making of the Underclass.* Cambridge, MA: Harvard University Press.

Mayer, Victoria. 2008. "Crafting a New Conservative Consensus on Welfare Reform: Redefining Citizenship, Social Provision, and the Public/Private Divide." *Social Politics* 15 (2): 154–81.

Maynard-Moody, Steven, and Michael Musheno. 2003. *Cops, Teachers, Counselors: Stories from the Front Lines of Public Service.* Ann Arbor: University of Michigan Press.

McCarty, Nolan. 2007. "The Policy Effects of Political Polarization." In *The Transformation of American Politics: Activist Government and the Rise of Conservatism*, edited by Paul Pierson and Theda Skocpol, 223–55. Princeton, NJ: Princeton University Press.

McCarty, Nolan, Keith T. Poole, and Howard Rosenthal. 2006. *Polarized America: The Dance of Ideology and Unequal Riches.* Cambridge, MA: MIT Press.

McGarty, Craig. 1999. *Categorization in Social Psychology.* London: Sage.

McGowan, Kathleen, and Jarrett Murphy. 1999. "No Job Too Big for New Welfare-to-Work Grants." *City Limits*, November 1.

Mead, Lawrence. M. 1986. *Beyond Entitlement: The Social Obligations of Citizenship.* New York: Free Press.

———. 1992. *The New Politics of Poverty: The Nonworking Poor in America.* New York: Basic.

———. 1996. "Welfare Policy: The Administrative Frontier." *Journal of Policy Analysis and Management* 15 (4): 592–98.

———. 1997a. "Citizenship and Social Policy: T. H. Marshall and Poverty." *Social Philosophy and Policy* 14: 197–230.

———. 1997b. *The New Paternalism: Supervisory Approaches to Poverty.* Washington, DC: Brookings Institution Press.

———. 1998. "Telling the Poor What to Do." *Public Interest* 132: 97–112.

———. 2001a. "The Politics of Conservative Welfare Reform." In *The New World of Welfare*, ed. Rebecca M. Blank and Ronald R. Haskins, 201–20. Washington, DC: Brookings Institution Press.

———. 2001b. "Review of Joe Soss, *Unwanted Claims: The Politics of Participation in the U.S. Welfare System.*" *Political Science Quarterly* 116 (4): 675–77.

———. 2002. "Welfare Reform: The Institutional Dimension." *Focus* 22 (1): 39–45.

———. 2004a. *Government Matters: Welfare Reform in Wisconsin.* Princeton, NJ: Princeton University Press.

———. 2004b. "The Great Passivity." *Perspectives on Politics* 2 (4): 671–75.

———. 2005. "Welfare Reform and Citizenship." In *Welfare Reform and Political Theory*, edited by Lawrence M. Mead and Christopher Beem, 172–99. New York: Russell Sage Foundation.

———. 2007. "Toward a Mandatory Work Policy for Men." *The Future of Children* 17 (2): 43–72.

Meier, Kenneth J. 1993. *Politics and the Bureaucracy.* Pacific Grove, CA: Brooks/Cole.

Melnick, R. Shep. 2005. "From Tax-and-Spend to Mandate-and-Sue: Liberalism after the Great Society." In *The Great Society and the High Tide of Liberalism*, edited by Sidney M. Milkis, 387–410. Amherst: University of Massachusetts Press.

Mendelberg, Tali. 2001. *The Race Card: Campaign Strategy, Implicit Messages, and the Norm of Equality.* Princeton, NJ: Princeton University Press.

Mettler, Suzanne. 1998. *Dividing Citizens: Gender and Federalism in New Deal Public Policy.* Ithaca, NY: Cornell University Press.

———. 2005. *Soldiers to Citizens: The G.I. Bill and the Making of the Greatest Generation.* New York: Oxford University Press.

———. 2007. "The Transformed Welfare State and the Redistribution of Political Voice." In *The Transformation of American Politics: Activist Government and the Rise of Conservatism*, edited by Paul Pierson and Theda Skocpol, 191–222. Princeton, NJ: Princeton University Press.

Mettler, Suzanne, and Joe Soss. 2004. "The Consequences of Public Policy for Democratic Citizenship: Bridging Policy Studies and Mass Politics." *Perspectives on Politics* 2 (1): 55–73.

Mettler, Suzanne, and Jeffrey M. Stonecash. 2008. "Government Program Usage and Political Voice." *Social Science Quarterly* 89 (2): 273–93.

Meyer, Bruce. 2002. "Labor Supply at the Extensive and Intensive Margins: The EITC, Welfare and Hours Worked." *American Economic Review* 92 (2): 373–79.

Meyers, Marcia K., Shannon Harper, Maria Klawitter, and Taryn Lindhorst. 2006. *Review of Research on TANF Sanctions*. Report to Washington State WorkFirst SubCabinet, West Coast Poverty Center, University of Washington, Seattle.

Mill, John Stuart.1983. *On Liberty*. Indianapolis: Liberty Fund Press.

Millard, Pete. 2000. "Staffing Firms Chafe as Maximus Skims Best Job Prospects." *Business Journal-Milwaukee*, January 21.

Miller, Carol Marbin. 2001. "State Jobs Agency Under Fire." *Miami Herald*, December 31.

Miller, Peter, and Nikolas Rose. 2008. *Governing the Present*. Malden, MA: Polity Press.

Miller, William H. 1998. "Surprise! Welfare Reform Is Working." *Industry Week*, March 16.

Mink, Gwendolyn. 1998. *Welfare's End*. Ithaca, NY: Cornell University Press.

Mittelstadt, Jennifer. 2005. *From Welfare to Workfare: The Unintended Consequences of Liberal Reform, 1945–1965*. Chapel Hill: University of North Carolina Press.

Moncada, Carlos. 2003. "Lawsuit Alleges Harassment in Woman's Suicide." *Tampa Tribune*, January 15.

Morgen, Sandra, Joan Acker, and Jill Weigt. 2010. *Stretched Thin: Poor Families, Welfare Work, and Welfare Reform*. Ithaca, NY: Cornell University Press.

Morris, Dick. 1998. *Behind the Oval Office: Getting Reelected Against All Odds*. Los Angeles: Renaissance.

Moynihan, Donald P. 2006. "Managing for Results in State Government: Evaluating a Decade of Reform." *Public Administration Review* 66 (1) (January/February): 77–89.

———. 2008. *The Dynamics of Performance Management: Constructing Information and Reform*. Washington, DC: Georgetown University Press.

Murray, Charles. 1984. *Losing Ground*. New York: Basic.

Nadasen, Premilla. 2005. *Welfare Warriors: The Welfare Rights Movement in the United States*. New York: Routledge.

Narayan, Uma. 1995. "Colonialism and Its Others: Considerations on Rights and Care Discourses." *Hypatia* 10 (2): 133–40.

Nathan, Richard P., and Thomas L. Gais. 1999. *Implementing the Personal Responsibility Act of 1996: A First Look*. Rockefeller Institute of Government. Albany: State University of New York.

NBC News. 1995. *NBC News Poll, June 8-12, 1995*. Roper Center at University of Connecticut, Public Opinion Online.

Nelson, Barbara J. 1984. "Women's Poverty and Women's Citizenship: Some Political Consequences of Economic Marginality." *Signs: Journal of Women's Culture and Society* 10 (2): 209–31.

———. 1990. "The Origins of the Two-Channel Welfare State: Workmen's Compensation and Mother's Aid." In *Women, the State, and Welfare*, edited by Linda Gordon, 123–51. Madison: University of Wisconsin Press.

Neubeck, Kenneth, and Noel Cazenave. 2001. *Welfare Racism: Playing the Race Card Against America's Poor*. New York: Routledge.

Nguyen, Dong-Phuong. 2003. "Goodwill: Rival Tainted Bid." *St. Petersburg Times*, June 26. http://www.sptimes.com/2003/06/26/Hillsborough/Goodwill__Rival_taint.shtml.

Noble, Charles. 1997. *Welfare as We Knew It: A Political History of the American Welfare State*. New York: Oxford University Press.

Norton, Anne. 2004. *Leo Strauss and the Politics of American Empire*. New Haven, CT: Yale University Press.

Novak, Michael, et al. 1987. *The New Consensus on Family and Welfare*. Washington, DC: American Enterprise Institute.

Oberfield, Zachery. 2008. "Becoming 'the Man': How Street-Level Bureaucrats Develop Their Identities and Views." PhD diss., Department of Political Science, University of Wisconsin–Madison.

Oliver, J. Eric, and Tali Mendelberg. 2000. "Reconsidering the Environmental Determinants of White Racial Attitudes."*American Journal of Political Science* 44 (3): 574–89.

Olson, Kevin. 2006. *Reflexive Democracy: Political Equality and the Welfare State.* Cambridge, MA: MIT Press.

Omi, Michael, and Howard Winant. 1986. *Racial Formation in the United States: From the 1960s to the 1980s.* New York: Routledge.

Orloff, Ann Shola. 2002. "Explaining U.S. Welfare Reform: Power, Gender, Race, and the U.S. Policy Legacy." *Critical Social Policy* 22 (1): 96–118.

Orr, Larry L. 1976. "Income Transfers as a Public Good: An Application to AFDC." *American Economic Review* 66 (3): 359–71.

Osborne, David, and Ted Gaebler. 1992. *Reinventing Government: How the Entrepreneurial Spirit Is Transforming the Public Sector.* Reading, MA: Addison-Wesley.

Page, Benjamin I., and Lawrence R. Jacobs. 2009. *Class War? What Americans Really Think about Economic Inequality.* Chicago: University of Chicago Press.

Pager, Devah. 2003. "The Mark of a Criminal Record." *American Journal of Sociology* 108: 937–75.

———. 2007. *Marked: Race, Crime, and Finding Work in an Era of Mass Incarceration.* Chicago: University of Chicago Press.

Parks, Kyle. 2000. "State Bill Reshapes Job Development." *St. Petersburg Times,* May 5.

Pateman, Carole. 2005. "Another Way Forward: Welfare, Social Reproduction, and a Basic Income." In *Welfare Reform and Political Theory,* edited by Lawrence Mead and Christopher Beem, 34–64. New York: Russell Sage Foundation.

Pavetti, LaDonna A. 2001. "Welfare Policy in Transition: Redefining the Social Contract for Poor Citizen Families with Children and for Immigrants." In *Understanding Poverty,* edited by Sheldon H. Danziger and Robert H. Haveman, 229–77. New York: Russell Sage Foundation.

Pavetti, LaDonna, Michelle Derr, and Heather Hesketh. 2003. *Review of Sanction Policies and Research Studies: Final Literature Review.* Report prepared for Office of the Assistant Secretary for Planning and Evaluation, Mathematica Policy Research, Washington, DC.

Pavetti, LaDonna, Michelle Derr, Gretchen Kirby, Robert Wood, and Melissa Clark. 2004. *The Use of TANF Work-Oriented Sanctions in Illinois, New Jersey and South Carolina.* Washington, DC: Mathematica Policy Research.

Pavetti, LaDonna A., Kathleen A. Maloy, Peter Shin, Julie Darnell, and Lea Scarpulla-Nolan. 1998. *A Description and Assessment of State Approaches to Diversion Programs and Activities under Welfare Reform.* Report prepared for Office of the Assistant Secretary for Planning and Evaluation, Mathematica Policy Research, Washington, DC.

Peck, Jamie. 1999. "Getting Real with Welfare-to-Work: (Hard) Lessons from America." *Renewal* 7 (4): 39–49.

———. 2001. *Workfare States.* Foreword by Frances Fox Piven and Richard A. Cloward. New York: Guilford Press.

———. 2002. "Political Economies of Scale: Fast Policy, Interscalar Relations, and Neoliberal Workfare." *Economic Geography* 78 (3): 331–60.

Peck, Jamie, and Nik Theodore. 2009. "Recombinant Workfare, across Americas: Transnationalizing 'Fast' Welfare Policy." *Geoforum* 41 (2): 195–208.

Peck, Jamie, and Adam Tickell. 2002. "Neoliberalizing Space." *Antipode* 34 (3): 380–404.

Peet, Richard. 2003. *Unholy Trinity: The IMF, World Bank and WTO.* London: Zed.

Peffley, Mark A., and Jon Hurwitz. 1999. *Perception and Prejudice: Race and Politics in the United States*. New Haven, CT: Yale University Press.

Peterson, Paul E. 1995. *The Price of Federalism*. Washington, DC: Brookings Institution Press.

Peterson, Paul E., and Mark C. Rom. 1990. *Welfare Magnets: A New Case for a National Standard*. Washington, DC: Brookings Institution Press.

Pierson, Paul. 1994. *Dismantling the Welfare State? Reagan, Thatcher, and the Politics of Retrenchment*. New York: Cambridge University Press.

———. 2006. "Public Policies as Institutions." In *Rethinking Political Institutions: The Art of the State*, edited by I. Shapiro, S. Skowronek, and D. Galvin, 114–31. New York: New York University Press.

———. 2007. "The Rise and Reconfiguration of Activist Government." In *The Transformation of American Politics: Activist Government and the Rise of Conservatism*, edited by Paul Pierson and Theda Skocpol, 19–38. Princeton, NJ: Princeton University Press.

Pierson, Paul, and Theda Skocpol. 2007. *The Transformation of American Politics: Activist Government and the Rise of Conservatism*. Princeton, NJ: Princeton University Press.

Pimpare, Stephen. 2004. *The New Victorians: Poverty, Politics, and Propaganda in Two Gilded Ages*. New York: New Press.

Piven, Frances Fox. 1981. "Deviant Behavior and the Remaking of the World." *Social Problems* 28 (5): 489–508.

———. 2002. "Globalization, American Politics, and Welfare Policy." In *Lost Ground: Welfare Reform, Poverty, and Beyond*, edited by R. Albelda and A. Withorn, 27–41. Boston: South End Press.

———. 2003. "Why Welfare Is Racist." In *Race and the Politics of Welfare Reform*, edited by Sanford F. Schram, Joe Soss, and Richard C. Fording, 323–36. Ann Arbor: University of Michigan Press.

———. 2006. *Challenging Authority: How Ordinary People Change America*. Lanham, MD: Rowman and Littlefield.

———. 2007. "Institutions and Agents in the Politics of Welfare Cutbacks." In *Remaking America: Democracy and Public Policy in an Age of Inequality*, edited by Joe Soss, Jacob S. Hacker, and Suzanne Mettler, 141–56. New York: Russell Sage Foundation.

———. 2010. "A Response to Wacquant." *Theoretical Criminology* 14 (1): 111–16.

Piven, Frances Fox, and Richard A. Cloward. 1971. *Regulating the Poor: The Public Functions of Welfare*. New York: Pantheon.

———. 1974. *The Politics of Turmoil*. New York: Vintage.

———. 1977. *Poor People's Movements: Why They Succeed, How They Fail*. New York: Vintage.

———. 1982. "The American Road to Democratic Socialism." *Democracy* 3 (3): 58–69.

———. 1988. *Why Americans Don't Vote*. New York: Pantheon.

———. 1993. *Regulating the Poor: The Public Functions of Welfare*. Updated ed. New York: Vintage.

Plotnick, Robert, and Richard F. Winters. 1985. "A Politico-Economic Theory of Income Redistribution." *American Political Science Review* 79:458–73.

Polanyi, Karl. 1957. *The Great Transformation: The Political and Economic Origins of Our Time*. Boston: Beacon Press.

Pollock, Micah. 2008. *Because of Race: How Americans Debate Harm and Opportunity in Our Schools*. Princeton, NJ: Princeton University Press.

Polsky, Andrew. 1991. *The Rise of the Therapeutic State*. Princeton, NJ: Princeton University Press.

Quadagno, Jill. 1988. *Transformation of Old Age Security: Class and Politics in the American Welfare State*. Chicago: University of Chicago Press.

———. 1994. *The Color of Welfare: How Racism Undermined the War on Poverty*. New York: Oxford University Press.

Quigley, William P. 1999. "Five Hundred Years of English Poor Laws, 1349–1834: Regulating the Working and Nonworking Poor." *Akron Law Review* 73:82–92.

Quillian, Lincoln. 2008. "Does Unconscious Racism Exist?" *Social Psychology Quarterly* 71 (1): 6–11.

Radin, Beryl A. 2006. *Challenging the Performance Movement: Accountability, Complexity, and Democratic Valuzes.* Washington, DC: Georgetown University Press.

Ragin, Charles. 2000. *Fuzzy Set Social Science.* Chicago: University of Chicago Press.

Rakis, John. 2005. "Improving the Employment Rates of Ex-Prisoners under Parole." *Federal Probation* 69 (1): 7–12.

Rector, Robert E., and Sarah E. Youssef. 1999. *The Determinants of Welfare Caseload Decline.* Center for Data Analysis Report No. 99–04. Washington, DC: Heritage Foundation.

Reed, Adolph. 1999. *Stirrings in the Jug: Black Politics in the Post-segregation Era.* Minneapolis: University of Minnesota Press.

———. 2004. "The Study of Black Politics and the Practice of Black Politics: Their Historical Relation and Evolution." In *Problems and Methods in the Study of Politics,* edited by Ian Shapiro, Rogers M. Smith, and Tarek E. Mamoud, 106–43. New York: Cambridge University Press.

Reese, Ellen. 2005. *Backlash against Welfare Mothers: Then and Now.* Berkeley: University of California Press.

Reichman, Nancy E., Julian O. Teitler, and Marah A. Curtis. 2005. "TANF Sanctioning and Hardship." *Social Service Review* 79 (2): 215–36.

Riccucci, Norma. 2005. *How Management Matters: Street-Level Bureaucrats and Welfare Reform.* Washington, DC: Georgetown University Press.

Rich, Andrew. 2004. *Think Tanks, Public Policy, and the Politics of Expertise.* New York: Cambridge University Press.

Ridzi, Frank. 2004. "Making TANF Work: Organizational Restructuring, Staff Buy-In, and Performance Monitoring in Local Implementation." *Journal of Sociology and Social Welfare* 31 (2): 27–48.

———. 2009. *Selling Welfare Reform: Work-First and the New Common Sense of Employment.* New York: New York University Press.

Rivlin, Alice M. 1992. *Reviving the American Dream: The Economy, the States, and the Federal Government.* Washington, DC: Brookings Institution Press.

Roberts, Dorothy. 2002. *Shattered Bonds: The Color of Child Welfare.* New York: Basic.

Rose, Dina R., and Todd R. Clear. 1998. "Incarceration, Social Capital and Crime: Implications for Social Disorganization Theory." *Criminology* 36 (3): 441–79.

Rosenberg, Tina. 2008. "Payoff Out of Poverty?" *New York Times,* December 19.

Rosenblatt, Rand E. 1982. "Legal Entitlement and Welfare Benefits." In *The Politics of Law: A Progressive Critique,* edited by David E. Kairys, 262–76. New York: Pantheon.

Rothstein, Jesse. 2009. "Is the EITC Equivalent to an NIT? Conditional Cash Transfers and Tax Incidence." NBER Working Paper No. w14966, National Bureau of Economic Research, Cambridge, MA. http://papers.ssrn.com/sol3/papers.cfm?abstract_id=1405974.

Sabol, William J., Heather C. West, and Matthew Cooper. 2009. *Prisoners in 2008.* NCJ 228417. Washington, DC: U.S. Department of Justice, Bureau of Justice Statistics.

Salamon, Lester. 1995. *Partners in Public Service: Government-Nonprofit Relations in the Modern Welfare State.* Baltimore: Johns Hopkins University Press.

Sampson, Robert J. 2001. "How Do Communities Undergird or Undermine Human Development? Relevant Contexts and Social Mechanisms." In *Does It Take a Village? Community Effects on Children, Adolescents, and Families,* edited by Alan Booth and Ann C. Crouter, 3–30. New York: Routledge.

Sandfort, Jodi R. 2010. "Reconstituting the Safety Net: New Principles and Design Elements to Better Support Low-Income Families." In *Old Assumptions, New Realities: Economic Security for Working Families in the 21st Century*, edited by Robert D. Plotnick, Marcia K. Meyers, Jennifer Romich, and Steven Rathgeb Smith, 214–41. New York: Russell Sage Foundation.

Sandler, Michael. 2004a. "Officials Demand Welfare-to-Work Contract Records." *St. Petersburg Times*, South Pinellas ed., September 1.

———. 2004b. "Welfare Contract at Center of Inquiry." *St. Petersburg Times*, South Pinellas ed., March 9.

———. 2004c. "Work Program Troubles Pinellas for Years." *St. Petersburg Times*, South Pinellas ed., March 15.

Sanger, M. Bryna. 2003. *The Welfare Marketplace: Privatization and Welfare Reform*. Washington, DC: Brookings Institution Press.

Schatz, Edward. 2009. "Introduction: Ethnographic Immersion and the Study of Politics." In *Political Ethnography: What Immersion Contributes to the Study of Power*, edited by Edward Schatz, 1–22. Chicago: University of Chicago Press.

Schneider, Anne, and Helen Ingram. 1997. *Policy Design for Democracy*. Lawrence: University Press of Kansas.

Schneider, Mary Beth, and Bob Ruthhart. 2009. "Indiana Axes Contract with IBM." IndyStar.com. October 16. Accessed November 4, 2009. http://www.222.indystar.com/apps/pbcs.dll/articles?AID=/200910016/.

Schneider, Saundra K. and Jacoby, William G. 1996. "Influences on Bureaucratic Policy Initiatives in the American States." *Journal of Public Administration Research and Theory* 6 (4): 495–522.

Schneider, Saundra K., and Jacoby, William G. 2005. "Elite Discourse and American Public Opinion: The Case of Welfare Spending." *Political Research Quarterly* 58 (3): 367–79.

Scholz, John Karl, Robert Moffitt, and Benjamin Cowan. 2009. "Trends in Income Support." In *Changing Poverty, Changing Policies*, edited by M. Cancian and S. Danziger, 203–41. New York: Russell Sage Foundation.

Schram, Sanford F. 1995. *Words of Welfare: The Social Science of Poverty and the Poverty of Social Science*. Minneapolis: University of Minnesota Press.

———. 2000. "In the Clinic: The Medicalization of Welfare. *Social Text* 18 (1): 81–107.

———. 2002. *Praxis for the Poor: Piven and Cloward and the Future of Social Science in Social Welfare*. New York: New York University Press.

———. 2005. "Contextualizing Racial Disparities in American Welfare Reform: Toward a New Poverty Research." *Perspectives on Politics* 3 (2): 253–68.

———. 2006. *Welfare Discipline: Discourse, Governance, and Globalization*. Philadelphia: Temple University Press.

Schram, Sanford F., and Joe Soss. 2001. "Success Stories: Welfare Reform, Policy Discourse, and the Politics of Research." *Annals of the American Academy of Political and Social Science* 557: 49–65.

Schram, Sanford F., Joe Soss, Richard C. Fording, and Linda Houser. 2009. "Deciding to Discipline: Race, Choice, and Punishment on the Frontlines of Welfare Reform." *American Sociological Review* 74: 398–422.

Schram, Sanford F., and J. Patrick Turbett. 1983. "Civil Disorder and the Welfare Explosion: A Two-Step Process," *American Sociological Review* 48 (3): 408–14.

Schultze, Steve. 2005. "W-2's Poor Stay Poor, Audit Finds: Most Still Earn Poverty Wages after Leaving Welfare Program." *Milwaukee Journal Sentinel*, April 7.

Schuman, Howard, Charlotte Steeh, Lawrence Bobo, and Maria Krysan. 1997. *Racial Attitudes in America: Trends and Interpretations*. Rev. ed. Cambridge, MA: Harvard University Press.

Scott, James. 1998. *Seeing Like a State: How Certain Schemes to Improve the Human Condition Have Failed*. New Haven, CT: Yale University Press.

Sears, David O., Jim Sidanius, and Lawrence Bobo, eds. 2000. *Racialized Politics: The Debate About Racism in America*. Chicago: University of Chicago Press.

Segal, Jacob. 2006. "The Discipline of Freedom: Action and Normalization in the Theory and Practice of Neo-Liberalism." *New Political Science* 28 (3): 323–34.

Selden, Sally C. 1997. *The Promise of Representative Bureaucracy*. Armonk, NY: M. E. Sharpe.

Sen, Amartya. 1999. *Development as Freedom*. New York: Knopf.

Serra, Narcis, and Joseph E. Stiglitz, eds. 2008. *The Washington Consensus Reconsidered: Towards a New Global Governance*. New York: Oxford University Press.

Shapiro, Ian. 1999. *Democratic Justice*. New Haven, CT: Yale University Press.

———. 2007. *The Flight from Reality in the Human Sciences*. Princeton, NJ: Princeton University Press.

Shaw, Kathleen M., Sara Goldrick-Rab, Christopher Mazzeo, and Jerry A. Jacobs. 2006. *Putting Poor People to Work: How the Work-First Idea Eroded College Access for the Poor*. New York: Russell Sage Foundation.

Sigurdson, Herbert R.1969. "Expanding the Role of the Nonprofessional." *Crime Delinquency* 15: 420–29.

Silverman, Phyllis R. 1982. "Transitions and Models of Intervention." *Annals of the American Academy of Political and Social Science* 464:174–87.

Simon, Herbert. 1997. *Administrative Behavior*. New York: Free Press.

Simon, Jonathan. 2007. *Governing through Crime: How the War on Crime Transformed American Democracy and Created a Culture of Fear*. New York: Oxford University Press.

Skocpol, Theda. 1992. *Protecting Soldiers and Mothers: The Political Origins of Social Policy in the United States*. Cambridge, MA: Belknap Press of Harvard University Press.

———. 1995. *Social Policy in the United States: Future Possibilities in Historical Perspective*. Princeton, NJ: Princeton University Press.

———. 1996. *Boomerang: Clinton's Health Security Effort and the Turn Against Government in U.S. Politics*. New York: Norton.

———. 2003. *Diminished Democracy: From Membership to Management in American Civic Life*. Norman: University of Oklahoma Press.

Skrentny, John D. 2002. *The Minority Rights Revolution*. Cambridge, MA: Belknap Press of Harvard University Press.

Smiley, Marion. 1989. "Paternalism and Democracy." *Journal of Value Inquiry* 23 (4): 299–318.

Smith, Anna Marie. 2007. *Welfare Reform and Sexual Regulation*. New York: Cambridge University Press.

Smith, Adam. 2003. "Red Ink Blues." *St. Petersburg Times*, February 16.

Smith, Mike. 2006. "Welfare Privatization? Reviews Get More Time." Associated Press, June 17.

Smith, Rogers M. 1997. *Civic Ideals: Conflicting Visions of Citizenship in U.S. History*. New Haven, CT: Yale University Press.

———. 2002. "Should We Make Political Science More of a Science or More about Politics?" *PS: Political Science and Politics* 35:200–201.

Sniderman, Paul M., Richard A. Brody, and Philip E. Tetlock. 1991. *Reasoning and Choice: Explorations in Political Psychology*. New York: Cambridge University Press.

Somers, Margaret. 2008. *Genealogies of Citizenship: Markets, Statelessness, and the Right to Have Rights*. New York: Cambridge University Press.

Somers, Margaret, and Fred Block. 2005. "From Poverty to Perversity: Ideas, Markets, and Institutions over 200 Years of Welfare Debate." *American Sociological Review* 70:260–87.

Sosin, Michael. 1986. "Legal Rights and Welfare Rights." In *Fighting Poverty: What Works, What Doesn't*, edited by Sheldon H. Danziger and Daniel H. Weingberg, 260–83. Cambridge, MA: Harvard University Press.

Soss, Joe. 2000. *Unwanted Claims: The Politics of Participation in the U.S. Welfare System*. Ann Arbor: University of Michigan Press.

Soss, Joe, Meghan Condon, Matthew Holleque, and Amber Wichowsky. 2006. "The Illusion of Technique: How Method-Driven Research Leads Welfare Scholarship Astray." *Social Science Quarterly* 87 (4): 798–807.

Soss, Joe, Richard C. Fording, and Sanford F. Schram. 2008. "The Color of Devolution: Race, Federalism, and the Politics of Social Control." *American Journal of Political Science* 52 (3): 536–53.

Soss, Joe, Jacob S. Hacker, and Suzanne Mettler, eds. 2007. *Remaking America: Democracy and Public Policy in an Age of Inequality*. New York: Russell Sage Foundation.

Soss, Joe, and Sanford F. Schram. 2007. "A Public Transformed? Welfare Reform as Policy Feedback." *American Political Science Review* 101 (1): 111–27.

———. 2008. "Coloring the Terms of Membership: Reinventing the Divided Citizenry in an Era of Neoliberal Paternalism." In *The Colors of Poverty: Why Racial and Ethnic Disparities Persist*, edited by D. Harris and A.C. Lin, 293–322. New York: Russell Sage Foundation.

Soss, Joe, Sanford F. Schram, Thomas Vartanian, and Erin O'Brien. 2001. "Setting the Terms of Relief: Explaining State Policy Choices in the Devolution Revolution." *American Journal of Political Science* 45 (2): 378–95.

Sparks, Holloway. 2003. "Queens, Teens, and Model Mothers: Race, Gender, and the Discourse of Welfare Reform." In *Race and the Politics of Welfare Reform*, edited by Sanford F. Schram, Joe Soss, and Richard Fording, 171–95. Ann Arbor: University of Michigan Press.

Spitzer, Steven. 1975. "Toward a Marxian Theory of Deviance." *Social Problems* 22 (5): 638–51.

Stahl, Roland. 2008. "Examining TANF Sanction Policies: Who Gets Sanctioned and What Are the Effects?" PhD diss., Graduate School of Social Work and Social Research, Bryn Mawr College.

Starobin, Paul. 1998. "The Daddy State." *National Journal*, March 28, 678–83.

Steenbergen, Marco R., and Bradford S. Jones. 2002. "Modeling Multilevel Data Structures." *American Journal of Political Science* 46 (1): 218–37.

Stefancic, Jean, Richard Delgado, and Mark Tushnet. 1996. *No Mercy: How Conservative Think Tanks and Foundations Changed America's Social Agenda*. Philadelphia: Temple University Press.

Stiglitz, Joseph E. 2002. *Globalization and Its Discontents*. New York: W. W. Norton.

Stoll, Michael A. 2010. "Race, Place, and Poverty Revisited." In *The Colors of Poverty: Why Racial and Ethnic Disparities Persist*, edited by David Harris and Ann Chih Lin, 201–31. New York: Russell Sage Foundation.

Stone, Deborah A. 1984. *The Disabled State*. Philadelphia: Temple University Press.

———. 1989. "Causal Stories and the Formation of Policy Agendas." *Political Science Quarterly* 104 (2): 281–300.

———. 2008. *The Samaritan's Dilemma: Should Government Help Your Neighbor?* New York: Nation.

Stonecash, Jeffrey M. 2000. *Class and Party in American Politics*. Boulder, CO: Westview.

Stricker, Frank. 2007. *Why America Lost the War on Poverty—and How to Win It*. Chapel Hill: University of North Carolina Press.

Strolovitch, Dara Z. 2008. *Affirmative Advocacy: Race, Class, and Gender in Interest Group Politics*. Chicago: University of Chicago Press.

Swain, Carol. 1995. *Black Faces, Black Interest*. Cambridge, MA: Harvard University Press.

Swartz, Teresa Toguchi, Amy Blackstone, Christopher Uggen, and Heather McLaughlin. 2010.

"Welfare and Citizenship: The Effects of Governmental Assistance on Young Adults' Civic Participation." *Sociological Quarterly* 50 (4): 633–65.

Tajfel, Henri. 1981. *Human Groups and Social Categories*. Cambridge: Cambridge University Press.

Talbot, Colin. 2005. "Performance Management." In *The Oxford Handbook of Public Management*, edited by E. Ferlie, L.E. Lynn, Jr., and C. Pollitt, 491–517. Oxford: Oxford University Press.

Tallahassee Democrat. 2005. "Scandalization." *Tallahassee Democrat*, July 27.

Tampa Tribune. 2006a. "Bush Should Demand Better from Child Welfare." *Tampa Tribune*, June 27.

Tampa Tribune. 2006b. "Corrections Scandal Another Case of Lax Oversight in Outsourcing." *Tampa Tribune*, July 8.

Tan, Shannon. 2004. "Former Pinellas Leader Drops Suit." *St. Petersburg Times*, South Pinellas ed., November 11.

Teles, Stephen M. 1996. *Whose Welfare? AFDC and Elite Policies*. Lawrence: University Press of Kansas.

———. 2008. *The Rise of the Conservative Legal Movement: The Battle for Control of the Law*. Princeton, NJ: Princeton University Press.

Thaler, Richard H., and Cass R. Sunstein. 2008. *Nudge: Improving Decisions about Health, Wealth, and Happiness*. New York: Penguin.

Theriault, Sean M. 2006. "Party Polarization in the U.S. Congress: Member Replacement and Member Adaptation." *Party Politics* 12 (4): 483–503.

Therneau, Terry M., and Patricia M. Grambsch. 2000. *Modeling Survival Data: Extending the Cox Model*. New York: Springer-Verlag.

Thompson, G. 2007. "The Good-Behavior Bribe: Can Cash Incentives Pull a Poor Family Out of Poverty?" *New York*, October 28. http://nymag.com/guides/money/2007/39955/.

Tolman, Richard M., and Jody Raphael. 2000. "A Review of Research on Welfare and Domestic Violence." *Journal of Social Issues* 56:655–81.

Torfing, Jacob. 1999. "Workfare with Welfare: Recent Reforms of the Danish Welfare State." *Journal of European Social Policy* 9 (1): 5–28.

Trattner, Walter I. 1999. *From Poor Law to Welfare State: A History of Social Welfare in America*. 6th ed. New York: Simon and Schuster.

Travis, Jeremy. 2005. *But They All Come Back: Facing the Challenges of Prisoner Reentry*. Washington, DC: Urban Institute Press.

Tronto, Joan C. 1993. *Moral Boundaries: A Political Argument for an Ethic of Care*. New York: Routledge.

Uccello, Cori E., Heather R. McCallum, and L. Jerome Gallagher. 1996. *State General Assistance Programs: 1996*. Assessing the New Federalism. Washington, DC: Urban Institute.

U.S. Department of Health and Human Services. Administration for Children and Families. 2004. *Temporary Assistance for Needy Families (TANF) Program, Sixth Annual Report to Congress*. Washington, DC: Government Printing Office.

U.S. Department of Health and Human Services. 2009. *Welfare Caseloads*. Washington, DC: U.S. Department of Health and Human Services. http://www.acf.hhs.gov/programs/ofa/data-reports/index.htm.

U.S. Department of Justice. 2009. *Prison Industry Enhancement Certification Program (PIECP)*. Washington, DC: U.S. Department of Justice, Bureau of Justice Assistance. http://www.ojp.usdoj.gov/BJA/grant/piecp.html.

U.S. Department of Labor. 2009. *The Work Opportunity Tax Credit (WOTC): An Employer-Friendly Benefit for Hiring Job Seekers Most in Need of Employment*. http://www.doleta.gov/business/Incentives/opptax/PDF/WOTC_Fact_Sheet.pdf.

U.S. General Accounting Office (GAO). 2000a. *Unemployment Insurance: Role as Safety Net for Low-Wage Workers Is Limited.* GAO-01-181. Washington, DC: GAO.

———. 2000b. *Welfare Reform: State Sanction Policies and Number of Families Affected.* GAO/HEHS-00-44. Washington, DC: GAO.

———. 2002. *Welfare Reform: Federal Oversight of State and Local Contracting Can Be Strengthened.* GAO-02-661. Washington, DC: GAO.

U.S. Government Accountability Office (GAO). 2010a. *Temporary Assistance for Needy Families: Fewer Eligible Families Have Received Cash Assistance Since the 1990s, and the Recession's Impact on Caseloads Varies by State.* Washington, DC: GAO.

———. 2010b. *Temporary Assistance for Needy Families: Implications of Changes in Participation Rates. Statement of Kay E. Brown, Director, Education, Workforce, and Income Security.* GAO-10-495T. Washington, DC: GAO.

U.S. Office of Management and Budget. 2010. "Budgets of the United States for Fiscal Years 2000–2008." http://www.gpoaccess.gov/usbudget/browse.html.

Valentino, Nicholas A., Vincent Hutchings, and Ismail K. White. 2002. "Cues that Matter: How Political Ads Prime Racial Attitudes During Campaigns." *American Political Science Review* 96:75–90.

Van Sant, Will. 2006. "Settling Dodge Lawsuit Costs County $350,000." *St. Petersburg Times,* March 16.

Venkatesh, Sudhir. 2006. *Off the Books: The Underground Economy of the Urban Poor.* Cambridge, MA: Harvard University Press.

Vestal, Christine. 2006. "States Stumble Privatizing Social Services." *Stateline,* August 4. http://www.stateline.org/live/details/story?contentId=131960.

Vogel, David. 1989. *Fluctuating Fortunes: The Political Power of Business in America.* New York: Basic.

Volden, Craig. 2002. "The Politics of Competitive Federalism: A Race to the Bottom in Welfare Benefits?" *American Journal of Political Science* 46 (2): 352–63.

Wacquant, Loïc. 2001a. "Deadly Symbiosis: When Ghetto and Prison Meet and Mesh." *Punishment & Society* 3 (1): 95–133.

———. 2001b. "The Penalisation of Poverty and the Rise of Neo-liberalism." *European Journal on Criminal Policy and Research* 9: 401–11.

———. 2002. "Four Strategies to Curb Carceral Costs: On Managing Mass Imprisonment in the United States." *Studies in Political Economy* 69 (Autumn): 19–30.

———. 2008. "Ordering Insecurity: Social Polarization and the Punitive Upsurge." *Radical Philosophy Review* 11 (1): 9–27.

———. 2009. *Punishing the Poor: The Neoliberal Government of Social Insecurity.* Durham, NC: Duke University Press.

———. 2010. "Crafting the Neoliberal State: Workfare, Prisonfare, and Social Insecurity." *Sociological Forum* 25 (2): 197–220.

Walker, Jack. 1969. "Diffusion of Innovation among the American States." *American Political Science Review* 63 (September): 880–99.

Walters, Jonathan. 2007. "The Struggle to Streamline." *Congressional Quarterly: Governing,* August 13. http://www.governing.com/topics/health-human-services/The-Struggle-to-Streamline.html.

Ward, Deborah E. 2005. *The White Welfare State: The Racialization of U.S. Welfare Policy.* Ann Arbor: University of Michigan Press.

Warren, Dorian T. 2010. "The American Labor Movement in the Age of Obama: The Challenges and Opportunities of a Racialized Political Economy." *Perspectives on Politics* 8 (3): 847–60.

Washington Technology. 2009. "Who's Who in the State and Local Market." *Washington Technology*, February 26. http://washingtontechnology.com/articles/2009/03/02/s-and-l-whos-who-big-chart.aspx?sc_lang=en.

Wasson, David. 2001. "Governor Leads Privatization Push." *Tampa Tribune*, February 25.

Watkins-Hayes, Celeste. 2009. *The New Welfare Bureaucrats: Situated Bureaucrats and Entanglements of Race, Class, and Welfare.* Chicago: University of Chicago Press.

Weaver, R. Kent. 2000. *Ending Welfare as We Know It.* Washington, DC: Brookings Institution Press.

———. 2002. "Polls, Priming, and the Politics of Welfare Reform." In *Navigating Public Opinion*, edited by J. Manza, F. L. Cook, and B. I. Page, 106–23. New York: Oxford University Press.

Weaver, Vesla M. 2007. "Frontlash: Race and the Development of Punitive Crime Policy." *Studies in American Political Development* 21:230–65.

Weaver, Vesla M., and Amy E. Lerman. 2010. "Political Consequences of the Carceral State." *American Political Science Review* 104:817–33.

Weick, Karl. 1995. *Sensemaking in Organizations.* Thousand Oaks, CA: Sage.

Weisbrod, Burton A. 1998. *To Profit or Not to Profit: The Commercial Transformation of the Nonprofit Sector.* New York: Cambridge University Press.

Weissert, Carol, ed. 2000. *Learning from Leaders: Welfare Reform Politics and Policy in Five Midwestern States.* Albany, NY: Rockefeller Institute.

Western, Bruce. 1997. *Between Class and Market: Postwar Unionization in the Capitalist Democracies.* Princeton, NJ: Princeton University Press.

———. 2006. *Punishment and Inequality in America.* New York: Russell Sage Foundation.

———. 2008. "Reentry: Reversing Mass Imprisonment." *Boston Review*, July/August. http://boston review.net/BR33.4/western.php.

Western, Bruce, and Katherine Beckett. 1999. "How Unregulated Is the U.S. Labor Market? The Penal System as a Labor Market Institution." *American Journal of Sociology* 104:1030–60.

Western, Bruce, Meredith Kleykamp, and Jake Rosenfeld. 2006. "Did Falling Wages and Employment Increase U.S. Imprisonment?" *Social Forces* 84: 2291–2312.

Western, Bruce, and Becky Petit. 2002. "Beyond Crime and Punishment: Prisons and Inequality." *Contexts* 1 (3): 37–43.

Westra, Karen, and John Routely. 2000. *Arizona Cash Assistance Exit Study, First Quarter 1998 Cohort: Final Report.* Phoenix: Arizona Department of Economic Security, Office of Evaluation.

White, Ahmed A. 2008. "The Concept of 'Less Eligibility' and the Social Function of Prison Violence in Class Society." *Buffalo Law Review* 56 (3): 737–820.

White, Lucie. 2002. "Care at Work." In *Laboring Below the Line*, edited by Frank Munger, 204–44. New York: Russell Sage Foundation.

Whyte, Dave. 2007. "The Crimes of Neoliberal Rule in Occupied Iraq." *British Journal of Criminology* 47 (2): 177–95.

Wichowsky, Amber, and Donald P. Moynihan. 2008. "Measuring How Administration Shapes Citizenship: A Policy Feedback Perspective on Performance Management." *Public Administration Review* 68 (5): 908–20.

Wildman, Stephanie M., and Adrienne D. Davis. 1996. "Making Systems of Privilege Visible." In *Privilege Revealed: How Invisible Preference Undermines America*, edited by Stephanie M. Wildman, 7–24. New York: New York University Press.

Williams, Linda. 2003. *The Constraint of Race: Legacies of White Skin Privilege in America.* University Park: Pennsylvania State University Press.

Wilson, James Q. 1975. *Thinking About Crime.* New York: Random House.

———. 1997. "Paternalism, Democracy, and Bureaucracy." In *The New Paternalism: Supervisory Ap-*

proaches to Poverty, edited by Lawrence M. Mead, 330–44. Washington, DC: Brookings Institution Press.

Wilson, William Julius. 1997. *When Work Disappears: The World of the New Urban Poor.* New York: Vintage.

Winant, Howard. 1994. *Racial Formation in the United States: From the 1960s to the 1990s.* 2nd ed. New York: Routledge.

Winston, Pamela, Andrew Burwick, Sheena McConnell, and Richard Roper. 2002. *Privatization of Welfare Services: A Review of the Literature.* A Report Submitted to the U.S. Department of Health and Human Services. Contract No. HHS-100-01-0011. Washington, DC.

Winter, Nicholas J. G. 2008. *Dangerous Frames: How Ideas about Race and Gender Shape Public Opinion.* Chicago: University of Chicago Press.

Winters, Jeffrey A., and Benjamin I. Page. 2009. "Oligarchy in the United States?" *Perspectives on Politics* 7 (4): 731–51.

Wolin, Sheldon S. 2008. *Democracy Incorporated: Managed Democracy and the Specter of Inverted Totalitarianism.* Princeton, NJ: Princeton University Press.

Wood, B. Dan, and Richard W. Waterman 1994. *Bureaucratic Dynamics: The Role of a Bureaucracy in a Democracy.* Boulder, CO: Westview.

Wright, Gerald C. 1976. "Racism and Welfare Policy in America." *Social Science Quarterly* 57 (1): 718–30.

Wu, Chi-Fang, Maria Cancian, Daniel R. Meyer, and Geoffrey Wallace. 2006. "How Do Welfare Sanctions Work?" *Social Service Review* 30 (1): 33–51.

Yanow, Dvora. 2006. "How Built Spaces Mean." In *Interpretation and Method: Empirical Research Methods and the Interpretive Turn*, edited by Dvora Yanow and Peregrine Schwartz-Shea, 349–66. Armonk, NY: M. E. Sharpe.

Yanow, Dvora, and Peregrine Schwartz-Shea. 2006. *Interpretation and Method: Empirical Research Methods and the Interpretive Turn.* Armonk, NY: M. E. Sharpe.

Yates, Jeff, and Richard C. Fording. 2005. "Politics and State Punitiveness in Black and White." *Journal of Politics* 67 (4): 1099–1121.

Yin, Robert K. 2003. *Case Study Research: Design and Methods.* 3rd ed. London: Sage.

Young, Iris Marion. 2000. *Inclusion and Democracy.* New York: Oxford University Press.

Ziliak, James P., David Figlio, Elizabeth Davis, and Laura Connolly. 2000. "Accounting for the Decline in AFDC Caseloads: Welfare Reform or the Economy?" *Journal of Human Resources* 35 (3): 570–86.

INDEX

—transformation of by reform movements, 2–3, 18
—unstable tactics, 2
—variation and contingency as defining features of, 11–12
—and visions of *civitas*, 5
poverty politics, as "race-making" mechanism, 64
poverty rate, decline from 1961 to mid-1970s, 95
"principle of less eligibility," 85, 89, 96, 112, 113, 114, 115, 139, 295
prison industries, 106
Prison Litigation Reform Act of 1996, 284
prisons: as America's largest mental institutions, 304; construction, 1979–1989, 103; state correctional spending, between 1982 and 1997, 103
prison work programs: benefits to employers at expense of the poor, 41, 272; similarity to welfare-to-work programs, 272
privatization, 10, 27, 42, 48, 129, 176, 178, 181–85, 196, 298, 301
probation programs, 47, 106, 272, 297
Progressive era, 44, 55–56
public assistance programs, prior to 1960s, 55; focus on poor single mothers and nonwhite Americans, 57; unfettered local implementation, 57, 155; weak and partial protections from the market, 204
public attitudes: average gap in perceived laziness of racial groups, by ideological identification of respondents, *161*; increase in opposition to reducing inequality and raising living standards for poor after welfare reform, 286–87; perceptions of poverty and welfare policy as important national problems, 1960–2000, 67; perceptions of welfare policy as important national problem in relation to black stereotypes, 1992–2000, 68–69; relationship between changing perceptions of black stereotypes and perceptions of welfare policy as important national problem, 1992–1996, 70–71; stereotype effects on white support for welfare paternalism, 74–75; "typical" welfare recipient as black woman, 73; values effects on white support for welfare paternalism and white opposition to welfare spending, 2002, 72–73, 75; and white racial stereotypes of sexual irresponsibility, 73
public good, 20

Quadagno, Jill, 13, 43, 54, 58, 62
Quigley, William P., 85
Quillian, Lincoln, 76, 259

race and poverty governance, 3–4, 12–15, 75; in early "two-tier" welfare state, 55–59; generation and toleration of racial bias, 16; historical perspective, 54–59; production of racial meanings and inequalities, 13; and public support for welfare paternalism, 65–75; and relation between gender and civic enforcement, 45; and rise of neoliberal paternalism, 10, 59–65. *See also* Florida Welfare Transition (WT) program
race-coded wedge issues, 61, 65–66, 82, 84, 105
"race death," 56
Racial Classification Model (RCM), 14, 54, 75–81, 85, 97, 117, 124–25, 140, 154, 220, 235; dependence of perceived categorical contrasts on salience of groups in policy domain, 79; dependence of racial salience on relative size of minority population, 131; dependence of stereotype activation on proximate contextual cues, 79; effect of perceived categorical contrasts on racially patterned policy outcomes, 79; effect of racial stereotypes on impact of racial classifications on policy choice, 79; implicit and contingent effects of client race, 260–61, 300; policy choices guided by assumptions about targeted populations, 76–81, 131; policymaker reliance on race as basis for social classification, 78; policymaker reliance on racial classification as basis for policy targets, 78; policymaker reliance on social classifications and group reputations, 77; and racial disparities in sanctioning, 162–63; variation in salience of race across policy domains, time periods, and political jurisdictions, 78–79
racial-dispersion effect, 131
racial incorporation, in 1960s, 12–13
racial stereotypes. *See* African Americans; Latinas/Latinos; public attitudes; welfare programs
Radin, Charles, 50, 208, 210
Rainbow Coalition, 66
Rakis, John, 47, 106
Reagan, Ronald, 21; coining of term "welfare queen," 33, 180; cut of federal investment in state unemployment insurance trust funds, 39; encouraged state applications for

Temporary Assistance for Needy Families
(TANF) program (*continued*)
—predicted change in caseload under alternative values of state socioeconomic and political variables, 270–71
—prime directives for case managers, 236
—run by for-profit contractors, 40
—sanctions: black families more likely than
white families to be exposed to localized
disciplinary governance, 135; cross-state
variations in disciplinary choices, 123;
effects of client race mediated by local political context in second-order devolution states,
172; full-family sanctions, 124, 125, 126; lack
of relationship between sanctions and state
differences in BWR, 125–26; quarterly client
earnings before and after first TANF spell,
by sanction status, 279–81, *280*; relation of
sanction patterns to client characteristics,
170; relationship between racial composition
of caseload and sanctioning, *170*; sanction
exits more likely in counties with larger
black populations, 171–72; targeting of most
disadvantaged clients, 279
—second-order devolution, 62, 128–33; black
TANF caseload and state incarceration
rates by TANF regime type, *137*; cumulative
exposure to devolution and discipline by
race, 2001, 135–36; effect of black percent
of state population at different levels of black
dispersion, 132–33, *140*, 154, 169; no effect
of state Latino population on devolution,
133; pervasive influence of race, 126–28;
and policy-based racial inequity, 134–38;
probability of devolution by stringency of
paternalism, *134*, *135*, 154; probability of
devolution in states with strong upper-class
bias in voter turnout, 132; probability of
devolution in states with tight labor markets
and higher welfare caseloads, 132; program
design, 123–33; regime scale measuring
devolution and discipline, 134; rigidity of
provisions, and black caseload percentage,
126–28, *127*, *140*; rigidity of provisions, and
state caseload-to-population ratios, 125;
sanctions at discretion of local officials,
155–56; similarity of policy choices between
ideologically liberal and conservative state
governments, 126
—work activities, 46
Tetlock, Philip E., 77
Texas: outsourcing of welfare centers, 183;
spending on prison operations, 103

Thaler, Richard H., 24
Thatcher, Margaret, 21
Theodore, Nik, 51
therapeutic state, 26–27
Theriault, Sean M., 31
think tanks, 31
Thomas, Lorrin R., 65
Thompson, G., 51
Thompson, Tommy, 116–17
"three strikes and you're out" rule, 181, 185
three-strikes laws, 23, 102
Tickell, Adam, 2, 42
Torfing, Jacob, 52
transitional welfare benefits, 7
Trattner, Walter I., 85, 86
Travis, Jeremy, 41, 64, 103, 106
Trice, Rakuya, 66
Tronto, Joan, 302
truth-in-sentencing laws, 102
Turbett, J. Patrick, 92
Turner, Jason, 184

Uccello, Cori E., 96, 100
Uggen, Christopher, 289
underclass pathology, racialized discourse of,
63, 82, 120, 126, 293, 299
undeserving poor, 235
undocumented immigrants, 33
Unemployment Insurance (UI), 39, 86
universalism, 20
unwed mothers, denial of aid to, 122
Urban-Brookings Tax Policy Center, 196
urban poverty, areas of concentration, 62–63
urban riots, 91, 92
U.S. Government Accountability Office
(GAO), 169–70, 264

Venkatesh, Sudhiz, 106
Verba, Sidney, 150
Vestal, Christine, 192
Vogel, David, 29, 30
Voting Rights Act of 1965, 58

Wacquant, Loïc, 2, 5–8, 18, 21, 38, 47, 48, 59,
64–65, 84, 103, 104, 108, 109, 110, 120,
130, 175, 180, 182, 284, 291, 294, 295, 296,
297
waiver requests, as paternalistic strategy,
116–17
Wakulla Correctional Institution, 195
Wallace, George, 32, 58, 102
Walters, Jonathan, 183
Wang, Hui-chen, 155, 158, 209

Made in the USA
San Bernardino, CA
07 February 2015